R Blackwell
Stamford Hill
November 1984.

# A Handbook of
# PERSONNEL
# MANAGEMENT
# PRACTICE

KU-330-870

# A Handbook of
# PERSONNEL
# MANAGEMENT
# PRACTICE

## Michael Armstrong

Kogan
Page

First published in 1977 and reprinted in 1978, 1979,
1980 and 1981 (twice). Second edition first published in
1984, and reprinted 1984, by Kogan Page Ltd,
120 Pentonville Road, London N1 9JN

Copyright © 1977, 1984 Michael Armstrong
All rights reserved

**British Library Cataloguing in Publication Data**

Armstrong, Michael, 1928-
    A handbook of personnel management practice.—
    2nd ed.
    1. Personnel management
    I. Title
    658.3      HF5549

    ISBN 0-85038-778-7
    ISBN 0-85038-779-5 Pbk

Printed and bound in Great Britain by
Billing & Sons Ltd, Worcester

# Contents

# Part III — Employee Resourcing

# Part IV — Employee Development

# Part V — Employee Relations

# Introduction

## Aim

The aim of this book is to present an integrated picture of personnel management as a key function in any organization and as a function which concerns all managers. Personnel management is not treated simply as something that personnel managers do. It is considered instead in relation to the needs of the business as a whole, where every manager is involved in obtaining, organizing, motivating, developing and interacting with the human resources he controls.

The book takes a contingency view of personnel management. That is, what personnel specialists do and how they do it depends or is contingent upon the organizational context within which they operate and upon the forces affecting the processes within that organization and influencing the behaviour of the individuals and groups who work in it.

## The second edition

This edition of the handbook has been prepared some eight years after the first edition was written. The substantial changes made to the original work have been based mainly on the new concepts that have emerged during these years.

Three important influences have affected the content of this edition. First, the work of Karen Legge on the 'contingency' approach to personnel management has reinforced the views expressed in the first edition – that personnel management has to adopt a diagnostic rather than a prescriptive approach. There are no textbook answers to personnel problems and it follows that the concepts of the behavioural scientists and the personnel management theorists provide us with no more than analytical tools which can be used to understand the situation we are in; relevant courses of action are developed in the light of that analysis.

The second influence has been my own experience over the last seven years, in which I have been in general management, and, as an executive board member with profit responsibility, have come to a better understanding of the role of personnel management as part of the total organization.

The third influence has been Charlotte Chambers, Dean of the School of Management Studies, Polytechnic of Central London, who has consistently over the years provided me with stimulating views about personnel management and has, on many occasions, successfully challenged my assumptions. I should like, belatedly, to thank her for all the help and advice she has given to me.

For the benefit of the many students of personnel management the book has been rearranged in accordance with the syllabus of the Institute of Personnel Management. Substantial new sections on organizational behaviour and the role of the personnel department have been added.

New sections have also been included on action learning, advertising, computers in personnel management, do-it-yourself training, negotiating and quality circles.

## Plan of the book

The book is divided into the following five parts:

**Part I – The Basis of Personnel Management** in which personnel management is defined and analysed into the areas covered in the last three parts of the book dealing with personnel management techniques and procedures.

**Part II – Organizational Behaviour** in which the organizational and human factors affecting personnel management are reviewed.

**Part III – Employee Resourcing** in which the main personnel activities are dealt with concerning organization, manpower planning, recruitment, appraisal, employment practices, pay, health and safety, welfare, and personnel record and information systems.

**Part IV – Employee Development** in which the principles and practice of training and developing people are explored. An extensive review of the main training techniques is contained in Appendix J.

**Part V – Employee Relations** which starts with an analysis of industrial relations principles before dealing with employee relations practice in the form of industrial relations procedures, negotiating, consultation, participation and communications.

*Part I*
# The Basis of Personnel Management

In this part, personnel management is considered as an integral part of the overall process of management for which all managers as well as personnel specialists are responsible. The various components of personnel management are analysed, and then the objectives, activities and role of the personnel function are described. Finally, and most importantly, personnel management is examined within the context of the environment in which it operates — the environment which, from a contingency point of view, will strongly influence the role and activities of the personnel function.

# 1 | What is Personnel Management?

## Definition of personnel management

Personnel management is concerned with:

☐ obtaining, developing and motivating the human resources required by the organization to achieve its objectives;
☐ developing an organization structure and climate and evolving a management style which will promote co-operation and commitment throughout the organization;
☐ making the best use of the skills and capacities of all those employed in the organization;
☐ ensuring that the organization meets its social and legal responsibilities towards its employees, with particular regard to the conditions of employment and quality of working life provided for them.

## Who are the personnel managers?

Personnel management, as defined above, deals with what the *organization* needs to do about one of its two key resources — people (the other is money). The organization is run by managers and those they manage. Because management is the process of getting things done through people, all managers are personnel managers. As the Institute of Personnel Management put it: 'Personnel management is a responsibility of all those who manage people, as well as being a description of those who are employed as specialists.'

Personnel management is therefore not a separate function of management. There are, however, a number of specific personnel activities carried out in organizations which use appropriate skills, techniques and procedures and are influenced by knowledge of how organizations function and how people behave at work. And, while these activities are carried out by all managers, advice, help and guidance may be provided by personnel specialists.

## What happens in personnel management?

Personnel management starts with objectives — what the organization is aiming to do about the people it employs. From these objectives are derived policies — guidelines on the approaches the organization wishes to adopt in achieving its personnel objectives. There are then a number of personnel activities carried out in organizations which are in line with agreed policies and which further the achievement of objectives.

## Personnel objectives

The overall aim of personnel management should be to make an effective contribution to the achievement of the objectives of the organization and to the fulfilment of its social responsibilities. Personnel objectives and the means for achieving them will, as mentioned above, depend on their context. There are no universal objectives, just as there are no absolute principles governing personnel policies and practices. There are only certain basic headings and guidelines which provide a framework within which the organization does what it needs to do in the way which best suits itself.

Personnel objectives can be set out in the form of a hierarchy as in figure 1.1. This states the overall and the main objectives concerned with organization, manpower, relationships and responsibility. Beneath each of these main objectives are listed possible sub-objectives. This is certainly not a universally applicable list. It begs a number of questions; for example, what is an 'effective organization'? What is 'effective effort'? To what extent is it appropriate to pursue the objective of achieving a 'co-operative climate of relationships'?

Effectiveness has to be defined, and it may be necessary and even desirable to accept a degree of conflict in working through problems of relationships. A bland, and, on the surface, a smooth-running organization is not necessarily an effective one in achieving the objectives of its owners, its management, its workpeople and the unions.

A hierarchy such as figure 1.1 and a statement of objectives such as the example given in Appendix A have their uses, however, as indicators of the main areas for concern in developing appropriate personnel policies and practices.

## Personnel policies

### What are personnel policies?

Personnel policies have been defined by Brewster and Richbell as 'a set of proposals and actions that act as a refererence point for managers in their dealings with employees'.[1] They are continuing guidelines on what should be done in different circumstances. They should be distinguished from personnel objectives. Objectives are what the organization wants to accomplish or where it wants to go. Policies are the practices which are used to implement plans. Personnel objectives define ends while personnel policies control means.

### Why have personnel policies?

In a sense, this is a non-question. All enterprises have some personnel policies in that there are certain approaches management usually adopts when confronted with certain personnel problems. The real question is: to what extent should these policies be formalized? The advantages of having written policies in terms of consistency and understanding seem to be obvious. But there are disadvantages. Written policies may be inflexible, platitudinous or both, and therefore useless or dangerous. To have a pay policy, for example, which sets salary levels at the upper quartile of market rates may provide a necessary guideline to salary administrators. But to reveal it as fixed policy to a trade union would undermine the company's negotiation stance if it could not afford to maintain its market position.

The definition and communication of policies is fraught with difficulties. They often have to be expressed in abstract terms and managers do not care for

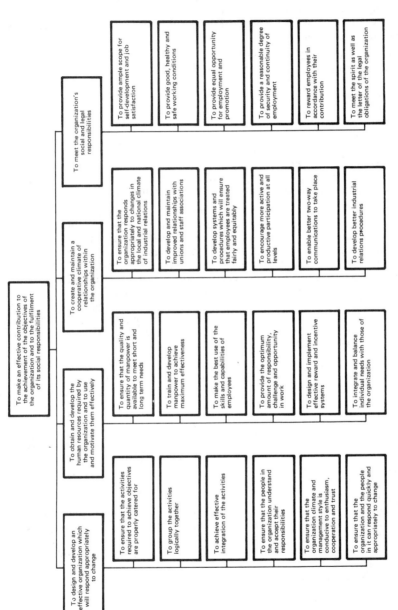

**Figure 1.1 Hierarchy of personnel objectives**

15

abstractions. But they do like to know how they should act in particular circumstances and the effort of thinking through personnel policies is worthwhile, even if it only produces the broadest of guidelines.

Actual policies will depend on the organizational context but the areas in which they can be defined are:

□ social responsibility
□ employment
□ pay
□ promotion
□ training
□ employee relations
□ health and safety.

### Social responsibility policies

Social responsibility policies express the attitude of the organization towards the people it employs, and they may be formulated in the following areas:

□ *Equity* – treating employees fairly and justly by adopting an 'even-handed' approach. This may include protecting individuals from the arbitrary decisions of their superiors, providing equal opportunities for employment and promotion and operating an equitable payment system.
□ *Consideration* – taking account of individual circumstances when making decisions which affect the prospects, security or self-respect of employees.
□ *Quality of working life* – increasing the sense of satisfaction people obtain from their work by, so far as it is possible, reducing monotony, increasing variety and responsibility and avoiding placing people under too much stress.
□ *Working conditions* – providing healthy, safe and, so far as practicable, pleasant working conditions.

It may be difficult to express these policies in anything but generalized terms and, although ideals of social justice and welfare are important, it should be remembered that, as Sadler and Barry expressed it: 'Organizations in general and business enterprises in particular, are established to achieve specific sets of objectives and not to satisfy the needs of their members.'[2]

Increasingly, however, organizations are having to recognize that they are subject to external as well as internal pressures which act as constraints on the extent to which they can disregard the higher standards of behaviour that are expected of employers.

### Employment policies

The basic employment policy issue is the level of people the organization wishes to employ as indicated by qualifications, experience and personal qualities. A company may decide, for example, that it wants to get and to keep higher quality staff than its competitors. This will directly affect its pay, promotion and training policies.

Employment policies will also cover the provision of equal opportunities.

### Pay policies

Pay policies deal with the level of pay and other benefits provided for employees. These are considered in relation to what other companies provide for similar jobs. If the organization wants higher quality staff it may have to adopt a policy of paying above the average.

**Promotion policies**
Companies often pay lip service to a policy of promotion from within. At the same time, and somewhat inconsistently, chief executives often express the wish to bring 'fresh blood into the organization'. Both these approaches are desirable in certain circumstances. A promotion policy would attempt to reconcile potential conflicts.

**Training policies**
Policies need to be determined on the scope of training and development schemes — who should be covered by formal training programmes, how much training should be provided, and the extent to which employees are going to be helped to acquire additional skills or qualifications.

Training policies will be influenced by the practical considerations of what the company needs and can afford to do in order to obtain qualified people, improve performance and provide for management succession. They will also be affected by the philosophy of the organization regarding development; the question might be asked: 'To what extent do we encourage employees to develop themselves as distinct from doing it for them?'

An example of a training policy is given in Appendix B.

**Employee relations policies**
Employee relations policies cover the following areas:

☐ *Union recognition* — the extent to which unions should be recognized and granted representational or negotiating rights and the terms and conditions of employment which are negotiable.

☐ *Union representation* — the preferred bargaining units that recognized unions should cover, that is, the categories of employees who should be represented by particular unions.

☐ *Participation* — the extent to which the company wants its employees to be involved in making decisions and to be consulted or informed about policies and plans that affect them.

**Health and safety policies**
Health and safety policies cover how the company intends to provide healthy and safe places and systems of work. An example of such a policy is given in Appendix C.

## Personnel management activities

The personnel management activities carried out in an organization can be grouped as follows:

EMPLOYEE RESOURCING. This area covers all aspects of the employment of people: how they are organized, obtained, motivated, treated, appraised and paid, the provision of health, safety and welfare programmes and the maintenance of records. The main employee resourcing activities are:

☐ *Organization design* — developing an organization structure which caters for all the activities required and groups them together in a way which encourages integration and co-operation and provides for effective communication and decision-making.

17

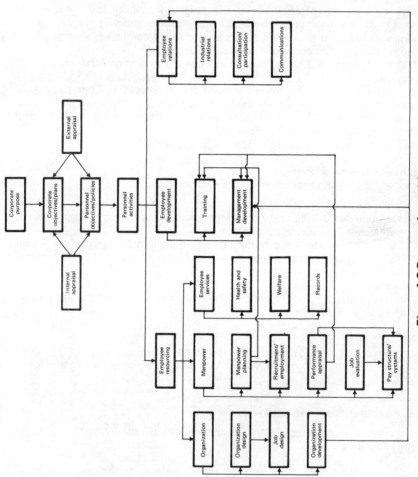

**Figure 1.2 Personnel activities**

| Activity | Organization | Manpower | Relationships | Responsibility |
|---|:---:|:---:|:---:|:---:|
| **Employee resourcing** | | | | |
| Organization design | ● | ● | | |
| Job design | ● | ● | | |
| Organization development | ● | | ● | |
| Manpower planning | ● | ● | | |
| Recruitment/employment | | ● | | ● |
| Performance appraisal | | ● | | |
| Job evaluation | | ● | | |
| Pay systems/structures | | ● | | ● |
| Health and safety | | | | ● |
| Welfare | | | | ● |
| Records | | ● | | |
| **Employee development** | | | | |
| Training | ● | ● | ● | |
| Management development | ● | ● | | |
| **Employee relations** | | | | |
| Industrial relations | | | ● | ● |
| Consultation/participation | ● | | ● | ● |
| Communications | ● | | ● | ● |

**Organization** — To design and develop an effective organization which will respond appropriately to change

**Manpower** — To obtain and develop the human resources needed by the organization and to use and motivate them effectively

**Relationships** — To create and maintain a cooperative climate of relationships within the organization

**Responsibility** — To meet the organization's social and legal responsibilities

**Figure 1.3 How personnel activities contribute to the achievement of personnel objectives**

☐ *Job design* – deciding on the content of a job: its duties and responsibilities and the relationships that exist between the job holder and his or her superior, subordinates and colleagues.

☐ *Organization development* – planning and implementing programmes designed to improve the effectiveness with which an organization functions and responds to change.

☐ *Manpower planning* – forecasting manpower requirements, making plans to achieve forecasts and taking steps to improve productivity.

☐ *Recruitment and selection* – getting the number and type of people the organization needs.

☐ *Performance appraisal* – reviewing and assessing an individual's performance in order to help him to do better and to develop potential.

☐ *Employment practices* – conditions of service, deploying and redeploying people, dealing with problems such as discipline and redundancy, ensuring that employment legislation is implemented.

☐ *Job evaluation* – establishing the relative value of jobs in a pay structure.

☐ *Pay* – developing and administering payment systems.

☐ *Health and safety* – administering health and safety programmes.

☐ *Welfare* – advising on and assisting with personal problems.

☐ *Personnel records* – maintaining information systems for personnel.

EMPLOYEE DEVELOPMENT. Employee development is concerned with:

☐ *Training* – systematically developing the knowledge and skills required to perform adequately a given job or task.

☐ *Management development* – ensuring that the organization has the effective managers it requires to meet its present and future needs.

EMPLOYEE RELATIONS. Employee relations is concerned with dealing with employees collectively in the following ways:

☐ *Industrial relations* – co-operating and negotiating with trade unions and staff associations.

☐ *Participation* – jointly involving management and employees in making decisions on matters of mutual interest.

☐ *Communications* – creating and transmitting information of interest to employees.

What activities actually take place and how they are carried out will be related to corporate objectives and plans, which are derived from internal and external appraisals in the context of the overall aims and purpose of the organization as shown in figure 1.2. This illustrates the considerable degree of interdependence between the activities. Although the book necessarily treats each activity and technique in separate chapters or sections, the extent to which they are related to and dependent on one another should never be forgotten. For example: job analysis, as a technique, has a bearing on almost every other personnel activity, and communications is an issue which pervades all aspects of personnel management. The relationships between personnel objectives and activities are shown in figure 1.3.

### References

1. Brewster, C. and Richbell, S. 'Getting managers to implement personnel policies', *Personnel Management*, December 1982.
2. Sadler, P.J. and Barry, B.A. *Organizational Development*. Longman, London, 1970.

# 2 | Role of the Personnel Function

## Overall role

The role of the personnel function should be to provide advice, services and functional guidance which will enable management to deal effectively with all matters concerning the employment of people and the relationships between the management of the organization and the people it employs.

The overall aim of the personnel function should be to make an effective contribution to the achievement of the objectives of the organization and to the fulfilment of its social and legal responsibilities. The particular aim should be to ensure that the personnel objectives of the organization are achieved, and the performance of the personnel function should be judged on the extent to which these objectives are met and on the efficiency with which advice, services and guidance are provided.

The personnel function is not the conscience of management. To state the reverse would be to adopt the arrogant posture that only personnel managers have a social conscience. But personnel managers are involved in the procurement, deployment and motivation of human resources on a full-time basis. Line managers may be equally concerned, but have other considerations to think about. It is the duty of personnel managers to alert line managers (line managers in this context include the managers of other functional departments as well as operational managers) to the human implications of what is happening to the organization and of what they are doing. They do this, not because they are inherently more aware of the implications, but because it is their job to use their time and analytical skills to consider all aspects of the utilization of human resources, while it is the job of line managers to be concerned about their own function as well as the people in it.

It must be emphasized, however, that all managers are concerned about human resources, not just personnel managers. The role of the personnel department is to help management to do this part of their job better and to provide services which it is more economical to group together under a functional head, where expertise is required which is unlikely to be shared equally amongst line managers.

In this chapter, attention is first given to the advisory, service and guidance aspects of the personnel function as a whole. The particular role of the personnel manager or specialist within the function is then examined, consideration being given to the extent to which personnel management can be described as a profession. The knotty problem of how to evaluate the effectiveness of the personnel function in carrying out its role is then discussed. Finally, a brief mention is made of organizational factors.

This chapter aims to outline the essence of what personnel departments and managers do. But how they operate will depend upon the organizational context, and this will be dealt with in chapter 3.

## Advisory role

The personnel function advises on personnel policies, procedures and methods and on the approach that should be adopted to deal with personnel and industrial relations problems.

### Advice on policy

Advice is given in the following policy areas:

☐ *Social responsibility* – the philosophy of the organization towards the people it employs, covering such areas as equity, consideration of individual needs and fears, the quality of working life.

☐ *Employment* – the level of personnel the company wishes to employ, the provision of equal opportunity and reasonable security.

☐ *Pay* – the level of pay and other benefits for employees and the extent to which pay systems are negotiated and disclosed.

☐ *Promotion* – the attitude of the company to providing long term career prospects and to promoting from within the organization.

☐ *Training* – the scope of training schemes and the extent to which the company proposes to subsidize education and training.

☐ *Industrial relations* – policies on union recognition, closed shops, the role of shop stewards and the approach to dealing with grievances, discipline and redundancy.

These are all policies which should be decided at the highest level by top management. They are not determined by the head of the personnel function but it is his job to persuade the chief executive and his colleagues to give proper thought to these matters and to formulate draft policies for their consideration.

To do this job effectively, the personnel function has to carry out research and keep in touch with current developments in legislation, social thought, the behavioural sciences and the views of the trade unions. It must be aware of what is happening in the outside world, but it must be equally capable of relating environmental changes to the situation within the organization. As much as anything, the personnel function should be concerned with advising on the policies required to manage change as it affects the people in the organization and the way in which they work together. The personnel function has therefore to keep closely in touch with trends within the company, measuring its employees' level of morale, motivation, commitment and general satisfaction with the company as employers. This requires the maintenance and analysis of records and statistics on labour turnover, absenteeism, sickness, accidents, disciplinary problems, disputes, grievances and productivity. Judicious use should be made of these statistics to persuade management that a change in policy is required.

### Advice on procedures and systems

The advice on procedures and systems should cover all those aspects of personnel administration with which top management and line management will be directly concerned. The personnel function should develop procedures and systems for the approval and use of line management in the following areas:

☐ *Manpower planning* – the preparation of manpower budgets; forecasting future deficits and surpluses, specifying requirements; recording and analysing information on labour turnover, absenteeism and movements between different levels and parts of the organization.

☐ *Recruitment* — requisitioning; the preparation of job specifications; advertising; interviewing; selection; fixing terms and conditions of employment.

☐ *Employment* — induction arrangements; fixing hours of work and shift and night duties; overtime arrangements; recording working hours; leave of absence; holiday arrangements and pay; flexi-time arrangements; promotion, transfer and redundancy procedures; fulfilling employment legislation requirements.

☐ *Training* — selecting personnel for courses; administrative arrangements on courses; following-up training; recording training carried out and the costs of training.

☐ *Performance appraisal* — appraisal forms; reporting arrangements; counselling methods.

☐ *Wages and payment by result systems* — fixing and altering wage rates and premium or other special payments; job evaluation; fixing and amending bonus or piece rates; payment of day rate; average earnings or lieu rates in particular circumstances (e.g. on transfer, new work, waiting time, special duties, or when a piece rate is in dispute).

☐ *Salary administration* — fixing salary levels on appointment, transfer or promotion; job evaluation; reviewing salaries; salary budgets.

☐ *Employee benefits* — arrangements for sick pay, pensions and other fringe benefits.

☐ *Industrial relations* — procedural agreements, including negotiating rights, closed shop arrangements, bargaining units, election of shop stewards and their rights, disputes procedure, disciplinary procedure, arrangements with regard to the *status quo.*

☐ *Joint consultation* — terms of reference; election arrangements; preparation of agenda and publication of minutes.

☐ *Communications* — briefing employees; using media.

☐ *Health and safety* — safety rules and regulations; arrangements for reporting incidents; inspection procedures.

☐ *Welfare* — arrangements for counselling and sick visiting.

The procedural aspects of personnel management, however, have to be treated with caution. One of the most dangerous traps a personnel manager can fall into is that of developing a massive bureaucratic machine which is resented by line management and ultimately defeats its own purpose by being ignored or by-passed. Personnel managers, like other managers in staff or service functions, are always liable to the accusation of empire-building. And too often this accusation is justified. At one time personnel managers who had not gained the respect of line managers could be dismissed as 'do-gooders'. It is even worse to be dismissed as 'bureaucratic do-gooders', and worst of all is the fate of being regarded as 'theoretical bureaucratic do-gooders'. Perhaps no one could fall into all three traps at once, but some personnel people seem to move in this direction by exhibiting a tendency to leap on to the latest personnel or behavioural science band-wagon without properly evaluating its practical use as seen through the eyes of line management. Drucker commented on this characteristic of personnel managers as long ago as 1955 when he wrote:

> The constant worry of all personnel administrators is their ability to prove that they are making a contribution to the enterprise. Their preoccupation is with the search for a 'gimmick' that will impress their management associates. Their persistent complaint is that they lack status.[1]

Unfortunately, this comment is just about as true today as it was then.

## Service role

The personnel function provides services to line management, especially in the fields of employment, recruitment, training, salary administration, employee relations, health and safety and the management of personnel information systems. These services are provided for one or more of the following reasons:

☐ members of the personnel department have particular skills;
☐ line managers need to be relieved of some aspects of personnel administration;
☐ it is more convenient and, possibly, economical to have a centralized function providing common services for a number of other departments.

## Functional guidance role

The functional guidance role of the personnel department is to interpret and help to communicate personnel policies and procedures approved by top management, and, on behalf of top management, to provide guidance to managers which will ensure that the policies and procedures are implemented and maintained.

This is perhaps the most difficult and delicate of all the roles that the personnel function carries out. It is not there to usurp or to interfere unduly with the legitimate authority of line management. But it is perfectly proper for top management to delegate some of its control duties to functional departments. The finance function controls budgets, the commercial function controls the wording of legal contracts and, in the same sense, the personnel function controls the implementation of personnel policies and procedures in order to ensure that they are consistently applied throughout the organization.

The word 'control' should really be in inverted commas. It is exercised in a very special sense. What, in effect, the personnel manager says is that 'this is the personnel policy of the company, ignore it at your peril'. He can seldom forbid anyone to do anything, except where it contravenes the law or a negotiated procedure, but he can refuse to authorize something – say a pay increase – if it is in his power to do so. And he can refer a matter to higher authority (the joint superior of the two managers concerned) and request that the action be delayed until a ruling has been made.

The principal matters upon which the personnel function might exercise control include:

☐ the application of contractual conditions of employment;
☐ alterations to rates of pay and pay structures;
☐ the implementation of agreed procedures; negotiating; grievance, discipline, redundancy, promotion and transfer;
☐ expenditure on recruitment and training;
☐ the quality and style of recruitment advertisements;
☐ the fulfilment of legal requirements concerning employment, health and safety.

In some companies the personnel department also exercises control over staff establishments. This is appropriate as long as the control is limited to ensuring that increases in establishment or replacements have been properly authorized, but it is not the job of personnel to fix establishment levels.

## The role of the personnel manager

### What he does

As a provider of services and, to a degree, functional guidance, the personnel manager is an administrator. He is there to get things done efficiently and effectively, although there are serious problems in measuring effectiveness, and these are referred to in the next section of this chapter.

As a provider of advice and, in some areas, guidance, the personnel specialist is a problem-solver. Karen Legge and others, such as Tom Lupton and Ann Crighton, see this as his main role. Indeed, in stressing this aspect of the job they seem to underestimate the existence of administration as an important though unglamorous activity in any personnel department. Personnel managers:

☐ innovate, i.e. devise and propose new policies, techniques and procedures;
☐ administrate, i.e. manage the activities for which the personnel department is responsible such as recruitment, training, pay administration, health and safety and record keeping;
☐ solve problems, i.e. general problems related to achieving corporate and personnel objectives and specific problems concerning disputes, grievances and disagreements with colleagues and superiors.

It is difficult to convey the flavour of what personnel specialists actually do because it depends so much on the context and the job. As examples, however, here is a selection of real problems thrown at a busy personnel department in a typical week. These were dealt with in addition to the normal innovating and administration functions.

1. A vacancy for a cost accountant has been outstanding for six months. Two offers have been rejected and one appointee resigned after six weeks for personal reasons. The agencies have no more applicants on their books and the manager doing the recruiting has come to the Personnel Department in a state of distress and frustration.
2. The Senior Financial Manager has approached Personnel about two other vacancies for accountants (*circa* £12,000). One has been outstanding for six months, the other has just arisen. They are difficult to fill as salaries are below market rate.
3. A senior manager complains that a manager appointed in his department about two months ago is not proving satisfactory.
4. Mrs Smith is complaining that she was held up by Personnel and was too late applying to DHSS for full National Insurance deductions. She claims, therefore, that she will be delayed 12 months in obtaining sick pay because of the company's inefficiency.
5. Four months ago a redundancy was avoided (embarrassing for a growing company) by redeploying a member of staff. Her manager is now complaining that she is not suited to the new job and wants to know what arrangements Personnel will make.
6. The senior representative of the staff union has confirmed with you that it is company policy for staff to see their own job descriptions on request. She has now told you that several people have been refused by their managers.
7. An employee with six weeks' service goes to the agency who placed her to complain she is being persecuted by colleagues because of her colour. The agency staff telephone to warn us.
8. Following an urgent set of re-grading applications, jobs in the Finance Depart-

ment have been graded higher when a professionally qualified accountant is required. This caused some concern with line management who eventually accepted the need for the qualification. Finance have now submitted a further job description which says this job would be carried out by someone with the experience of a qualified accountant, i.e. someone who is not necessarily a qualified accountant. The job is organizationally at the same level as qualified accountants.

9. The company has an agreement with the staff union to consult prior to altering prices of food to employees. Two incidents upset the staff representatives:
   (a) A letter from the catering company to the Office Manager was opened in the wrong office and refers to an agreement to raise drink prices by 2p per cup.
   (b) Rolls and sandwiches were increased in price by the catering company's restaurant manager as he thought, wrongly, that consultations had been carried out.

## How he does it

A personnel specialist carries out his advisory and administrative tasks in essentially the same way as any manager. He ensures that systems and procedures are operated or implemented properly and within predetermined timescales and budgets. He maintains records and communicates information. This applies to such typical activities as recruitment, performance appraisal, training and salary administration, although in each case setting up the systems, evaluating their effectiveness and amending them in the light of experience or because of changed circumstances will involve problem-solving.

As a problem-solver, the personnel manager does three things:

1. He *defines* the nature of the problem or, in the words of McFarland,[2] he conceptualizes it — becoming aware of the difficulty or the need for improvement and analysing the circumstances leading to and surrounding the situation.
2. He *diagnoses* the cause(s) of the problem or the reason(s) for the situation arising. This process of diagnosis accompanies the process of definition and it is often iterative, i.e. possible explanations may reveal the need for further analysis which will lead to a different diagnosis which may indicate that more data is required, and so on.
3. He *decides* on a course of action, having weighed up the relative merits of a number of alternatives.

The emphasis throughout the process is on analysis. And this analysis has to cover the organizational context in which it is all happening. It ought therefore to be carried out against the background of an understanding of the organizational processes that are taking place, i.e. organizational behaviour.

To a degree, the personnel manager has to accept that what he does and how he does it will be contingent on a number of variable and often uncertain factors. Contingency theory, as expounded by Lawrence and Lorsch, suggests that 'organizational variables are in a complex inter-relationship with one another and with conditions in the environment'[3] and that these environmental contingencies, which include the technological character of the work, will act as both constraints and opportunities and influence the organization's internal structures and processes. How a contingency approach can be used in personnel management is discussed in the next chapter.

Meanwhile, it is worth re-emphasizing that the personnel manager in his analytical and diagnostic capacity needs, in Karen Legge's words, 'a body of knowledge or frame of reference on which to base his diagnosis'.[4] Most commentators have suggested that this body of knowledge should be based on behavioural science. It is interesting to note, however, that some commentators, including Legge, do not appear to admit that the knowledge required includes an understanding of the range of techniques that can be used, selectively, to solve problems. Be that as it may, there *is* a body of knowledge available to personnel practitioners and this leads naturally to a consideration of the extent to which, because of this fact, personnel management can be regarded as a profession.

## Personnel management as a profession

If the term is used loosely, personnel managers are professional because they display expertise in doing their work. A professional occupation such as medicine or the law could, however, be defined more rigidly as one which gives members of its association exclusive rights to practise their profession. A profession is not so much an occupation as a means of controlling an occupation. Personnel management is not in this category.

A 'profession' may alternatively be identified using the following less rigid criteria: skill based on theoretical knowledge; the provision of training and education; a test of the competence of members administered by a professional body; a formal professional organization which has the power to regulate entry to the profession; and a professional code of conduct. By these standards personnel management could be regarded as a profession, especially in the U.K. where the Institute of Personnel Management carries out all the functions of a professional body.

Sir Peter Parker, chairman of British Rail for many years, has no doubts on this subject: 'I am an ardent advocate of professionalism in personnel management. There must be a core of disciplined expertise at the heart of its effectiveness.'[5] But he was not saying that personnel management is a 'profession'.

David Guest and Robert Horwood took a somewhat different stance as a result of their research into the role of the personnel manager:

The [research] data also highlights the range of career types in personnel management. Given the diversity of personnel roles and organizational contexts, this is surely something to be welcomed. It is tempting but wrong to view personnel managers as homogeneous. Their different backgrounds and fields of operations raise doubts about the value of a professional model and of any attempt to view personnel problems as amenable to solution through a primary focus on professionalism.[6]

The debate continues, but it is an academic one. What matters is that personnel managers need expertise and have to use it responsibly. In other words, they should act professionally but do not *have* to be members of a professional association to do that. Such associations, however, have an important part to play in setting and improving professional standards.

## Evaluating the personnel function

It is not easy to evaluate the personnel function — to measure its contribution to achieving the organization's objectives. Guest and Horwood have commented on 'the considerable effort involved in attempting to define and evaluate effectiveness, either for the personnel function or indeed for individual roles'.

It is facile to say that people are the most important resource in an enterprise and that therefore the department that specializes in people is important. The head of an advertising agency once said that his 'inventory goes up and down in the lift'; but that did not mean that he attached any importance to the role of the personnel manager − if he had one − in looking after that inventory. This is the difficulty. People may be regarded as the vital resource − at least plenty of lip service is paid to this concept by company chairmen in their annual statements − but many managers find it difficult to appreciate where the personnel department fits in, except in the simplest terms as a procurement and fire-fighting function.

Chief executives are often perfectly happy with their personnel manager if he runs an efficient recruitment service ('he always gets his man − or woman'), keeps labour turnover down, is good at calming down shop stewards, keeps the company out of legal difficulties, and generally seems to please management and keep the workers happy. All this is highly desirable but somewhat subjective. If a personnel department can do all that, it is doing reasonably well, within limits, but it will still be difficult to measure the extent to which the work is contributing to profitability. Perhaps the most that can be said in many companies is that the personnel department has a role in providing the basis upon which profitability can be built up − i.e. the people; and it is also concerned in a negative way in helping to avoid situations where productivity is diminished − by minimizing disputes and removing causes of dissatisfaction.

The personnel function should, of course, do much more than that. Its true role is to make a positive contribution to organizational health and effectiveness by ensuring that well trained and well motivated people are there to work effectively and co-operatively together in the achievement of objectives which are recognized to be mutually beneficial to management and workers. This is the strategic role of personnel in the fields of organization development, manpower planning, management development, motivation and industrial relations. It is the key policy-formulating function and it is the one that is most difficult to evaluate. It is much easier to assess the effectiveness of the maintenance functions at office and shop floor level where the local personnel officer is there to provide efficient recruitment, employment, training, negotiating and record keeping services.

The personnel function is best evaluated under the headings of its three roles: advisory, service and guidance. The first and last roles present the greatest difficulties.

## Evaluating the advisory role

For the personnel department's advisory role, the first level of evaluation will be made by management on the basis of whether the advice on policy sounds practical and is delivered in a positive, persuasive and straightforward manner. They will expect the personnel manager to anticipate problems and come up with realistic answers to them. Whether proposals are made orally or in writing they must be succinct and well argued; they must define the problem, explain why it must be solved, describe how it should be solved − by whom and when − set out clearly the costs involved, and end with a clear statement of the benefits that should result from the proposal. This provides at least some basis for evaluating the function from a cost/benefit point of view. There is nothing that damages the reputation of a personnel manager more than being woolly in his proposals; especially if he is the sort of individual who is so steeped in behavioural science and organization development jargon that he cannot put a proposition into language that management understands, let alone finds acceptable.

The second level of evaluation is, of course, whether the advice works. Unfortunately, in the personnel field, this evaluation will be largely subjective, except where specific advice is given on dealing with a specific problem; for example, how to handle a labour dispute or to deal with a discipline issue.

Advice on procedures can be evaluated by monitoring the effectiveness of the procedures. Do they run smoothly? Are managers using them properly? Do they produce the expected results? The procedural aspect of the advisory role overlaps with the service role, but when developing procedures, the personnel manager can be set targets such as the date when they should be in operation, the results they should obtain, and the costs of using them. Performance can then be measured against those targets.

The advisory aspect of personnel management is often concerned with projects designed to implement strategies and procedures. Where work can be set up on a project basis it is always easier to acquire a cost/benefit analysis before starting the project, to set precise time and targets and cost budgets for completing the project, to lay down procedures for reporting on progress, performance and costs, and to ensure that continuous steps are taken to measure cost-effectiveness. A project approach along these lines provides the most promising basis for evaluating the advisory aspects of personnel performance. The problem of evaluating the personnel manager's advisory role is, as Legge has said, that 'useful advice has a habit of becoming the property of the recipient and, unlike bad advice, its origins lost in the allocation of praise'.[3]

### Evaluating the service role

The service role should be the easiest to evaluate. Standards can be set and the personnel department can be required to operate within a defined budget in meeting these standards. In this way cost-effectiveness can be measured, in theory at least. The difficulty is in selecting areas where realistic standards can be defined.

Some of the possible areas where quantitative standards or targets can be determined include:

□ recruitment − speed in filling vacancies, advertising costs, recruitment cost per head, number of unfilled vacancies;
□ employment − reduction in wastage rates and absenteeism;
□ training − throughput of training schemes, time taken to develop and introduce new courses, impact of training on performance;
□ management development − availability of trained managers to provide for management succession;
□ industrial relations − number of disputes, extent to which disputes are resolved, time taken to progress a grievance through the procedure at each stage;
□ communications − speed with which briefing groups are convened; speed with which information is generally disseminated amongst employees;
□ personnel costs − expenditure in relation to budget, cost of personnel function per employee.

In all or any of these areas, however, quantification may be impossible. In these circumstances, evaluation is inevitably carried out in qualitative terms. Subjective judgements are made about the efficiency of the service and the speed, willingness and degree of success achieved by members of the personnel function. The successful personnel manager is the one who can persuade top management and his management colleagues that he is providing them with a good service. This success is more likely to be achieved if the personnel manager can demonstrate that he is willing and able to help. It is less likely to happen where the personnel manager is too 'pushy' and attempts to steamroller his colleagues into trying out his latest idea.

The value of the personnel function in all areas is often best demonstrated by providing a small service cheerfully and efficiently and thus preparing people to accept that they are likely to benefit from an extension of the service. The Fabian approach of making progress one step at a time has much to commend it in the personnel world. It may, for example, be far easier to convince management of the virtues of a comprehensive training programme if a number of pilot-scheme courses are run to which senior managers are invited as observers and speakers.

### Evaluating the guidance role

The guidance role can only be evaluated by top management who can observe the way in which the personnel department exercises functional control in accordance with the powers delegated to it. Information on effectiveness in providing control can be established by analysing the extent to which pay-roll costs or numbers of employees exceed budget, managers ignore personnel procedures in taking action, sub-standard employees are engaged, and the company is subjected to legal actions and references to industrial tribunals.

## Organization

The organization of the personnel department will clearly depend upon the organizational context within which it operates and the role assigned to the function.

There are two basic principles of organization, however, that should apply within any company. First, the head of the personnel function should be a member of the top policy-forming body of the enterprise — the board or executive committee — and should be directly responsible to the chief executive. Only thus can he make his proper contribution to the formulation of personnel policies and strategies which are clearly within the context of and supportive to the overall objectives, policies and strategies of the firm. Without taking a full part in policy deliberations and without having ease of access to the chief executive, the personnel function too easily becomes a peripheral body.

Second, the personnel organization should ensure that the day-to-day services required by management in the different divisions and departments can readily be made available. In a large divisionalized organization this may require the appointment of divisional personnel managers or factory personnel officers who may report directly to divisional or company line management. They would have a functional relationship with the chief personnel executive on the implementation of corporate personnel policies and the handling of issues such as union negotiations which may have corporate implications.

### References

1. Drucker, P.F. *The Practice of Management*. Heinemann, London, 1955.
2. McFarland, D.E. *Personnel Management: Theory and Practice*. Macmillan, New York, 1968.
3. Lawrence, P.R., and Lorsch, J.W. *Developing Organizations. Addison-Wesley,* Reading, Mass, 1969.

4. Legge, K. *Power, Innovation and Problem Solving in Personnel Management*. McGraw-Hill, Maidenhead, 1978.
5. Parker, P. 'How I See the Personnel Function'. *Personnel Management*, January 1983.
6. Guest, D. and Horwood, R. 'Perceptions of Effectiveness in Personnel Management', *Personnel Management*, May 1981.

# 3 | Personnel Management in Practice

## The significance of context

Personnel managers, as well as those who write about personnel management, can fall into the trap of treating the subject in isolation. It is too easy to divorce personnel management from the context in which it operates – the organization and its environment.

It is interesting to observe how changes in the environment – economic pressures and the climate of opinion – have changed the role of personnel managers over the years. At one time personnel management was seen as a welfare activity – providing tea and sympathy. Then in the immediate post-war years, personnel management blossomed as a profession, advocating and deploying 'scientific' techniques for recruitment, job evaluation, and performance appraisal and training. Then, in the expansive 1960s, the behavioural scientists took over: organization development, job enrichment and concerns for the creation of organizational health, job satisfaction and involvement became pre-eminent. Management by objectives became a popular cult. The euphoria of the swinging (or socially conscious) 1960s spilled over into the early 1970s. But increasingly, as economic gloom took over, life became more real and earnest for personnel practitioners. They became aware that what mattered was survival as well as growth and job satisfaction. They became involved in tough redundancies. They had to take part in even tougher confrontations with trade unions as top management decided that enough was enough so far as union disruption was concerned. Participation and involvement was no longer the key to success. Productivity was what mattered. And this was *real* productivity, not the give-away productivity bargaining that had been indulged in previously. Personnel departments took part in and were subjected to cost-cutting exercises. And quality improvement by means of quality circles became the latest gimmick – if the Japanese can do it, why can't we?

Personnel managers were no longer able to be self-righteous about what was good for their enterprise. This is how they had fallen into the trap of being over-prescriptive. As Legge[1] pointed out, personnel management specialists and textbook writers had tended to decide what was right for the organization on theoretical grounds without basing their views on a proper analysis of the situation or context in which their policies and procedures have to exist.

Definitions of aims and policy areas, lists of activities and analyses of the role of the personnel department, as contained in the first two chapters of this book, are no more than generalizations. What actually happens depends on three factors:

1. *Organization context* – purpose, environment, performance, people, management style and climate.
2. *Relationships* between personnel and general or line managers.

32

3. *Constraints* — the problems and limitations created by organizational context, relationships and the way in which organizations operate, which affect the degree to which personnel managers can achieve their aims.

This chapter therefore deals initially with these factors and then goes on to discuss first their impact on the role of the personnel manager and then how he should deal with them.

## Organization context

Charles Handy[2] has suggested six factors of crucial importance in the development of organizations and resulting behaviour patterns: history and ownership; size; technology; goals and objectives; the environment; and the people. These provide a good basis for analysing organization behaviour and as such are discussed fully in the next chapter. But they need to be modified and extended if they are to help in understanding organization context from the viewpoint of personnel management.

The factors which particularly influence personnel objectives, policies, activities and the role and organization of the personnel function are:

☐ purpose
☐ external environment
☐ internal environment
☐ size
☐ structure
☐ performance
☐ people
☐ management style
☐ organization climate.

These factors are interconnected, as shown in figure 3.1. They are described below.

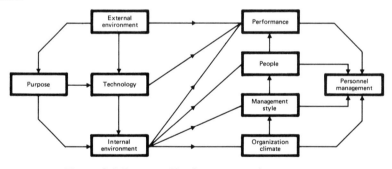

**Figure 3.1 Factors affecting personnel management**

### Purpose
Organizations exist to achieve a purpose. In the public sector or in a non-profit-making organization the purpose may be defined as the provision of certain services for national or local government, the community, or the members of the organization.

The purpose of a business will be to create and satisfy customer demands for goods or services, to provide customers with value for money and to generate an acceptable rate of return on the investment of its owners. As Drucker said, 'a business cannot be defined or explained in terms of profit'[3] and profit-making is not the sole purpose of a company. But unless shareholders are satisfied that they are getting a reasonable return on their investment and unless sufficient cash is generated to finance trading and development, the business will not survive or grow.

The steps taken to achieve the purposes of the organization may conflict with the needs of its employees. As Douglas McGregor[4] has pointed out, the biggest challenge to personnel managers is to integrate the needs of the organization with the needs of those who work in it. It is not an impossible challenge, and there are a number of ways in which it can be met, as described later in this book. But none of these approaches will work unless the personnel manager understands what the organization is setting out to achieve just as clearly as he understands what individuals need and want.

### The external environment
Organizations will be affected by factors in their external environment such as competition, changes in markets, economic forces, government policies, public opinion and trade unions. Turbulence in the environment can create conditions which significantly alter personnel policies and practices, the most obvious example being shortage of work leading to cutbacks and redundancies. Change is perhaps the biggest challenge facing personnel managers. Techniques for managing change are discussed in chapter 5, but without an understanding of what is happening outside the organization, these techniques will be ineffective.

### The internal environment
The internal environment consists of the characteristics of the organization itself, namely its technology, its size and its structure.

### Size
On the whole, large organizations are more formalized, and specialist functions such as personnel departments are more likely to exist. Size, however, brings with it problems of integration and communication with which personnel managers have to contend. Schumacher's proposition 'small is beautiful' has its attractions to anyone concerned with managing and motivating people.

### Structure
The structure of an organization is related to its technology and size, which will influence the degree of formality in defining roles and relationships, the extent to which the organization is de-centralized and the numbers of levels of management or supervision that exist. In turn, these factors will influence the procedural aspects of personnel management (e.g. the use of formal job descriptions) and the ways in which people are managed and communications take place.

### Performance
Performance in achieving purpose will be largely determined by the people in the organization, but will also be subjected to environmental influences. Clearly, personnel management is an entirely different affair in troubled times when costs are being cut and morale is suffering than when business is booming. Personnel managers must be prepared to adjust their methods accordingly.

### People

Purpose and technology will determine what sort of people the organization employs and will therefore influence personnel policies and techniques. The personnel manager dealing with scientists in a high technology company has a quite different job from the personnel manager of a large mechanical baker. The basic activities of recruitment, training, pay administration and employee relations may have the same names and share some basic concepts. But their application will be entirely different.

History, external influences and the feelings of management and employees will affect the degree to which the latter are organized into trade unions or staff associations. The strength of unions, if they exist, and the attitudes of management towards them will exert major influences on the role and activities of a personnel manager.

### Management style

The role of management is to ensure that the organization achieves its purpose. To this end, management sets objectives, budgets and targets, prepares plans to achieve objectives, obtains the resources required by the plans (people, finance, plant, etc.), directs the use of these resources and monitors performance, taking corrective action if plans are not achieved.

Obtaining and using resources effectively is one of the key tasks of management. And people are obviously a major resource, alongside finance. So managers will be concerned with leading, motivating and developing their staff. However, they are there to achieve results and in this process they will be encouraged, indeed commanded, in Robert Heller's words, 'to do the most possible with the least possible'.[5] They may attach a lot of importance to how they manage their staff but they will know that in the last analysis it is 'the bottom line that counts', i.e. the profits they achieve are *the* measure of their performance.

This emphasis on results in the minds of general or line managers, especially those responsible for achieving output or sales targets, can present a problem to personnel managers. The latter will be regarded as peripheral if they cannot demonstrate that what they are doing will make a direct and, preferably, measurable impact on the results the line manager is expected to achieve.

The way in which managers set about achieving results — their management style — will vary between organizations. The degree to which they are autocratic, democratic or permissive will depend partly on themselves and partly on the context in which they work, which includes technology and the climate of the organization. The personnel manager will, however, have to be prepared to cope with different management styles and ones with which he has little sympathy. He will want to bring his influence to bear on changing inappropriate styles but should never underestimate the size of his task.

### Organization climate

The climate or culture of an organization is dependent on or related to all the factors mentioned above. Historical as well as technological factors may exert influence, as will the management style of the chief executive, or, if they are involved, those in overall control — the owners, the politicians, or the members, as the case may be. As Katz and Kahn put it:

> Every organization develops its own culture and climate; with its own taboos, folkways and mores. The climate or culture of the system reflects both the norms and values of the formal system and their reinterpretation in the informal system.

> Organizational climate reflects also the history of internal and external struggles, the types of people the organization attracts, its work processes and physical layout, the modes of communication, and the exercise of authority within the system.[6]

The climate of the organization will consist not only of the norms and values of management about such matters as equity or participation but also of the attitudes of workpeople to their job and the company. The behaviour of trade unions and the way they are dealt with by management will also contribute to the organization climate, where the extremes may be continuous hostility on the one hand or total co-operation on the other, but where various degrees of hostility and co-operation between these extremes are more likely to exist.

The personnel manager has to know his way around this maze if he is going to exert any influence or get anything worthwhile done. And every move he makes to change a policy or to introduce a new technique must be thought through against the background of his knowledge of the organization's climate.

## Relationships between personnel and other managers

The context within which personnel managers operate is not only the organization and its internal and external environment, but also the network of relationships that exist between themselves and their bosses and colleagues.

The essence of the problem faced by personnel specialists in these relationships is that, because all managers are, in effect, personnel managers, it is more difficult for them to accept that personnel specialists have the same level of professional expertise as, say, accountants and lawyers. To most laymen, accountancy and the law are subjects that they are quite glad to leave to other people. Line managers do not want to draw up a trial balance — most cannot even read a balance sheet. Neither have they any wish to get involved in the technicalities of commercial law. They are glad to leave these things to the experts. But many find it more difficult to accept that personnel managers have certain expertise which they themselves lack. And it is no good personnel people saying 'I know about behavioural science and you do not, therefore you should listen to me'. Your typical line manager does not know behavioural science when he meets it and would not believe it if he did. The personnel manager may indeed be able to convince his colleagues that they need someone around to look after the administration of recruitment, training, or pay and records, not to speak of the canteen. They may, more recently, have persuaded their bosses that there has to be someone around who understands the ramifications of employment law or, in the U.K., the ghastly administrative problems produced by the government's statutory sick pay scheme. But they find it more difficult to demonstrate that they know things about dealing with people which their line colleagues do not. And personnel specialists suffer the additional disadvantage of being perceived as living in an ivory tower and 'not being at the sharp end'.

A variety of attitudes, typical of those found amongst chief executives and line managers, are described below. The personnel function will be encouraged or inhibited, depending on how it is regarded by colleagues. How the appreciation, indifference or hostility of others affects the ability of the personnel manager to influence policy and decision-making is discussed later in this chapter.

### Attitudes towards personnel managers

In a series of articles published in 1982/83 in *Personnel Management*,[8] a number of well known chief executives in large, forward-looking British firms described how they saw the personnel function. The following are some of the more significant comments, each attributing a key role to personnel management.

> Skills of a very high order of professionalism, such as the Institute of Personnel Management exists to foster, will be increasingly required of the personnel function. These personnel skills will touch every point of the business and so I see the personnel function being drawn more and more into the general management of the business.
>
> We take it for granted that the finance specialist, the production specialist, the engineer, the materials and equipment specialist, the marketing expert will have their say in general management decisions. All too often the personnel contribution in the past has been a reactive one rather than a harnessing of human resources to maximize achievement. The time has come for this to change to a more positive role.
>
> *– Sir Derek Ezra (now Lord Ezra), Chairman, National Coal Board*

> It is relevant here to quote part of a policy statement issued by our board: 'Involvement means that all employees are able to make known their views and ideas about the pattern of their everyday work, to contribute to decisions that affect its development and change, and are made aware of the wider issues affecting their well-being and security.'
>
> This greater involvement of all employees in the content and purpose of their jobs should apply whatever their particular role and working group. It should create an understanding of the individual contribution of all employees to achieving the prime objective of the company.
>
> The most important role of personnel is probably to develop and enhance the commitment of managers and supervisors to this end, in ways compatible with collective bargaining arrangements agreed with recognized trade unions; and to help in providing the necessary training, education and communication of relevant commercial, financial and production information.
>
> If personnel management is about people at work and their effective contribution to the business, personnel managers can have little fear about the importance of their future role and of the task that lies ahead of them.
>
> *– Sir Alex Jarrett, Chairman, Reed Paper Group*

> Summing up on the things I expect from personnel, there are two or three themes that recur. One of these is professionalism; another is the need to be outward-looking and in touch with other industries and society at large. The third is the need to operate on two distinct timescales. Personnel must develop long-term policies and strategies and it must also be in there pitching when day-to-day problems arise, when tough negotiations are being faced, when the line managers need their skill and experience to the full. In a sense, there is the creative, philosophical role, the preventative role and the day-to-day role. The job is not purely fire-fighting but we must recognize that even with the best long-term strategies, some fires will inevitably break out.                                    *– Sir Peter Parker, Chairman, British Rail* [9]

There is no evidence of negative attitudes here, but chief executives do not all feel so bullish about personnel management. Peter Prior, Chairman of HP Bulmer, did indeed state that:

> ...the personnel manager obviously has a key role... It is a specialist role and his or her skill and advice are called upon when the problem to be resolved involves people. Apart from this ... the main task is to see that people problems do not arise, to ensure that people do not slow down the organization when it gets into top gear.

But later on, he wrote:

> All too often, personnel people have claimed to have approached the problems of the individual through social science but, with the greatest respect, the present state of human and industrial relations in many critical areas of British business says little for the success of their efforts. [10]

And that arch-iconoclast, Robert Townsend, headed his section on personnel management in *Up the Organization* with the words 'Sack the personnel department'. [11]

Legge quotes a variety of comments by line managers about the personnel function derived from her research into the role of personnel management in a number of organizations.

> The trouble with the Personnel Department here is that they try to introduce gimmicky new theories through general management channels. They should stick to welfare – that's what personnel's job is – looking after routine welfare matters.
> *– Assistant Works Manager (Engineering)*

> We're all personnel managers here. We have to be, as the only resource we've got is people. *– Director*

> The Personnel Department is important in that both the Industrial Relations Officer and the Personnel Superintendent are anchor men who provide continuity of experience and interpretation of company policy. *– Assistant Works Manager (Operations)*

> The Personnel Department have little understanding of line management's problems.
> *– Work Study Manager*

> The Personnel Department here is, as it should be, a service to the line. For example, if we want more labour they get it, train it, and arrange for it to be paid. They provide information for negotiations too, but I do the real negotiating.
> *– General Works Manager*

Kingsley Manning, writing in *Management Today*, made the following comments about the personnel function:

> The challenge and the opportunity for the personnel function remain as great as ever. The people a firm employs are still its largest cost and most important asset. Though the importance of getting the best performance out of that asset has not changed, personnel management as a discipline has yet to meet that challenge and make the significant impact it surely should.
> The failure to do so raises fundamental questions about the whole personnel function. Of all the major areas of management, personnel has the weakest conceptual base and the poorest technology. It is not surprising that personnel departments often exhibit little unity of purpose; but this effectively ensures that the departments contribute little to the company's decision-making process. If personnel management is to rise to the challenge of the turbulent 1980s it must review its most basic concepts and practices. What is needed is the sort of analytic and creative thinking that has been demonstrated so successfully in disciplines like marketing and finance.[12]

Support for the personnel function, especially in large progressive companies, is often to be found at the top, and elaborate new approaches such as organization development and job enrichment programmes have often been launched at this level, although not always successfully. A case study of what happened a few years after an organization development exercise was initiated by top management in ICI showed that middle managers were generally hostile or indifferent to the programme, which consequently made little impact.

The attitudes of middle managers can be mixed. They are the ones who deal day-to-day with the personnel department. Some understand and appreciate the services and advice offered. Others do not. Tony Watson reported the fact that relationships with line managers were the major problem for his sample of personnel managers. As one of them said of line managers:

> They come along and dump a 'people problem' on us. When we try to get them to do something or see something in a wider perspective, they say 'That's your pigeon – that's Personnel – now't to do with us.[13]

The challenge to personnel managers is to get to grips with this aspect of the context in which they work in order to exert whatever influence they can to modify the attitudes of line managers, when they are negative, or to make the best use of positive attitudes, when they exist. There are, however, constraints on what can be done, and these are discussed below.

## Constraints on personnel management

A hostile or turbulent environment which changes the role or affects the performance of the organization can restrict the positive things that personnel managers can do. What some managements regard as fringe activities, e.g. training, are the first in troubled times to be cut. Personnel departments go into reverse, removing rather than recruiting people. General and line managers become more hard-nosed.

There are, however, more fundamental and permanent constraints on what personnel departments can do. Legge wrote that it is easy to state that good personnel management should aim for 'the optimum utilization of the organization'.[1] In reality, however, this aim is difficult to define for the following reasons:

1. The goals and objectives of organizations are often hard to pin down and the targets for personnel aims and policies are therefore less clear.
2. Even when primary organizational goals can be defined (e.g. mazimize profit) the secondary goals required to achieve them may not be obvious. In other words, while it is sometimes relatively easy to define ends there is often conflict over the best means to achieve these ends.
3. The concept of 'optimization' is not so clear as it seems. There are many interests in organizations, e.g. management and workers, not to speak of the state, the owners and the public. These groups may legitimately have different interests which are incompatible with one another and consequently difficult if not impossible to reconcile (the concept of the plurality of legitimate groups in organizations).
4. Although managers confess to aim for optimization, in practice they are often forced into choosing the just adequate or 'good enough' course of action. This is because choice is limited by constraints operating in or on the organization, limited knowledge, and the perceived need to avoid uncertainty and make decisions that will at least work even if they are not necessarily the 'best' decisions.
5. The ends (primary goals) and the means (secondary goals) will be influenced by the context of the organization – its environment, role, structure, management style, technology, etc. What is required and works well in one organization will not necessarily be appropriate or work in another setting.
6. The power of the personnel function to influence policies may be constrained by the values of the organization and the part the function is allowed to play in the decision-making process.

## Impact of constraints on the role of personnel managers

As Keith Thurley has said, personnel managers, in Britain at least, are often 'working against the grain of British culture and values' and 'it is judged that attempts to break out of this situation by developing overall strategies are difficult due to the constraints under which organizations have to work'.[14] Variations in the organizational context, and environmental changes mean that there is no fixed pattern for what personnel specialists do or how they do it. And ambiguity in the role of the personnel function often results in confusion between ideals and reality. Shaun Tyson[15] also sees a contrast between the ideology and the actual realities of organizational life to which personnel managers as 'organization men' have to conform.

The main impact of this ambiguity and the constraints discussed above is on the power that personnel managers can exert and on the degree to which they can influence personnel policies.

## Power

Power in organizations depends on three main factors as analysed by Handy:[2]

☐ *Position* — the right to do something because of position or rank in an organization. The value of position as a source of power depends on the value placed on that position within the organization. It is also related to the resources controlled by the position holder.

☐ *Expertise* — the power that is vested in someone because of acknowledged expertise: 'authority goes to the one who knows'. This power can only be given by those over whom it is exercised.

☐ *Personal* — the most elusive form of power, which resides in the person and in his personality and is fanned by success and self-confidence or can evaporate in defeat.

Personnel managers hope that their power will rest on position and expertise with an admixture of personal charisma. But, as Handy comments: 'Too often personnel departments of organizations are forced to rely on position or resource power when their expert power proves to be unrecognized.' Legge established that, because the position power held by personnel management in company decision-making is often ambiguous,

> ... the personnel management considerations involved in production, marketing, and finance decisions were not so much overruled as went by default. In other words, non-specialists, while formally recognising the importance of effectively utilizing human resources, lacking as they did the expertise to develop a systematic view of what this entailed in terms of personnel strategies and action, *in practice* tended to underestimate the importance of the human resource variables in decision-making on issues that were not explicitly 'personnel management'. While in theory they recognized that the effective use of manpower was of vital importance to their organizations, in practice the very pervasiveness of manpower management meant that, being taken for granted, it was neglected as a dimension to most problems under discussion and emerged as an issue worthy of concentrated consideration only if a specifically 'manpower' crisis threatened. Hence, although theoretically strategic to the organization, personnel management, even in its broadest sense, often was not perceived or treated as such.[1]

## Policy formulation and implementation

Constraints, ambiguity and restricted power combine to limit the extent to which personnel managers can influence personnel policies in the sense that these define the organization's approach to its employees.

Brewster, Gill and Richbell, in their paper on the application of industrial relations policies,[16] distinguished between the *instigators* of policies (usually top management, who may or may not be advised by a personnel specialist), the *implementors* of policies (the line managers) and the *facilitators* (industrial relations specialists). In their research in a variety of companies they observed differences between 'espoused' policies — what the instigators intended to happen — and operational policies — what the implementors saw as their priorities and put into practice. Espoused and operational personnel policies were not always the same because personnel specialists were often not directly involved in their implementation: 'The personnel manager is frequently left on the touchline — there to give advice but not allowed to play.'[20] The line manager tends to assess the various demands upon him and acts in accordance with his own abilities and limitations. As Brewster and Richbell commented:

> Sometimes it seems as though a great many very talented personnel specialists are wasting an awful lot of time. They carefully watch developments in the industrial relations, political and labour market environments, they develop sensible, well thought-out personnel policies that would make their company one of the most progressive and highly respected of employers. And then they see their efforts continually frustrated and subverted by a management team that seems determined to ignore most of what the personnel department does. [17]

## What should the personnel manager do?

At first sight, the results of the Brewster, Gill and Richbell research make depressing reading. Personnel managers must sometimes wonder what they *can* do, never mind what they should do, to cope with the complexity and changeability of their organizational context, the indifferent or even negative attitudes of line managers and the constraints placed upon the personnel function.

But all is not lost. The personnel specialist can not only cope, he can triumph over these adversities as long as he does not rely upon his position and expertise to prescribe what the organization must do.

Alan Fowler, Head of Manpower Services, Hampshire County Council, gave some good advice at the Institute of Personnel Management's 1982 conference:

> Efficient and effective personnel departments display certain characteristics. They are recognized and used as the central repository of all knowledge on personnel matters — not only of the organization itself, but concerning legislation, the industry, trends, etc. They take a positive advisory role, offering ideas and advice rather than simply answering questions. They show a willingness to delegate and decentralize many personnel functions which can be part of uniform company policy and to bend rules to get things done. Their officers have a genuine interest in operational matters and are as keen as other line managers and directors to get all-round efficiency; at the same time they show an ability to involve others in personnel work.[18]

To make the approach suggested by Fowler work, personnel managers must develop and apply analytical skills to gain an understanding of the organizational context, the attitudes of their fellow managers, the constraints they have to live with *and* themselves — their own abilities, values and attitudes. It will help if the personnel specialist has adequate status and access to information and resources to exert influence and implement decisions. The use of collaborative problem-solving methods will achieve even better results. But understanding is the most important thing to achieve. As Brewster and Richbell put it:

> The realization of personnel policies demands an understanding of how policies are implemented within the organization. It should not be assumed that simply having a policy accepted at the formal level is the end of the exercise. There is a need to see 'policy' from the point of view of its implementors — frequently line and general managers — and to develop a deeper awareness of the many pressures and demands that make the implementation of espoused personnel policies difficult for them. Line managers do not decide to accept or reject policies arbitrarily; rather, they are, most of the time, trying to conform with the values and priorities of senior executives.[17]

## Using a contingent approach

Understanding derived from analysis will enable personnel managers to adopt a contingent approach as advocated by Legge, i.e. 'the design and implementation of policy that matches, or is *contingent* upon specified organizational requirements and circumstances'. This requires five steps:

1. An objective-setting exercise, based on a diagnosis of what specific objectives are appropriate to the organizational context.
2. An analytical classification of the alternatives, whether new techniques, or managerial styles or different approaches to reorganizing work.
3. An analysis of the context in which the alternatives are to apply.
4. The selection of one of the alternatives on the basis that it 'fits' the context in which it is to operate in such a way as to facilitate the achievement of the specified objective.
5. A recognition of the need to evaluate systematically, not only the basis for selecting a specific alternative in the first instance, but also its degree of success following implementation.

Thus, before leaping on to the latest bandwagon, say quality circles, the personnel manager must go through the analytical process to decide first if it would fit the organization and, second, how it should be introduced. This would mean preliminary research on whether the technology and circumstances of the organization are right or ripe for quality circles. Is there a quality control problem? What is being done about it now? Does management feel that enough is being done? How ready are supervisors, workpeople and trade unions to co-operate in the participative approach fundamental to quality circles? And, based on *first-hand* studies of quality circles in action in firms of a similar size and with a similar technology (not relying on the blandishments of management consultants or the self-laudatory articles or lectures of exponents of quality circles), will it work in our circumstances? And what are the ingredients for success? If the answers to these questions are favourable, objectives can be set, alternative methods can be identified and after a more detailed analysis of the context in which the quality circles are to operate, the most appropriate alternative can be selected.

Fundamental to this whole approach is the need to analyse and understand the attitudes and needs of the line managers affected by it. New techniques or answers to old problems have to be sold to managers. And they have to be sold in a way which will convince them of the necessity, practicality and value of the innovation or solution.

Political sensitivity to where power lies in the organization and, therefore, how it can be influenced, is another important characteristic required for success in personnel management. Sadly, good ideas do not always sell themselves. People have to be convinced, and the art is first to establish who needs to be convinced (i.e. who has the power not only to make the decision but also to ensure its success or failure in implementation), and then to decide on the best method of convincing them.

## Summary

To summarize, the personnel manager needs to ensure that:

☐ ideas for improvement or innovation are thoroughly tested against an analysis of the characteristics and true needs of the organization;
☐ ideas are sold to management on the basis of the practical and, wherever

possible, measurable benefits that will result from their implementation (it is not the idea itself that is saleable but the result it can achieve);

☐ new procedures or techniques are pilot-tested to make sure they work in practice and to provide evidence of the benefits they produce;

☐ the procedures or techniques are presented with great care to management as providing direct help to them in running the organization or their department more effectively than before;

☐ unobtrusive assistance, guidance and encouragement is provided in implementing new techniques — not from the stance of a would-be professional who knows it all, but from the point of view of a colleague who can give practical help in achieving something worthwhile.

## References

1. Legge, K. *Power, Innovation and Problem-Solving in Personnel Management.* McGraw-Hill, Maidenhead, 1978.
2. Handy, C.B. *Understanding Organizations.* Penguin Books, Harmondsworth, 1974.
3. Drucker, P. *The Practice of Management.* Heinemann, London, 1955.
4. McGregor, D. *The Human Side of Enterprise.* McGraw-Hill, New York, 1960.
5. Heller, R. *The Naked Manager.* Barrie and Jenkins, London, 1972.
6. Katz, D. and Kahn, R.L. *The Social Psychology of Organizations.* John Wiley and Sons, New York, 1964.
7. Ezra, Sir Derek, 'How I see the Personnel Function', *Personnel Management*, July 1982.
8. Jarrett, Sir Alex, 'How I see the Personnel Function', *Personnel Management*, June 1982.
9. Parker, Sir Peter, 'How I see the Personnel Function', *Personnel Management*, January 1983.
10. Prior, P. 'Toll the Knell for Leadership. The Personnel Man Cometh', *Personnel Management*, October 1981.
11. Townsend, R. *Up the Organization.* Michael Joseph, London, 1970.
12. Manning, K. 'The Rise and Fall of Personnel', *Management Today*, March 1983.
13. Watson, T. *The Personnel Managers.* Routledge and Kegan Paul, London, 1977.
14. Thurley, K. 'Personnel Management in the UK — A Case for Urgent Treatment', *Personnel Management*, August 1981.
15. Tyson, S. 'Taking Advantage of Ambiguity', *Personnel Management*, February 1983.
16. Brewster, C.J., Gill, C.G., and Richbell, S. 'Developing an Analytical Approach Of Industrial Relations Policy', *Personnel Review*, Vol 10, No 2, 1981.
17. Brewster, C.T., and Richbell, S. 'Getting Managers to Implement Personnel Policies', *Personnel Management*, December 1982.
18. Fowler, A., as reported in *IPM Digest*, November 1982.

## Part II
# Organizational Behaviour

The study of organizational behaviour is the study of how organizations function, in terms of their structure and processes, and how the people within organizations act, individually or in groups.

Personnel managers perform their jobs within complex systems called organizations. Managers in general, and personnel managers in particular, exist to influence behaviour in a desired direction. Skills in the analysis and diagnosis of patterns of organizational behaviour are therefore important. They help in the definition of organizational context, and, as Nadler and Tushman have said:

> The manager needs to be able to *understand* the patterns of behaviour that are observed, to *predict* in what direction behaviour will move (particularly in the light of managerial action), and to use this knowledge to *control* behaviour over the course of time... Effective managerial action requires that the manager be able to diagnose the system he or she is working in.[1]

The purpose of this part of the book is to outline a basic set of concepts and to provide analytical tools which will enable the personnel manager to diagnose organizational behaviour and to take appropriate actions. The actions will include the use of techniques to design organizations and jobs, to develop more effective organizations and people, to manage change and conflict, to motivate people to work and to deal with problems concerning individuals or groups. These techniques should be developed and operated in the knowledge of the processes at work in the organization as they affect and are affected by the behaviour of the people in it.

Chapter 4 considers how organizations are structured, taking into account the human factors involved. In chapter 5 the way in which organizations function is examined by studying the various processes that take place within them — change, leadership, power, conflict, stress and group behaviour. Chapter 6 deals with the factors that influence individual behaviour at work — motivation and how people adapt to their roles.

### Reference
1. Nadler, D.A. and Tushman, M.L. *A Congruence Model for Diagnosing Organizational Behaviour*, Resource Book in Macro-Organizational Behaviour, R.H. Miles (ed). Goodyear Publishing, Santa Monica, 1980.

# 4 | Organization Structure

Organizations exist to get work done. The organization itself is an entity which is there for a purpose. This determines what it sets out to do, but *what* it actually does and *how* it does it will be influenced by a number of external and internal forces, including the environment and the history of the organization.

The process of organizing can be described as the design, development and maintenance of a system of co-ordinated activities in which individuals and groups of people work co-operatively under authority and leadership towards commonly understood and accepted goals. The key word in that definition is 'system'. Organizations are systems which, as affected by their environment, have a structure which has both formal and informal elements.

All organizations have some form of structure, which has been defined by John Child as comprising 'all the tangible and regularly occurring features which help to shape its members' behaviour'.[1] This chapter deals with the considerations that affect the structure of organizations. It does this by reviewing the various organization 'models' developed by the theorists on this subject. These concepts are intended to provide a background against which the design of organizations and jobs as discussed in part III of this book can be carried out.

## Basic considerations

Organizations vary in their complexity, but in every case it is necessary to divide the overall management task into a variety of activities and to establish means of co-ordinating and controlling these activities. This design process leads to the development of a formal organization structure consisting of units and positions between which there are relationships involving the exercise of authority and the communication and exchange of information.

The structure must be appropriate to the organization's purpose and to the situation in which it exists. As Lupton says: 'Organizations are seen as patterns of human tasks and relationships, shaped so as to allow at least survival, at most growth and development, in environments which constrain, but which also offer opportunities.'[2]

The personnel manager is, or should be, involved in the design and development of organizations. He should base his contribution on an understanding of the forces shaping his own organization. To do this he needs tools which will help him to analyse and appreciate what is happening. These tools are provided in the form of 'models' developed by a number of writers and researchers on organization development.

The original model derived from the work of the *classical school* of organization theorists, who believed that the design of the structure should conform to certain general principles. The *human relations school*, however, emphasized that the way organizations function and how, therefore, they should be structured, is

47

primarily dependent on how people behave, interact and create the informal organization. The *bureaucratic model* developed by Weber suggested that there were circumstances in which organizations did require formal hierarchies and clear definitions of responsibilities. The *systems* and *contingency schools* stressed correctly that the way organizations functioned and were structures was closely related to their environment, technology and the amount of change and differentiation to which they were subjected.

It should be remembered, however, that while these models either contribute to our understanding of the different forms of organization or provide a basis for tackling organizational problems, they do not add up to a universal theory of organization. As Perrow wrote: 'We know enough about organizations now to recognize that most generalizations that are applicable to all organizations are too obvious or too general to be of much use for specific predictions.'[3] And the earliest models produced by the scientific management or so-called 'classical' school fell into this trap, which is why, as will emerge later, the contingency approach seems to have most to offer.

## Scientific management

The scientific management or classical school as represented by Fayol, Taylor and Urwick believed in control, order and formality. Organizations need to minimize the opportunity for unfortunate and uncontrollable informal relations, leaving room only for the formal ones. From these overriding principles the following concepts are derived:

1. *Structure*. Formal structures are required to provide orderly relationships between functions. The basic structure contains the line organization, which exercises delegated authority in performing the functions of the enterprise, and the staff organization which offers advice and provides services required by the line organization. Structural considerations include the span of control, which relates to the number of subordinates an executive can manage and the number of levels in the hierarchy.
2. *Specialization*. As the human organization grows, work must be broken down along lines as natural as possible to provide well defined areas of specialization. This is the classical economic theory of the division of labour and all other scientific-management principles are derived from it.
3. *Co-ordination*. The need for specialization creates the need for co-ordination. The many different functions performed by the members of an organization must be co-ordinated or tied together so that they contribute jointly to the end result. To achieve this members have to carry out their work as and when required so that each contribution fits the contribution of others.
4. *Authority*. Organizations achieve order and regularity by the use of authority implemented through a defined hierarchy or chain of command.
5. *Continuity*. Organizations should be designed to achieve continuity, stability and predictability. This must be done by minimizing disruptions caused by personality and individual idiosyncrasy. The organization consists of replaceable members and its design should not be affected by the people who happen to be employed in it.

The scientific management model has been attacked vigorously because it is too rigid and because it makes no allowance for situational factors such as the environment or technology. Neither does it take account of change or human factors, including the informal organization. But this approach, with its emphasis on organization charts and manuals, job descriptions, clear definitions of responsibility and authority and limited spans of control, still thrives. As Lupton pointed out: 'The attraction of the classical design from the point of view of top management is that it seems to offer them control.'[2] Managers like to think they are rational and this has all the appearance of a rational approach. Many line managers when asked to describe their organizations will draw hierarchical charts, produce job descriptions and use such expressions as chain of command, levels of authority, line and staff and span of control. This is the language of classical theory.

## The human relations school

The scientific management school reigned supreme until the late 1930s and still holds sway in the 1980s, as mentioned above. But in 1938 a business executive named Chester Barnard suggested that organizations are co-operative systems, not the products of mechanical engineering. He stressed natural groups within the organization, upward communication, authority from below rather than from above, and leaders who functioned as a cohesive force. Barnard also emphasized the importance of the informal organization — the network of informal roles and relationships which, for better or worse, strongly influences the way the formal structure operates. He wrote: 'Formal organizations come out of and are necessary to informal organization: but when formal organizations come into operation, they create and require informal organizations.'[4] Much more recently, Child[1] has pointed out that it is misleading to talk about a clear distinction between the formal and the informal organization. Formality *and* informality can be designed into structure. Unofficial policies do exist in organizations but they are not to be confused with informality. Organization designers recognize the relevance of informal relationships but do not implement unofficial structures.

In 1938 Roethlisberger and Dickson[5] reported on the Hawthorne Studies — the first large-scale investigation of productivity and industrial relations, which took place at the Hawthorne plant at Western Electric. This highlighted the importance of informal groups, work restriction norms and decent, humane leadership.

It was widely, if unfairly, believed that supporters of the human relations school approach only wanted organizations to be nice to people. This criticism became stronger as the original ideas were extended to suggest that, in all organizations, there were a number of things that were bad for the morale of individuals and groups — routine and specialized tasks, submission to authority, ignorance of objectives and centralized decision-making. In the 1960s a number of behavioural scientists emerged who would not like to be described as part of the human relations school, but did in fact subscribe to many of the fundamental beliefs of that school, although these beliefs were refined and re-presented on the basis of further study and research. The most notable contributors to this post-war development were McGregor, Likert and Argyris.

### Douglas McGregor

Douglas McGregor is best known for his classification of assumptions about human nature into Theories X and Y. Theory X is the traditional view that the average human being dislikes work and wishes to avoid responsibility and that, therefore, 'most people must be coerced, controlled, directed, threatened with

49

punishment to get them to put forward adequate effort towards organizational objectives.'[6] The more progressive, some would say optimistic, assumptions contained in Theory Y are that, given the chance, people will not only accept but also seek responsibility: 'The capacity to execute a relatively high degree of imagination, ingenuity and creativity in the solution of organizational problems is widely, not narrowly, distributed in the population.'

The central principle of organizations that McGregor derived from Theory Y is that of integration — the process of recognizing the needs of both the organization and the individual and creating conditions which will reconcile their needs so that members of the organization can work together for its success and share in its rewards: 'Man will exercise self-direction and self-control in the service of objectives to which he is committed.'

### Rensis Likert

Rensis Likert derived his concept of organizations based on supportive relationships from the programmes of research at the University of Michigan where he was director. The initial studies distinguished between job-centred and employee-centred supervisors and established that employee-centred supervisors were higher producers than the job-centred ones. The studies also distinguished between general and close supervision and showed that general rather than close supervision is more often associated with a high rather than a low level of productivity.

From his analysis of high-producing managers Likert found that their operations were characterized by attitudes of identification with the organization and its objectives and a high sense of involvement in achieving them. This situation was created by 'harnessing effectively all the major motivational forces which can exercise significant influence in an organizational setting and which, potentially, can be accompanied by co-operative and favourable attitudes.'[7]

The integrating principle of supportive relationships was derived from this analysis. This principle states that:

> The leadership and other processes of the organization must be such as to ensure a maximum probability that in all interactions and all relationships with the organization each member will, in the light of his background, values and expectations, view the experience as supportive and one which builds and maintains his sense of personal worth and importance.[7]

### Chrys Argyris

The research carried out by Argyris into personality development in organizations suggested to him 'that the formal organization creates in a healthy individual feelings of failure and frustration, short time perspective and conflict'.[8] He further concluded that the formal work organization requires many members to act in immature rather than adult ways: 'At all levels there is behaviour that is not productive in the sense of helping the organization achieve its objectives. For example, at the lower levels we found apathy, indifference and non-involvement. .. At the upper levels we found conformity, mistrust, inability to accept new ideas, and fear of risk taking.'[9]

To overcome this problem Argyris wants the individual to feel that he has a high degree of self-control over setting his own goals and over defining the paths to these goals. The strategy should be to 'develop a climate in which the difficulties can be openly discussed, the employee's hostility understood and accepted, and a programme defined which everyone can participate in attempting to develop new designs. Wherever this is impossible, the attempt will be made to design new work worlds that can be integrated with the old and that help the employee obtain more opportunity for psychological success.'[9] Lest this seems too idealistic (a tendency shared by all members of the human relations school) Argyris stresses the need for some structure to provide 'the firm ground on which to anchor one's security'. Organization design has therefore to plan for integration and involvement, although these processes will probably have to take place within the traditional pyramidal structure.

## The behavioural science movement

The behavioural science movement, pioneered by the writers mentioned above, but furthered by people such as Herzberg and Blake, continued to emphasize that in organizations the proper study of mankind is man. The research conducted by Herzberg and his colleagues[10] suggested that improvements in organization design must centre on the individual job as the positive source at motivation. If the individual feels that the job is stretching him he will be moved to perform it well. (Herzberg's theories are dealt with in more detail in chapter 6.)

Blake[11] concentrates on management style − the way in which managers manage, based on their beliefs and values. He suggests that there are two factors: 'concern for people' and 'concern for production' (this is in line with the distinction made by the Ohio State University researchers Halpin and Winer[12] between leadership styles based on 'consideration' or 'initiating' structure.) Blake's managerial grid presents a matrix of 81 styles based on nine degrees of concern for people and nine degrees of concern for production. A manager scoring 9 for people and 1 for production would be a 9/1 manager − the softy who lets production slide in case he offends anyone; someone who scores 1 for people and 9 for production would be too tough, the no-nonsense man who gets the staff out of the door and doesn't care whom he hurts in the process. Ideally, one should be 9/9 but most people are probably 5/5 or thereabouts. Blake believes that the process of analysing managerial style along the lines of discussing how to progress to 9/9 is the best way to seek organizational efficiency.

The concepts of these and other behavioural scientists provided the impetus for the organization development movement whose beliefs were summarized by Bennis as follows:

(a) A new concept of man based on increased knowledge of his complex and shifting needs which replaces an oversimplified, innocent, push-button idea of man;
(b) a new concept of power, based on collaboration and reason, which replaces a model of power based on coercion and threat;
(c) a new concept of organization values, based on humanistic-democratic ideals, which replaces the mechanistic value system of bureaucracy.[13]

## Views on the human relations school

No one can quarrel with the values expressed by the human relations school and these behavioural scientists associated with it − we are all in favour of virtue. But there are a number of grounds on which the more extreme beliefs of the school can be criticized:

1. It claims that its concepts are universally applicable, yet organizations come in all shapes and sizes, types of activity and context.
2. It ignores the real commercial and technological constraints of industrial life. Instead, it reflects more of an ideological concern for personal development and the rights of the individual rather than a scientific curiosity about the

factors affecting organizational efficiency.

3. It overreacts against the excessive formality of the scientific management school by largely ignoring the formal organization and attaching too much importance to informal work-group processes.

4. Its emphasis on the need to minimize conflict overlooks the point that conflict is not necessarily undesirable, and may rather be an essential concomitant of change and development.

To be fair, not all behavioural scientists were so naive. Although McGregor's Theory Y was somewhat idealistic, he at least recognized that 'industrial health does not flow automatically from the elimination of dissatisfaction, disagreement, or even open conflict. Peace is not synonymous with organizational health; socially responsible management is not co-extensive with permissive management.'[6]

## The bureaucratic model

Meanwhile, as Perrow put it:

> In another part of the management forest, the mechanistic school was gathering its forces and preparing to outflank the forces of light. First came the numbers men – the linear programmers, the budget experts, the financial analysts... Armed with emerging systems concepts, they carried the 'mechanistic' analogy to its fullest – and it was very productive. Their work still goes on, largely untroubled by organizational theory; the theory it seems clear, will have to adjust to them, rather than the other way around... Then the works of Max Weber, not translated until the 1940s ... began to find their way into social science thought.[14]

Max Weber coined the term 'bureaucracy' as a label for a type of formal organization in which impersonality and rationality are developed to the highest degree. Bureaucracy, as he conceived it, was the most efficient form of organization because it is coldly logical and because personalized relationships and non-rational, emotional considerations do not get in its way. The ideal bureaucracy, according to Weber, has the following features:

☐ maximum specialization;
☐ close job definition as to duties, privileges and boundaries;
☐ vertical authority patterns;
☐ decisions based on expert judgement, resting on technical knowledge and on disciplined compliance with the directives of superiors;
☐ policy and administration are separate;
☐ maximum use of rules;
☐ impersonal administration of staff.

At first, with his celebrations of the efficiency of bureaucracy, Weber was received with only reluctant respect, even hostility. Most writers were against bureaucracy. But it turned out, surprisingly, that managers are not. They prefer clear lines of communication, clear specifications of authority and responsibility and clear knowledge of whom they are responsible to. Admittedly, in some situations, as Burns and Stalker point out,[15] they might want absolute clarity but they can't get it. On the other hand there are circumstances when the type of work carried out in an organization requires a bureaucratic approach in the Weberian, not the pejorative 'red tape' sense. The apparently conflicting views of the human relations and bureaucratic schools of thought had to be reconciled. Much of what they said was right, but it was insufficiently related to context.

The first step was to look at how organizations worked as systems related to their environment – this was taken by the systems school. At the same time a number of researchers were looking at organizations primarily in relation to their environment; they constitute what may be termed the contingency school.

## The systems school

The systems approach to organizations as formulated by Miller and Rice[16] states that organizations should be treated as open systems which are continually dependent upon and influenced by their environments. The basic characteristic of the enterprise as an open system is that it transforms inputs into outputs within its environment.

As Katz and Kahn wrote: 'Systems theory is basically concerned with problems of relationship, of structure and of interdependence.'[7] As a result there is a considerable emphasis on the concept of transactions across boundaries – between the system and its environment and between the different parts of the system. This open and dynamic approach avoided the error of the classical and human relations theorists who thought of organizations as closed systems and analysed their problems with reference to their internal structures and processes of interaction, without taking account of external influences and the changes they impose or of the technology in the organization.

### The socio-technical model

The basic idea of the organization as a system was extended by the Tavistock Institute researchers into the socio-technical model of organizations. The basic principle of this model is that in any system of organization, technical or task aspects are interrelated with the human or social aspects. The emphasis is on interrelationships between, on the one hand, the technical processes of transformation carried out within the organization, and on the other hand, the organization of work groups and the management structures of the enterprise.

The socio-technical model originated from two major studies carried out by members of the Tavistock Institute: first, the Longwall study in the mines of Durham and, second, the study of the textile mills in Ahmedabad, India. In the mining study it was found that two very different forms of organization were operated in the same seam and with identical technology. The conventional Longwall system combined a complex formal structure with simple work roles. The miner was committed to only one task and entered into a very limited number of unvarying social relations that were sharply divided between those within the particular task group and those who were outside. With those 'outside' he shared no sense of belongingness and recognized no responsibility to them for the consequences of his actions. The composite Longwall system, in contrast, combined a simple formal structure with complex work roles. The miner in this system had a commitment to the whole group task and consequently found himself drawn into a variety of tasks in co-operation with different members of the work group. As Trist wrote:

> That two such contrasting social systems can effectively operate the same technology is clear enough evidence that there exists an element of choice in designing a work organization. However, it is far from a matter of indifference which form of organization is selected... The technological system and the effectiveness of the total production system will depend upon the adequacy with which the social system is able to cope with these requirements.[18]

The research demonstrated that the composite system showed superiority over the conventional in terms of production and costs. It enabled miners to operate more flexibly and thereby cope better with changing conditions. It made better provision for the personal needs of miners and reduced stress as measured by absenteeism.

The analysis of the Longwall study suggested that when changes are being made in technology, it is necessary to choose carefully from among the alternatives available for the division in labour, the working practices and the reward system. While the aim should be to exploit the new technology, care should be taken not to threaten the existing social system.

The textile studies in India conducted by A.K. Rice were concerned with the re-design of an organization and based upon the socio-technical model. The reorganization was based on the following principles:

1. There is an optimum level of grouping activities which can be determined only by an analysis of the requirements of the technological system.
2. Grouping should be such that the workers are primarily related to each other by way of the requirements of task performance and task interdependence.
3. Supervisory roles should be designed after analysing the system's requirements for control and co-ordination. The aim should be to create unified commands which correspond to natural task groupings. This should free the supervisor for his tasks of planning, co-ordinating and controlling, first by enabling him to detect and to manage the boundary conditions which relate his individual commands to the larger system, and second by maximizing the autonomous responsibility of the work groups for internal control and co-ordination.

## The contingency school

The contingency school consists of writers such as Burns and Stalker, Joan Woodward, Laurence and Lorsch, and Perrow who have analysed a variety of organizations and concluded that their structures and methods of operation are a function of the circumstances in which they exist. They do not subscribe to the view that there is one best way of designing an organization or that simplistic classifications of organizations as formal or informal, bureaucratic or non-bureaucratic are helpful. They are against those who see organizations as mutually opposed social systems (what Burns and Stalker refer to as the 'Manichean world of the Hawthorne studies')[15] which set up formal against informal organizations, and against those who impose rigid principles of organization irrespective of the technology or environmental conditions.

### Burns and Stalker
Burns and Stalker based their concept of mechanistic and organic organizations on research into a number of Scottish firms in the electronics industry. They emphasized the rate of change in the environment of the organization as being the key factor in determining how it could operate.

In stable conditions a highly structured or 'mechanistic' organization will emerge with specialized functions, clearly defined roles, strict administrative routines and a hierarchical system of exercising authoritarian control. In effect, this is the bureaucratic system. However, when the environment is volatile, a rigid system of ranks and routines will inhibit the organization's speed and sensitivity of response. In these circumstances the structure is, or should be, 'organic' in the sense that it is a function of the situation in which the enterprise finds itself rather than conforming to any predetermined and rigid view of how it should operate. Individual responsibilities are less clear cut and members of the organization must constantly relate what they are doing to its general situation and specific problems.

Perhaps the most important contribution made by Burns and Stalker was the stress they placed on the suitability of each system to its own specific set of conditions. They concluded their analysis by writing:

> We desire to avoid the suggestion that either system is superior under all circumstances to the other. In particular, nothing in our experience justifies the assumption that mechanistic systems should be superseded by organic in conditions of stability. The beginning of administrative wisdom is the awareness that there is no one optimum type of management system.

## Woodward

Woodward's ideas about organization derived from a research project carried out in Essex designed to discover whether the principles of organization laid down by the classical theorists correlate with business success when put into practice. She found considerable variations in patterns of organization which could not be related to size of firm, type of industry or business success. She also found that there was no significant correlation between adherence to the classical principles relating to matters such as span of control or number of levels in the hierarchy, and business success. After further analysis, she concluded:

> When, however, the firms were grouped according to similarity of objectives and techniques of production, and classified in order of the technical complexity of their production systems, each production system was found to be associated with a characteristic pattern of organization. It appeared that technical methods were the most important factor in determining organizational structure and in setting the tone of human relationships inside the firms. The widely accepted assumptions that there are principles of management valid for all types of production systems seemed very doubtful.[19]

Woodward's main contribution to organization theory is, therefore, her belief that different technologies demand different structures and procedures and create different types of relationships.

## Laurence and Lorsch

Laurence and Lorsch[20] developed their contingency model on the basis of a study of six firms in the plastics industry. Organization, as they define it, is the process of co-ordinating different activities to carry out planned transactions with the environment. The three aspects of environment upon which the design of the organization is contingent are the market, the technology (i.e. the tasks carried out) and research and development. These may be differentiated along such dimensions as rate of change and uncertainty. This process of reacting to complexity and change by *differentiation* creates a demand for effective *integration* if the organization as a whole is to adapt efficiently to the environment. This concept of differentiation and integration is, in fact, the greatest contribution of Laurence and Lorsch to organization theory.

They suggested that:

> As organizations deal with their external environments, they become segmented into units, each of which has as its major task the problem of dealing with a part of the conditions outside the firm... These parts of the system need to be linked together towards the accomplishment of the organization's overall purpose.

Their research showed that the two organizations with the most successful records had, in fact, achieved the highest degree of integration of the six, and were also amongst the most highly differentiated. The differentiation of the various units was more in line with the demands of the environment for those two organizations than for the others.

One of the most important implications of the Laurence and Lorsch model for organization designers is that, although differentiation demands effective integration, this must not be achieved by minimizing differences and producing a common bland outlook. Instead, integration should be achieved by allowing each department to be as different in its outlook and its structure as its tasks demand — that is to be highly distinctive — but to use mediating devices such as committees, *ad hoc* project groups and assigned 'integrators' who stand midway between the functions with which they are concerned and are not dominated by any of them. Integration can therefore be achieved by structural means as well as by organizational development interventions designed to increase trust and understanding between groups and to confront conflict.

## Perrow

The model developed by Perrow[3] recognizes the importance of structure and the inevitable tendency towards routinization, standardization and bureaucracy in organizations. In accordance with the views of other members of the contingency school, he suggests that different structures can exist within the same firm and that a bureaucratic structure is as appropriate for some tasks as a non-bureaucratic structure is for other tasks.

## Application of organization theory

The different schools of organization theory provide a number of ways of analysing organizations from the point of view of the formal structure, individual behaviour, the organization as a system and the environmental influences which affect the shape and climate of an organization. The most pragmatic approach is provided by the contingency school. They say: first ensure that you understand the environment, the technology and the existing systems of social relationships, and then design an organization which is *contingent* upon the circumstances of the particular case. There is always some choice, but the designer is trying to achieve the best fit he can. But in making his choice, he should be aware of the structural, human and systems factors which will influence the design and of the context within which the organization operates. He must also take into account the culture of the organization, the processes that take place in it, namely change and the exercise of leadership and power, and the effect all this has on relationships (conflict), on individuals (stress) and on groups within the organization. These factors are discussed in the next chapter.

## References

1. Child, J. *Organization, A Guide to Problems and Practice*. Harper and Row, London, 1977.
2. Lupton, T. '"Best Fit" in the design of organizations', *Personnel Review,* **4**, 1, 1975.
3. Perrow, C. *Organizational Analysis. A Sociological View*. Tavistock Publications, London, 1970.
4. Barnard, C. *Functions of the Executive*. Harvard University Press, Cambridge, Mass, 1938.
5. Roethlisberger, F.J. and Dickson, W.J. *Management and the Worker*. Harvard University Press, Cambridge, Mass, 1939.

6. McGregor, D. *The Human Side of Enterprise.* McGraw-Hill, New York, 1966.
7. Likert, R. *New Patterns of Management.* McGraw-Hill, New York, 1961.
8. Argyris, C. *Personality and Organization.* Harper, New York, 1957.
9. Argyris, C. *Integrating the Individual and the Organization.* John Wiley, New York, 1964.
10. Herzberg, F. *et al, The Motivations to Work.* John Wiley, New York, 1959.
11. Blake, R.R. and Mouton, J.S. *The Managerial Grid.* Gulf Publishing, Houston, 1964.
12. Halpin, A.W. and Winer, B.J. *A Factorial Study of the Leader Behaviour Description.* Ohio State University, 1957.
13. Bennis, W. *Organization Development.* Addison-Wesley, Reading, Mass, 1969.
14. Perrow, C. *The Short and Glorious History of Organizational Theory,* Resource Book in Macro-Organizational Behaviour, R.H. Miles (ed). Goodyear Publishing, Santa Monica, 1980.
15. Burns, T. and Stalker, G.M. *The Management of Innovation.* Tavistock Publications, London, 1961.
16. Miller, E. and Rice, A.K. *Systems of Organization.* Tavistock Publications, London, 1967.
17. Katz, D. and Kahn, R.L. *The Social Psychology of Organizations.* John Wiley, New York, 1964.
18. Trist, E.L. *et al, Organizational Choice.* Tavistock Publications, London, 1963.
19. Woodward, J. *Industrial Organization.* Oxford University Press, 1965.
20. Laurence, P.R. and Lorsch, J.W. *Organization and Environment.* Harvard University Press, Cambridge, Mass, 1967.

# 5  How Organizations Function

The way in which organizations function within their environment is affected by their culture and the following processes: change, leadership, power, conflict, stress and the way in which groups operate. The factors which influence culture and the various organizational processes are discussed in turn in this chapter. The chapter ends with a review of how these and other factors affect organizational performance.

## Organization culture

Organization culture, as defined by Handy, is the pervasive way of life or set of norms and values that evolve in an organization over a period of time – the 'deep-set beliefs about the way work should be organized, the way authority exercised, people rewarded, people controlled'.[1]

Alternatively, the working atmosphere of the enterprise could be described as 'organization climate'. This comprises the ways in which the following aspects of organizational behaviour manifest themselves: teamwork and co-operation; commitment; communications; creativity; conflict resolution; participation; and confidence and trust between individuals and groups and between managers and their subordinates.

### Types of culture
Handy distinguishes between four types of culture:

1. *The power culture*, which depends on a central power source as in a small entrepreneurial organization. The organization works on precedent, on anticipating the wishes and decisions of the central sources of power. There are few rules and procedures. 'These cultures put a lot of faith in the individual, little in committees. They judge by results and are tolerant of means.' They are tough and abrasive but morale is often low and they can easily fall apart.
2. *The role culture*, another name for a bureaucratic organization which works by logic and rationality. Work is controlled by procedures for roles (i.e. job descriptions), procedures for communications and rules for the settlement of disputes. A role culture offers security and predictability but can be frustrating to individuals who want to get results quickly.
3. *The task culture* is job or project orientated. Groups, project teams or task forces are formed for a specific purpose and can be reformed, abandoned or continued without difficulty. The 'matrix' organization is a structural form of the task culture. This combines functional hierarchies related usually to a skill or a scientific, technical or professional discipline, with a task-performing entity related to a project, an assignment or a product. There will be a manager for each functional hierarchy and a manager or leader for each

project. Task cultures or matrix organizations exist in research and development industries such as aerospace, or professional firms of engineers or consultants who exist on projects. This culture is very adaptable and is appropriate where flexibility and sensitivity to the market or environment are important. On the whole, people like working in task cultures although they can induce feelings of insecurity (role ambiguity and conflict) if things go wrong. And control is difficult. Task cultures in hard times can revert to a power or role base and this causes frustration.

4. *The person culture*, where the organization exists only to serve and assist the people in it — some professional partnerships and consultancy firms come into this category. Organizations where this culture prevails may be rare, but within many enterprises there are individual specialists who are more orientated to their own discipline than the role assigned to them by the organization. Such individuals can be difficult to manage.

None of these cultures is necessarily preferable to another. To a degree they are inevitable consequences of the history, environment and technology of the organization. Each type of culture creates its own kind of problems but these are accentuated if an attempt is made to impose a culture which is inappropriate to the situation.

There are six factors which influence culture and, therefore, structure:

☐ *History and ownership.* Centralized ownership will lead towards a power structure with more control over resources. Family firms exhibit the same tendency.

☐ *Size.* Increasing size pushes an organization towards a role culture. Large organizations tend to be more formalized and develop specialized groups which need systematic co-ordination.

☐ *Technology* — routine, programmable operations or mass production are more suitable to a role culture. Non-continuous operations (one-off or batch) and rapidly changing technologies are suited to power or task cultures. The tendency towards increased automation and high investment in technology pushes organizations into a role culture.

☐ *Goals and objectives* — goals vary between organizations and both influence and are influenced by cultures. Growth goals are more prevalent in power or task cultures, while quality of product goals are more easily monitored in a role organization.

☐ *The environment* — rapid changes in the economic environment or the market require a task culture which is sensitive, adaptable and quick to respond. Threats or danger in the environment are best countered by power cultures. Firms with undiversified markets and products with a long life-cycle usually have a role culture.

☐ *The people* — certain types of people will be happy and successful in one culture, not in another. According to Handy, 'a match between organization, culture and an individual's psychological contract (i.e. his expectations from the organization) should lead to a satisfied individual'. Individuals with high needs for security and low tolerance for ambiguity will prefer role cultures. Those with a need to establish their identity at work and to make the maximum impact with their skills and talents will be more at home in a power or task culture.

### Implications

Organizations are subject to change and have to be restructured. As they grow, differentiation takes place. Adaptive mechanisms such as integration have to be deployed. Different approaches to defining roles and managing people may be required. These processes of change, leadership and power result in conflict and stress. To achieve organizational effectiveness it is necessary to analyse the situation in terms of the different types of culture and the circumstances in which one or other is appropriate.

## Change

### The problem

Change is the only thing that remains constant in organizations. As Alfred Sloan said:

> The circumstances of an ever-changing market and an ever-changing product are capable of breaking any business organization if that organization is unprepared for change — indeed in my opinion if it has not provided procedures for anticipating change.[2]

Change is imposed by the external environment, e.g. the economy, the market, government. But it can also arise internally from the introduction of new tasks, technologies and systems.

People resist change because it is seen as a threat to familiar patterns of behaviour as well as to status and financial rewards. Woodward made this point clearly:

> When we talk about resistance to change we tend to imply that management is always rational in changing its direction, and that employees are stupid, emotional or irrational in not responding in the way they should. But if an individual is going to be worse off, explicitly or implicitly, when the proposed changes have been made, any resistance is entirely rational in terms of his own best interest. The interests of the organization and the individual do not always coincide.[3]

If not properly managed, change can decrease morale, motivation and commitment and create conditions of conflict within an organization.

### Managing change

Resistance to change will be less if:

☐ those affected by change feel that the project is their own, not one imposed on them by outsiders;

☐ the change has the wholehearted support of top management;

☐ the change is seen as reducing rather than increasing present burdens;

☐ the change accords with well established values;

☐ the programme for change offers the kind of new experience which interests participants;

☐ participants feel that their autonomy and security are not threatened;

☐ participants have jointly diagnosed the problem;

☐ the change has been agreed by group decisions;

☐ those advocating change can understand the feelings and fears of those affected and take steps to relieve unnecessary fears;

☐ it is recognized that new ideas are likely to be misunderstood and ample provision is made for the discussion of reactions to proposals to ensure complete understanding of them.

In carrying out the process of managing change the three mechanisms suggested by Lewin[4] can be used:

1. *Unfreezing* – altering the present stable equilibrium which supports the present behaviour and attitudes. This process must take account of the inherent threat that change presents and motivate those affected to attain the natural state of equilibrium by accepting change.
2. *Changing* – developing new responses based on new information.
3. *Refreezing* – stabilizing the change by integrating the new responses into the personality of those concerned.

# Leadership

The function of the leader is to achieve the task set for him with the help of his group. The leader and his group are therefore interdependent.

## Main roles

The leader has two main roles. First he must achieve the task. Secondly, he has to maintain effective relationships between himself and his group and the individuals in it – effective in the sense that they are conducive to achieving the task. These two roles were first identified by the Ohio State researchers (Halpin and Winer)[5] who identified the two dimensions of leadership behaviour:

☐ Initiating structure – specifying ways and means of accomplishing the goals of the group and co-ordinating the activities of its members.
☐ Consideration – motivating the members of the group to accept the group goals and to work at the group task while at the same time maintaining internal harmony and satisfaction.

In fulfilling his role the leader has to satisfy the following needs:

1. *Task needs*. The group exists to achieve a common purpose or task. The leader's role is to ensure that this purpose is fulfilled. If it is not he will lose the confidence of the group and the result will be frustration, disenchantment, criticism and, possibly, the ultimate disintegration of the group.
2. *Group maintenance needs*. To achieve its objectives the group needs to be held together. The leader's job is to build up and maintain team spirit and morale.
3. *Individual needs*. Individuals have their own needs which they expect to be satisfied at work. The leader's task is to be aware of these needs so that where necessary he can take steps to harmonize them with the needs of the task and the group.

As John Adair[6] pointed out, these three needs are interdependent. The leader's actions in one area affect both the others; thus successful achievement of the task is essential if the group is to be held together or the individual is to be motivated to give his best effort to the job. Action directed at meeting group or individual needs must be related to the needs of the task. It is impossible to consider individuals in isolation from the group or to consider the group without referring to the individuals within it. If any need is neglected, one of the others will suffer and the leader will be less successful.

## Exercising leadership

The kind of leadership exercised will be related to the nature of the task and the people being led. It will also depend on the environment and, of course, on the leader himself. Analysing the qualities of leadership in terms of intelligence, initiative, self-assurance and so on has only limited value. The qualities required may be different in different situations. It is more useful to adopt a contingency approach and take account of the variables the leader has to deal with; especially the task, the group and his own position in the group.

Fiedler, in particular, concentrated upon the relationship between the leader and his group and the structure of the task as determinants in the choice of the most effective style of leadership. His research indicated that the leaders of the more effective groups tended to maintain greater distance between themselves and their subordinates than the leaders of less effective groups. He found that an 'initiating structure' approach was most effective when the situation was either very favourable or unfavourable to the leader, while 'consideration' was more appropriate when the situation was only moderately favourable. Fiedler also emphasized the 'situational' aspects of leadership':

> Leadership performance then depends as much on the organization as on the leader's own attributes. Except perhaps for the unusual case, it is simply not meaningful to speak of an effective leader and an ineffective leader; we can only speak of a leader who tends to be effective in one situation and ineffective in another.[7]

### Leadership style
The most effective leaders fit their style to the situation, which includes their own preferred style of operating and personal characteristics as well as the nature of the task and the group.

Leadership style is the way in which managers exercise their leadership role — it characterizes their approach to managing people. Leadership styles tend to be defined in terms of extremes:

| | |
|---|---|
| authoritarian | — democratic |
| autocratic | — participative |
| job-centred | — people-centred |
| close, directive | — general, permissive |

In fact, most managers develop an approach somewhere between the two extremes. There is no one style appropriate to all situations. Managers must be prepared to adjust their style according to the circumstances. This does not imply inconsistency. Effective managers adopt the same approach in similar situations.

A continuum of leadership behaviour based on the work of Tannenbaum and Schmidt[8] (figure 5.1) suggests that there are five basic styles: tell, sell, consult, join and delegate. These styles move from the authoritarian to the democratic, but it is not suggested that one is better than the other. There will be circumstances when a manager has to *tell* someone to do something; in other circumstances he may have to sell the idea or consult his subordinates in one way or another. The job of the leader is to analyse the situation and apply the most appropriate style in accordance with his knowledge of his own capabilities and limitations.

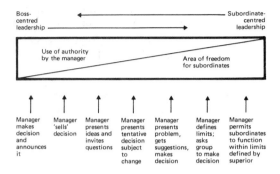

**Figure 5.1 Continuum of leadership behaviour**

# Power

Organizations exist to get things done and in the process of doing this people or groups will exercise power. Directly or indirectly the use of power in influencing behaviour is a pervading feature of organizations, whether it is exerted by managers, specialists, informal groups or trade union officials.

### Sources of power

Power is clearly linked to position and rank. But to a certain degree it has to be earned. Managers give orders to their subordinates but they will get more out of them if they obtain their willing co-operation rather than their grudging submission. Power is bestowed upon managers, but they also have to justify their use of it. There are, however, other sources of power, namely:

☐ *Access to people with power*. Proximity or a direct line obviously gives people more scope to exert influence, actual or perceived. That is why secretaries are important.

☐ *Control over information*. 'Knowledge is power' or, alternatively, 'authority goes to the one who knows'. If people are in the know, they are in a better position to control events or, if they want to play politics, to put a spoke in other people's wheels.

☐ *Control over results*. Power goes to those who can control what the organization achieves. When trade unions strike, they are exercising this sort of power.

☐ *Control over resources*. If control is exercised over resources such as money, manpower, equipment or services that anyone else needs, the person in that position will have power.

☐ *Control over rewards and punishments*. People have power if they can give rewards or punishments or influence others who control them.

☐ *Expertise*. People gain and keep power if they can convince others that they are the experts.

☐ *Identification*. Power can be achieved over others if they identify with what is being done or with the individual concerned. This is what charismatic leaders do by enthusiasm, dedication, getting people involved and by sheer force of personality.

63

## Using power

John Kotter[9] interviewed over 250 managers who were in a position to use power. He found that the successful ones had the following characteristics:

1. They use their power openly and legitimately. They are seen as genuine experts in their field and consistently live up to the leadership image they build for themselves.
2. They are sensitive to what types of power are most effective with different types of people. For example, experts respect expertise.
3. They develop all their sources of power and do not rely too much on any particular technique.
4. They seek jobs and tasks which will give them the opportunity to acquire and use power. They constantly seek ways to invest the power they already have to secure an even higher positive return.
5. They use their power in a mature and self-controlled way. They seldom if ever use power impulsively or for their own aggrandisement.
6. They get satisfaction from influencing others.

# Conflict

## The sources of conflict

Conflict is inevitable in organizations because they function by means of adjustments and compromises among competitive elements in their structure and membership. These elements produce conflict of two kinds: horizontal conflict between functions, departments and groups, and vertical conflict between different levels in the hierarchy.

Conflict also arises when there is change, because it may be seen as a threat to be challenged or resisted, or when there is frustration — this may produce an aggressive reaction: fight rather than flight. Conflict is not to be deplored. It is an inevitable result of progress and change and can and should be used constructively.

Conflict between individuals raises fewer problems than conflict between groups. Individuals can act independently and sort out their differences. Members of groups may have to accept the norms, goals and values of their group. The individual's loyalty will usually be to his own group if it is in conflict with others.

## Approaches to managing conflict

The basic assumptions about conflict made by Blake, Shepart and Mouton[10] are that:

☐ conflict is inevitable, agreement is impossible;
☐ conflict is not inevitable, yet agreement is not possible;
☐ although there is conflict, agreement is possible.

The third assumption is clearly the most hopeful. There are three approaches that can be adopted if this assumption is held:

1. *Peaceful co-existence*. People are encouraged to work happily with one another. There is the maximum amount of information, contact and exchange of views, and people move freely between groups. This is a pleasant ideal but it may lead to smoothing over real differences and is not practicable in all circumstances.
2. *Problem-solving*. The joint development of solutions to the problem and the

sharing of responsibility to see that the solutions work. This is clearly the best approach. It emphasizes the need to find a genuine solution to the problem, rather than simply accommodating different points of view.

3. *Compromise.* Splitting the difference by negotiation or bargaining. This approach assumes that there is no right or best answer and is essentially pessimistic, although it may be inevitable if the other two approaches are tried and do not work.

## Stress

Unfortunately, stress is a feature of organizational life associated with getting work done, relating to other people, being subjected to change, supervision and the exercise of power.

### Causes of stress
The main causes of stress are:

☐ the work itself − over-pressurized, actual or perceived failure;
☐ role in the organization − ambiguity in what is expected of the individual or conflict between what he wants to do and can do;
☐ poor relationships within the organization − with the boss, colleagues or subordinates;
☐ impact of the organization − lack of information, little effective consultation, restrictions on behaviour, office politics;
☐ feelings about job or career − lack of job security, over-promotion or under-promotion;
☐ external pressures − clash between demands made by the organization and those made by the family or other external interests.

### Coping with stress
How people deal with stress will depend on their personality, tolerance for ambiguity and ability to live with change. Some people revel in highly pressurized jobs. Others cannot cope. Motivation also comes into it. Motivation is a form of pressure. People can be too highly motivated and pressure becomes stress when they cannot achieve what they are setting out or expected to do.

Stress can be coped with by adaptive behaviour. An overworked manager may adapt successfully by delegating some work, but someone else may accept the overload with the result that his performance deteriorates. And, as Torrington and Cooper[11] point out, a manager who adapts successfully to role ambiguity will seek clarification with his superior or colleagues, but a manager who cannot adapt will withdraw from some aspect of his work role.

### Managing stress
The three basic ways in which stress can be managed by an organization are:

☐ job design − reducing the scope for placing people under stress and clarifying roles;
☐ placement and career development − placing people in jobs with which they can cope and advancing their careers in accordance with their capabilities;
☐ motivation − using methods of motivation and leadership which do not place undue demands on people.

Further refinements to these basic methods have been suggested by Torrington and Cooper. These include:

□ using performance reviews as a basis for discussion between the superior and the subordinate about the latter's progress in a job;
□ counselling – giving the individual the chance to talk over his problems with a member of the personnel department or the company medical officer;
□ training – helping people to understand and to carry out their jobs better.

## Group behaviour

Organizations consist of groups of people working together. Interactions take place within and between groups and the degree to which these processes are formalized will vary according to the organizational context. To understand and influence organizational behaviour it is necessary to understand how groups behave. In particular this means considering the nature of:

□ formal groups
□ informal groups
□ the processes that take place within groups
□ the factors that make for group effectiveness.

### Formal groups
Formal groups are set up by organizations to achieve a defined purpose. People are brought together with the necessary skills to carry out the tasks and a system exists for directing, co-ordinating and controlling the group's activities. The structure, composition and size of the group will depend largely on the nature of the task; although tradition, organizational culture and management style may exert considerable influence. The more the task is routine or clearly defined the more structured the group will be. In a highly structured group the leader will have a positive role and may well adopt an authoritarian style. The role of each member of the group will be precise and a hierarchy of authority is likely to exist. The more ambiguous the task the more difficult it will be to structure the group. The leader's role is more likely to be supportive – he will tend to concentrate on encouragement and co-ordination rather than on issuing orders. The group will operate in a more democratic way and individual roles will be fluid and less clearly defined.

### Informal groups
Informal groups are set up by people in organizations who have some affinity for one another. It could be said that formal groups satisfy the needs of the organization while informal groups satisfy the needs of their members. One of the main aims of organization design and development should be to ensure, so far as possible, that the basis upon which activities are grouped together and the way in which groups are allowed or encouraged to behave satisfy both these needs. The values and norms established by informal groups can work against the organization. This was first clearly established in the Hawthorne studies which revealed that groups could regulate their own behaviour and output levels irrespective of what management wanted. An understanding of the processes that take place within groups can, however, help to make them work for, rather than against, what the organization needs.

**Group processes**

As mentioned above, the way in which groups function will be affected by the task and by the norms in the organization. An additional factor will be size. There will be a greater diversity of talent, skills and knowledge in a large group, but individuals will find it more difficult to make their presence felt. According to Handy,[1] for best participation and for highest all-round involvement, the optimum size is between five and seven. But to achieve the requisite breadth of knowledge the group may have to be considerably larger, and this makes greater demands on the skills of the leader in getting participation.

The main processes that take place within groups are:

INTERACTION. There are three basic channels of communication within groups, as illustrated below:

  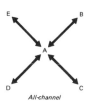

Wheel     Circle     All-channel

These patterns were defined by Leavitt,[12] and he and subsequent researchers found the following to be true:

☐ Wheel groups, where the task is straightforward, work faster, need fewer messages to solve problems and make fewer errors than circle groups, but they are inflexible if the task changes.
☐ Circle groups are faster in solving complex problems than wheel groups.
☐ All-channel groups are the most flexible and function well in complex open-ended situations.
☐ The level of satisfaction for individuals is lowest in the circle, fairly high in the all-channel and mixed in the wheel, where the leader is more satisfied than the outlying members.

TASK AND MAINTENANCE FUNCTIONS. The following functions need to be carried out in groups:

☐ task – initiating, information seeking, diagnosing, opinion-seeking, evaluating, decision-managing;
☐ maintenance – encouraging, compromising, peace-keeping, clarifying, summarizing, standard-setting.

It is the job of the group leader or leaders to ensure that these functions operate effectively. Leaderless groups can work, but only in special circumstances. A leader is almost essential – whether official or self-appointed. The style adopted by the leader will affect the way the group operates. If he is respected, this will increase the group's cohesiveness and its ability to get things done. An inappropriately authoritarian style will create tension and resentment. An over-permissive style will mean that respect for the leader will diminish and the group will not function so effectively.

GROUP IDEOLOGY. In the course of interacting and carrying out its task and maintenance functions, the group develops an ideology which affects the attitudes and actions of its members and the degree of satisfaction which they feel.

IDENTIFICATION. An individual will identify with his group if he likes the other members, approves of the purpose and work of the group and wishes to be associated with the standing of the group in the organization. Identification will be more complete if the standing of the group is good.

### Group effectiveness

An effective group is likely to be one in which the structure, leadership and methods of operation are relevant to the requirements of the task. The Tavistock Institute Longwall and Ahmedabad studies referred to in chapter 4 emphasized the importance of commitment to the whole group task and the need to group people in a way which ensures that they are related to each other by way of the requirements of task performance and task interdependence.

In an effective group, its purpose is clear and its members feel that the task is important both to them and the organization (the concept of saliency). According to McGregor[13] the main features of a well functioning creative group are as follows:

1. The atmosphere tends to be informal, comfortable, relaxed.
2. There is a lot of discussion in which initially everyone participates, but it remains pertinent to the task of the group.
3. The task or objective of the group is well understood and accepted by the members. There will have been free discussion of the objective at some point until it was formulated in such a way that the members of the group could commit themselves to it.
4. The members listen to each other. Every idea is given a hearing. People do not appear to be afraid of being considered foolish by putting forth a creative thought even if it seems fairly extreme.
5. There is disagreement. Disagreements are not suppressed or overridden by premature group action. The reasons are carefully examined, and the group seeks to resolve them rather than to dominate the dissenter.
6. Most decisions are reached by a kind of consensus in which it is clear that everybody is in general agreement and willing to go along. Formal voting is at a minimum; the group does not accept a simple majority as a proper basis for action.
7. Criticism is frequent, frank and relatively comfortable. There is little evidence of personal attack, either openly or in a hidden fashion.
8. People are free in expressing their feelings as well as their ideas both on the problem and on the group's operation.
9. When action is taken, clear assignments are made and accepted.
10. The leader of the group does not dominate it, nor on the contrary does the group defer unduly to him. There is little evidence of a struggle for power as the group operates. The issue is not who controls but how to get the job done.

These characteristics together present an ideal which might be striven for but is seldom attained. The extent to which it is possible or even desirable for them to be achieved will depend on the situation. A mechanistic or bureaucratic type of enterprise — where this is appropriate to the technology — cannot allow its formal organizational units to function just like this, although it should try to ensure that any committees, task forces or project teams that are set up do exhibit these forms of behaviour.

## Organizational effectiveness

An organization could be said to be effective if it achieves its purpose. But at what cost? It is necessary to be concerned not only with what an organization achieves but how it achieves it. The behavioural scientists who wrote about organization development, such as Richard Beckhard,[14] were concerned about organizational behaviour in terms of what they referred to as organizational health. Beckhard has defined a healthy organization as having the following characteristics:

1. The total organization, the significant sub-parts, and individuals manage their work against goals and plans for the achievement of these goals.
2. Form follows function (the problem, or task or project, determines how the human resources are organized).
3. Decisions are made by and near the source of information, regardless of where these sources are located on the organization chart.
4. The reward system is such that managers and supervisors are rewarded (and punished) comparably for (a) short-term profit or production performance, (b) growth and development of their subordinates, and (c) creating a viable working group.
5. Communication laterally and vertically is relatively undistorted. People are generally open and confronting. They share all the relevant facts, including feelings.
6. There is a minimum amount of inappropriate win/lose activities between individuals and groups. Constant effort exists at all levels to treat conflict and conflict situations as problems subject to problem-solving methods.
7. There is a high 'conflict' (clash of ideas) about tasks and projects, and relatively little energy spent in clashing over interpersonal difficulties because they have been generally worked through.
8. The organization and its parts see themselves as interacting with each other *and* with a *larger* environment. The organization is an 'open system'.
9. There is a shared value, and management strategy to support it, of trying to help each person (or unit) in the organization to maintain his (or its) integrity and uniqueness in an interdependent environment.
10. The organization and its members operate in an 'action research' way. General practice is to build in feedback mechanisms so that individuals and groups can learn from their own experience.

This is an ideal view of how organizations should behave, and it seems to represent the philosophy adopted by most organization development practitioners. But there is some danger in adopting these values as ends in themselves and neglecting the fact that organizations exist to serve a purpose. The values are important because they can promote the effectiveness of an organization as well as its health.

### Factors affecting organizational performance

John Child[15] examined the factors affecting organizational performance on the basis of research in 82 British companies. He found that where the following propositions were operating, performance was better:

1. In conditions of environment variability, successful organizations will tend to have structures with the following characteristics: (a) arrangements to reduce and structure uncertainty; (b) a relatively high level of integration achieved through flexible, rather than formalized processes. This is in accordance with contingency theory whereby different approaches to organization design are conducive to high performance, depending on whether or not the environment in which the organization operates is variable and complex in nature, or stable and simple.
2. Organizations that increase their degree of formalization to parallel their growth in size will tend to achieve higher levels of performance. Child found that in each industry the more profitable and faster growing companies were those that developed a bureaucratic type organization when they had more than about 2000 employees.
3. Organizations that group their basic activities into divisions once these activities become diversified will tend to achieve higher levels of performance.
4. Organizations that carefully design their work flow control and support technology will tend to achieve higher levels of performance.
5. Organizations that adopt forms of administrative structure consistent with the expectations and perceived needs of their employees will tend to achieve higher levels of performance. This proposition may be a truism but it emphasizes the need to understand the *perceived* needs and expectations of employees. This means looking at the factors affecting their behaviour as individuals – their motivation and the way they adapt to their roles. These matters are considered in the next chapter.

## References

1. Handy, C.B. *Understanding Organizations*. Penguin Books, Harmondsworth, 1976.
2. Sloan, A.P. *My Years with General Motors*. Doubleday, New York, 1964.
3. Woodward, J. 'Resistance to Change', *Management International Review*, Vol. 8, 1968.
4. Lewin, K. *Field Theory in Social Science*. Harper and Row, New York, 1951.
5. Halpin, A.W. and Winer, B.J. *A Factorial Study of the Leader Behaviour Descriptions*. Ohio State University, 1957.
6. Adair, J. *The Action Centred Leader*. McGraw-Hill, London, 1973.
7. Fiedler, F.E. *A Theory of Leadership Effectiveness*. McGraw Hill, New York, 1967.
8. Tannenbaum, R. and Schmidt, W.H. 'How to Choose a Leadership Pattern', *Harvard Business Review*, May-June 1973.
9. Kotter, J.P. 'Power, Dependence and Effective Management', *Harvard Business Review*, May-June 1973.
10. Blake, R.R., Shepart, H.A. and Mouton, J.S. *Managing Intergroup Conflict in Industry*. Gulf Publishing, Houston, 1964.
11. Torrington, D.P. and Cooper, C.L. 'The Management of Stress in Organizations and the Personnel Initiative', *Personnel Review*, Summer 1977.
12. Leavitt, H.J. 'Some Effects of Certain Communication Patterns on Group Performance', *Journal of Abnormal Psychology*, 1951.
13. McGregor, D. *The Human Side of Enterprise*. McGraw-Hill, New York, 1966.
14. Beckhard, R. *Organization Development: Strategy and Models*, Addison-Wesley, Reading, Mass, 1969.
15. Child, J. 'What Determines Organization Performance?', *Organization Design, Development and Behaviour, A Situational View*. K.O. Magnusen (ed), Scott Foreman, Glenview, Illinois, 1977.

# 6 The Individual at Work –
## Motivation and Roles

The way in which an individual behaves at work will depend on:

☐ the organization context, which includes the work he has to do, the culture or climate of the organization, management style and relationships with co-workers;
☐ his own drives, attitudes, personality, attributes and personal circumstances.

The organization context has been dealt with in the previous two chapters. This chapter is primarily concerned with the worker as an individual – his motivation, what makes him tick, and the way in which he adjusts to his role in the organization.

## Motivation

Motivation is about what makes people act or behave in the way they do. When we observe people behaving in a particular manner, we ask: what are their motives? If we want them to behave in a certain way, we ask: how can we motivate them?

At work we can observe some people working harder or more effectively than others. We can experience difficulties in recruiting and retaining staff and obtaining the sort of effort and commitment we want from them. Managerial action is required if these difficulties prevent the organization from achieving its objectives. This action must be based on an understanding of various aspects which are considered individually later on in this chapter:

☐ the process of motivation;
☐ the factors that affect motivation;
☐ the concept of job satisfaction and how it affects performance;
☐ the relationship between motivation and performance;
☐ the various approaches to motivating people.

Motivation is a complex process. Numerous studies have been made of it which have produced a wide variety of theories. The aim of this chapter is to review the main concepts in some detail; to avoid confusion, the following summary of motivation theory is provided as a framework for the more detailed analysis in later sections.

### Summary of motivation theory

Motivation is inferred from or defined by goal-directed behaviour. It is anchored in two basic concepts: (a) the *needs* that operate within the individual and (b) the *goals* in the environment toward or away from which the individual moves. In its simplest form the process of motivation is initiated by the conscious or unconscious recognition of an unsatisfied need. A goal is then established which, it is thought, will satisfy that need, and a course of action is determined that will lead towards the attainment of the goal. The process of motivation is fundamentally about providing people with the means to achieve their goals.

The complexity of the motivation process arises because people have different needs and varied perceptions about them. Consequently, they have a wide variety of goals and of perceptions about the actions which are likely to help them achieve those goals. Motivation is very much a matter of perceptions which will be influenced by past experiences and the present environment.

The degree to which people are motivated will depend not only upon the perceived value of the outcome of their actions – the goal or reward – but also upon their perceptions of the likelihood of obtaining the reward. They will be more highly motivated if they can control the means to attain their goals.

Motivation at work can be either extrinsic – provided by the employer in the context of the job, or intrinsic – derived from the content of the job. Extrinsic rewards provided by the employer, including pay, can be important in attracting and retaining employees and, in the short term, increasing effort and minimizing dissatisfaction. Intrinsic rewards related to responsibility, achievement and the work itself may have a longer-term and deeper effect in creating and increasing satisfaction.

The basic requirements for job satisfaction may include comparatively higher pay, an equitable payment system, real opportunities for promotion, considerate and participative supervision, a reasonable degree of social interaction at work, interesting and varied tasks and a high degree of control over work pace and work methods. The degree of satisfaction obtained by individuals, however, will depend largely upon their own needs and expectations and the environment in which they work.

But research has not established any strongly positive connection between satisfaction and performance. A satisfied worker is not necessarily a high producer, and a high producer is not necessarily a satisfied worker. Some people claim that good performance produces satisfaction rather than the other way round, but their case has not been proved.

The overriding consideration in motivation is that the members of an organization contribute to the organization in return for the inducements that the organization offers them. In the words of H.A. Simon: 'Individuals are willing to accept organization membership when their activity in the organization contributes, directly or indirectly, to their own personal goals.'[1] The task of the organization is to analyse its own circumstances and the particular needs and requirements of its employees to determine the mix of extrinsic and intrinsic motivating factors needed to attract and retain good quality staff and to obtain consistently high standards of performance from them.

## Schools of motivation theory

The theory of motivation presented above is an eclectic one, derived from a number of schools of thought. To obtain some perspective of this complicated subject it is helpful to summarize the main approaches that have been developed, using the classification developed by Schein:[2]

☐ rational-economic man
☐ social man
☐ self-actualizing man
☐ complex man.

## Rational-economic man

According to this view, man is primarily motivated by economic rewards. It assumes that a person will be motivated to work if rewards and penalties are tied directly to his performance; thus the awards are contingent upon effective performance. This approach has its roots in the scientific management methods of Taylor who wrote: 'It is impossible, through any long period of time, to get workmen to work much harder than the average men around them unless they are assured a large and permanent increase in their pay.'[3]

This approach has been described by 'the law of effect' or 'the principle of reinforcement'. This states that if a person undertakes an action and this action is followed by a reward, the probability that the action will be repeated is increased. On the other hand, if the person undertakes an action which is ignored or followed by a punishment, that behaviour is less likely to be repeated.

Motivation using this approach has been and still is widely adopted and can be successful in some circumstances. But it is based exclusively on a system of external controls and fails to recognize a number of other human needs. It also fails to appreciate the fact that the formal control system can be seriously affected by the informal relationship existing between workers.

## Social man

Elton Mayo and his colleagues observed this shortcoming and developed an approach which emphasized man's social needs. The need for belonging was seen as providing the basic motivation for individuals to work. The social controls set up by cohesive work groups can be a powerful countervailing force to management's efforts to use financial rewards and organizational controls to achieve what it wants. This concept rapidly developed into the human relations school which believed that productivity was directly related to job satisfaction and that an individual's output will be high if he likes his co-workers and is given pleasant supervision.

To a certain extent, this approach is akin to paternalism, where it is assumed that people can be induced to work out of a feeling of gratitude for the system.

## Self-actualizing man

The social man/human relations school was seen by many psychologists as somewhat naive, especially in its apparent assumption that a contented individual is necessarily highly productive. Man was seen by people such as Maslow, McGregor, Argyris and Herzberg to be motivated by a number of different needs. The most important of these needs from the point of view of long-term motivation are the higher order needs for esteem and self-fulfilment or actualization. These needs are intrinsic to the work people and are not subject to an external control system. The key point in McGregor's Theory Y – 'that people will exercise self-direction and self-control in the achievement of organizational objectives to the degree that they are committed to those objectives'[4] – is fundamental to this concept. Argyris[5] also sees each individual person as having a potential which can be fully realized and believes that such self-realization or self-actualization benefits not only the individual but also those around him and the organization in which he works.

The other significant contributor to this school was Herzberg, whose basic theme is that opportunities for self-actualization are the essential requirements of both job satisfaction and high performance.

### Complex man

The concept of complex man was originated by Schein[2] and developed by Lawrence and Lorsch.[6] It absorbs much of the earlier ideas, especially those of Herzberg, but also makes use of more recent empirical research findings. The scheme indicates that an individual can usefully be conceived of as a system of biological needs, psychological motives, values and perceptions. The individual's system operates so as to maintain its internal balance in the face of the demands placed upon it by external forces and it develops in response to his basic needs to solve the problems presented by his external environment. But each individual system will have unique characteristics because, as Lawrence and Lorsch say:

1. Different individual systems develop with different patterns of needs, values and perceptions.
2. Individual systems are not static, but continue to develop as they encounter new problem experiences.

## The process of motivation

An individual is motivated when he acts purposively with reference to some object, event or person in his environment. The process consists of four elements:

1. *Homeostasis* — the tendency to move towards equilibrium.
2. *The need-goal model* — behaviour seen as a means of satisfying needs by achieving goals.
3. *Reinforcement* — the process of learning by trial and error, reward and punishment.
4. *Expectancy* — the influence of expectations on the choice of behaviour.

### Homeostasis

The human organism, like all other living organisms, is constantly in a state of disequilibrium. It expends energy to stay alive and must replenish this energy. Automatic mechanisms exist to maintain a normal body temperature. This is called the homeostatic principle and it underlies all behaviour and motivation. The drive to satisfy unsatisfied needs is actuated by the constant move towards equilibrium.

Another concept which has some affinity with the principle of homeostasis is the desire to master one's immediate environment. Individuals subjectively organize their environment by reference to past experience, present needs and future expectations. This develops into a pattern which is taken for granted until some external influence affects it. The individual then engages in interpretative or problem-solving activity in an attempt to absorb or resist the change.

### Needs and goals

An unsatisfied need creates tension and a state of disequilibrium. To restore the balance a goal is identified which will satisfy the need, and a behaviour pathway is selected which will lead to the achievement of the goal. All behaviour is therefore motivated by unsatisfied needs. This process is illustrated in figure 6.1.

Not all needs are equally important for a person at any one time — some may provide a much more powerful drive towards a goal than others, depending on the individual's background and present situation. Complexity is further increased because there is no simple relationship between needs and goals. The same need can be satisfied by a number of different goals and the stronger the need and the longer its duration, the broader the range of possible goals. At the same time, one goal may satisfy a number of needs — a new car provides transport as well as an opportunity to impress the neighbours.

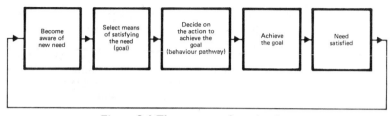

**Figure 6.1 The process of motivation**

If management wishes to increase productivity it has to bear in mind, in the words of Georgopoulos:

> Individual productivity is, among other things, a function of one's motivation to produce at any given level; in such motivation depends upon (a) the particular needs of the individual as reflected in the goals towards which he is moving, and (b) his perception regarding the relative usefulness of productivity behaviour as an instrumentality, or as a path to the attainment of these goals.[7]

Thus the individual's main concern is to assess the benefits that will accrue to him from doing what the organization wants him to do, and the penalties that may result from a failure to act as the organization requires. The organization has to make assumptions about what people want in deciding how they should be motivated. This is the problem of motivation. Many such assumptions are invalid because they are based on generalizations and an inadequate understanding of the process of motivation. Even if attitude surveys are used to assess needs and wants they can easily produce misleading results because of the difficulties of administration and interpretation. (Attitude surveys are considered in more detail later in this chapter.) Finally, there is the problem that all managers meet — it is easy to observe behaviour, it is much more difficult to interpret and attach reasons for that behaviour when it has been motivated by a set of hidden needs and goals.

### Reinforcement

As experience is gained in taking action to satisfy needs, people perceive that certain actions help to achieve their goals while others are less successful. Some actions bring rewards, others result in failure or even punishment. Reinforcement theory as developed by Hull[8] is derived from the previously mentioned law of effect. It suggests that successes in achieving goals and rewards act as positive incentives and reinforce the successful behaviour which is repeated the next time a similar need emerges. The more powerful, obvious and frequent the reinforcement, the more likely it is that the behaviour will be repeated until, eventually, it can become a more or less unconscious reaction to an event. Conversely, failures or punishments provide negative reinforcement which suggests that it is necessary to seek alternative means of achieving goals.

The degree to which experience shapes future behaviour does, of course, depend first on the extent to which an individual correctly perceives the connection between the behaviour and its outcome and, secondly, on the extent to which he is able to recognize the resemblance between the previous situation and the one that now confronts him. Perceptive ability varies between people as does the ability to identify correlations between events. For these reasons, some people are better at learning from experience than others, just as some people are more easily motivated than others.

It has been suggested that theories based on the law of effect or the principle of reinforcement are limited because they imply, in Allport's phrase, a 'hedonism of the past'.[9] They assume that the explanation of the present choices of an individual is to be found in an examination of the consequences of his past choices. Insufficient attention is paid in the theories to the influence of expectations, and no indication is given of any means of distinguishing in advance the class of outcomes which would strengthen responses and those which would weaken them.

### Expectancy theory

The assumption of the needs-goal concept is that people will direct their efforts towards the goals which they value. But, as Cooper says: 'The existence of a valued goal is not a sufficient condition for action; people will act only when they have a reasonable expectation that their actions will lead to desired goals.'[10] The concept of expectancy was defined by Vroom as follows:

> Whenever an individual chooses between alternatives which involve uncertain outcomes, it seems clear that his behaviour is affected not only by his preferences among these outcomes but also by the degree to which he believes these outcomes to be possible. An expectancy is defined as a momentary belief concerning the likelihood that a particular act will be followed by a particular outcome. Expectancies may be described in terms of their strength. Maximal strength is indicated by subjective certainty that the act *will* be followed by the outcome, while minimal (or zero) strength is indicated by subjective certainty that the act *will not* be followed by the outcome.[11]

The strength of expectations may be based on past experiences (reinforcement), but individuals are frequently presented with new situations — a change in job, payment system or working conditions imposed by management — where past experience is an inadequate guide to the implications of the change. In these circumstances, motivation may be reduced.

Motivation is only likely when a clearly perceived and usable relationship exists between performance and outcome, and the outcome is seen as a means of satisfying needs. This explains why extrinsic motivation — for example, an incentive or bonus scheme — only works if the link between effort and reward is clear and the value of the reward is worth the effort. It also explains why intrinsic motivation arising from the work itself can be more powerful than extrinsic motivation; intrinsic motivation outcomes are more under the control of the individual who can place greater reliance on his past experiences to indicate the extent to which positive and advantageous results are likely to be obtained by his behaviour.

## Factors affecting motivation

The process of motivation is affected by a number of factors, which influence it to a greater or lesser degree depending on circumstances. The main factors considered below are:

☐ the patterns of needs that initiate drives towards goals, as classified by Maslow and McClelland;

☐ the circumstances in which needs are satisfied or dissatisfied, as analysed by Herzberg;

☐ the influence of the extrinsic and intrinsic motivating forces which are related to needs, and the circumstances in which they operate.

## Needs

Because individuals differ so much it is hard to establish with precision a general model of human needs. The most famous classification is the one formulated by Maslow.[12] He suggested that there are five major need categories which apply to people in general, starting from the fundamental physiological needs and leading through a hierarchy of safety, social and esteem needs to the need for self-fulfilment, the highest need of all. Maslow's hierarchy is as follows:

1. *Physiological* – the need for oxygen, food, water and sex.
2. *Safety* – the need for protection against danger and the deprivation of physiological needs.
3. *Social* – the need for love, affection and to be accepted as belonging to a group.
4. *Esteem* – the need to have a stable, firmly based high evaluation of oneself (self-esteem) and to have the respect of others (prestige). These needs may be classified into two subsidiary sets: first, 'the desire for achievement, for adequacy, for confidence in the face of the world, and for independence and freedom' and second, the desire for reputation or status defined as respect or esteem from other people, and manifested by recognition, attention, importance or appreciation.
5. *Self-fulfilment* (self-actualization) – the need to develop potentialities and skills, to become what one believes one is capable of becoming.

Maslow's theory of motivation states that when a lower need is satisfied the next highest becomes dominant and the individual's attention is turned to satisfying this higher need. The need for self-fulfilment, however, can never be satisfied. He said that man is a 'wanting animal'; only an unsatisfied need can motivate behaviour and the dominant need is the prime motivator of behaviour. Psychological development takes place as people move up the hierarchy of needs, but this is not necessarily a straightforward progression. The lower needs still exist, even if temporarily dormant as motivators, and individuals constantly return to previously satisfied needs. The schematic representation of the progressive development of needs is shown in figure 6.2.

One of the implications of Maslow's theory is that the higher order needs for esteem and self-fulfilment provide the greatest impetus to motivation – they grow in strength on satisfaction, while the lower needs decline in strength on satisfaction. But the jobs people do will not necessarily satisfy their needs, especially when they are routine or de-skilled.

An alternative way of classifying needs was developed by McClelland[13] who based it mainly on studies of managerial staff. He identified three needs as being most important:

1. *The need for achievement*, defined as the need for competitive success measured against a personal standard of excellence.
2. *The need for affiliation*, defined as the need for warm, friendly, compassionate relationships with others.
3. *The need for power*, defined as the need to control or influence others.

Different individuals have different levels of these needs. Some have a greater need for achievement, others a stronger need for affiliation, and still others a stronger need for power. While one need may be dominant, however, this does not mean that the others are non-existent.

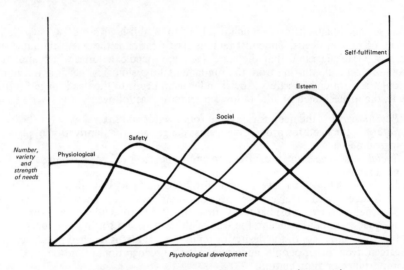

**Figure 6.2 Progressive development of needs (Maslow)**

### Herzberg's two-factor model

The two-factor model of satisfiers and dissatisfiers was developed by Herzberg following an investigation into the sources of job satisfaction and dissatisfaction of accountants and engineers. As Vroom comments, the methods used by the researchers were neither correlational (between satisfaction and productivity) nor experimental. It was assumed that people have the ability and the motivation to report accurately the conditions which made them satisfied and dissatisfied with their jobs. Accordingly, the subjects were asked to tell their interviewers about the times during which they felt exceptionally good and exceptionally bad about their jobs and how long their feelings persisted. It was found that the stories told about 'good' periods most frequently concerned the content of the job. Achievement, recognition, advancement, responsibility, and the work itself were the most frequently coded themes in such stories. On the other hand, stories concerned with 'bad' periods most frequently concerned the context of the job. Company policy and administration, supervision, salary and working conditions more frequently appeared in these stories than in those told about 'good' periods. As Herzberg comments, the main implications of this research are that:

> The wants of employees divide into two groups. One group revolves around the need to develop in one's occupation as a source of personal growth. The second group operates as an essential base to the first and is associated with fair treatment in compensation, supervision, working conditions and administrative practices. The fulfilment of the needs of the second group does not motivate the individual to high levels of job satisfaction and to extra performance on the job. All we can expect from satisfying (this second group of needs) is the prevention of dissatisfaction and poor job performance.[14]

These groups form the two factors in Herzberg's model: one consists of the satisfiers or motivators, because they are seen to be effective in motivating the individual to superior performance and effort. The other consists of the dissatisfiers which essentially describe the environment and serve primarily to prevent job dissatisfaction, while having little effect on positive job attitudes. These were named the *hygiene* factors in the medical use of the term, meaning preventive and environmental.

Herzberg's theory has been strongly attacked. The research method has been criticized because no attempt was made to measure the relationship between satisfaction and performance. It has been suggested that the two-factor nature of the theory is an inevitable result of the questioning method used by the interviewers. It has also been suggested that wide and unwarranted inferences have been drawn from small and specialized samples and that there is no evidence to suggest that the satisfiers do improve productivity. In an extended critique of the theory, Opsahl and Dunnette stated that the data on feelings about salary 'seem inconsistent with the interpretations and lend no substantial support to hypotheses of a so-called differential role for money in leading to job satisfaction or job dissatisfaction.'[15]

In spite of these criticisms (or perhaps because of them, as they are all from academics) the Herzberg theory continues to thrive; partly because for the layman it is easy to understand and seems to be based on 'real-life' stories rather than academic abstractions, and partly because it fits in well with the highly respected ideas of Maslow and McGregor in its emphasis on the positive value of the intrinsic motivating factors. It is also in accord with a fundamental belief in the dignity of labour and the protestant ethic – that work is good in itself. As a result, Herzberg has had immense influence on the job enrichment movement which seeks to design jobs in a way which will maximize the opportunities to obtain intrinsic satisfaction from work.

### Extrinsic and intrinsic motivation

The motivation theories of Maslow, McGregor, Herzberg and others emphasize the distinction between extrinsic and intrinsic factors. As defined by Cooper:

> Extrinsic motivation occurs when outcomes are mediated by an agent external to the person, and behaviour is perceived as originating in conditions outside the person's control, e.g., physical needs. In contrast, in intrinsic motivation outcomes are mediated by the person himself, and behaviour is perceived as originating from his own forces.[10]

The belief in intrinsic motivation has been fostered by researchers and humanists such as L.K. Taylor who wrote:

> It does make sense in terms of increased productivity if we treat people as people – creative, imaginative and with wishes and desires peculiar to each individual, rather than as parts of a machine some of which do not work as consistently as the other parts.[16]

Intrinsic job satisfaction is seen by Katz and many others as the motivational pathway to high productivity and to high quality production: 'The job itself must provide sufficient variety, sufficient complexity, sufficient challenge and sufficient skill to engage the abilities of the worker.'[17]

Following Herzberg, the believers in intrinsic motivation deny the importance of pay and other extrinsic factors except as causes of dissatisfaction. 'A person will still be dissatisfied even if he is extremely well paid, if his job does not allow him to achieve satisfaction of all his needs and carry a sense of personal responsibility.'[16] They may concede that pay can be a motivator in special circumstances, but only in the short term. In Britain they point out the high incidence of labour unrest amongst the well paid workers in the motor industry.

An apparent counterblast to this belief was provided by the study of skilled and semi-skilled workers in Luton by Goldthorpe. This revealed that the 'affluent' workers interviewed by the research team valued work largely for extrinsic reasons:

> Considerations of pay and security appear most powerful in binding men to their present job... Workers in all groups within our sample tend to be particularly motivated to increase their power as consumers and their domestic standard of living, rather than their satisfaction as producers and the degree of their self-fulfilment in work.[18]

It has been pointed out, however, that in this case, pay and security were the dominant factors in the *choice* of employer. There was no evidence that they influenced satisfaction with the work itself or productivity.

The debate of intrinsic versus extrinsic motivators centres on the relevance of money. The original Herzberg theory relegated it to the role of a hygiene factor, but though he still insists that money is not a true motivator and that it has no long-term effect on performance, he now agrees that:

> Because of its ubiquitous nature relating to most other factors, salary commonly shows up as motivational as well as hygiene. Although primarily a hygiene factor it also takes on some of the properties of a motivator with dynamics similar to recognition for achievement.[19]

The Goldthorpe study mentioned above highlighted the significance of pay to Luton manual workers. Another study carried out by McDougall of Ashridge College[20] concerned the attitudes of management to remuneration in a major British company. Managers were asked to rate the importance to them of each of 31 tangible or intangible rewards which might be associated with their jobs. An analysis of the replies into six motivational groups showed that the largest group, comprising 25 per cent of the managers, was mainly interested in material reward expressed in money, fringe benefits and opportunities for advancement. This group was younger and potentially more mobile than the others and included a high proportion of production staff and accountants. The groups, however, varied considerably in their preferences, which led the research team to conclude that it is dangerous to make any generalized assumptions about values and motives when considering the role of money and the type of remuneration system a company ought to provide.

Money is a major factor in getting and keeping people. It can also serve as a tangible recognition of success, but its main relevance as a motivator, as Gellerman points out,[21] is that it is a means to an end, and can be used to satisfy a number of intangible needs. In itself, of course, it has no intrinsic meaning. It acquires motivating power only when it comes to symbolize intangible goals or provides the means to attaining them. But this sort of satisfaction is achieved outside work. To achieve sustained motivation within the organization it is still necessary to take account of the intrinsic motivation provided by the job.

## Job satisfaction

The term 'job satisfaction' refers to the attitudes and feelings people have about their work. Positive and favourable attitudes towards the job indicate job satisfaction, and negative and unfavourable attitudes towards the job indicate job dissatisfaction.

Morale is often defined as being equivalent to job satisfaction. Thus Guion defines morale as 'the extent to which the individual's needs are satisfied and the extent to which the individual perceives that satisfaction as stemming from his total work situation'.[22] Other definitions stress the group aspects of morale; for example, Gilmer suggests that morale 'is a feeling of being accepted by and belonging to a group of employees through adherence to common goals'.[23] And he, like others, distinguishes between morale as a group variable, related to the degree to which group members feel attracted to their group and desire to remain a member of it, and job attitude as an individual variable related to the feeling the employee has about his job.

### Factors affecting job satisfaction
The following factors affect job satisfaction:

1. *The intrinsic motivating factors*. These relate to job content, especially variety, challenge, responsibility, control over work methods, control over work pace, the opportunity to use skills and abilities and influence in decision-making.
2. *The extrinsic factors*. These relate to pay and the context in which the work is carried out.
3. *The quality of supervision*. The Hawthorne studies resulted in the claim that supervision is the most important determinant of worker attitudes. The Ohio State Leadership Studies[24] later identified two major independent dimensions of leadership behaviour (while other studies distinguished between employee orientation and production orientation). The first dimension was called 'consideration' and includes supervisory behaviour 'indicative of friendship, mutual trust, respect and warmth'. The second dimension was termed initiating structure, which includes behaviour in which the supervisor organizes and defines group activities and his relation to the group. A number of subsequent studies have suggested that the display of consideration of supervisors has increased employee satisfaction and resulted in lower labour turnover, less absenteeism and fewer grievances. But they have not shown that there is a direct relationship between consideration, satisfaction and productivity. Herzberg, however, claimed that the importance of supervision has been overrated and it seems clear that considerate supervision is only one out of many factors that can affect attitudes and satisfaction.
4. *The work group*. Elton Mayo believed that 'a man's desire to be continuously associated in work with his fellows is a strong, if not the strongest human characteristic'.[25] And it is true that social interaction can be highly rewarding to most people, and that experiences with one's fellow workers can be a major satisfaction at work. Research has shown that larger groups where less interaction is possible have lower cohesiveness or morale than smaller groups. The social isolation which exists on assembly lines is a known cause of dissatisfaction.
5. *Success or failure*. Success will obviously create satisfaction, especially if it enables the individual to prove to himself that he is using his skills effectively. And it is equally obvious that the reverse is true of failure.

## Job satisfaction and performance

It is a commonly held and apparently not unreasonable belief that an increase in job satisfaction will result in improved performance. The whole human relations movement was based on the belief that productivity could be increased by making workers more satisfied. The first real blow to this view came from the Survey Research Centre studies in an insurance company[26] and a railroad.[27] No differences were found in either study between the satisfaction with wages, satisfaction with job status, or satisfaction with fellow workers in high and low productivity sections.

A review of the extensive literature on this subject by Brayfield and Crockett[28] concluded that there was little evidence of any simple or appreciable relationship between employee attitudes and the effectiveness of their performance. An updated version of their analysis by Vroom[11] covered 20 studies, in each of which one or more measures of job satisfaction or employee attitudes was correlated with one or more criteria of performance. The median correlation of all these studies was 0.14, which is not high enough to suggest any marked relationship between satisfaction and performance. Our own observations confirm the results of this analysis. We are constantly coming across people who are perfectly content to do the minimum that will keep them in employment.

It has been suggested that it is not increases in satisfaction that produce improved performance but improved performance that increases satisfaction. This is certainly true in the sense that individuals are motivated to reach certain goals and will be satisfied if they achieve those goals through improved performance. But individual goals can be satisfied in other ways besides working harder or better. Improved performance is not a necessary or the only factor in improving satisfaction. As Brayfield and Crockett suggested:

> Productivity is seldom a goal in itself but is more commonly a means to goal attainment. Therefore ... we might expect high satisfaction and high productivity to occur together when productivity is perceived as a path to certain important goals and when these goals are achieved. Under other conditions, satisfaction and productivity might be unrelated or even negatively related.

Increases in satisfaction may therefore reduce staff turnover, absenteeism and grievances but they do not necessarily result in increases in productivity. Satisfaction and performance are often related but the precise effect on one another depends upon the working situation and the people in it. Motivation is not simply a matter of increasing job satisfaction. The common sense view that people are only motivated when they have something to strive for accords with Maslow's suggestion that only an unsatisfied need motivates behaviour. A measure of dissatisfaction and a desire for more achievement or power may be the best motivator for some people. But it will all depend on the people concerned and the environment in which they are working.

### Measuring job satisfaction

Some indication of the level of job satisfaction can be derived from the analysis of labour turnover, absenteeism or grievance rates. But these are only symptoms. A proper analysis of job satisfaction leading to a diagnosis of the cause of any problems is best carried out by an attitude survey. A properly conducted attitude survey can provide general information on attitudes and feelings as a basis for formulating policies: Attitude surveys can also be used to:

☐ provide particular information on the preferences of employees, for example, on a union recognition issue;

☐ give warning on potential trouble spots;

☐ diagnose the cause of particular troubles;
☐ compare morale in different parts of the organization;
☐ evaluate training;
☐ assess how organizational and other policy changes have been received;
☐ observe the effects of policies and actions over a period of time;
☐ provide people with the opportunity to express their views — attitude surveys are therefore in themselves a means of increasing job satisfaction as long as feelings of frustration do not arise because of lack of action on the part of management after the survey;
☐ provide an additional means of communication, especially if the survey includes some discussions with employees on their attitudes and what actions they would like management to take.

APPROACH. The best approach to the measurement of job satisfaction is first to identify the individual's needs and then to assess the extent to which these needs are being met. This means using two questionnaires. The first questionnaire would ask people how they feel about various things for *any* job they might do, not just their present job. Thus, against the heading of 'good wages' they would be asked to indicate how they feel by ticking the appropriate heading — absolutely top priority, very important, fairly important, not very important. The second questionnaire would ask them to express their feelings about different aspects of their present job. For example, indicating against 'pay' whether their feelings about it are very good, good, neither good nor bad, bad, very bad.

METHODS OF CONDUCTING ATTITUDE SURVEYS. There are three methods of conducting attitude surveys:

1. By the use of *structured questionnaires* issued to all or a sample of employees. The questionnaires must be standardized ones such as the Brayfield and Rothe Index of Job Satisfaction, or they may be developed specially for the organization. The advantage of using standardized questionnaires is that they have been thoroughly tested and in many cases norms are available against which results can be compared. Additional questions specially relevant to the company can be added to the standard list. A tailor-made questionnaire can be used to highlight particular issues but if it is thought to be essential, it is advisable to obtain professional help from an experienced psychologist who can carry out the skilled work of drafting and pilot-testing the questionnaire and interpreting the results. Questionnaires have the advantage of being relatively cheap to administer and analyse, especially when there are large numbers involved.
2. By the use of *interviews*. These may be 'open-ended' or depth interviews where the discussion is allowed to range quite freely. Or they may be semi-structured in that there is a checklist of points to be covered, although the aim of the interviewer is to allow discussion to flow around the points so that the frank and open views of the individual are obtained. Alternatively, and more rarely, interviews can be highly structured so that they become no more than the spoken application of a questionnaire. Individual interviews are to be preferred because they are more likely to be revealing and are easier to analyse. But they are expensive and time consuming. Group discussions are a quicker way of reaching a large number of people, but the results are not so easy to

quantify and some people may have difficulty in expressing their views in public.

3. By a combination of *questionnaire and interview*. This is the ideal approach because it will combine the quantitative data from the questionnaire with the qualitative data from the interviews. It is always advisable to accompany questionnaires with some depth interviews, even if time permits only a limited sample. An alternative approach is to administer the questionnaire to a group of people and then discuss the reactions to each question with the group. This ensures that a quantified analysis is possible but enables the group, or at least some members of it, to express their feelings more fully.

ASSESSING RESULTS. It is an interesting fact that when people are asked directly if they are satisfied with their job, most of them (70 to 90 per cent) will say they are. This is regardless of the work being done and often in spite of strongly held grievances. The probable reason for this phenomenon is that while most people are willing to admit having grievances — in fact, if invited to complain, they will complain — they may be reluctant to admit, even to themselves, to being dissatisfied with a job which they have no immediate intention of leaving. Many employees have become reconciled to their work, even if they do not like some aspects of it, and have no real desire to do anything else. So they are, in a sense, satisfied enough to continue, even if they have complaints. Finally, many people *are* satisfied with their job overall, although they will grumble about many aspects of it.

Overall measures of satisfaction do not, therefore, always reveal anything interesting. It is more important to look at particular aspects of satisfaction or dissatisfaction to decide whether or not anything needs to be done. In these circumstances, the questionnaire will only indicate a line to be followed up. It will not provide the answers. Hence the advantage of individual meetings or group discussions to explore in depth any issue raised.

## Motivation and performance

Although there is some doubt about the relationship between motivation and satisfaction, it seems obvious that the link between motivation and performance is a positive one: increased motivation results in more effort and improved performance. But there are two qualifications to this point of view. First, there is the effect of ability, and second, there are the possible detrimental effects of too much motivation. There is also the whole question of the impact of such factors as rewards and the individual's understanding of the kinds of activities and behaviour he should engage in to perform his job successfully (role perceptions).

### Motivation and ability

However keen someone is to do something, he will not be able to do it unless he has the required abilities. Vroom suggested on the basis of a number of experiments that:

> The effects of motivation on performance are dependent on the level of ability of the worker, and the relationship of ability to performance is dependent on the motivation of the worker. The effects of ability and motivation on performance are not additive but interactive. The data presently available on this question suggest something more closely resembling the multiplicative relationship depicted in the following formula:
>
> $$\text{Performance} = \int (\text{Ability} \times \text{Motivation})[11]$$

This formula expresses more than the truism that you cannot perform a task without some ability *and* some motivation. The emphasis is on the multiplicative relationship between the two factors, from which it follows that when ability is low increases in motivation will result in smaller increases in performance than when ability is high. Similarly, when motivation is low, increases in ability will result in smaller increases in performance than when motivation is high.

The implication is that it is as necessary to concentrate on improving ability by means of good selection and training as it is to concentrate on improving motivation by some manipulation of the extrinsic and intrinsic factors affecting it. At the same time, more is to be gained from increasing the motivation of those who are high in ability than of those who are low in ability, and more is to be gained from increasing the ability of those who are highly motivated than of those who are relatively less well motivated.

### Effects of high motivation

There is a second qualification to the concept that higher motivation always results in greater productivity. It is possible for someone to be too highly motivated; to want something so much that he becomes over-anxious and therefore prone to indecision and error or to ignoring relevant information. Vroom proposed three hypothetical relationships between the amount of motivation and performance, as shown in figure 6.3. He suggests that while it is possible for performance to improve steadily as in the straight line on figure 6.3, it is equally possible that the rate at which performance increases diminishes until there is no further increase, as in the dotted line. Another plausible relationship is shown by the broken line, where performance reaches its maximum point under moderate levels of motivation and then drops off under high levels of motivation. The latter view is supported by a number of research studies.

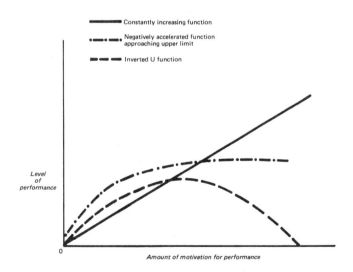

**Figure 6.3 Hypothetical relationships between motivation
and performance**

## Motivation/performance model

When looking at the relationships between motivation and performance it is necessary to answer the two basic questions posed by Porter and Lawler: 'What factors determine the *effort* a person puts into his job? What factors affect the relationship between effort and performance?'[29] Their conceptual model is shown in figure 6.4. This model suggests that there are two factors determining the effort a person puts into his job:

1. The value of the rewards to the individual in so far as they are likely to satisfy his needs for security, social esteem, autonomy and self-actualization.
2. The probability that rewards depend on effort, as perceived by the individual — in other words, his expectations about the relationships between effort and reward.

Thus, the greater the value of a set of awards and the higher the probability that receiving each of these rewards depends upon effort, the greater the effort that will be put forth in a given situation.

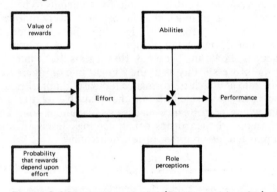

**Figure 6.4 Motivation model (Porter and Lawler)**

But effort is not enough. It has to be effective effort if it is to produce the desired performance. The two additional variables to effort which affect task achievement are:

☐ ability — individual characteristics such as intelligence, manual skills, know-how;
☐ role perceptions — what the individual wants to do or thinks he is required to do. These are good from the viewpoint of the organization if they correspond with what it thinks the individual ought to be doing. They are poor if the views of the individual and the organization do not coincide.

The Porter-Lawler model has been verified quantitatively to some extent for North American managerial employees and seems to represent the best available guide to motivation/performance relationships, at least at this level. It has been further developed by Schwab and Cummings,[30] as shown in figure 6.5. The refinements introduced into this model are first, that performance results in intrinsic or extrinsic rewards which, through a feedback loop, affect perceptions about the relationships between effort and reward and hence the amount of effort. Second, the model suggests that satisfaction is affected not only by the existence of reward but also by perceptions about the extent to which the reward

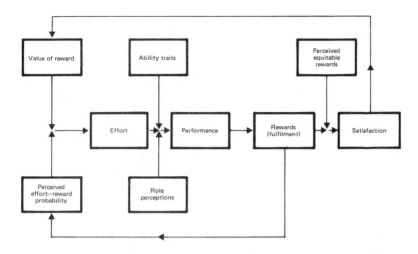

**Figure 6.5 Motivation model (Schwab and Cummings)**

is fair and equitable. By a feedback process this determines the value of the reward, which also influences the amount of effort. The model clearly shows the interactive nature of performance and satisfaction. Satisfaction is contingent upon the receipt of equitable rewards following performance, but it also influences perceptions about the value of rewards and, therefore, effort and performance.

## Techniques of motivation

It has been suggested by Katz that there are three basic types of behaviour that are essential for a functioning organization:

1. People must be induced to enter and remain within the system.
2. They must carry out their role assignments in a dependable fashion.
3. There must be innovative and spontaneous activity in achieving organizational objectives which go beyond the role specifications.[17]

The following methods are available to achieve these aims:

1. *The extrinsic reward system* which consists of basic pay, incentives, fringe benefits, security, promotion, recognition, status symbols, and pleasant working conditions. It is possible to distinguish between system rewards and individual rewards. System rewards are obtained by everyone in the organization and help to attract and retain them there. They include competitive and equitable pay structures, across-the-board pay increases, common fringe benefits, good working conditions and, in some circumstances, the organization climate, if it is friendly and supportive. Individual rewards include pay related to performance and effort and recognition awards such as promotion, status symbols and praise. If pay incentives are to work they must be perceived as:

   ☐ large enough in amount to justify the additional effort required to obtain them;

□ directly related to the required performance and follow directly on its accomplishment;

□ equitable, both by those who receive them and by those to whom they are not awarded.

If these conditions cannot be achieved, the effectiveness of individual incentive schemes is limited. It is difficult to devise and maintain an individual bonus scheme which is accepted by all concerned as fair, and informal norms are quickly developed to protect the group against efforts which are seen as divisive or exploitative.

2. *Intrinsic rewards* contained in the content of the job which provide satisfaction by enabling people to feel a sense of accomplishment, to express and use their abilities and to exercise their own decision-making powers. Motivating by means of intrinsic rewards is mainly a matter of job design and job enrichment as discussed in chapter 8. But it is also dependent upon the quality of management and supervision and the style they adopt. Organization development and training activities can help to produce a climate in which people are more likely to feel that their jobs are intrinsically rewarding.

3. *Improving ability levels*, which can be achieved by using more effective selection procedures and by training. It is also important to deploy abilities properly by improving the design of organization structures and jobs, manpower planning and systems development.

4. *Increasing understanding and acceptance of roles* by clearer role definitions, target setting techniques, training and better supervision.

5. *Increasing a sense of commitment and identification with the organization and its objectives* by organization design and development activities which achieve the better integration of activities and people (see chapters 7 and 9) and by adopting a more participative or democratic style of management.

6. *Ensuring an appropriate degree of compliance with legitimate rules.* Motivation is not simply a matter of providing incentives and rewards. People have to know what they are expected to do and what will happen if they do not do it. They should be aware of the standards of performance and behaviour they are expected to achieve if they wish to remain with the organization. The standards of performance and codes of behaviour must, of course, be reasonable and they must be legitimate in the sense that they are accepted as appropriate by the members of the organization. If disciplinary sanctions have to be used they should be applied justly and equitably.

There is no question of one approach being better than another. All may be required. What must be done is to analyse the situation and the changes taking place in it — the environment, the organization, the work systems and the people concerned. Motivation is a complex process because human beings are complex. There is no quick and easy answer to it.

## Roles

An individual at work — and elsewhere — occupies a role in relation to other people (his 'role set'). He will have expectations about the behaviour he should exhibit. If he lives up to these expectations he will have successfully performed the role.

An individual's performance in a role will be a product of the interaction between his own personality and the situation he is in. Situational factors are important, but the role he performs will both shape and reflect his personality. Stress and inadequate performance will result when roles are ambiguous, incompatible or in conflict with one another.

ROLE AMBIGUITY. When an individual is unclear about what his role is, what he is expected to do or how he is getting on he may become insecure or lose confidence in himself.

ROLE INCOMPATIBILITY. Stress and poor performance may be caused by someone's role having incompatible elements, as when there is a clash between what other people expect from the role and what the individual believes it is.

ROLE CONFLICT. Role conflict results when even if the role is clearly defined and there is no incompatibility between expectations, the individual has to carry out two antagonistic roles. For example, conflict can exist between the role of the individual at work and his role at home.

## The implications of motivation and role theory

Motivation theory helps us to understand why people behave in the way they do and what we can do about it. There are, however, no easy answers. Motivation is a complex process. The relationship between satisfaction and performance is not so clear as some people would have us believe. Motivation can be extrinsic or intrinsic but the relative importance of these to an individual will depend on his personality and his expectations, and the latter are not always predictable. Motivation theory does not, therefore, provide us with all the answers. But it does give us a set of analytical tools which we can use to assess the situation and consider what actions are most likely to be appropriate in the circumstances.

The importance of role theory is that it emphasizes the fact that people at work are placed in situations where they have to play roles which are not always ones that suit them and which can result in stress and poor performance. However well motivated someone is, he may get into difficulties because his role is ambiguous or incompatible with what he wants to do or can do.

Motivation theory shows the importance of establishing the right mix of extrinsic and intrinsic rewards which meet the expectations of people at work. Role theory adds to this concept the need for people to be fitted, so far as possible, into jobs that suit them, to be trained in how to use their skills, and to be managed in a way which enables them to deploy their capacities effectively in their jobs.

## References

1. Simon, H.A. *Administrative Behaviour*. Macmillan, New York, 1957.
2. Schein, E.H. *Organizational Psychology*. Prentice-Hall, New Jersey, 1965.
3. Taylor, F.W. 'The Principles of Scientific Management', *Scientific Management*, Harper, New York, 1947.
4. McGregor, D. *The Human Side of Enterprise*. McGraw-Hill, New York, 1960.
5. Argyris, C. *Personality and Organization*. Harper and Row, New York, 1957.
6. Lawrence, P.R. and Lorsch, J.W. *Developing Organizations*. Addison-Wesley, Reading, Mass, 1969.
7. Georgopoulos, B.S., Mahoney, G.M. and Jones, N.W. 'A path-goal approach to productivity', *Journal of Applied Psychology*, Vol. 41, pp. 345-53.
8. Hull, C.L. *Essentials of Behaviour*, Yale University Press, New Haven, 1951.
9. Allport, G. 'The historical background of modern social psychology'. In G. Lindzey (ed) *Handbook of Social Psychology*, Addison-Wesley, Cambridge, Mass, 1954.

10. Cooper, C. *Job Motivation and Job Design*, Institute of Personnel Management, London, 1974.
11. Vroom, V.H. *Work and Motivation*. John Wiley and Sons, New York, 1964.
12. Maslow, A.H. *Motivation and Personality*. Harper, New York, 1954.
13. McClelland, D. *The Achieving Society*, New York, D. Van Nostrand, 1961.
14. Herzberg, F.W., Mausner, B. and Snyderman, B. *The Motivation to Work*, Wiley, New York, 1957.
15. Opsahl, R.C. and Dunnette, M.D. 'The role of financial compensation in industrial motivation', *Psychological Bulletin*, Vol. 56, 1966, pp. 94-118.
16. Taylor, L.K. *Not for Bread Alone*. Business Books, London, 1972.
17. Katz, D. 'The motivation basis of organizational behaviour', *Behavioural Science*, Vol. 9, 1964, pp. 131-36.
18. Goldthorpe, J.H., Lockwood, D.C., Bechofer, F. and Platt, J. *The Affluent Worker: Industrial Attitudes and Behaviour*. Cambridge University Press, 1968.
19. Herzberg, F.W. 'To be efficient and to be human', *Harvard Business Review*, Sept/Oct 1974.
20. McDougall, C. 'How well do you reward your managers?', *Personnel Management*, March 1973.
21. Gellerman, S.V. *Motivation and Productivity*. American Management Association, New York, 1963.
22. Guion, R.M. 'Industrial morale (a symposium) – The problem of terminology', *Personnel Psychology*, 11, 1958, pp. 59-64.
23. Gilmer, B. van Haller *Industrial Psychology*. McGraw-Hill, New York, 1961.
24. Halpin, A.W. and Winer, B.J. 'A factorial study of the leader behaviour descriptions'. In R.M. Stogdill and A.E. Coons (eds) *Leader Behaviour: Its Description and Measurement*, Ohio State University, Columbus, 1957.
25. Mayo, E. *The Human Problems of an Industrial Civilization*. Harvard University, Boston, 1945.
26. Katz, D., Macoby, N. and Morse, N.C. *Productivity, Supervision and Morale in an Office Situation*. Survey Research Center, University of Michigan, Ann Arbor, 1950.
27. Katz, D., Macoby, N. Gurin, G. and Floor, L.G. *Productivity, Supervision and Morale Among Railroad Workers*. Survey Research Center, University of Michigan, Ann Arbor, 1951.
28. Brayfield, A.H. and Crockett, W.H. 'Employee attitudes and employee performance,' *Psychological Bulletin*, Vol. 52, 1955, pp. 346-424.
29. Porter, L.W. and Lawler, E.E. *Managerial Attitudes and Performance*. Irwin-Dorsey, Homewood, Illinois, 1968.
30. Schwab, D.P. and Cummings, L.L. 'Theories of Performance and Satisfaction', *Industrial Relations*, Vol. 9 (4), 1970.

## Part III

# Employee Resourcing

This part deals with the techniques and procedures used by personnel specialists in helping the organization to obtain and deploy the manpower resources it needs. Chapter 7 describes how organizations in general are designed; chapter 8 examines the design of individual jobs; and chapter 9 considers methods of developing organizations to improve their effectiveness. Chapters 10 and 11 deal with the basic functions of personnel management – deciding how many and what sort of people are required and how to obtain them.

Having got the manpower it needs, an organization must ensure that it is used effectively, and performance appraisal, as discussed in chapter 12, is concerned with the basic information required to do this. Personnel management is also about the day-to-day business of dealing with people's problems and ensuring that people are deployed effectively. Chapter 13 considers the range of employment practices used in all organizations to deal with discipline, grievances, redundancy, transfers and promotions.

The next three chapters deal with how employees are paid. The basis of all pay structures is job evaluation and this subject is covered in chapter 14; salary administration and wage payment systems are dealt with in chapters 15 and 16 respectively.

Finally, this part deals with three important services provided by personnel departments: health and safety (chapter 17), welfare (chapter 18) and personnel record systems (chapter 19).

# 7 | Organization Design

Much of personnel management in its broadest sense is concerned with providing answers to questions such as 'who does what?', 'how should functions and people be grouped together?', 'what lines and means of communication need to be established?' and 'how should people be helped to understand their roles in relation to the objectives of the organization and the roles of their colleagues?'.

Organization design deals with the structural aspects of organizations; it aims to analyse roles and relationships so that collective effort can be explicitly organized to achieve specific ends. It is necessary to divide the overall management task into a variety of activities and to establish means of co-ordinating and controlling these activities. This design process leads to the development of an organization structure consisting of units and positions between which there are relationships involving the exercise of authority and communication and exchange of information. Organization design may thus lead to the definition and description of a more or less formal structure but it cannot ignore the existence of the informal organization – the network of informal social roles and relationships, as described in chapters 4 to 6.

It may be appropriate to think in terms of organization re-design or modification. Organizations are in a constant state of change and anyone with responsibilities for organization has to be able to move fast. But action should be based upon an understanding of the objectives, activities, decision-making processes and relationships within the organization. And this must be developed against the background of an understanding of the historical background to the organization – how it got to where it is; the personalities involved – who exerts influence, how and why; the power relationships between people; the reward system; the economic and cultural environment; and the dynamics of the organization – what is happening to it and where it is going.

The first stage in an organization design review is therefore an analysis of the present and future circumstances of the enterprise. This is followed by the detailed planning and implementation stages. Within each stage a number of steps are carried out as shown in figure 7.1.

## Organization analysis

Organization analysis is the process of defining the aims, objectives, activities and structure of an enterprise in the light of a study of its external environment and internal circumstances. The aims of the analysis are to assess the strengths and weaknesses of the organization and to determine the activities it should carry out prior to designing its structure and planning how it should be implemented. Clearly, the scale of the study will vary according to the size and complexity of the organization under review, but the general approach to organization analysis discussed below is appropriate in most circumstances.

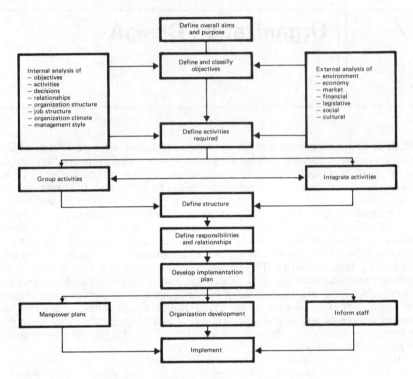

**Figure 7.1 Organization survey programme**

Organization analysis should move from the general to the particular. The general stages are: first, to obtain a broad understanding of the overall aims and purpose of the enterprise and second, to define and analyse the environment in which the organization exists and the changes that are taking place in it. The initial stages are followed by the more detailed step by step analysis of these aspects of the organization:

☐ objectives
☐ activities
☐ decisions
☐ relationships
☐ organization structure
☐ job structure
☐ organization climate
☐ management style
☐ manpower resources.

Each of these general and particular aspects of organization analysis is discussed below.

**Defining overall aims and purpose**
The initial stage is to define the overall aims and purpose of the enterprise. In a

profit-making concern this means answering Drucker's famous question 'what business are we in?' as well as identifying the basic aims of growth, survival, corporate excellence and social responsibility.

When analysing aims, the first question to answer is whether or not they seem to be relevant to the present and future circumstances of the enterprise. The second question is whether or not the aims provide an adequate guide to the establishment of the more specific objectives which will determine where the enterprise is going. Neither of these questions can be answered in full until the organization's external environment and its specific objectives have been analysed.

## Analysing the external environment
The external environment consists of the economic, market, financial, legislative, social and cultural climate within which the enterprise operates. The analysis of the environment should determine first, the extent to which it is turbulent or stable, and second, the rate and direction of any changes that may be taking place. The constraints, threats and opportunities imposed or presented by the environment should then be assessed. For the whole enterprise, this means looking at economic and market indicators as well as considering the implications of legislation and social change. For individual functions within the enterprise, it will mean looking at particular external influences. For example growth in white collar trade unionism may affect the role and the organization of the personnel function.

## Analysing objectives
Objectives are the specific aims or targets to be achieved if the organization is to fulfil its purpose. In a profit-making concern these would be set out under such headings as profits, level of investment, future ownership, product development, market standing, manufacturing facilities, personnel policies and social responsibilities. The objectives of departments or individuals would then be determined by reference to their function or role. These could be expressed quantitatively (e.g. profit, volume), or qualitatively (e.g. level of service, quality of advice).

In a non-profit-making organization the objectives would be defined by reference to the areas in which services are provided for the government, for members of the organization or for the public. Thus a professional institution might set out its objectives under such headings as developing and maintaining high professional standards, improving the technical competence of its members, providing information and other services for its members and representing the interests of the profession to the government and the public at large.

The analysis of objectives should concentrate on establishing the extent to which they are clearly defined, understood and relevant.

## Analysing activities
Activity analysis establishes what work is done and what needs to be done if the enterprise is to achieve its objectives. The analysis should start with a broad look at the basic functions and technologies of the enterprise. Is it profit-making or non-profit-making? Is it primarily an administrative service, manufacturing or selling organization? To what extent does the work involve planning, research and development, administration, selling or production? Is the work continuous or subject to constant changes, as in project or case work? What type of production system is used: unit, mass, process, batch or flow? To what extent is the work routine or innovative? How much numerical analysis is used? To what extent are systems computerized?

The analysis of activities should establish what is and what is not being done, who is doing it, where it is being done and how much i; being done. The most important points to be established are that everything is being done that needs to be done and nothing is being done that does not need to be done. Whether or not the activities are being done in the right place and by the right people can be established when looking at the structure of the organization.

### Analysing decisions
The analysis of activities and tasks leads naturally into the analysis of decisions. This will establish how work is being delegated or decentralized and how and where interrelated decisions are being made.

Decision analysis is most helpful when it cuts across vertical and horizontal boundaries: vertical between levels of management in the hierarchy; horizontal between individuals in different functions who jointly contribute to making corporate decisions.

Decision analysis moves horizontally across functions but may also incorporate some vertical analysis of the division of responsibility between managers and their subordinates. The aim is to establish who ultimately has the authority to make the operating decision. The analysis should also show who is responsible for formulating the policy guidelines which determine the boundaries within which the decision is made, and who is contributing to the decision by providing information and advice. It should help, therefore, to identify information flows and areas where co-operation is required as well as clarifying the responsibilities and authorities for decision-taking.

Questions on decisions should concentrate on the extent to which decisions are being made in the right place and on the degree to which there is adequate information, communications and consultation during the process of decision-making.

### Analysing relationships
Relationships should be analysed from the point of view of the communications that take place between people and units in the organization and the contacts that are regularly made by individuals inside and outside the company with colleagues, customers and outside bodies. The analysis should provide information which can be used to assess whether the grouping of activities, lines of communication, information system and organization climate generally are conducive to effective management, co-operation and decision-taking. The relationship analysis should also cover the power structure of the organization — who exerts influence, who gets things done.

### Analysing the organization structure
The structural aspects of the organization that should be analysed are:

(a) how activities are grouped together;
(b) the span of control of managers and supervision;
(c) the number of levels in the hierarchy.

GROUPING ACTIVITIES. The analysis should establish which activities are carried out by the different functions and in the different organizational units. The two main points to be covered are: first, the extent to which the activities are grouped logically together and second, whether or not there is any unnecessary duplication of activities.

The analysis of how activities are grouped should also consider the need to integrate closely related activities to avoid problems of co-ordination and communication and to enable those responsible for the function or group of activities to have adequate control of all the resources they require.

SPAN OF CONTROL. Spans of control should be analysed in order to find out if they are too wide or too narrow. However, the organization designer must avoid falling into easy assumptions about what is an optimum span. It is an almost instinctive reaction to say that more means worse. But there have been many instances where what might appear to be over-extended spans of control have worked perfectly well because the manager was a good delegator.

Very small spans of control can work just as badly. In one instance, the chief executive had only two direct subordinates. But they formed themselves into armed camps and because the chief executive identified himself with the operational wing of the enterprise (there is a tendency towards polarization in these situations), the other administrative and financial wing was left out in the cold. As a result, operational decisions were made without proper regard to their financial implications and the enterprise rapidly became insolvent.

The organization designer must also beware of imposing mechanistic span of control assumptions. If work alters rapidly or if it is carried out by frequently changing project teams, span of control in the classical sense may no longer be a valid concept when analysing structures. In these circumstances, the analyst must concentrate more on establishing that the project teams or task forces are set up properly in the sense that they know what they are there to do and are in a position to do it — because they have the resources they need and, when necessary, are able to integrate their work with others.

MANAGEMENT LEVELS. The number of management levels in the hierarchy should be studied to establish whether communications are being affected by the existence of too many barriers or whether unnecessary layers of management have been inserted in the structure.

### Analysing job structure

The analysis of the organization structure concentrates on the grouping of activities into units and on the relationships between these units. The next stage is to look at the structure of the individual jobs within those units in terms of the range of tasks to be carried out, the demands made on the job holders, the amount of authority and responsibility they are given and their relationship with other people.

The analyst should find out if tasks have been grouped logically together into jobs, whether job holders have been given sufficient responsibility and authority and if they understand what they are expected to do. The design of individual jobs is dealt with in chapter 8.

### Analysing organization climate

In general, organization climate is the working atmosphere of the enterprise. In particular, it is the ways in which the following aspects of behaviour in the organization manifest themselves:

□ teamwork and co-operation
□ commitment

☐ communications
☐ creativity
☐ conflict resolution
☐ participation
☐ confidence and trust between individuals and groups and between management and their staff.

These are a reflection of the norms and values of the organization as they have evolved over time and they constitute the headings under which the climate should be analysed.

The analysis should look at the current situation, but it should also examine its antecedents and the likely ways in which it might develop in the future. The importance of examining organization climate is that the study will help to explain how the structure has evolved into its present state as well as identifying the factors that have to be taken into account in changing the structure and in implementing change. These are the human factors which determine the health of the organization and they must be appreciated at this stage of a survey.

### Analysing management style
The analysis of management style should concern itself with questions on the degree to which management is authoritarian, democratic or *laissez-faire*, the way in which rewards and punishments are meted out, and methods of delegating authority and communicating information. The traditional or prevailing style, whether it is open and democratic, or closed and authoritarian, will have influenced the way in which the organization has been structured and must be taken into account when considering changes.

### Analysing manpower resources
Management and manpower resources need to be analysed from two points of view: first, the extent to which the existing structure has been built round the personalities and strengths or weaknesses of the key people in the organization; second, the availability of the quality and quantity of people required to enable any necessary changes in organization structure to take place.

All but the most bureaucratic or mechanistic type organizations will allow the structure to adapt itself to the people available — to a certain degree. This may be unavoidable and it could be desirable in the more organic type of organization where room has to be provided for entrepreneurs, innovators and others with special administrative and technical skills. But it can go too far, and the analyst must try to assess if the structure has been unnecessarily distorted by empire-building or by weakly accommodating people whose skills are by no means unique. This information is required because the designer may have to accept that pure logic has to bow to necessity. But he should not accept it too readily. The case has to be made.

Organization design leads into organization planning — assessing implications of structural changes on future manpower requirements and taking steps to meet those requirements. The organization analyst has therefore to take an inventory of existing manpower resources in terms of numbers and skills, and, for management and other key jobs, in terms of strengths, weaknesses and potential. This may be a purely statistical exercise, or in some situations it may mean making or obtaining individual assessments of people.

## Organization planning

Organization planning is the process of converting the analysis into the design. It determines structure, relationships, roles, manpower requirements and the lines along which changes should be implemented. The organization analysis should have provided all the information required to undertake the three planning steps:

☐ listing and evaluating alternative approaches to the organization design and deciding what, on balance, is the best approach;
☐ preparing definitions of the organization's structure, relationships, and roles;
☐ identifying problems of implementing the organization, and preparing an implementation plan.

### Evaluating and deciding on the design

There is no one best design. There is always a choice between alternatives. Logical analysis will help in the evaluation of the alternatives but the law of the situation will have to prevail. The final choice will depend upon the present and future circumstances of the organization. It will be strongly influenced by personal and human considerations – the inclinations of top management, the strengths and weaknesses of management generally, the availability of people to man the new organization and the need to take account of the feelings of those who will be exposed to change. Cold logic may sometimes have to override these considerations. If it does, then it must be deliberate and the consequences must be appreciated and allowed for when planning the implementation of the new organization.

It may have to be accepted that a logical re-grouping of activities cannot be introduced in the short term because no one is available with the experience to manage the new activities, or because a capable individual is so firmly entrenched in one area that to uproot him would cause serious damage to his morale and would reduce the overall effectiveness of the new organization. This frequently happens when planning a highly structured organization, where one of the most difficult tasks facing the designer is that of reconciling ideal requirements with the practical realities of the situation. But it can also happen in non-structured situations, although the problem may not be so well recognized. The designer may wish to develop a more loosely defined organic type of organization, but he could find that many people like structure and feel threatened if the well-defined framework within which they live their lives is taken away from them. The organic concept may have to be modified and some structure left behind.

The worst sin that an organization designer can commit is that of imposing his own ideology on the organization. His job is to be eclectic in his knowledge, sensitive in his analysis of the situation and deliberate in his approach to the evaluation of alternatives.

## Implementation

The implementation stage has to ensure: first, that people concerned understand how they are personally affected by the change; secondly, that they understand how their relationships with other people will change and thirdly, and most importantly, that they accept the reasons for the change and will participate gladly in its implementation.

It is not too difficult to tell people what they are expected to do; it is much harder to get them to understand and accept how and why they should do it. The implementation plan should therefore cover not only the information that is to be given but also how it should be presented. The presentation will be easier if in the analysis and design stage full consultation has taken place with the individuals and groups who will be affected by the change. Their contribution is vital, both because they will have information and ideas which are invaluable to the designer and because they are more likely to 'own' the solution if they feel that they have played an important part in producing it. Too many re-designed organizations have failed because they have been imposed from above or from outside without proper consideration for the views or feelings of those who are most intimately concerned.

Implementation can be attempted by purely formal means – issuing edicts, circulating job descriptions or distributing organization manuals. These are useful as far as they go, but while they may provide information, they do not necessarily promote understanding and acceptance. This can only be achieved on an informal but direct basis. Individuals must be given the chance to talk about what the changes in their responsibilities involve – they should already have had the chance to contribute to the thinking behind the change, so final discussions should follow quite naturally. There is no guarantee that individuals who feel threatened by change will accept it, however much they are consulted. But the attempt should be made. Departmental sectional and inter-functional meetings can also help to increase understanding.

The process of managing change and improving teamwork are two important aspects of organization development which, as an approach to the implementation of new or changed organizations as well as the improvement of the overall health and effectiveness of an enterprise, are discussed in chapter 9.

## Who does the work?

Organization design may be carried out by line management with or without the help of members of the personnel function or internal consultants, or it may be done by outside consultants. Personnel management should always be involved because organization design is essentially about people and the work they do – subjects on which personnel managers should be capable of giving sound advice. The advantage of using outside consultants is that an entirely independent and dispassionate view is obtained. They can cut through internal organizational pressures, politics and constraints and bring experience of other organizational problems they have dealt with. Sometimes, regrettably, major changes can only be obtained by outside intervention. But there is a danger of consultants suggesting theoretically ideal organizations which do not take sufficient account of the problems of making them work with existing people. They do not have to live with their solutions as do line and personnel managers. If outside consultants are used, it is essential to involve people from within the organization so they can ensure that they are able to implement the proposals smoothly.

<table>
<tr><td>8</td><td>**Job Design**</td></tr>
</table>

## What is job design?

Job design is the process of deciding on the content of a job in terms of its duties and responsibilities; on the methods to be used in carrying out the job, in terms of techniques, systems and procedures; and on the relationships that should exist between the job holder and his superiors, subordinates and colleagues.

Job design has two aims: first, to satisfy the requirements of the organization for productivity, operational efficiency and quality of product or service, and second, to satisfy the needs of the individual for interest, challenge and accomplishment. Clearly, these aims are interrelated and the overall objective of job design is to integrate the needs of the individual with those of the organization.

The process of job design must start from an analysis of what work needs to be done — the tasks that have to be carried out if the purpose of the organization or an organizational unit is to be achieved. This is where the techniques of work study, process planning, organization and methods and organizational analysis are used. Inevitably, these techniques are directed to the first aim of job design: the maximization of efficiency and productivity. They concentrate on the work to be done, not the worker. They may lead to a high degree of task specialization and assembly line processing, of paper work as well as physical products. This in turn can lead to the maximization of individual responsibility and the opportunity to use personal skills.

It is necessary, however, to follow Drucker and distinguish between efficiency and effectiveness. The most efficient method may maximize outputs in relation to inputs in the short run, but it may not be effective in the longer term in that it fails to achieve the overall objectives of the activity. Short term profits may be achieved by efficient stock control which minimizes inventory levels; in the long run, however, customer dissatisfaction because of delays in providing spares may have a detrimental effect on sales which wipes out the initial profits. Similarly, in job design, the pursuit of short term efficiency by imposing the maximum degree of task specialization may reduce longer term effectiveness by demotivating job holders and increasing labour turnover and absenteeism.

Job design has therefore to start from work requirements because that is why the job exists — too many writers on job design seem to imply that job design is *only* concerned with human needs. When the tasks to be done have been determined it should then be the function of the job designer to consider how the jobs can be set up to provide the maximum degree of intrinsic motivation for those who have to carry them out. Consideration has also to be given to the third implied aim of job design: to fulfil the social responsibilities of the organization to the people who work in it by improving the quality of working life, which, as stated in Wilson's report on this subject, 'depends upon both efficiency of performance and satisfaction of the worker'.[1]

The technical aspects of job design are outside the scope of this book and this chapter concentrates on the human aspects of, in Robert Ford's phrase, 'motivation through the work itself'.[2] The process of trying to improve the motivational content of tasks has come to be known as 'job enrichment' which was defined by Paul and Robertson as follows:

> Job enrichment seeks to improve both task efficiency and human satisfaction by building into people's jobs, quite specifically, greater scope for personal achievement and recognition, more challenging and responsible work, and more opportunity for individual advancement and growth.[3]

This chapter is therefore about job enrichment as an approach to job design. Before looking at job enrichment programmes, however, it is necessary to consider the factors affecting job design and the motivation that can be obtained from the work itself.

## Factors affecting job design

Job design is fundamentally affected by the technology of the organization and the changes that are taking place to that technology and the environment in which the organization operates. Job design has therefore to be considered within the context of organizational design, as described in chapter 7, but it must also take into account the following factors:

☐ the process of intrinsic motivation;
☐ the characteristics of task structure;
☐ the motivating characteristics of jobs;
☐ the implications of group activities.

### The process of intrinsic motivation

The case for using job enrichment techniques in the design of jobs is based on the premise that effective performance and genuine satisfaction in work follow mainly from the intrinsic content of the job. This is related to the fundamental concept that people are motivated when they are provided with the means to achieve their goals. Work provides the means to earn money, which as an extrinsic reward satisfies basic needs and is instrumental in providing ways of satisfying higher level esteem and self-fulfilment needs. But work also provides intrinsic rewards which are under the direct control of the worker himself. The main assumption of motivation theory is that intrinsic rewards contribute more to the achievement of job satisfaction in the longer term than extrinsic rewards.

### Characteristics of task structure

Job design requires the assembly of a number of tasks into a job or a group of jobs. An individual may carry out one main task which consists of a number of interrelated elements or functions. Or task functions may be split between a team working closely together or strung along an assembly line. In more complex jobs, individuals may carry out a variety of connected tasks, each with a number of functions, or these tasks may be allocated to a group of workers or divided between them. Complexity in a job may be a reflection of the number and variety of tasks to be carried out, or the range and scope of the decisions that have to be made, or the difficulty of predicting the outcome of decisions.

The internal structure of each tasks consists of three elements: *planning* (deciding on the course of action, its timing and the resources required), *executing* (carrying out the plan), and *controlling* (monitoring performance and progress and taking corrective action when required). A completely integrated job will include all these elements for each of the tasks involved. The worker, or group of workers, having been given objectives in terms of output, quality and cost targets, decides on how the work is to be done, assembles the resources, performs the work, and monitors output, quality and cost standards. Responsibility in a job is measured by the amount of authority someone has to do all these things.

The ideal arrangement from the point of view of intrinsic motivation is to provide for fully integrated jobs containing all three task elements. In practice, management and supervisors are concerned with planning and control, leaving the worker responsible for execution. To a degree, this is inevitable, but one of the main aims of job design and job enrichment is to extend the responsibility of workers into the functions of planning and control.

### Motivating characteristics of jobs

Three characteristics have been distinguished by Lawler[4] as being required in jobs if they are to be intrinsically motivating.

1. *Feedback.* The individual must receive meaningful feedback about his performance, preferably by himself evaluating his own performance and defining the feedback he needs. This implies that he should ideally work on a complete product, or a significant part of it which can be seen as a whole.
2. *Use of abilities.* The job must be perceived by the individual as requiring him to use abilities that he values in order for him to perform the job effectively.
3. *Self-control.* The individual must feel that he has a high degree of self-control over setting his own goals and over defining the paths to these goals.

## Job enrichment

Job enrichment aims to maximize the interest and challenge of work by providing the employee with a job that has these characteristics:

☐ It is a complete piece of work in the sense that the worker can identify a series of tasks or activities that end in a recognizable and definable product.
☐ It affords the employee as much variety, decision-making responsibility and control as possible in carrying out the work.
☐ It provides direct feedback through the work itself on how well the employee is doing his job.

Job enrichment is not just increasing the number or variety of tasks, neither is it the provision of opportunities for job rotation. These approaches may relieve boredom, but they do not result in positive increases in motivation.

### Job enrichment techniques

There is no one way of enriching a job. The technology and the circumstances will dictate which of the following techniques or combination of techniques is appropriate:

☐ increasing the responsibility of individuals for their own work;
☐ giving employees more scope to vary the methods, sequence and pace of their work;
☐ giving a person or a work group a complete natural unit of work — i.e. reducing task specialization;

- [ ] removing some controls from above while ensuring that individuals or groups are clearly accountable for achieving defined targets or standards;
- [ ] allowing employees more influence in setting targets and standards of performance;
- [ ] giving employees the control information they need to monitor their own performance;
- [ ] encouraging the participation of employees in planning work, innovating new techniques and reviewing results;
- [ ] introducing new and more difficult tasks not previously handled;
- [ ] assigning individuals or groups specific projects which give them more responsibility and help them to increase their expertise.

### Steps to job enrichment

When developing job enrichment the following approach should be adopted:

- [ ] Select those jobs where better motivation is most likely to improve performance.
- [ ] Set up a controlled pilot scheme before launching the full programme of job enrichment – do not try to do too much too quickly.
- [ ] Approach these jobs with a conviction that they can be changed – it is necessary to challenge assumptions at this stage, especially about the ability of people to take on responsibility and the scope for changing established work methods.
- [ ] Brainstorm a list of changes that may enrich the jobs, without concern at this stage for their practicability.
- [ ] Screen the list to concentrate on motivation factors such as achievement, responsibility and self-control.
- [ ] Ensure that the changes are not just generalities like 'Increase responsibility' but list specific differences in the way in which the jobs are designed and carried out.
- [ ] Do not be too concerned about achieving a high degree of participation from employees in changing their jobs. Improvement is to be achieved by changing the *content* of jobs, not making employees feel happier because they have been consulted.
- [ ] Make the maximum use of line management and supervision in enriching jobs, but make sure that they have the training, guidance, encouragement and help they need.
- [ ] Bear in mind that job enrichment may develop into a major change programme and appreciate that change may be resisted and will have to be introduced with care.
- [ ] Set precise objectives and criteria for measuring success and a time-table for each project, and ensure that control information is available to monitor progress and the results achieved.

### Impact of job enrichment

The advocates of job enrichment have been so dedicated to their cause that one cannot help feeling sometimes that their enthusiasm for the philosophy of their movement has clouded their judgement of its real benefits to the organization, let alone to the individuals who are supposed to have been 'enriched'.

There have been plenty of case studies which have indicated success, although this has often been measured in subjective terms. Volvo is the famous example, although ICI has carried out a number of job enrichment programmes in the UK, and in the United States there are the well known examples of American Telephone and Telegraph and Texas Instruments. In Robert Ford's report on the AT & T programme he said that 'of the 19 studies, nine were rated outstandingly successful'. He goes on to admit that:

> No claim is made that these 19 trials cover a representative sample of jobs and people within the Bell system. For example, there were no trials among the manufacturing or laboratory employees, nor were all operating companies involved. There are more than a thousand different jobs in the Bell system, not just the nine in these studies.[2]

Douglas McGregor has said that 'unless there is opportunity *at work* to satisfy these higher level needs (esteem and self-actualization) people will be deprived, and their behaviour will reflect this deprivation'.[5] But extensive research into the effects of job enrichment has not found this belief to be universally applicable. For example, Reif and Schoderbek's[6] study of 19 United States companies who had introduced job enrichment revealed that only four thought their experience was very successful. They found that only 15 per cent of the companies had attempted to enrich unskilled jobs, and in follow-up interviews three major reasons emerged why it was more difficult to get unskilled workers to accept job enrichment: (a) the unskilled preferred the *status quo*; (b) the unskilled seemed to prefer highly specialized work, and (c) the unskilled showed a lack of interest in improvements in job design which require learning new skills or assuming greater responsibility. A representative comment was: 'Most unskilled workers prefer the routine nature of their jobs, and it has been my experience that they are not eager to accept responsibility or learn new skills.' Numerous studies quoted by Reif and Luthans[7] have pointed out that repetitive work can have positively motivating characteristics for some workers. Maurice Kilbridge[8] found that assembly line workers in television factories did not necessarily regard repetitive tasks as dissatisfying or frustrating.

A study by Hulin and Blood[9] of all relevant research on job enrichment concluded that the effects of job enrichment on job satisfaction or worker motivation are generally overstated and in some cases unfounded. They argue convincingly that many shop floor workers are not alienated from the work environment but are alienated from the work norms and values of the middle class, especially its belief in the work-related elements of the protestant ethic and in the virtue of striving for the attainment of responsible positions.

Fein's study of worker motivation came up with essentially the same conclusion. He states:

> Workers do not look upon their work as fulfilling their existence. Their reaction to their work is the opposite of what the behaviouralists predict. It is only because workers *choose* not to find fulfilment in their work that they are able to function as healthy human beings. By rejecting involvement in their work which simply cannot be fulfilling, workers save their sanity... The concepts of McGregor and Herzberg regarding workers' needs to find fulfilment through their work are sound *only for those workers who choose to find fulfilment through their work*... Contrary to their postulates, the majority of workers seek fulfilment outside their work.[10]

## References

1. Wilson, N.A.B. *On the Quality of Working Life*. Her Majesty's Stationery Office, London, 1973.
2. Ford, R. *Motivation Through the Work Itself*. American Management Association, New York, 1969.
3. Paul, W.J. and Robertson, K.B. *Job Enrichment and Employee Motivation*. Gower Press, London, 1970.

105

4. Lawler, E.E. 'Job Design and Employee Motivation', *Personnel Psychology*, Vol. 22, 1969, pp. 426-35.
5. McGregor, D. *Leadership and Motivation*. The MIT Press, Cambridge, Mass, 1966.
6. Reif, W.E. and Schoderbek, P.F. *Job Enlargement* University of Michigan, Ann Arbor, 1969.
7. Reif, W.E. and Luthans, F. 'Does Job Enrichment Pay Off?', *California Management Review*, Vol. XV, No. 1, 1973.
8. Kilbridge, M.D. 'Do Workers Prefer Larger Jobs?', *Personnel*, Sept-Oct 1960.
9. Hulin, C.L. and Blood, M.R. 'Job Enlargement, Individual Differences and Worker Responses', *Psychological Bulletin*, Vol. 69, No. 1, 1968.
10. Fein, M. *Approaches to Motivation*. Hillsdale, New Jersey, 1970.

# 9 | Organization Development

## What is organization development?

Organization development is concerned with the planning and implementation of programmes designed to improve the effectiveness with which an organization functions and responds to change. The programmes will be based on a variety of behavioural science concepts and techniques, but these will be carefully integrated so that a coherent approach is used to change for the better the ways in which people carry out their work and interact with others.

Organization development should be distinguished from management development, although the two often overlap. Management development (as discussed in chapter 21) is mainly aimed at the improvement of the performance and potential of individuals, while organization development is more concerned with improving the overall effectiveness of the organization; in particular, the way its various processes function and how people work together.

### Methods of organization development

Organization development programmes are usually characterized by three main features:

1. They are managed, or at least strongly supported, from the top but make use of third parties or 'change agents' to diagnose problems and to manage change by various kinds of planned activity of 'intervention'.
2. The plans for organization development are based upon a systematic analysis and diagnosis of the circumstances of the organization and the changes and problems affecting it.
3. They use behavioural science knowledge and aim to improve the way the organization copes in times of change with such processes as interaction, communications, participation, planning and conflict. Typical activities include:
   □ introducing new systems or structures;
   □ working with teams on team development;
   □ working on inter-group relationships either in defining roles or resolving conflict;
   □ educational activities for improving personal skills, especially interactive skills concerned with relationships between people.

Organization development programmes can consist of any one or a mix of these activities, and this is why it is difficult to describe 'OD', as it is familiarly known, in a satisfactorily comprehensive way. In some companies an OD programme is no more than a glorified management development package, using a few team-building exercises, informal training courses and, perhaps, dabbling in some interactive skills training such as transactional analysis. In others the programme embraces a number of different but related activities, all designed to achieve a measurable improvement in the performance of the organization.

## Analysis and diagnosis

The success of an organization development programme depends upon the thoroughness and accuracy of the initial analysis and diagnosis of the problems and opportunities faced by the organization. This should lead to a definition of the objectives of the programme and the preparation of action plans. A model of this process is shown in figure 9.1.

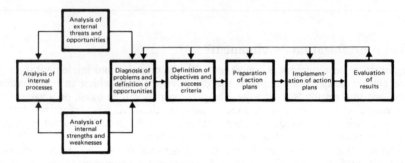

**Figure 9.1 Organization development — planning model**

A satisfactory diagnosis of problems and opportunities depends upon a thorough analysis of the internal processes of the organization as they are affected by change imposed externally or from within. When carrying out their diagnosis, most organization development practitioners take a normative view. In other words, they establish in their minds norms of behaviour or values to which they think the organization should conform. A list of typical values produced by Richard Beckhard was set out in chapter 5. The OD consultant then analyses the differences between actuality and his norms, and these are the gaps to be filled by the OD programme of interventions. The analysis is carried out by observations and by means of largely unstructured interviews and group meetings. A more structured approach is to use a questionnaire to uncover attitudes and opinions as well as indicating how the various processes of interaction, planning, participation and consultation operate. Questionnaires can be fairly simple, as in the example shown opposite used by Douglas McGregor in 1964 at Union Carbide.

In *Organizational Development*[1] Sadler and Barry give another example of a simple questionnaire which they used for diagnostic purposes in a printing works. More elaborate questionnaires have been produced by Likert[2] and, for ICI, by Maugham, Shaw and Wilson.[3]

The writer's own experience of using questionnaires suggests that the best approach is to design a special questionnaire following a brief pilot study conducted by means of a small sample of unstructured interviews. This does not frighten the participants or top management, who can be worried by what appears to be an over-detailed and time-consuming exercise. A short, specially designed questionnaire can easily be completed and discussed during interviews and group meetings and saves the inevitable difficulties of explanation when a longer questionnaire has to be distributed and completed in advance. Brevity also makes for easier analysis.

| | *Degree of Mutual Trust* | |
|---|---|---|
| 1. High suspicion (1) | ——————————— | (7) High trust |
| | *Communications* | |
| 2. Guarded, cautious (1) | ——————————— | (7) Open, authentic |
| | *Degree of Mutual Support* | |
| 3. Every man for himself (1) | ——————————— | (7) Genuine concern for each other |
| | *Team Objectives* | |
| 4. Not understood (1) | ——————————— | (7) Clearly understood |
| | *Handling Conflicts Within Teams* | |
| 5. Through denial, avoidance (1) | ——————————— | (7) Acceptance and 'working through' conflicts |
| | *Utilization of Member Resources* | |
| 6. Competencies used by team (1) | ——————————— | (7) Competencies not used |
| | *Control Methods* | |
| 7. Control is imposed (1) | ——————————— | (7) Control from within |
| | *Organizational Environment* | |
| 8. Restrictive, pressure for conformity (1) | ——————————— | (7) Free, supportive, respect for differences |

**Table 9.1 Team development scale (used by groups for self-assessment)**

## Planning organization development programmes

The steps required after the diagnosis has been completed are to:

☐ define the objectives of the programme – as specifically as possible;
☐ establish criteria for measuring the ultimate effectiveness of the programme and for monitoring its progress during intermediate stages;
☐ prepare the action plan.

When preparing the action plan it should be remembered that there will be a number of alternative choices, depending on the situation. At one end of the scale it may simply be a matter of introducing new systems or structures. This could be accomplished by information, education and discussion. At the other end of the scale, the requirement may be for a fundamental change in attitudes and values. Many OD practitioners are wary of any suggestion that their job is to change attitudes. To them it smacks of manipulation and borders on the unethical. But people's attitudes to change may be unconstructive and even if they cannot be changed, at least they can be given the opportunity to recognize for themselves why their attitudes might have to be modified. In between these extremes are the situations where there is a specific problem, but the solution requires a rather more pronounced change in behaviour or modification of attitudes than is necessary in a simple change of systems or structures.

The plan will have to consider which of the various organizational development processes should be used. These include team development activities, inter-group relations work and educational programmes and are examined in more detail in the next section of this chapter. It is usual to combine a number of these, and a typical approach would be to start with a general education programme such as laboratory training, Coverdale or Blake's grid, continue with on the job team building or inter-group relations work and add, as required, further educational programmes to follow up the initial activities. Such a sequence is illustrated in figure 9.2.

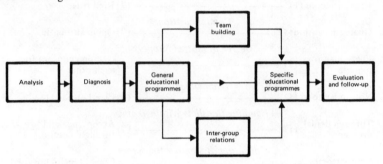

**Figure 9.2 Organization development programme**

In large organizations, varied environments produce a multitide of different development problems. The extent to which the programme is to cover the whole organization or selected parts of it has therefore to be considered. It may be decided that the educational phase at least should cover all management, supervision and key technical and administrative staff, and this approach has been adopted by British companies such as Esso and Unigate. Obviously this is a massive investment and it is wise to start with a pilot scheme. Alternatively, the plan might be to tackle the organization on a divisional or functional basis, although provision could be made for extending the activities across interrelated functions or for including both head office and divisional departments to assist with integration. The scope of the programme must depend upon the diagnosis of the problem, the resources available and the degree to which management is committed to the value of organization development.

## Organization development activities

Organization development activities can be classified into four main areas:

1. Implementing changed systems or structures.
2. Team development.
3. Inter-group relations.
4. Educational programmes.

### Implementing changed systems and structures

The need to introduce new systems or structures may have been established at the diagnosis stage. Their introduction would have to take account of potential resistance to change and should therefore try to ensure that staff will understand, accept and 'own' the change. Two examples of this type of activity with which the writer was concerned are first, a Civil Service department where, because the role of the department was changing, a fundamental change to the structure required. The broad outlines of the revised structure were discussed extensively with the members of the department. When they had been agreed, the management and supervisors of each of the new units were brought together for a week to discuss how the work should be organized and what their staff requirements were. During the week various educational activities were carried out to give the participants an insight into the main organization issues. The second example was in a manufacturing company where the introduction of a new performance review system was used as a reason for setting up a number of 'workshops' for managers and supervisors in which they agreed what was required, helped to design the system and received training in its operation.

## Team development

Team development activities are aimed at improving the ways in which work groups function. The need might emerge naturally from a systems or structures review, or it might result from a specific study of group processes in the organization and the resulting diagnosis that teamwork within groups needs to be improved. The aim would be to develop the group along the lines suggested by Douglas McGregor.

1. A group meeting in which issues are explored under the guidance of a group leader and agreement is reached on what the team development exercise is expected to achieve.
2. The presentation by the leader of his understanding of what needs to be done in such areas as structure, systems, relationships and methods of operation and communications.
3. Contributions from each member of the group on matters affecting him in the areas referred to by the leader.
4. A joint discussion to resolve any areas of disagreement.
5. The joint preparation of detailed action plans to improve teamwork and communications.

This approach could be made slightly less structured by confining the group leaders's role to the organization of discussion, and allowing the group to develop its own ideas without too much prompting from the leader. Team development work may be related to general issues or specific projects and it may be combined with educational activities of one kind or another as described under the headings 'Group exercises' and 'Group dynamics' in Appendix J.

## Inter-group relations

Inter-group relations activities deal with conflict situations, or problems relating to communication or roles which may lead to conflict. They may also be concerned with the conflicts or misapprehensions that arise when two companies or departments have to be merged.

Conflict resolution is the basis of most inter-group relations work. The simplest and crudest approach is a confrontation meeting in which the two parties get together with a third party on the side-lines to help them work through their differences.

A more refined version of this approach is to get the third party to hold discussions with each of the groups separately to agree on the issues and on an agenda for discussion. This can be time-consuming, but in the writer's experience the time is well-spent. Fairly long discussions with the separate parties in which they do all the talking are of value in themselves as a means of relieving feelings and bringing hidden issues out into the open. It is especially in this area that the OD specialist has to be able to gain confidence and trust — and be a good listener.

## Educational activities

Educational activities in organization development programmes aim to improve skill, especially in the processes of teamwork, interaction, problem-solving, objective-setting and planning. Some knowledge may have to be imparted on the basic factors affecting the processes, but this is incidental, The emphasis should be on active learning by experiencing and analysing the various processes.

The educational activities can be more or less unstructured, as in laboratory or 'T-group' training. Or they can be built round a series of projects as in Coverdale Training, which could be described as semi-structured — the participants are asked to carry out in groups a series of set tasks, but they are given the maximum amount of scope to discover for themselves the processes at work and to analyse the lessons they have learned. A slightly more structured approach is provided by the managerial grid series of programmes devised by Blake and Mouton. These activities are described in more detail in Appendix J.

## Management of organization development

One of the basic tenets of the OD movement is that an organization development programme should be 'managed from the top'. If this means that the chief executive should personally take charge of planning the programme and should actively participate in its implementation, then it is an unrealistic requirement in all but the smallest organizations. If it means that the chief executive should give active rather than passive support, then it is more feasible. Such support is clearly desirable, and the writer's own knowledge of OD programmes that have failed suggests that one of the prime reasons for failure has been because an experiment has been forced on to the company by an outsider or by an internal staff specialist without gaining the real interest of top management.

The implications of the managed from the top view are that OD can only succeed if it is organization-wide. Ideally, of course, it should cover the whole enterprise, but practical experience has shown that programmes covering separate functions or units have been quite successful, as long as the head of the function really believes in them.

Almost by definition, OD programmes need to be run by a third party. In the jargon of the OD trade — and like all new movements, it abounds in jargon — the third party is the 'change agent' who makes 'interventions' in the 'client system'. It is usually assumed that the third party should be a qualified behavioural scientist. He may come from outside or inside the organization.

An external consultant should be able to bring to the organization a wide range of experience and knowledge. He is not involved in the day-to-day politics of the enterprise and can be seen as objective and dispassionate. He should be able to act as a true catalyst — bringing about change without being changed himself. The internal consultant or adviser has the advantage that he knows something about the processes at work in the organization and should be able to reach management easily. He may be able to work more continuously than the outsider and can play a key role in implementing agreed actions following an OD programme — something the external consultant may not be given the time to do. But the internal consultant may find it difficult to keep in touch both with top and middle management in order to maintain the confidence of all concerned — a prophet is not always honoured in his own country. The external adviser may well be in a better position because he is engaged by top management but is also given ample opportunity to use his skills to make himself acceptable to middle management.

The choice depends on the situation. If the enterprise has trained people available or thinks that it is worth recruiting them, then there is much to be said for an internally managed programme. Otherwise, it may be best to get outside help, but the consultant should preferably work closely with members of the organization who will be responsible for implementation.

The factors required for success when introducing OD are:

☐ the credibility of the advocate — he must show that he knows what he is talking about, he must be able to refer to successful experience in the field and he must look and sound like the sort of person the people taking part in the programme will trust;
☐ a presentation to management which will show that the specialist appreciates their problems and can describe them in language they understand;
☐ a description of the proposed activities which will indicate what is going to take place, why this approach is being adopted, the results that should be achieved and how these results should help to overcome the problems and benefit the organization;
☐ a clear indication of the time and resources required and the cost of the programme, so that this can be measured against the potential benefits;
☐ the avoidance at all times of the use of OD jargon — terms such as 'change agent', 'intervention', 'client system', 'experiential learning' and 'confrontation meeting' may be convenient shorthand to the specialist, but mean nothing to the typical manager and are usually positively off-putting;
☐ a continuing programme of communication and discussion with line managers which is aimed at convincing them that organization development will work for them;
☐ the programme must take account of the values of the organization as well as that of the interventionist.

## Does organization development work?

Organization development programmes are based on a set of values. The first question to ask in evaluating OD is: 'Are these values appropriate to the organization?' Organization development has lost a degree of credibility in recent years because the messianic zeal displayed by some practitioners has been at variance with the circumstances and real needs of the organization. Values have been imposed and have therefore been resisted. As Adrian McLean has commented:

> It is becoming increasingly apparent that there exists a considerable discrepancy between OD as practised and the prescriptive stances taken by many OD writers... The theory of change and change management which is the foundation of most OD programmes is based on over-simplistic generalizations which offer little specific guidance to practitioners faced with the confusing complexity of a real change situation.[4]

The somewhat naive beliefs of many behavioural scientists who started the OD movement have shifted in recent years to a contingency approach as advocated by Karen Legge and Tom Lupton. This emphasizes the need to decide from the start how the process of planned change should be evaluated and then recognize that viewpoints for values will change during the course of the programme. As Lupton and Warnington state: 'Not only the strategy but the specific goal itself is likely to change as the strategy develops and better understanding of the dynamics of the system is achieved through the monitoring process.'[5]

## The future of organization development

In his persuasive article on the future of OD, McLean concluded:

> There seems to be a growing awareness of the inappropriateness of some of the fundamental value stances, models and prescriptions inherited from the 1960s. Writers are facing up to the naivete of early beliefs and theories in what might be termed a climate of sobriety and new realism. There is an increasing recognition of the existence of human traits other than those of trust, love, openness and sharing. Such traits as competitiveness, political ambition, distrust and dislike are coming to be seen as endemic and enduring features of organizational life. The signs are that more recent theories and concepts are beginning to incorporate these new perspectives.[4]

This new climate of realism coupled with a contingency approach means that OD has still something to offer because it recognizes that change and other organizational processes should not be allowed to drift. They must be managed.

There are a number of management approaches available but they are all based on analysis followed by diagnosis. Evaluation is based not on a rigid set of values but a viewpoint which is developed in the light of an assessment of the situation.

Knowledge of the contribution of the behavioural sciences to the understanding of the processes of change, conflict, interaction, group dynamics, motivation and role playing will help but will not dictate the choice of the most appropriate method in the circumstances. Less reliance will be placed on the OD packages developed in the 1960s. A more empirical approach is required which will use individual sessions and group meetings to increase understanding of what needs to be done so that those concerned will do it for themselves. Argyris summarized this approach when he defined the three primary tasks of the OD practitioner or interventionist as being to:

☐ generate and help clients to generate valid information that they can understand about their problems;

☐ create opportunities for the clients to search effectively for solutions to their problems, to make free choices;

☐ create conditions for internal commitment to these choices and apparatus for the continual monitoring of the action taken.[6]

## References

1. Sadler, P.J. and Barry, B.A. *Organizational Development*. Longmans, Green and Co, London, 1970.
2. Likert, R. *The Human Organization*. McGraw-Hill, New York, 1967.
3. Maugham, I.L., Shaw, D. and Wilson, B. *Managing Change*. British Institute of Management, London, 1971.
4. McLean, A. 'Organization Development: A Case of the Emperor's New Clothes?', *Personnel Review*, Vol. IV, No. 1, 1981.
5. Lupton, T. and Warnington, W.A. *A systems approach to determining the criteria for successful change in the context of a particular action research programme*. Manchester Business School Working Paper No. 6, 1974.
6. Argyris, C. *Intervention Theory and Method: A Behavioural Science View*. Addison-Wesley, Reading, Mass, 1970.

<table>
<tr><td>*10*</td><td># Manpower Planning</td></tr>
</table>

## Aims and activities

The aims of manpower planning are to ensure that the organization:

☐ obtains and retains the quantity and quality of manpower it needs;
☐ makes the best use of its manpower resources;
☐ is able to anticipate the problems arising from potential surpluses or deficits of manpower.

Manpower planning consists of six interrelated areas of activity:

1. *Demand forecasting* – estimating future manpower needs by reference to corporate and functional plans and forecasts of future activity levels.
2. *Supply forecasting* – estimating the supply of manpower by reference to analyses of current resources and future availability, after allowing for wastage.
3. *Determining manpower requirements* – analysing the demand and supply forecasts to identify future deficits or surpluses.
4. *Productivity and cost analysis* – analysing manpower productivity, capacity, utilization and costs in order to identify the need for improvements in productivity or reductions in cost.
5. *Action planning* – preparing plans to deal with forecast deficits or surpluses of manpower, to improve utilization and productivity or to reduce manpower costs.
6. *Manpower budgeting and control* – setting manpower budgets and standards and monitoring the implementation of the manpower plans against them.

Although these are described as six separate areas, and are analysed as such in later sections of this chapter, they are, in fact, closely interrelated and often overlap. For example, demand forecasts are estimates of future requirements, and these can only be prepared on the basis of assumptions about the productivity of employees. But the supply forecast will also have to consider productivity trends and how they might affect the supply of manpower.

A flow chart of the process of manpower planning is shown in figure 10.1.

## Demand forecasting

Demand forecasting is the process of estimating the future quantity and quality of manpower required. The basis of the manpower forecast should be the annual budget and longer term corporate plan, translated into activity levels for each function and department. In a manufacturing company the sales budget would be translated into a manufacturing plan giving the numbers and types of products to be made in each period. From this information the number of man hours by skill categories to make the quota for each period would be computed. A man-

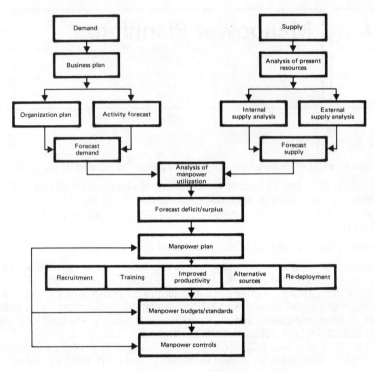

**Figure 10.1 The process of manpower planning**

power plan for a van sales operation would start from the sales plan setting out a programme for establishing new rounds. In an insurance company, forecasts of new business would be translated into the number of proposals that would have to be processed by the underwriting department. In a mail order company, forecasts would be made of the number of orders that have to be processed, assembled and dispatched.

Details are required of any organization plans which would result in increased or decreased demands for staff. For example, setting up a new regional organization, creating a new sales department, decentralizing a head office function to the regions.

The planning data would refer to expected changes in productivity or manpower levels arising from changes in working methods or procedures, automation or mechanization. These could be set out as a crude percentage increase in productivity which could be used to adjust the required man hours for a given level of output. Or they might give specific instances of cases where the manning for a machine, a production line, a clerical section or a sales office is to be increased or decreased.

### Demand forecasting methods
There are three basic demand forecasting methods:

1. Managerial judgement.
2. Statistical techniques, including ratio-trend analysis and econometric models.
3. Work study techniques.

These are described separately below, although in many cases a combination of, say, managerial judgement and statistical techniques would be used.

## Managerial judgement

The most typical method of forecasting used in smaller companies, or those who do not have access to work study data, is managerial judgement. This simply requires managers to sit down, think about their future workloads and decide how many people they need. It might be done on a 'bottom-up' basis with line managers submitting proposals for agreement by senior management.

Alternatively, a 'top-down' approach can be used in which company and departmental forecasts are prepared by top management, possibly acting on advice from the personnel and organization and methods departments. These forecasts are reviewed and agreed with departmental managers. A less directive approach is for top management to prepare planning guidelines for departmental managers setting out the planning assumptions and the targets they should try to meet. The personnel and organization and methods of work study departments then discuss and agree budgets with departmental managers.

Perhaps the best way of using managerial judgement is to adopt both the 'bottom-up' and 'top-down' approach. Guidelines for departmental managers should be prepared which indicate broad company assumptions about future activity levels which will affect their departments. Targets are also set where necessary. Armed with these guidelines, departmental managers prepare their forecasts to a laid-down format. They are encouraged to seek help at this stage from personnel, O & M, or work study. Meanwhile, the personnel department, in conjunction as necessary with planning, O & M and work study departments, prepares a company manpower forecast. The two sets of forecasts are then reviewed by a manpower planning committee consisting of functional heads. This committee reconciles with departmental managers any discrepancies between the two forecasts and submits the final amended forecast to top management for approval. This is sometimes called the 'right-angle method'.

An example of a staff forecast form using managerial judgement is shown in figure 10.2.

## Statistical techniques

The most commonly used statistical manpower forecasting technique is ratio-trend analysis. More complex and less used techniques include regression analysis and econometric models.

RATIO-TREND ANALYSIS. In its crudest form, ratio-trend analysis is carried out by studying past ratios between, say, the number of direct and indirect workers in a manufacturing plant, and forecasting future ratios, having made some allowance for changes in organization or methods. Activity level forecasts are then used to determine direct labour requirements and the forecast ratio of indirects to directs is used to calculate the number of indirect workers needed. For example, table 10.1 shows how ratio-trend analysis could be used to forecast the number of inspectors required in an assembly plant. Similar techniques could be used to develop fairly crude ratios between activity levels and numbers of staff.

| Category of staff .............................. | | Year ............. |
|---|---|---|
| *Staff members and movements* | *No. of staff to be provided* | *Remarks* |
| 1. Number of staff at 1.1.....<br>(excluding known resignations) 75 | — | Age groups:<br>Under 25           30<br>25 - 34              20<br>35 - 44              15<br>45 and over      10 |
| 2.(a) Expected retirements,<br>      transfers out and<br>      promotions during year    8<br>   (b) Less expected transfers in,<br>      promotions and new<br>      appointments already made   3 | 5 | (dates to be specified) |
| 3.(a) Number of staff<br>      required at 1 January,<br>      next year            80<br>   (b) Less present staff      75 | 5 | Increase in number to be substantiated by O & M report |
| 4. Expected staff losses due to<br>   normal wastage of existing<br>   staff                        15 | 15 | Estimated by age groups:<br>Under 25           12<br>25 - 34               2<br>35 - 44               1<br>45 and over      — |
| 5. Expected losses of staff to be<br>   recruited in the period     5 | 5 | Short service staff turnover at<br>20% of 25 (events 2. + 3. + 4<br>above) |
| 6. Total staff to be provided<br>   during period | 30 | 5 to be recruited by 1 February —<br>others to be programmed later |

**Figure 10.2 Staff forecast form**

| | | No. of Employees | | Ratio |
|---|---|---|---|---|
| | Year | *Production* | *Inspector* | **Inspector : Production** |
| *Actual* | - 3<br>- 2<br>Last year | 1500<br>1800<br>2000 | 150<br>180<br>180 | 1 : 10<br>1 : 10<br>1 : 11 |
| *Forecast* | Next year<br>+2<br>+3 | 2200*<br>2500*<br>2750 | 200†<br>210†<br>230† | 1 : 11<br>1 : 12<br>1 : 12 |
| * calculated by reference to forecast activity levels<br>† calculated by applying forecast ratio to forecast activity levels | | | | |

**Table 10.1 Demand forecast — inspectors**

Table 10.2 shows how an analysis of actual and forecast ratios between the number of routine proposals to be processed by an insurance company underwriting department and the number of underwriters employed could be used to forecast future requirements.

| | Year | No. of underwriters | No. of proposals per week | Ratio Underwriters : Proposals |
|---|---|---|---|---|
| *Actual* | - 3 | 10 | 2,000 | 1 : 200 |
| | - 2 | 10 | 2,500 | 1 : 250 |
| | Last Year | 12 | 3,600 | 1 : 300 |
| *Forecast* | Next Year | 14 | 4,200 | 1 : 300 |
| | +2 | 16 | 4,800 | 1 : 300 |
| | +3 | 18 | 5,400 | 1 : 300 |

Table 10.2 Demand forecast — underwriters

These techniques, although crude, are easy to understand and use. Their value depends upon accurate records and realistic estimates of future activity levels and the effect of improved performance or changed methods.

ECONOMETRIC MODELS. To build an econometric model for manpower planning purposes it is necessary to analyse past statistical data and to describe the relationship between a number of variables in a mathematical formula. The variables affecting manpower requirements may be identified under headings such as investment, sales or the complexity of the product line. The formula could then be applied to forecasts of movements in these variables to produce a manpower forecast. This is a complex process only suitable for large organizations. (The use of computers in manpower planning is dealt with in chapter 19.)

WORK STUDY TECHNIQUES. Work study techniques can be used when it is possible to apply work measurement to calculate how long operations should take and the amount of labour required. The starting point in a manufacturing company is the production budget prepared in terms of volumes of saleable products for the company as a whole, or volumes of output for individual departments. The budgets of productive hours are then compiled by the use of standard hours for direct labour, if standard labour times have been established by work measurement. The standard hours per unit of output are then multiplied by the planned volume of units to be produced to give the total planned hours for the period. This is divided by the number of actual working hours for an individual operator to show the number of operators required. Allowance may have to be made for absenteeism and forecast levels of idle time. The following is a highly simplified example of this procedure:

(a) Planned output for year             : 20,000 units
(b) Standard hours per unit             : 5 hours
(c) Planned hours for year              : 100,000 hours
(d) Productive hours per man/year
    (allowing normal overtime,
    absenteeism and down time)          : 2,000 hours
(e) Number of direct workers
    required (c/d)                      : 50

Work study techniques for direct workers can be combined with ratio-trend analysis to calculate the number of indirect workers needed. Clerical staff requirements may also be estimated by these methods if clerical work measurement techniques can be used.

## Supply forecasting

Manpower resources comprise the total effective effort that can be put to work as shown by the number of people and hours of work available, the capacity of employees to do the work and their productivity. Supply forecasting measures the quantity of manpower that is likely to be available from within and outside the organization, having allowed for absenteeism, internal movements and promotions, wastage and changes in hours and other conditions of work. The supply analysis covers:

☐ existing manpower resources;
☐ potential losses to existing resources through labour wastage;
☐ potential changes to existing resources through internal promotions;
☐ effect of changing conditions of work and absenteeism;
☐ sources of supply from within the firm.

### Analysing existing manpower resources

The basic analysis should classify employees by function or department, occupation, level of skill and status.

The aim should be to identify from this analysis 'resource centres' consisting of broadly homogeneous groups for which forecasts of supply need to be made. There is endless scope for cross analysis in preparing manpower inventories, but the manpower planner has to beware of collecting useless data. He must subject the analytical scheme he devises to rigorous analysis, and for each category ask the questions: 'Why do we need this information?' and 'What are we going to do with it when we get it?'

Some detailed analysis may be essential. For example, the review of current resources may need to cut across organizational and occupational boundaries to provide inventories of skills and potential. It may be important to know how many people the organization has with special skills or abilities; for example, chemists, physicists, mathematicians, economists or linguists. From the point of view of management succession planning and the preparation of management development programmes it may be equally important to know how many people with potential for promotion exist and where they can be found.

An analysis of manpower by age helps to identify problems arising from a sudden rush of retirements, a block in promotion prospects, or a preponderance of older employees. Age distribution can be illustrated graphically as in figure 10.3 which shows that a large number of staff will retire shortly and that the proportion of employees in the older age brackets is unduly high.

Length of service analysis may be even more important because it will provide evidence of survival rates, which, as discussed later, are a necessary tool for use by planners in predicting future resources.

The analysis of current resources should look at the existing ratios between different categories of staff; for example, supervisors to employees, skilled to semi-skilled, direct to indirect, clerical to production. Recent movements in these ratios should be studied to provide guidance on trends and to highlight areas where rapid changes may result in manpower supply problems.

### Labour wastage

Labour wastage should be analysed in order to forecast future losses and to identify the reasons for people leaving the organization. Plans can then be made to attack the problems causing unnecessary wastage and to replace uncontrollable

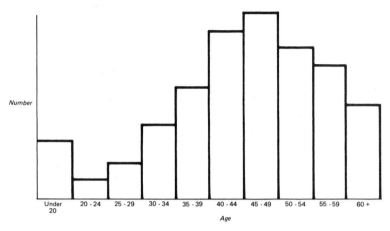

Figure 10.3 Analysis of age distribution

losses. The manpower planner therefore has to know how to measure wastage and how to analyse its causes.

MEASURING LABOUR WASTAGE. This can be done in various ways:

*Labour Turnover Index.* This is the traditional formula for measuring wastage:

$$\frac{\text{Number of leavers in a specified period (usually 1 year)}}{\text{Average number of employees during the same period}} \times 100$$

This method is in common use because it is easy to calculate and to understand. It is a simple matter to work out that if last year 30 out of an average force of 150 skilled fitters left (20% turnover), and this trend continues, then the company will have to recruit 110 fitters during the following year, in order to increase and to hold the labour force at 200 in that year (50 extra fitters, plus 40 to replace the 20% wastage of the average 200 fitters employed, plus 20 to replace wastage of the 90 recruits).

This wastage formula is simple to use. But it can be positively misleading. The main objection to the measurement of labour turnover, in terms of the proportion of the labour force who leave in a given period, is that the figure may be inflated by the high turnover of a relatively small proportion of the labour force, especially in times of heavy recruitment. Thus, a company employing 1,000 people might have had an annual wastage rate of 20%, meaning that 200 jobs had become vacant during the year. But this could have been spread throughout the company, covering all occupations and long as well as short service employees. Alternatively it could have been restricted to a small sector of the labour force — only twenty jobs might have been affected although each of these had to be filled ten times during the year. These are totally different situations, and unless they are appreciated, inaccurate forecasts would be made of future requirements and inappropriate actions would be taken to deal with the problem. The labour wastage percentage is also suspect if the average number of employees upon which the percentage is based is unrepresentative of recent trends because of considerable increases or decreases during the period in the numbers employed.

121

*Labour Stability Index*. This measure is considered by many to be an improvement:

$$\frac{\text{Number with 1 year's service or more}}{\text{Number employed 1 year ago}} \times 100$$

This index provides an indication of the tendency for longer service employees to remain with the company, and therefore shows the degree to which there is a continuity of employment. But this too can be misleading because the index will not reveal the vastly different situations that exist in a company or department with a high proportion of long-serving employees in comparison with one where the majority of employees are short service.

*Length of Service Analysis*. This disadvantage of the labour stability index may be partly overcome if an analysis is also made of the average length of service of people who leave, as in table 10.3.

This analysis also gives the index of labour turnover. It is still fairly crude, because it only deals with those who leave. A more refined analysis would compare for each service category the numbers leaving with the numbers employed. If, in the example shown, the total numbers employed with less than three months' service was 80 and the total with more than five years was 80, the proportion of leavers in each category would be, respectively, 50% and 10% — much more revealing figures, especially if previous periods could be analysed to reveal adverse trends.

*Survival Rate*. Another method of analysing labour turnover which is particularly useful for manpower planners is the survival rate: the proportion of employees who are engaged within a certain period who remain with the firm after so many months or years of service. Thus an analysis of apprentices who have 'finished their time' might show that after two years, ten of the original 'cohort' of twenty ex-apprentices were still with the company, a survival rate of 50%.

The distribution of losses for each entry group or 'cohort' can be plotted in the form of a 'survival curve' as shown in figure 10.4.

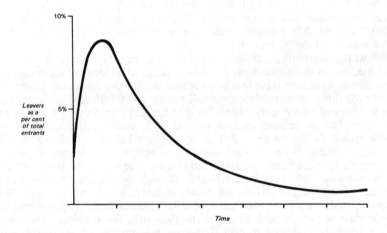

**Figure 10.4 A survival curve**

| Occupation | Leavers by Length of Service 19..... | | | | | | Total no. leaving | Average no. employed | Index of labour turnover |
| | less than 3 months | 3 - 6 months | 6 months - 1 year | 1 - 2 years | 3 - 5 years | 5 or more years | | | |
|---|---|---|---|---|---|---|---|---|---|
| | | | | | | | | | % |
| Skilled | 5 | 4 | 3 | 3 | 2 | 3 | 20 | 200 | 10 |
| Semi-skilled | 15 | 12 | 10 | 6 | 3 | 4 | 50 | 250 | 20 |
| Unskilled | 20 | 10 | 5 | 3 | 1 | 1 | 40 | 100 | 40 |
| Totals | 40 | 26 | 18 | 12 | 6 | 8 | 110 | 550 | 20 |

**Table 10.3 Analysis of leavers by length of service**

The basic shape of this curve has been found to be similar in many situations, although it has been observed that the peak of the curve may occur further along the time scale and/or may be lower when it relates to more highly skilled or trained entry cohorts. Table 10.4 would tell the manpower planner that he has to allow for half the number of recruits in any one year to be lost over the next five years, unless something can be done about the factors causing wastage. Thus, to achieve a requirement of 50 trained staff in five years' time, 100 people would have to be engaged this year.

| Entry cohort | Original strength | No. surviving to end of year after engagement | | | | |
|---|---|---|---|---|---|---|
| | | Year 1 | Year 2 | Year 3 | Year 4 | Year 5 |
| A | 40 | 35 | 28 | 26 | 22 | 20 |
| B | 32 | 25 | 24 | 19 | 18 | 17 |
| C | 48 | 39 | 33 | 30 | 25 | 23 |
| D | 38 | 32 | 27 | 24 | 22 | 19 |
| E | 42 | 36 | 30 | 26 | 23 | 21 |
| Average survival rate | 100% | 83% | 71% | 62% | 55% | 50% |

**Table 10.4 Survival rate analysis**

*Half-Life Index.* A simpler concept derived from survival rate analysis is that of the half-life index, which is defined as the time taken for a group or cohort of starters to reduce to half its original size through the wastage process (five years in the above example). Comparisons can then be made for successive entry years or between different groups of employees in order to show where action may have to be taken to counter undesirable wastage trends.

*Choice of Measurement.* It is difficult to avoid using the conventional labour turnover index as the easiest and most familiar of all methods of measurement. But it needs to be supplemented with some measure of stability — an analysis of labour wastage as part of a manpower planning exercise requires detailed information on the length of service of leavers to identify problem areas and to provide a foundation for manpower supply forecasts.

### Analysing the effect of promotions and transfers
The supply forecast should indicate the number of vacancies that will have to be filled to meet the demand forecast. Vacancies arise because people leave but the exit of a senior manager may produce a chain reaction of replacements. Transfers between departments and divisions may also have to be allowed for.

In a large organization, persistent patterns of promotion or transfer may develop and it may be possible to predict the proportions of employees in particular categories who are likely to be promoted or moved in the future by starting with a forecast of the chain reaction factor, to give a broad indication of the number of displacements that may occur. For example, where there are three levels of management:

3rd line management    :    1 promotion    =    3 moves
2nd line management    :    5 promotions    =    10 moves
1st line management    :    25 promotions    =    25 moves

**Total promotions/moves    31                    38**

But this is very crude, and in most companies management succession planning has to be worked out specifically by reference to known retirements and transfers.

### Assessing changes in conditions of work and absenteeism

This assessment should cover factors operating within the firm such as changes in: normal weekly hours of work; overtime policies; the length and timing of holidays; retirement policy; the policy for employing part-timers; and shift systems.

The effect of absenteeism on the future supply of labour should also be allowed for, and trends in absenteeism should be analysed to trace causes and identify possible remedial actions.

### Analysing sources of supply

Internal sources will include the output from established training schemes or management development programmes and the reservoirs of skill and potential that exist within the organization. But the availability of manpower from outside as well as inside the enterprise is a vital factor when preparing development plans. Too often, corporate or functional plans make assumptions about the availability of labour, locally or nationally, which could easily be proved wrong after a brief investigation. It is particularly necessary to identify at an early stage any categories of employees where there might be difficulties in recruiting the numbers required, so that action can be taken in good time to prepare a recruiting campaign, to tap alternative sources, or to develop training or re-training programmes to convert available manpower to meet the company's needs. The factors which can have an important bearing on the supply of manpower are listed below:

LOCAL FACTORS
1. Population densities within reach of the company.
2. Current and future competition for labour from other employers.
3. Local unemployment levels.
4. The traditional pattern of employment locally, and the availability of people with the required qualifications and skills.
5. The output from the local educational system and government or other training establishments.
6. The pattern of immigration and emigration within the area.
7. The attractiveness of the area as a place to live.
8. The attractiveness of the company as a place to work in.
9. The availability of part-time labour such as for married women.
10. Local housing, shopping and transport facilities.

NATIONAL FACTORS
1. Trends in the growth of the working population.
2. National demands for special categories of manpower — graduates, professional staff, technologists, technicians, craftsmen, secretaries.
3. The output of the universities, polytechnics and professional institutions.
4. The effect of changing educational patterns — children staying longer at schools, or different emphases in university or school curriculae.
5. The impact of national government training schemes and, in Britain, the industrial training boards.
6. The impact of government employment regulations such as, in Britain, the Employment Protection Act, the Sex Discrimination Act or the Equal Pay Act.

## Determining manpower requirements

Manpower requirements are determined by relating the supply to the demand forecasts and establishing any deficits or surpluses of manpower that will exist in the future. Table 10.5 shows how demand and supply forecasts can be scheduled over a period of five years to indicate the number of fitters to be recruited.

| | | Year 1 | Year 2 | Year 3 | Year 4 | Year 5 |
|---|---|---|---|---|---|---|
| **Demand** | 1. Numbers required at beginning of year | 120 | 140 | 140 | 120 | 120 |
| | 2. Changes to requirements forecast during year | +20 | Nil | - 20 | Nil | Nil |
| | 3. Total requirements at end of year (1+2) | 140 | 140 | 120 | 120 | 120 |
| **Supply** | 4. Numbers available at beginning of year | 120 | 140 | 140 | 120 | 120 |
| | 5. Gains from transfers and promotions in | 5 | 5 | -- | -- | -- |
| | 6. Losses through: | | | | | |
| | (a) retirements | 3 | 6 | 4 | 1 | 3 |
| | (b) wastage | 15 | 17 | 18 | 15 | 14 |
| | (c) transfers and promotions out | 2 | 4 | 6 | 3 | -- |
| | (d) total losses | 20 | 27 | 28 | 19 | 17 |
| | 7. Total available at end of year (4+5-6) | 105 | 118 | 112 | 101 | 103 |
| **Requirement** | 8. Deficit (d), or surplus (s): (3-7) | 25(d) | 22(d) | 8(d) | 19(d) | 17(d) |
| | 9. Losses of those recruited during year | 3 | 6 | 2 | 4 | 3 |
| | 10. Additional numbers required during year (8+9) | 28 | 28 | 10 | 23 | 20 |

**Table 10.5 Forecast of recruitment needs for fitters**

The first year of the forecast could be the labour budget for the year and the forecast would be updated annually, or more frequently if there are rapid changes in demand. In some situations it might be impossible to forecast as far ahead as five years, and in others there might be no point in doing so because no action could be taken by the company more than one or two years in advance.

An example of a more detailed one-year manpower budget for a sales organization is shown in table 10.6

The reconciliation of demand and supply forecasts shows how many people may have to be recruited or made redundant and this forms the basis for the manpower plan proper — drawing up recruitment campaigns and training programmes or preparing for redundancy.

But manpower planning is not only about obtaining people. It is also concerned with how efficiently they are used. The raw assumptions built into the supply and demand forecasts need to be reconsidered to find out if there is any scope for satisfying future demands by improved manpower utilization and controlling costs.

| | Current establish-ment | New appoint-ments during year | Forecast losses of existing staff during year | | | | Requirements during year | | | Losses of staff recruited during year | Number to be recruited during year |
|---|---|---|---|---|---|---|---|---|---|---|---|
| | | | Retire-ment | Wastage | Promo-tion out | Total | Total (2+6) | By promotion | By recruitment | | |
| | (1) | (2) | (3) | (4) | (5) | (6) | (7) | (8) | (9) | (10) | (11) |
| General Sales Manager | 1 | – | 1 | – | – | 1 | 1 | 1 | – | – | – |
| Regional Sales Managers | 6 | 1 | 1 | – | 1 | 2 | 3 | 3 | – | – | – |
| Area Sales Managers | 18 | 2 | – | 2 | 3 | 5 | 7 | 6 | 1 | – | 1 |
| Sales Representatives | 165 | 10 | 1 | 15 | 6 | 22 | 32 | – | 32 | 3 | 35 |

**Table 10.6 Sales manpower budget : year commencing . . .**

127

## Manpower productivity and costs

Manpower planning is just as concerned with making the best use of people as with forecasting and getting the numbers required. An increase in activity levels can be catered for by improving productivity as well as by recruiting more staff. This means looking at productivity and manpower costs as well as the possibility of treating human resources as assets rather than liabilities, to be invested in, maintained and allocated on the same rational basis that is used for all other assets.

### Productivity

Fundamentally, productivity represents the output of goods and services which can be obtained from a given input of employees. Within the firm, productivity should be monitored by using such measures as manpower costs per unit of output, manpower costs as a ratio of sales value, sales value per employee, tons of product handled per man hour, or labour costs as a percentage of added value (the difference being production costs and sales value). Internal and external comparisons may then reveal areas where improvement is required by mechanization, automation, improved management or other means.

### Manpower costs

Manpower costs can be grouped under the seven headings drawn up by the Manpower Society:

1. *Remuneration costs:*
    (a) pay — basic, bonuses, profit-sharing, overtime and shift payments, merit pay, other supplementary pay;
    (b) direct fringe benefits — pensions, life insurance, holidays, car, luncheon vouchers/subsidized meals, share ownership schemes, housing schemes, housing assistance, education loans;
    (c) statutory costs — national insurance and pension fund contributions, training board levies (offset by grants), employer's liability insurance.
2. *Recruitment costs:*
    (a) preparation of job specifications and advertisements;
    (b) advertising and general promotional activities;
    (c) sifting applications, interviewing and corresponding with applicants;
    (d) selection testing;
    (e) medical examinations;
    (f) induction.
3. *Training costs* (offset, where applicable, by grants):
    (a) remuneration and expenses of trainees and trainers;
    (b) preparing and maintaining training programmes;
    (c) training materials, equipment and premises;
    (d) lower efficiency of trainees until fully trained.
4. *Relocation costs:*
    (a) travel, accommodation and disturbance allowances;
    (b) housing assistance;
    (c) hostel charges.
5. *Leaving costs:*
    (a) loss of production between leaving and replacement;
    (b) statutory redundancy payments, less rebates;
    (c) *ex gratia* payments.

6. *Support costs:*
   (a) indirect fringe benefits — social and sports facilities, medical, welfare, rehabilitation and convalescent schemes, canteens, preferential purchase schemes, house magazines, music-while-you-work, library;
   (b) long-service awards;
   (c) suggestions schemes;
   (d) safety facilities;
   (e) car parking;
7. *Personnel administration costs:* personnel department costs, other than those allocated under other headings.

It may be difficult to collect and allocate expenses under all these headings, but the more detailed the analysis the better the control that can be exercised over manpower costs.

## Action planning

The manpower plan should be prepared on the basis of an analysis of manpower requirements and a study of the implications of the information on productivity and costs. The main elements, depending on circumstances, will consist of:

1. *The recruitment plan* which will set out:
   (a) the numbers and types of people required and when they are needed;
   (b) any special supply problems and how they are to be dealt with;
   (c) the recruitment programme.
2. *The re-development plan* which will set out programmes for transferring or re-training existing employees.
3. *The redundancy plan* which will indicate:
   (a) who is to be redundant and where and when;
   (b) the plans for re-development or re-training, where this has not been covered in the re-development plan;
   (c) the steps to be taken to help redundant employees find new jobs;
   (d) the policy for declaring redundancies and making redundancy payments;
   (e) the programme for consulting with unions or staff associations and informing those affected.
4. *The training plan* which will show:
   (a) the number of trainees or apprentices required and the programme for recruiting or training them;
   (b) the number of existing staff who need training or re-training and the training programme;
   (c) the new courses to be developed or the changes to be made to existing courses.
5. *The productivity plan* which will set out:
   (a) programmes for improving productivity or reducing manpower costs by such means as:
       — improving or streamlining methods, procedures or systems;
       — mechanization or automation;
       — productivity bargaining;
       — training;
       — the use of financial incentives: payment by result schemes, bonuses, profit-sharing;
       — the development of other methods of improving motivation and

commitment: organization development programmes, re-designing jobs, increased participation;
  (b) productivity or efficiency targets such as:
    — remuneration or total employment costs as a percentage of sales revenue;
    — sales per employee;
    — net profit after tax as a percentage of remuneration cost;
    — remuneration or labour cost per unit of output;
    — labour costs as a percentage of added value;
    — standard hours as a percentage of actual hours worked.
6. *The retention plan* which will describe the actions required to reduce avoidable wastage under the following headings:
  (a) pay problems — increasing pay levels to meet competition; improving pay structures to remove inequities, altering payment systems to reduce excessive fluctuations; introducing procedures for relating rewards more explicitly to effort or performance;
  (b) employees leaving to further their career — providing better career opportunities and ensuring that employees are aware of them; extending opportunities for training; adopting and implementing 'promotion from within' policies and introducing more systematic and equitable promotion procedures; deliberately selecting employees who are not likely to want to move much higher than their initial job.
  (c) employees leaving due to conflict — introducing more effective procedures for consultation, participation and handling grievances; improving communications by such means as briefing groups; using the conflict resolution and team-building techniques of organization development programmes; re-organizing work and the arrangement of offices or workshops to increase group cohesiveness; educating and training management in approaches to improving their relationships with employees;
  (d) the induction crisis — improving recruitment and selection procedures to ensure that job requirements are specified accurately and that the people who are selected fit the specification; ensuring that candidates are given a realistic picture of the job, pay and working conditions, developing better induction and initial training programmes;
  (e) shortage of labour, improving recruitment, selection and training for the people required; introducing better methods of planning and scheduling work to smooth out peak loads;
  (f) changes in working requirements — ensuring that selection and promotion procedures match the capacities of individuals to the demands of the work they have to do; providing adequate training or adjustment periods when working conditions change; adapting payment by result systems to ensure that individuals are not unduly penalized when they are only engaged on short runs;
  (g) losses of unstable recruits — taking more care to avoid recruiting unstable individuals by analysing the characteristics of applicants which are likely to cause instability and using this analysis to screen results.

In each of the six areas of the manpower plan it will be necessary to estimate the costs involved so that they can be assessed against the potential benefits. It will also be necessary to indicate who is responsible for implementing the plan, for reporting on progress and for monitoring the results achieved.

130

## Manpower control

The manpower plan should include budgets, targets and standards. It should also clarify responsibilities for implementation and control and establish reporting procedures which will enable achievements to be monitored against the plan. These may simply report on the numbers employed against establishment (identifying both those who are in-post and those who are in the pipeline) and on the numbers recruited against the recruitment targets. But they should also report manpower costs against budget and trends in wastage and the manpower ratios. Procedures and forms for preparing and presenting manpower statistics are discussed in chapter 19 on personnel records.

# 11 Recruitment and Selection

## The recruitment and selection process

The overall aim of the recruitment and selection process should be to obtain at minimum cost the number and quality of employees required to satisfy the manpower needs of the company. This chapter discusses three stages of recruitment and selection:

1. *Defining requirements* – preparing job descriptions and specifications; deciding terms and conditions of employment.
2. *Attracting candidates* – reviewing and evaluating alternative sources of applicants, inside and outside the company; advertising; using agencies and consultants.
3. *Selecting candidates* – sifting applications, interviewing, testing, assessing candidates; offering employment, obtaining references; preparing contracts of employment.

The last section of the chapter covers induction and follow-up procedures for new employees.

The flow of work and main decisions required in a recruitment and selection procedure are shown in figures 11.1 and 11.2

## Defining requirements

The numbers and categories of manpower required should be specified in the recruitment programme, which is derived from the manpower plan. In addition, there will be demands for replacements or for new jobs to be filled, and these demands should be checked to ensure that they are justified. It may be particularly necessary to check on the need for a replacement or the level or type of employee that is specified.

In a large organization it is useful to have a form for requisitioning staff, as illustrated in figure 11.3. However, even when a requisition form is completed, it may still be necessary to supplement the brief information contained in the form about the job, and it will almost certainly be necessary to check on the specification. If a requisition form is not available, then the job has to be analysed and a job description and job specification prepared. Existing descriptions and specifications should be checked to ensure that they are up-to-date. It is also necessary to establish or check on the terms and conditions of employment at this stage.

### Job descriptions

A job description defines the overall purpose or role of the job and the main tasks to be carried out. A good job description is vital to the success of a selection procedure because it is the foundation upon which all the other processes are

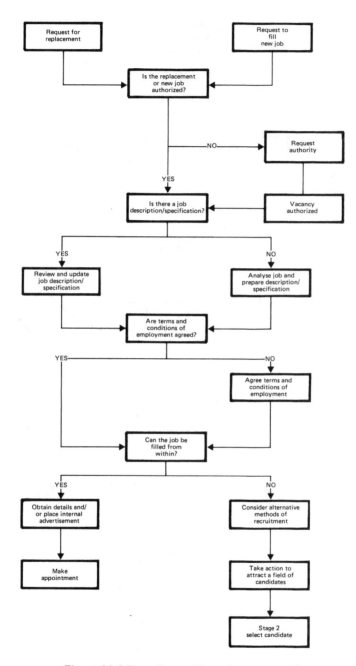

**Figure 11.1 Recruitment flow chart — stage 1
preliminary stages**

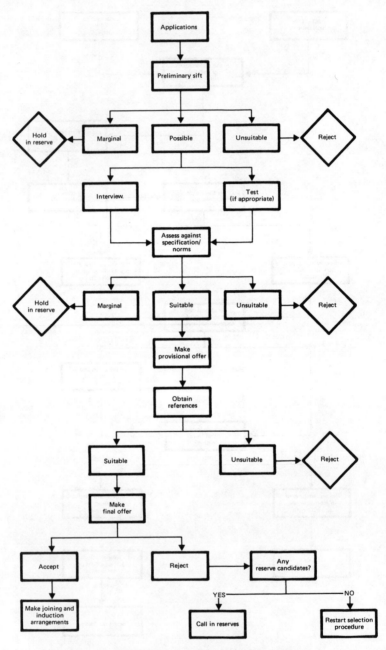

**Figure 11.2 Recruitment flow chart — stage 2
interviewing and selection stages**

| STAFF REQUISITION | | | |
|---|---|---|---|
| To<br>Personnel Department | From | Department | Date |

### REQUIREMENTS

| Job title | Permanent ☐ | Temporary ☐ |
|---|---|---|
| Salary grade | Date needed | |
| | If temporary, specify the period<br>from           to | |
| Brief outline of main duties | Education and qualifications required | |
| | Experience required | |
| | Special skills, mental or personality<br>requirements | |
| | Age limits (if any) | |
| | Who will supervise<br>the employee? | |
| | Whom will the<br>employee supervise? | |

### IF A REPLACEMENT, COMPLETE THE FOLLOWING

| Employee replaced | Job title | Salary | Date terminated |
|---|---|---|---|
| Reason for termination | | | |
| Performance<br>☐ Above average  ☐ Satisfactory  ☐ Unsatisfactory | | Would you re-engage?<br>☐ Yes  ☐ No | |

### IF INCREASE IN ESTABLISHMENT, COMPLETE THE FOLLOWING

| What has created the need for an increase? | | |
|---|---|---|
| Explain why it is not possible to avoid this increase by organizational or other<br>re-arrangements | | |
| Increase in establishment approved | Signed | Date |

**Figure 11.3 Staff requisition form**

based. The job specification and, in turn, the advertisement and the interviewing, testing and assessment procedures will all be derived from it.

The main points to be included in a job description are:

- ☐ the location of the job – division, department, branch or section;
- ☐ the title of the job;
- ☐ the job title of the individual to whom the job holder is responsible;
- ☐ the job grade;
- ☐ the job titles of any individuals responsible to the job holder and the numbers of employees he supervises;
- ☐ a brief description of the overall purpose of the job;
- ☐ the main tasks carried out by the job holder – these should be listed separately in chronological order or in order of importance;
- ☐ details of the equipment or tools used or any special requirements to deal with people, inside or outside the company;
- ☐ the location of the job and the amount of travelling that may be required;
- ☐ special circumstances such as shifts or night work, considerable overtime or weekend working, heavy lifting, exceptionally monotonous work, unpleasant or dangerous working conditions.

### Job specifications

A job specification defines the qualifications, experience and personal qualities required by the job holder and any other necessary information on the special demands made by the job, such as physical conditions, unusual hours, or travelling away from home. It should also set out or refer to terms and conditions of employment such as salary, fringe benefits, hours and holidays.

The information on qualifications, experience and qualities should be derived from an analysis of the knowledge and skills needed to carry out the job. These should therefore be specified: for example, the skills a machine operator requires to operate a machine or group of machines; the ability to read engineering drawings needed by a tool room fitter; the knowledge of double entry book-keeping an accounts clerk may have to possess; or the persuasive ability needed by a salesman. The list should be as exact as possible so that at the interviewing stage the interviewer can ask direct questions about what the applicant knows or can do.

The biggest danger to be avoided at this stage is that of overstating the qualifications required. Perhaps it is natural to go for the best, but setting an unrealistically high level for candidates increases the problems of attracting applicants, and results in dissatisfaction amongst recruits when they find their talents are not being used. Understating requirements can, of course, be equally dangerous, but it happens much less frequently.

When the requirements have been agreed, they should be analysed under suitable headings. There are various ways of doing this; the most familiar being the seven-point plan developed by Alec Rodger[1] and the five-fold grading system produced by Munro Fraser.[2]

THE SEVEN-POINT PLAN (RODGER). The seven-point plan covers:

1. *Physical Make-up* – health, physique, appearance, bearing and speech.
2. *Attainments* – education, qualifications, experience.
3. *General Intelligence* – fundamental intellectual capacity.
4. *Special Aptitudes* – mechanical, manual dexterity, facility in the use of words or figures.

5. *Interests* — intellectual, practical — constructional, physically active, social, artistic.
6. *Disposition* — acceptability, influence over others, steadiness, dependability, self-reliance.
7. *Circumstances* — domestic circumstances, occupations of family.

THE FIVE-FOLD GRADING SYSTEM (MUNRO FRASER). The five-fold grading system covers:

1. *Impact on others* — physical make-up, appearance, speech and manner.
2. *Acquired Qualifications* — education, vocational training, work experience.
3. *Innate Abilities* — natural quickness of comprehension and aptitude for learning.
4. *Motivation* — the kinds of goals set by the individual, his consistency and determination in following them up, his success in achieving them.
5. *Adjustment* — emotional stability, ability to stand up to stress and ability to get on with people.

CHOICE OF METHOD. Each of these systems has its staunch advocates and the writer has used both of them quite satisfactorily (on separate occasions, of course). The seven-point plan is more comprehensive and has the longer pedigree. The five-fold grading scheme is simpler, in some ways, and places more emphasis on the dynamic aspects of the applicant's career. Both provide a good framework for interviewing although a more simple approach used by many interviewers is to start from the analysis of the knowledge and skills required and go on from there to define the minimum and the optimum education, qualifications, training and experience needed to succeed in the job. This leads on naturally to a specification of the personal and physical attributes required and to a definition of other requirements such as age limits, location of work, travelling, night or shift work. This information can be recorded on a job specification form as shown in figure 11.4.

## Attracting candidates

Attracting candidates is primarily a matter of identifying, evaluating and using the most appropriate sources of applicants. However, in cases where difficulties in attracting or retaining candidates are being met or anticipated, it may be necessary to carry out a preliminary study of the factors that are likely to attract or repel candidates — the strengths and weaknesses of the organization as an employer.

### Analysis of recruitment strengths and weaknesses

The analysis of strengths and weaknesses should cover such matters as the national or local reputation of the company, pay, fringe benefits and working conditions, the intrinsic interest of the job, security of employment, opportunities for education and training, career prospects, and the location of the office or plant. These need to be compared with competition so that a list of what are, in effect, selling points, can be drawn up as in a marketing exercise, in which the preferences of potential customers are compared with the features of the product so that those aspects which are likely to provide the most appeal to the consumers can be emphasized. Candidates are, in a sense, selling themselves, but they are

137

| Part 1: JOB DESCRIPTION | |
|---|---|
| Department | Section |
| Job title | Job grade |
| Reporting to (job title) | |
| Reporting to job holder (job titles) | |
| Overall purpose of job | |
| Main activities/tasks | |
| Special requirements (tools and equipment used, external contacts, etc.) | |
| Other features of job: shift or night work, travelling, working conditions, etc. | |
| Location of job | |

**Figure 11.4(a) Job specification form (part 1)**

| Part 2: JOB REQUIREMENTS |
|---|
| Knowledge and skills |
| Education, qualifications and special training |
| Experience |
| Personality requirements |
| Physical requirements |
| Other requirements<br><br>Age<br><br>Travel<br><br>Hours<br><br>Other |

**Figure 11.4(b) Job specification form (part 2)**

also buying what the company has to offer. If, in the latter sense, the labour market is a buyer's market, then the company which is selling itself to candidates must study their needs in relation to what it can provide.

The aim of the study might be to prepare a better image of the company for use in advertisements, brochures or during interviews. Or it might have the more constructive aim of showing where the company needs to improve if it is to attract more or better candidates. The study could make use of an attitude survey to obtain the views of existing employees. One such survey mounted by the writer in an engineering company wishing to attract science graduates elicited the response that the main concern of the graduates was that they would be able to use and develop the knowledge they gained at university. As a result, special brochures were written for each major discipline giving technical case histories of the sort of work graduates carried out. These avoided the purple prose used in some brochures (which the survey established was distinctly off-putting to most students) and were found to be a most useful recruitment aid. Steps were also taken to encourage research managers to make proper use of the graduates they recruited.

## Sources of candidates

The main sources of candidates are:

☐ internal, by means of a search or 'trawl', as the Civil Service puts it more expressively, or by internal advertisements;
☐ external advertisements;
☐ employment agencies – private or government;
☐ education and training establishments;
☐ other external sources, unsolicited letters or casual callers, and recommendations from employees.

One source may suffice, or it may be necessary to tap a number of alternative sources. It depends upon the type of job to be filled, the relative difficulty of attracting candidates, the area in which the company operates and the history of success or failure in using different methods.

Clearly, if the job can be filled from inside, so much the better. Failing that, unsolicited inquiries and/or personal recommendations are to be preferred, if they are known to work and if the cost of maintaining an employment office to deal with inquiries is taken into account.

From a cost point of view, an approach to government employment agencies, schools, universities, or ex-servicemen employment agencies may be preferred to advertising or to the use of private agencies or consultants. But the effectiveness of the alternative sources must be taken into account as well as the indirect costs of using them or of having to put up with a longer waiting period before recruits can be obtained. External advertising may have to be used as the only reliable method of attracting candidates or to supplement other sources, but it is essential to evaluate such advertising properly in terms of cost per reply from each insertion.

The first choice of method may depend on the type of job, and typical methods for different categories of jobs are shown opposite:

| *Job Category* | *Typical Sources* |
|---|---|
| 1. Juveniles | Schools, youth employment agencies |
| 2. Clerical and secretarial staff | Private employment agencies |
| 3. Manual workers | Government employment and training centres |
| 4. Professional staff | Advertisement, including the professional institutions themselves, where they operate an employment service and the Professional and Executive Recruitment Service (U.K.) |
| 5. Graduates | Direct from universities, polytechnics and business schools |
| 6. Managerial staff | Advertisements, consultants, the Professional and Executive Recruitment Service |

## Advertising

Advertising is the most obvious method of attracting candidates. Nevertheless, the first question to ask is whether an advertisement is really justified. This means looking at the alternative sources mentioned above and confirming, preferably on the basis of experience, that they will not do. Consideration should be given as to whether it might be better to use an agency or a selection consultant. When making the choice, refer to the three criteria of cost, speed and the likelihood of providing good candidates. The objectives of an advertisement should be to:

☐ *attract attention* – competing for the interest of potential candidates against other employees;

☐ *create and maintain interest* – the advertisement has to communicate in an attractive and interesting way information about the job, the company, the terms and conditions of employment and the qualifications required;

☐ *stimulate action* – the message needs to be conveyed in a manner which will not only focus people's eyes on the advertisement but will also encourage them to read to the end and stimulate action in the form of a sufficient number of replies from good candidates.

To achieve these aims six things need to be done:

1. Analyse requirement.
2. Decide who does what.
3. Write the copy.
4. Design the advertisement.
5. Plan media.
6. Evaluate response.

### Analyse requirement

First it is necessary to establish how many jobs have to be filled and by when. Then turn to the job description and specification to obtain information on responsibilities, qualifications and experience required, age limits, and any other data needed to draft the advertisement.

The next step is to consider where suitable candidates are likely to come from, the companies, jobs or education establishments they are in and the parts of the country where they can be found.

Finally, think about what is likely to attract them about the job or the company so the most can be made of these factors in the advertisement. Consider also what might put them off; for example, the location of the job, so that objections can be anticipated. Analyse previous successes or failures to establish what does or does not work.

### Decide who does what

When planning a campaign or when recruiting key people there is much to be said for using an advertising agency. An agency can provide expertise in producing eye-catching headlines and writing good copy. It can devise an attractive house style and prepare layouts which make the most of the text, the logo and any 'white space' around the advertisement. Moreover, it can advise on ways of achieving visual impact by the use of illustrations and special typographical features. Finally, an agency can advise on media, help in response analysis and take up the burden of preparing blocks and placing advertisements.

The following steps should be taken when choosing an advertising agency:

1. Check experience in handling recruitment advertising.
2. See examples of its work.
3. Check with clients on the level of service provided.
4. Meet the staff who will be working on the advertisements.
5. Check the fee structure.
6. Discuss methods of working.

### Write the copy

A recruitment advertisement should start with a compelling headline and then contain information on:

☐ the company
☐ the job
☐ the person required
☐ the benefits provided
☐ the location
☐ the action to be taken.

The headline is all important. The simplest and most obvious approach is to set out the job title in bold type. To gain attention it is advisable to quote the salary (if it is worth quoting) and to put 'plus car' if a company car is provided. Salaries and cars are major attractions and should be stated clearly. Applicants are rightly suspicious of phrases such as 'salary will be commensurate with age and experience'. This usually means either that the salary is so low that the company is afraid to reveal it, or that salary policies are so incoherent that the company has no idea what to offer until someone tells them what he wants.

The name of the company should be given. (Do not use box numbers – if you want to be anonymous use a consultant.) Add any selling points such as growth or diversification and any other areas of interest to potential candidates. The essential features of the job should be conveyed by giving a brief description of what the job holder will do and, as far as space permits, the scope and scale of activities. Create interest in the job but do not oversell it.

The qualifications and experience required should be stated as factually as possible and age limits (if any) should be given. There is no point in overstating requirements and seldom any point in specifying exactly how much experience is wanted. This will vary from candidate to candidate and the other details about the job and the salary should provide them with enough information about the sort of experience required. Be careful about including a string of personal qualities such as drive, determination and initiative. These have no real meaning to candidates. Phrases such as 'proven track record' and 'successful experience' are equally meaningless. No one will admit to not having either of them.

The advertisement should end with information on how the candidate should apply. 'Brief but comprehensive details' is a good phrase. Candidates can be asked to write, but useful alternatives are asking them to telephone or to come along for an informal chat at a suitable venue.

Remember that the Sex Discrimination Act 1975 makes it unlawful to discriminate in an advertisement by favouring either sex, the only exceptions being a few jobs which can only be done by a man or a woman. Advertisements must therefore avoid sexist job titles such as salesman or stewardess. They must refer to a neutral title such as 'sales representative' or amplify the description to cover both sexes by stating 'steward or stewardess'. It is accepted, however, that certain job titles are unisex and therefore non-discriminatory. These include director, manager, executive and officer. It is best to avoid any reference to the sex of the candidate by using neutral or unisex titles and referring only to the 'candidate' or the 'applicant'. Otherwise you must specify 'man or woman' or 'he or she'.

The Race Relations Act 1976 has similar provisions making unlawful an advertisement which discriminates against any particular race. As long as race is never mentioned or even implied in an advertisement, you should have no problem in keeping within the law.

## Design the advertisement
The main types of advertisement are:

1. *Classified/run-on*, in which copy is run-on, with no white space in or around the advertisement and no paragraph spacing or indentation. They are cheap but suitable only for junior or routine jobs.
2. *Classified/semi-display*, in which the headings can be set in capitals, paragraphs can be indented and white space is allowed round the advertisement. They are fairly cheap and semi-display can be much more effective than run-on advertisements.
3. *Full display*, which are bordered and in which any typeface and illustrations can be used. They can be expensive but obviously will make the most impact for management, technical and professional jobs.

Professional advice in designing display advertisements is desirable. The aim should be simplicity. Logos, illustrations, pre-set headings and borders and different typefaces can all help to achieve impact, but avoid creating too cluttered an impression. Use of 'white spaces' can be very effective.

## Plan media
An advertising agency can advise on the choice of media (press, radio, television) and its cost. *British Rates and Data* (BRAD) can be consulted to give the costs of advertising in particular media.

The quality papers are best for managerial, professional and technical jobs. The popular papers can be used to reach less qualified staff such as sales representatives and technicians. Local papers are obviously best for recruiting clerical, secretarial and manual workers. Professional and trade journals can reach your audience directly, but results can be erratic and it is often best to use them to supplement a national campaign.

Avoid Saturdays and be cautious about repeating advertisements in the same medium. Diminishing returns can set in rapidly.

### Evaluate response

Measure response to provide guidance on the relative cost effectiveness of different media. Cost per reply is the best ratio.

## Using agencies

Most private agencies deal with secretarial and clerical staff. They are usually quick and effective but quite expensive. London agencies charge a fee averaging 15 per cent of the first year's salary for finding someone. It can be cheaper to advertise, especially when the company is in a buyer's market. Shop around to find the agency which suits the company's needs at a reasonable cost.

Agencies should be briefed carefully on what is wanted. They will produce unsuitable candidates from time to time but the risk is reduced if they are clear about your requirements.

## Using selection consultants

Selection consultants generally advertise, interview and produce a shortlist. They provide expertise and reduce workload. The company can be anonymous if it wishes. Most selection consultants charge a fee based on a percentage of the basic salary for the job, ranging from 15 to 20 per cent. The following steps should be taken when choosing a selection consultant:

1. Check reputation with other users if there are any doubts.
2. Look at the advertisements of the various firms. An idea of the quality of a consultancy and the type and level of jobs with which it deals can thus be gained.
3. Check on special expertise. The large accountancy firms, for example, are obviously skilled in recruiting accountants.
4. Meet the consultant who will work on the assignment to assess his quality.
5. Compare fees, although the differences are likely to be small, and the other considerations will usually be more important.

When using a selection consultant do the following:

1. Brief them clearly on their terms of reference.
2. Give every assistance to the consultant in defining the job and the company's requirements. He will do much better if he knows what type of person is most likely to fit well into the company.
3. Check carefully the proposed programme and the draft text of the advertisement.
4. Clarify the basis upon which fees and expenses will be charged.
5. Ensure that arrangements are made to deal directly with the consultant who will handle the assignment.

## Using executive search consultants

Use an executive search consultant or 'head hunter' for senior jobs where there are only a limited number of suitable people and a direct lead to them is wanted. They are not cheap. Head hunters charge a fee of 30-50 per cent of the first year's salary, but they can be quite cost effective.

Head hunters first approach their own contacts in the industry or profession concerned; the more numerous the contacts the better the head hunter. Some may be interested in the job themselves, others may provide leads to people who can be approached. If this fails, the consultant will telephone likely people, even if there is no indication that they are interested. Those who receive unexpected calls from a head hunter are often flattered or interested enough to agree to see him. A fairly relaxed and informal meeting then takes place and the consultant forwards the names of suitable and interested candidates to his client.

There are some good and some not-so-good executive search consultants. Do not use one unless a reliable recommendation is obtained.

## Sifting applications

Assuming that the vacancy or vacancies have been advertised and that a fair number of replies have been received, the typical sequence of steps required to process and sift applications is as follows:

1. List the applications on a standard control sheet such as the one illustrated in figure 11.5.

| Ref. | | Vacancy | | | | | |
|------|------|------|------|------|------|------|------|
| Media | | | | | | | |
| No. | Media Ref. | Name | Address | Grading | Acknow-ledge | Inter-view | Final letter |
| 1 | | | | | | | |
| 2 | | | | | | | |
| 3 | | | | | | | |
| 4 | | | | | | | |
| 5 | | | | | | | |
| 6 | | | | | | | |
| 7 | | | | | | | |
| 8 | | | | | | | |
| 9 | | | | | | | |
| 10 | | | | | | | |

**Figure 11.5 Recruitment control sheet**

145

2. Send a standard acknowledgement letter to each applicant unless an instant decision can be made to interview or reject. If there is insufficient information in the initial letter, the applicant could be asked to complete and return an application form. To save time, trouble, expense and irritation, it is best to make a decision on the initial letter rather than ask for a form.
3. Compare the applications with the key criteria in the job specification: qualifications, training, experience, age and location, and sort them initially into three categories:
   □ possible
   □ marginal
   □ unsuitable.
4. Scrutinize the possibles again to draw up a shortlist for interview. This scrutiny could be carried out by the personnel or employment specialist, and, preferably, the manager.
5. Invite the candidates to interview, using a standard letter where large numbers are involved. At this stage candidates should be asked to complete an application form, if they have not already done so.
6. Review the remaining possibles and marginals and decide if any are to be held in reserve. Send reserves a standard 'holding' letter and send the others a standard rejection letter. This should express thanks to the candidate for the interest he has shown and inform him briefly, but not too brusquely, that he has not been successful. A typical reject letter might read as follows:

Since writing to you on ......... we have given careful consideration to your application for the above position. I regret to inform you, however, that we have decided not to ask you to attend for an interview. We should like to thank you for the interest you have shown.

### Application forms

Application forms are required as a means of setting out the information on a candidate in a standardized format. They provide a basis both for the interview and for the subsequent actions in offering an appointment and in setting up personnel records.

Application forms come in many shapes and sizes. An example of a fairly simple form is shown in figure 11.6. A more elaborate form is shown in figure 11.7.

## Interviewing

The interviewing arrangements will depend partly on the procedure being used, which may consist of individual interviews, an interviewing panel, a selection board or some form of group selection procedure. The main features of these alternative procedures are described later in this section but, in most cases, the arrangements for the interviews should conform broadly to the following pattern:

□ The candidate who has applied in writing or by telephone should be told where and when to come and whom to ask for. The interview time should be arranged to fit in with the time it will take to get to the company. It may be necessary to adjust times for those who cannot get away during working hours. If the company is difficult to find, a map should be sent with details of public transport. The receptionist or security guard should be told who is coming. Candidates are impressed to find that they are expected.

## GENERAL APPLICATION FORM

Position applied for

| Surname (block letters) | First names |
|---|---|
| Address | Telephone number |

| Age now | Date of birth | Place of birth | State of health (mention any disability) |
|---|---|---|---|

| Marital status | Number, age and sex of children |
|---|---|

## EDUCATION AND TRAINING

| Schools (after 11 yrs) | Dates | Examinations passed and qualifications |
|---|---|---|
| Universities/Colleges | | |
| Professional/craft/ other training | | |

## EXPERIENCE
(start with most recent employer and work backwards. Include military service)

| Name of employer and nature of business | Dates From    To | Position held and reason for leaving |
|---|---|---|
| | | |

Any other information you would like to give about yourself or your experience

May we contact any of your previous employers?  YES/NO  (no approach will be made to present employers at this stage)

If yes, please give below the names of any of your previous managers with whom we may speak about you

If selected when could you start?

To be completed by interviewer

**Figure 11.6 General application form**

## SENIOR STAFF APPLICATION FORM

Position applied for

| Surname (block capitals) | First names |
|---|---|

| Address | Telephone number<br><br>Home<br><br>Business |
|---|---|

| Age now | Date of birth | Nationality | Place of birth |
|---|---|---|---|

| Marital status | Children  1     2     3     4<br><br>sex<br><br>age |
|---|---|

| State of health (mention any disability or serious illness) | Height<br><br>Weight |
|---|---|

## EDUCATION AND TRAINING

| | Dates | Details, including dates, of examinations passed, diplomas and degrees (give class) |
|---|---|---|
| Schools (after 11 yrs) | | |
| Universities/Colleges | | |
| Part time/other courses | | |

Professional and technical bodies (indicate grade of membership)

| Languages (indicate fluency) | Reading<br>Fluent   Fair | Writing<br>Fluent   Fair | Speaking<br>Fluent   Fair |
|---|---|---|---|

**Figure 11.7(a) Senior staff application form**

| PRESENT (OR LAST) APPOINTMENT | | |
|---|---|---|
| Employer's name and address | | |
| Nature of business | Company turnover | Number employed |
| Position held | | Number supervised |
| Responsible to (name and status) | | |
| Basic salary | Other emoluments (bonus, profit-sharing, etc.) | Benefits (car, free house, etc.) |
| Date appointed | Date left and reason for leaving | Notice required |
| Draw organization chart, indicating your own position | | |
| Describe responsibilities and duties performed | | |

**Figure 11.7(b) Senior staff application form (2)**

## PREVIOUS APPOINTMENTS
Start with the most recent and work backwards. Include military service

| Dates<br>From    To | Name of employer<br>and nature of<br>business | Position held and<br>reason for leaving | Last salary |
|---|---|---|---|
| | | | |

## SUPPLEMENTARY INFORMATION

Please give any other relevant particulars about your career and achievements

## REFERENCES

Please give the addresses of three persons to whom reference may be made (business references preferred)
N.B. Referees will not be approached without your permission

_____

_____

Signed . . . . . . . . . . . . . . . . . . . . . . . . .    Date . . . . . . . . . . . . . . . . . . . . . . . .

**Figure 11.7(c) Senior staff application form (3)**

☐ Applicants should have somewhere quiet and comfortable in which to wait for the interview, with reading material available and access to cloakroom facilities.

☐ The interviewers or interviewing panel should have been well briefed on the programme. Interviewing rooms should have been booked and arrangements made, as necessary, for welcoming candidates, for escorting them to interviews, for meals and for a conducted tour round the company.

☐ Comfortable private rooms should be provided for interviews with little, if any, distractions around them. Interviewers should preferably not sit behind their desks as this creates a psychological barrier.

☐ During the interview or interviews, time should be allowed to tell the candidate about the company and the job and to discuss with him conditions of employment. Negotiations about salaries and other benefits may take place after a provisional offer has been made, but it is as well to prepare the ground during the interviewing stage.

☐ Candidates should be told what the next step will be at the end of the interview. They may be asked at this stage if they have any objections to references being taken up.

☐ Follow-up studies should be carried out of the performance of successful candidates on the job compared with the prediction made at the selection stage. These studies should be used to validate the selection procedure and to check on the capabilities of interviewers.

INDIVIDUAL INTERVIEWS. The individual interview is the most familiar method of selection. It involves face-to-face discussion and provides the best opportunity for the establishment of close contact — *rapport* — between the interviewer and the candidate. If only one interviewer is used, there is more scope for a biased or superficial decision, and this is one reason for using a second interviewer or an interviewing panel.

INTERVIEWING PANELS. Two or three people gathered together to interview one candidate may be described as an interviewing panel. The most typical situation is when a personnel man and a line manager see the candidate at the same time. This has the advantage of enabling information to be shared and reducing overlaps. The two interviewers can discuss their joint impressions of the candidate's behaviour at the interview and modify or enlarge any superficial judgements.

SELECTION BOARDS. Selection boards are more formal and, usually, larger interviewing panels convened by an official body because there are a number of parties interested in the selection decision. Their only advantage is that they enable a number of different people to have a look at the applicants and compare notes on the spot. The disadvantages are that the questions tend to be unplanned and delivered at random, the prejudices of a dominating member of the board can overwhelm the judgements of the other members, and the candidates are unable to do justice to themselves because they are seldom allowed to expand. Selection boards tend to favour the confident and articulate candidate, but in doing so they may miss the underlying weaknesses of a superficially impressive individual. They can also underestimate the qualities of someone who happens to be less effective in front of a formidable board, although he would be fully competent in the less formal or artificial situations that would face him in the job.

GROUP SELECTION. A group selection procedure involves gathering a number of candidates together (ideally six to eight) in the presence of a group of interviewers/observers (ideally two to three). The candidates are subjected to a series of exercises and tests which are supplemented by individual or panel interviews.

The group exercised may be of the 'analogous' type in which the group is given a case study to discuss, which includes features and problems similar to those they would meet if they joined the organization. Or the group may be asked to discuss a general social or economic problem. They may even be sat down and asked to agree amongst themselves what they are going to discuss.

Members of the group may be tested on leadership qualities by being asked to take turns in leading the group, or the groups may not have appointed leaders, so that leadership qualities can emerge in discussion.

The observers will rate or rank participants in respect of a set of factors such as:

☐ ability to think in a logical manner about the problem posed;
☐ realistic practical approach to the problem;
☐ confidence in putting his views to the group;
☐ willingness to follow and consider other people's opinions;
☐ tendency to emerge as a leader in the group;
☐ willingness to accept criticisms of his ideas.

Ranking on each of these characteristics is sometimes preferred to rating on a numerical scale because of the difficulty of ensuring that the raters maintain a uniform standard of judgement.

In addition to the group discussions, candidates may be tested on their ability to express themselves in writing by being given paper exercises. Their ability to express themselves and to present a case orally may be tested by asking them to deliver 'lecturettes' or to make a presentation of a proposal to the group based on the study of a brief.

Individual abilities and qualities can be discussed by administering a battery of intelligence, personality and aptitude tests.

Group selection procedures are time-consuming and expensive to run but they appear to be a more comprehensive method of making selection decisions, i.e. they have 'face validity'. This is because they expose candidates to a number of more or less realistic situations and enable interviewers to see them in action with others as well as individually. A number of studies have been carried out on their *true* validity — that is, their value as a means of predicting future performance in the job, and one conducted for the Civil Service Commission showed that the selection procedure as a whole had a considerable degree of validity when judged in the light of follow-up information about the performance of successful candidates.

But Vernon sounded the following warning on group selection procedures:

> They are likely to be somewhat superior to the conventional interview method of assessing people, because they provide a more prolonged and varied set of situations in which to observe and interpret. But they are just as dependent as the interview on the skill, experience and impartiality of the observer and they should be applied with all the more caution because they engender in the observers an undue measure of confidence in the accuracy of their judgements.[3]

### The interview
The purpose of the interview is to obtain and assess information about a candidate which will enable a valid prediction to be made of his future performance

on the job in comparison with the predictions made for any other candidates. Interviewing therefore involves processing and evaluating evidence about the capabilities of a candidate in relation to the job specification. Some of the evidence will be on the application form but this must be supplemented by the more detailed or specific information about experience and personal characteristics that can be obtained in a face-to-face meeting. Further evidence may be obtained from selection tests or from references but the interview remains the main source of information.

An interview has been described as a conversation with a purpose. It is a conversation because the candidate should be drawn out to talk freely with his interviewer about himself and his career. But the conversation has to be planned, directed and controlled to achieve the main purpose of the interview, which is to make an accurate prediction of the candidate's future performance in the job for which he is being considered.

Interviewers, however, have other aims. One is to provide the candidate with information about the job and the company. An interview is basically an exchange of information which will enable both parties to make a decision: to offer or not to offer a job; to accept or not to accept the offer. A further aim is to give the candidate a favourable impression of the company. This should encourage the good candidate to join and should leave the rejected candidates without any ill-feelings.

A good interviewer knows what he is looking for, then knows how to set about finding it. Finally, he has a method for recording his analysis of the candidate against a set of assessment criteria.

KNOWING WHAT TO LOOK FOR. Knowing what to look for is a matter of knowing the job specification and the information needed to confirm whether or not the candidate meets the specification under each of its headings: qualifications, experience, knowledge, skills, physical and personality characteristics, personal circumstances.

KNOWING HOW TO FIND IT. Knowing how to find the information required is a matter first of planning the interview and then of conducting it in a way which will obtain all the data needed to make a balanced decision.

The interview should be planned around the candidate's application form to cover each of the headings on the job specification. It is therefore essential to read the application form thoroughly before the interview to decide on the line of questions and any areas where probing may be required. The aim is to establish exactly what the applicant knows and can do or to fill any gaps in his employment record. A biographical approach is usually best, starting with the applicant's education (especially younger candidates) and then moving progressively and naturally through his work experience, job by job, discussing for each job: why he took it, what he did, what knowledge and skills he acquired and why he left it. Clearly, the interview should concentrate on the most recent experience. There is no point in dwelling for long on the earlier experience of someone who has been in employment for a number of years.

The information required in an interview can seldom be obtained in less than 20 minutes, but it is usually unproductive to extend the information-gathering part of the interview beyond 30 to 40 minutes. Allowance has also to be made for the information-giving part of the interview and for the candidate's questions. For a managerial interview, a longer period may be necessary to discuss recent experience and ambitions more thoroughly. Time must also be allowed for information about the company and the job, and for the candidate to ask questions. The best approach is to start with a few welcoming remarks and explain how the interview is to be planned. Then carry out the biographical interview before telling the candidate about the job and discussing conditions of employment, including pay and fringe benefits. There is no point in giving a lengthy dissertation about the company or the work to someone who is clearly unsuitable or uninterested. Allow time at the end for questions and round off the interview by telling the candidate what the next step will be. It is normally better not to announce the final decision during the interview. It may be advisable to obtain references and, in any case, time is required to reflect on the information received. Moreover, some candidates, especially senior staff and students, do not like to think that snap decisions are being made about them, even if they are favourable.

| Do | Don't |
|---|---|
| ☐ plan the interview<br>☐ establish an easy and informal relationship<br>☐ encourage the candidate to talk<br>☐ cover the ground as planned<br>☐ probe where necessary<br>☐ analyse career and interests to reveal strengths, weaknesses, patterns of behaviour<br>☐ maintain control over the direction and time taken by the interview | ☐ start the interview unprepared<br>☐ plunge too quickly into demanding questions<br>☐ ask leading questions<br>☐ jump to conclusions on inadequate evidence<br>☐ pay too much attention to isolated strengths or weaknesses<br>☐ allow the candidate to gloss over important facts<br>☐ talk too much |

**Table 11.1 Do's and dont's of interviewing**

ASSESSMENT CRITERIA. The criteria for assessing candidates and the method of recording assessments should either be standardized for regular recruitment exercises or, if a one-off recruitment is being carried out, they should be drawn up in advance of the interviewing stage.

The criteria should obviously be those used in drawing up the job specification: for example, the seven points or the five factors in the two schemes referred to earlier in this chapter.

Admirable though these systems may be when they are used by a skilled personnel practitioner or a trained manager, they sometimes prove too complex for the typical line manager or selection board. It may therefore be necessary to devise a simplified set of criteria for their use which can be expressed in terms a layman can understand with the minimum of training.

In any situation in which non-specialists are making selection decisions it is best to use criteria which can be defined simply in familiar language and can easily be related to a job specification. The following criteria, which were mentioned earlier in this chapter when discussing job specifications, are used by managers in practice even if they do not necessarily analyse them under precisely similar headings:

☐ qualifications and training;
☐ experience;
☐ knowledge and skills – as required by experience, training and education or the natural abilities the individual possesses;

☐ overall impression – appearance, manner and speech, physique, health (physical characteristics);
☐ personality characteristics – leadership, drive, dependability, persistence, self-reliance, sociability.

An interview record form using these criteria is illustrated in figure 11.8.

| Vacancy | Candidate | | | | | |
|---|---|---|---|---|---|---|
| *Factor* | *Comments* | *Rating* A | B | C | D | E |
| Qualifications and training | | | | | | |
| Experience | | | | | | |
| Knowledge and skills | | | | | | |
| Personality characteristics | | | | | | |
| Overall impression | | | | | | |
| Recommendation | | | | | | |
| A = Very much above average; B = Above average; C = Average; D = Below average; E = Very much below average. | | | | | | |

**Figure 11.8 Interview assessment form**

Whatever assessment criteria are used, it is essential to follow up interviews to find out if the assessments and predictions have been validated by performance on the job. This is the only way in which interviewers can ever find out how effective they are. It takes time and trouble, and valid criteria are not always easy to identify, but it is well worthwhile.

## Selection tests

The purpose of a selection test is to provide an objective means of measuring individual abilities or characteristics. Tests involve the application of standard procedures to subjects which enable their responses to be quantified. The differences in the numerical scores represent differences in abilities or behaviour.

A good test has the following four characteristics:

1. It is a *sensitive measuring instrument* which discriminates well between subjects.
2. It will have been *standardized* on a representative and sizeable sample of the population for which it is intended so that any individual's score can be interpreted in relation to that of others.
3. It is *reliable* in the sense that it always measures the same thing. A test aimed at measuring a particular characteristic, such as intelligence, should measure

155

the same characteristic when applied to different people at the same or a different time, or to the same person at different times.
4. It is *valid* in the sense that it measures the characteristic which the test is intended to measure. Thus an intelligence test should measure intelligence (however defined) and not simply verbal facility. A test meant to predict success in a job or in passing examinations should produce reasonably convincing (statistically significant) predictions.

The main types of tests used for selection are intelligence tests, aptitude and attainment tests, and personality tests.

INTELLIGENCE TESTS. Intelligence tests are the oldest and most frequently used psychological tests. The first test was produced by Binet and Simon in 1905, and shortly afterwards, Stern suggested that the test scores should be expressed in the form of intelligence quotients, or IQs. An IQ is the ratio of the mental age as measured by a Binet-type test to the actual (chronological) age. When the mental and chronological age correspond, the IQ is expressed as 100. It is assumed that intelligence is distributed normally throughout the population, that is, the frequency distribution of intelligence corresponds to the normal curve shown in figure 11.9.

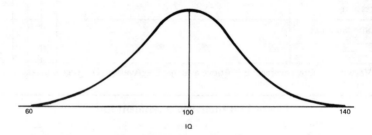

**Figure 11.9 A normal curve**

The most important characteristic of the normal curve is that it is symmetrical — there are an equal number of cases on either side of the mean, the central axis. Thus the distribution of intelligence in the population as a whole consists of an equal number of people with IQs above and below 100.

The difficulty with intelligence tests is that they have to be based on a theory of what constitutes intelligence and then have to derive a series of verbal and non-verbal instruments for measuring the different factors or constituents of intelligence. But intelligence is a highly complex concept. There is no agreed definition of it amongst psychologists and the variety of theories about intelligence and the consequent variations in the test instrument or battery available makes the choice of an intelligence test a difficult one. For general selection purposes, a test which can be administered to a group of candidates is the best, especially if it has been properly validated and it is possible to relate test scores to 'norms' in such a way as to indicate how the individual taking the test compares with the rest of the population, in general or in a specific area.

APTITUDE AND ATTAINMENT TESTS. Aptitude tests are designed to predict the

156

potential an individual has to perform a job or specific tasks within a job. They can cover such areas as clerical aptitude, numerical aptitude, mechanical aptitude and dexterity. They may come in the form of well-validated single tests, or as a battery of tests such as those developed some years ago by the British National Institute of Industrial Psychology for selecting apprentices.

All aptitude tests should be properly validated. The usual procedure is to determine the qualities required for the job by means of a job analysis. A standard test or a test battery is then obtained from a test agency such as, in Britain, the National Foundation for Educational Research. Alternatively, a special test is devised by or for the company. The test is then given to employees already working on the job and the results compared with a criterion, usually supervisor's ratings. If the correlation between test and criterion is sufficiently high, the test is then given to applicants. To validate the test further, a follow-up study of the job performance of the applicants selected by the test is usually carried out. This is a lengthy procedure, but without it no real confidence can be attached to the results of any aptitude test. Many do-it-yourself tests are worse than useless because they have not been properly validated.

Attainment tests measure abilities or skills that have already been acquired by training or experience. A typing test is the most typical example. It is easy to find out how many words a minute a typist can type and compare that with the standard required for the job.

PERSONALITY TESTS. Personality tests attempt to assess the type of personality possessed by the applicant in terms of personality traits (styles of behaviour such as aggressiveness or persistence) or personality types (salient features which characterize the individual such as extraversion or introversion).

They need to be treated with great caution. For selection purposes they are almost meaningless if they have not been validated by a thorough correlation of test results with subsequent behaviour. And such validations present great difficulties.

THE USE OF TESTS IN A SELECTION PROCEDURE. Tests are most likely to be helpful when they are used as part of a selection procedure for occupations where a large number of recruits are required, and where it is not possible to rely entirely on examination results or information about previous experience as the basis for predicting future performance. In these circumstances it is economic to develop and administer the tests and a sufficient number of cases can be built up for the essential validation exercise.

Intelligence tests are particularly helpful in situations where intelligence is a key factor but there is no other reliable method of measuring it. It may, incidentally, be as important to use an intelligence test to keep out applicants who are too intelligent for the job as to use one to guarantee a minimum level of intelligence. A validation exercise with which the author was concerned on tests for van salesmen established that applicants above a certain level of intelligence should be rejected, unless they have promotion potential, because they could not settle down in the job.

Aptitude and attainment tests are most useful for jobs where specific and measurable skills are required, such as typing or computer programming. Personality tests are potentially of greatest value in jobs such as selling where 'personality' is important and where it is not too difficult to obtain quantifiable criteria for validation purposes.

In some situations a battery of tests may be associated, including various types of intelligence, aptitude and personality tests. These may be a standard battery supplied by a test agency, such as the National Foundation for Educational Research (Great Britain), or a custom-built battery may be used. The biggest pitfall to avoid is adding extra tests just for the sake of it, without ensuring that they make a proper contribution to the success of the predictions for which the battery is being used.

## Offers and references

After the interviewing and testing procedure has been completed a provisional decision to make an offer orally by telephone or in writing can be made. This will normally be 'subject to satisfactory references' and the candidate should, of course, be told that these will be taken up. If there is more than one eligible candidate for a job it may be advisable to hold one or two people in reserve. Applicants can often change their minds, especially those whose only purpose in applying for the job was to carry out a 'test marketing' operation, or to obtain a lever with which to persuade their present employers to value them more highly.

### References

The purpose of a reference is to obtain in confidence factual information about a prospective employee and opinions about his character and suitability for a job.

The factual information is straightforward and essential. It is simply necessary to confirm the nature of the previous job, the period of time in employment, the reason for leaving (if relevant), the salary or rate of pay and, possibly, the attendance record.

Opinions about character and suitability are less reliable and should be treated with caution. The reason is obvious. Previous or present employers who give references tend to avoid highly detrimental remarks either out of charity or because they think anything they say or write may be construed as slanderous, or libellous (references are, in fact, privileged as long as they are given without malice and are factually correct).

Personal referees are, of course, entirely useless. All they prove is that the applicant has at least one or two friends.

Written references save time, especially if they are standardized. They may take the form of an invitation to write a letter confirming the employment record and commenting on the applicant's character in general. If brief details about the job are included (these may be an extract from the advertisement — they should certainly not be an over-elaborate job description), the previous employer can be asked to express his views about the suitability of the individual for the job. But this is asking a lot. Unless the job and companies are identical, how well can any existing or ex-employer judge the suitability of someone he may not know particularly well for another job in a different environment?

More precise answers may be obtained if a standard form is provided for the employer to complete. The questions asked on this form should be limited to the following:

(a) What was the period of employment?
(b) What was the job title?
(c) What work was carried out?
(d) What was the rate of pay or salary?

(e) How many days' absence over the last twelve months?
(f) Would you re-employ (if not, why not)?

Question (f) is the key one, if it is answered honestly.

Telephone references may be used as an alternative or an addition to written references. The great advantage of a telephone conversation is that people are more likely to give an honest opinion orally than if they have to commit themselves in writing. It may also save time to use the telephone.

Employer references are necessary but they are unreliable. A satisfactory reference has to be treated at its face value — all one can be reasonably certain about is that the factual details will be correct. A very glowing reference may arouse suspicion, and it is worth comparing it with a reference from another employer (two employment references are desirable in any case). Poor or grudging references must create some alarm if only because they are so infrequent. But allowance should be made for prejudice and a check should be made, by telephone if possible.

### Confirming the offer

The final stage in the selection procedure is to confirm the offer of employment after satisfactory references have been obtained and the applicant has passed the medical examination required for pension and life assurance purposes or because a certain standard of physical fitness is required for the work. The contract of employment should also be prepared at this stage.

## Contracts of employment

The basic information that should be included in a written contract of employment will vary according to the level of job, but the following checklist sets out the typical headings:

☐ job title;
☐ duties, including a phrase such as 'The employee will perform such duties and will be responsible to such person, as the Company may from time to time direct';
☐ date when continuous employment starts and basis for calculating service;
☐ rate of pay, allowances, overtime and shift rates, method of payment;
☐ hours of work including lunch break and overtime and shift arrangements;
☐ holiday arrangements:
  — days paid holiday per year;
  — calculation of holiday pay;
  — qualifying period;
  — accrual of holidays and holiday pay;
  — details of holiday year;
  — dates when holidays can be taken;
  — maximum holiday that can be taken at one time;
  — carry over of holiday entitlement;
  — public holidays;
☐ sickness:
  — pay for time lost;
  — duration of sickness payments;
  — deductions of national insurance benefits;
  — termination due to continued illness;

- notification of illness (medical certificate);
- [ ] length of notice due to and from employee;
- [ ] grievance procedure (or reference to it);
- [ ] disciplinary procedure (or reference to it);
- [ ] works rules (or reference to them);
- [ ] arrangements for terminating employment;
- [ ] arrangements for union membership (if applicable);
- [ ] special terms relating to rights to patents and designs, confidential information and restraints on trade after termination of employment;
- [ ] employer's right to vary terms of the contract subject to proper notification being given.

## Induction

Induction is the process of receiving and welcoming an employee when he first joins a company and giving him the basic information he needs to settle down quickly and happily and start work. Induction has three aims:

- [ ] to smooth the preliminary stages when everything is likely to be strange and unfamiliar to the new starter;
- [ ] to establish quickly a favourable attitude to the company in the mind of the new employee so that he or she is more likely to stay;
- [ ] to obtain effective output from the new employee in the shortest possible time.

### Company induction

The first stage in induction is when the employee arrives at the company. He or she should be welcomed by a responsible person (not simply a commissionaire or a junior wages clerk) who can provide basic information about the company and terms and conditions of employment. Some of the information will confirm what the employee has already been told, some will be new, but there is a limit to how much can be conveyed at this stage.

An employee handbook is useful for this purpose. It need not be too glossy, but it should convey clearly and simply what new staff need to know under the following headings:

- [ ] a brief description of the company – its history, products, organization and management;
- [ ] basic conditions of employment – hours of work, holidays, pension scheme, insurance;
- [ ] pay – pay scales, when paid and how, deductions, queries;
- [ ] sickness – notification of absence, certificates, pay;
- [ ] leave of absence;
- [ ] works rules;
- [ ] disciplinary procedure;
- [ ] grievance procedure;
- [ ] promotion procedure;
- [ ] union and joint consultation arrangements;
- [ ] education and training facilities;
- [ ] health and safety arrangements;
- [ ] medical and first-aid facilities;
- [ ] restaurant and canteen facilities;

160

☐ social and welfare arrangements;
☐ telephone calls and correspondence;
☐ travelling and subsistence expenses.

If the organization is not large enough to justify a printed handbook, the least that can be done is to prepare a typed summary of this information.

Company induction procedures, however, should not rely on the printed word. The member of the personnel department or other individual who is looking after new employees should run through the main points with each individual or, when larger numbers are being taken on, with groups of people. In this way, a more personal touch is provided and queries can be answered.

When the initial briefing has been completed the new employee should be taken to his place of work and introduced to his manager or supervisor for the departmental induction programme. Alternatively, he may go straight to a training school and join the department later.

### Departmental induction

The departmental induction programme should, wherever possible, start with the departmental manager, not the immediate supervisor. The manager may limit his remarks to a general welcome and a brief description of the work of the department before handing the new employee over to his supervisor for the more detailed induction. But it is important for the manager to be involved at this stage so that he is not seen as a remote figure by the new employee. And at least this means that the new starter will not be simply a name or a number to him.

The detailed induction is probably best carried out by the immediate supervisor. He should have five main aims:

☐ to put the new employee at his ease;
☐ to interest him in his job and the company;
☐ to provide basic information about working arrangements;
☐ to indicate the standards of performance and behaviour expected of him;
☐ to tell him about training arrangements and how he can get on with the company.

## Follow up

It is essential to follow up newly engaged employees to ensure that they have settled in and to check on how well they are doing. If there are any problems it is much better to identify them at an early stage rather than allowing them to fester.

Following up is also important as a means of checking on the selection procedure. If by any chance a mistake has been made, it is useful to find out how it happened so that the selection procedure can be improved. Misfits can be attributed to a number of causes, for example: an inadequate job description or specification, poor sourcing of candidates, weak advertising, poor interviewing techniques, the use of inappropriate or invalidated tests, or prejudice on the part of the selector. If any of these are identified steps can be taken to prevent their recurrence.

### References
1. Rodger, A. *The Seven-Point Plan*. National Institute of Industrial Psychology, London, 1952.

2. Munro Fraser, J. *A Handbook of Employment Interviewing*. Macdonald and Evans, London, 1954.
3. Vernon, P.E. 'The Validation of Civil Service Board Selection Procedures', *Occupational Psychology*, Vol. 24, 1950, pp. 75-95.

<table>
<tr><td>

**12**

</td><td>

# Performance Appraisal

</td></tr>
</table>

## Purpose of performance appraisal

Performance appraisal is the process of reviewing an individual's performance and progress in a job and assessing his potential for future promotion. It is a systematic method of obtaining, analysing and recording information about a person that is needed:

☐ for the better running of the business;
☐ by the manager to help him improve the job holder's performance and plan his career;
☐ by the job holder to assist him to evaluate his own performance and develop himself.

There are three main groups of performance review activities:

1. *Performance reviews* which relate to the need to improve the performance of individuals and thereby to improve the effectiveness of the organization as a whole.
2. *Potential reviews* which attempt to deal with the problem of predicting the level and type of work that the individual will be capable of doing in the future.
3. *Reward reviews* which relate to the distribution of such rewards as pay, power and status.

## Performance reviews

The purpose of a performance review is to analyse what a person has done and is doing in his job in order to help him to do better, by developing his strengths or by overcoming his weaknesses. The phrase 'performance review' suggests a deliberate stocktaking exercise. Some people deny that this is necessary. They claim that managers must be making judgements about their subordinates all the time – why go through the artificial and, to some, painful process of summing up in a few platitudinous phrases how well or how badly someone is doing? He ought to know anyway.

The answer to this objection is that managers do not know – they only obtain a series of random impressions. They need to take time off, not only to analyse and record their impressions systematically, but also to think about how they can help their subordinates to improve. Even when managers have formed a balanced view, they often find it difficult to carry out the most important task of conveyeing it to their subordinates unless they are stimulated into doing so.

But it is not easy to do well. Assessing people properly is a difficult task not simply because, in McGregor's phrase, 'Managers are uncomfortable when they are put in the position of playing God'[1] – everyone forms judgements about other people, and are quite happy to; what they do not like is to justify their views in writing or, worse still, face to face with the person they are assessing. The fundamental problems are:

☐ the development and understanding of characteristics and standards against which people can be assessed objectively and consistently, which means that those who develop and use performance review procedures must appreciate the factors affecting assessments of people;
☐ the method of recording judgements, when the task is to choose a performance review technique which encourages managers to set out their views within an understood framework, but does not impose an unreasonable burden of form filling;
☐ ensuring that counselling sessions do take place between managers and their subordinates which make good use of the appraisal to show the way to improvements in performance.

### Factors affecting assessments

Assessments require the ability to judge people, and good judgement is a matter of using fixed standards, considering only relevant evidence, avoiding projection (the process of ascribing to other persons one's own unacceptable wants and faults) and combining probabilities in their correct weight.

The factors affecting assessments are those arising from:

☐ the characteristics of the manager, including his ability to judge people, and his attitudes to the process of assessment;
☐ the interaction between the manager and the interviewee;
☐ the way in which the person being assessed is regarded by the manager — stereotyping;
☐ the methods used to measure performance.

CHARACTERISTICS OF THE MANAGER. Most managers think they are good judges. One seldom if ever meets anyone who admits to being a poor judge of people, just as one seldom hears anyone confessing that he is a bad driver — although accident rates suggest that bad drivers do exist — and mistakes in selection, placement and promotion indicate that some managers are worse than others at judging people.

Differences in personality characteristics will affect the type of judgements made and also the consistency and fairness of the judgements. As a result, the attitudes of managers to their staff will vary so that different managers will appraise the same people quite differently. One manager will, for example, rate everyone very strictly so that the average level of his ratings will be much lower than that of another manager who is less strict. A major reason for differences in level arises because managers do not have common standards to judge by.

It has also been discovered that if two managers are required to rate the same people, not only do they tend to rate against different standards, but the spread or scatter of their ratings will vary. One person, for example, will tend to produce ratings that group fairly closely around the man, whereas another judge's ratings will be much more widely scattered. It has been found that people who make snap judgements or jump to conclusions quickly tend to produce a wider scatter of judgements than people who are more deliberate and painstaking. It has also been found that people who produce a wide scatter in judgements tend to see things in extremes — as black or white rather than in shades of grey. The well-known 'halo effect' or its less known opposite, the 'horns effect', are associated with the spread factor. These effects arise when the manager is aware of some prominent or recent example of good or bad performance and assumes from this that all aspects of the job holder's performance are equally good or bad.

Knowledge of these factors has strongly influenced the design of the various performance review systems described later in this chapter. In an attempt to ensure consistency in judgements, assessment characteristics have been defined and scales have been drawn up against which the ratings are made. Elaborate statistical devices have been developed to eliminate variations.

These systems have universally failed and the emphasis has turned to improving managers' skills in judging by:

☐ encouraging them to define and agree standards and measures of effectiveness beforehand with those concerned;
☐ encouraging and training people to avoid jumping to conclusions too quickly by consciously suspending judgement until all the relevant data available have been examined;
☐ providing managers with practice in exercising judgements which enable them to find out for themselves their weaknesses and thus improve their techniques.

INTERACTION BETWEEN THE MANAGER AND THE INTERVIEWEE. Assessments are made by observation and discussion during interviews. But their validity is affected by the following problems:

☐ poor perception — not noticing things or events for what they are;
☐ wishful thinking — noticing only those things one wants to see;
☐ poor interpretation — putting one's own interpretation on information;
☐ projection — seeing one's own faults in other people.

Empathy is required to obtain an accurate interpretation of a person's behaviour. Empathy is the ability to put oneself into someone else's shoes when trying to understand why he or she is behaving in a certain way.

The development of an effective performance review system is more a matter of overcoming the problems of making assessments and of improving empathy than of introducing elaborate procedures, whether these are traditional merit rating-schemes, or slightly more up-to-date management by objectives programmes. There is a limit to which empathy can be induced — it is a skill and an attitude which people have mainly to develop for themselves. But they can be helped to improve their ability to understand others by gaining a greater knowledge of the forces and drives that affect people and by being given practice in using skills of gathering and analysing information about them carefully, objectively and systematically.

Performance appraisal is a skilled process which, unfortunately, many managers are not very good at. Training is necessary to develop the skills required and to encourage an attitude of mind which ensures that managers will give this important aspect of their duties the emphasis is deserves.

STEREOTYPING. Judgements are affected by the universal tendency to stereotype. We all tend to carry around with us a collection of mental pictures of what we imagine certain people to be like, and these preformed pictures or stereotypes are used as an easy way to classify those with whom we come into contact. Familiar stereotypes include curates, retired colonels and students. It is difficult to avoid stereotyping people as typical salesmen, accountants or personnel managers, but managers should be encouraged to control a tendency to stereotype because it is only when they can learn to see people as individuals that they are able to make an objective assessment of performance.

FACTORS AFFECTING THE MEASUREMENT OF PERFORMANCE. Appraisal schemes have been in existence since before World War I, when W.D. Scott invented the man-to-man comparison scale. Various schemes of merit rating were developed, mainly in the U.S.A. between the wars, and came into increasing use in the U.K. after World War II. To a large extent, however, they are greeted by line management with hostility or indifference as an administrative burden imposed on them by a power-seeking personnel department. In particular, managers resist them because of:

☐ a mistrust of the validity of the scheme itself;
☐ a dislike of criticizing subordinates to their face;
☐ lack of skill in handling appraisals and interviews;
☐ dislike of new procedures.

As Douglas McGregor pointed out, this resistance was met by imposing controls; but assessments are then done as a matter of routine and the forms gather dust in the personnel department — forgotten and ignored. McGregor suggested in his highly influential article 'An Uneasy Look at Performance Appraisal'[1] that the emphasis should be shifted from appraisal to analysis:

> This implies a more positive approach. No longer is the subordinate being examined by the superior so that his weaknesses may be determined; rather he is examining himself; in order to define not only his weaknesses but also his strengths and potentials... He becomes an active agent, not a passive 'object'. He is no longer a pawn in a chess game called management development.

McGregor went on to suggest that the emphasis should be on the future rather than the past in order to establish realistic targets and to seek the most effective ways of reaching them. The accent of the review is therefore on performance, on actions relative to goals:

> There is less tendency for the personality of the subordinate to become an issue. The superior, instead of finding himself in the position of a psychologist or a therapist, can become a coach helping the subordinate to reach his own decisions on the specific steps that will enable him to reach his targets.

In short, the main factor in measuring performance should be the analysis of the behaviour required to achieve agreed results, not the assessment of personality. This is, in effect, management by objectives, which is concerned with planning and measuring results in relation to agreed targets and standards. It is possible, however, that McGregor and others overstated their case when they placed so much emphasis on planning for the future. Surely, future behaviour cannot be determined without an analysis of what is right or wrong with current behaviour. Results are what count, but it is still necessary to consider how better results can be achieved by changing behaviour and by acquiring new knowledge and improved skills.

The factors affecting the measurement of performance were also studied in the U.K. by Kay Rowe who carried out an extensive research project into the effectiveness of the more traditional methods of appraisal which use largely subjective ratings of personality traits. This study confirmed that managers did not like using these schemes and were using them badly. She noted that assessors were required to answer such questions as 'Is he tactful?', 'Has he a pleasant personality?', 'Is he vindictive?' and commented: 'No appraiser has the moral right to press judgement on such matters, except in so far as they are directly and demonstrably relevant in the subordinate's job.'[2] The view was reaffirmed that if appraisals are meant to help people to improve their performance they must consider how the results were achieved. It was suggested that one of the bonuses of results-orientated appraisals is that they would be more acceptable to both appraiser and appraised.

### Performance review techniques

There has been a steady growth in the use of results-orientated appraisals over the past seven years, largely due to the influence of management by objectives. There is no doubt that, properly conducted, this is the best approach. It is necessary, however, to review briefly the other techniques available before considering how results-orientated schemes can be made to work. The main types are:

☐ overall assessment
☐ guideline assessment
☐ grading
☐ merit rating
☐ critical incident
☐ results-orientated schemes.

OVERALL ASSESSMENT. This approach simply asks a manager to write down in narrative form his comments about the employee. He may be given a checklist of personality characteristics to consider such as reliability, enthusiasm, appearance, acceptability and, with a slight bow to the McGregor philosophy, he may be asked to comment on results achieved against targets.

This is the simplest approach and at least ensures that managers have to collect their thoughts together and put them down on paper. But different people will consider different aspects of performance and there will be no conspiracy in the criteria selected for assessment. The value of the exercise will also depend on the ability of the manager to express himself in writing. And he will tend to be evasive. As Kay Rowe reported on the comments made in the six schemes she studied:

> A few suggested careful thought and a conscientious effort to say something meaningful but the vast majority were remarkable for their neutrality. Glib, generalized, enigmatic statements abounded. Typical of such statements was 'a loyal, conscientious and hard-working employee'. Such a statement may well have been true but it is not very revealing.[2]

GUIDELINE ASSESSMENT. The guideline assessment approach is an attempt to obtain more specific judgements from assessors who are asked to comment separately on a number of defined characteristics; for example, industry and application, loyalty and integrity, co-operation, accuracy and reliability, adaptability, knowledge of work and use of initiative. When assessing a characteristic such as industry and application, managers might be asked to: 'Consider his application to work and the enthusiasm with which he approaches a task. Does he work quickly and stick to the job or is he slow and inclined to slack if not watched?'

In theory this method should help managers to be more precise but in practice the guidelines are so vague that comments are uninformative, especially if they are about generalized characteristics such as industry and application.

GRADING. Grading is a further development of the guideline approach which attempts to provide a framework of reference by defining a number of levels at which the characteristic is displayed and asking managers to select the definition which most closely describes the individual they are assessing. For example, in rating effective output the manager in a typical grading scheme is asked to choose between:

(a) Outstanding – outstanding output of high quality work;
(b) Satisfactory – satisfactory level of output and effort;
(c) Fair – completes less than the average amount of effective work;
(d) Poor – low output and poor worker.

In themselves, definitions of this type are not particularly helpful – they are generalized and fail to establish actual standards against which judgements can be made. Assessments are therefore just as subject to variations and inconsistencies as in the other schemes.

MERIT RATING. Merit rating is similar to grading except that numerical values are attached to the judgements so that each characteristic is rated on a scale of, say, one to 20. The ratings are then added up to produce a total score.

A variation of this approach is the graphic rating scale in which the assessor ticks the place on a line running from very high to very low to indicate the employee's standing on each quality. In its most Machiavellian form, this method requires an *eminence grise* in the personnel department to attach values to ratings and adjust them when it is thought that a manager is tending to over- or under-assess his staff.

These schemes have rightly been discredited. Their only reason for survival is that they satisfy those people who are not happy unless they can quantify everything, even the patently unquantifiable judgements of personality characteristics. The other problem with this type of scheme, as with all the others, is that it does not ensure that the assessor bases his judgements on systematic and objective observations of the job behaviour of the people he is asked to describe.

CRITICAL INCIDENT METHOD. The critical incident method is an attempt to overcome the fundamental defect of the other schemes by focusing attention on behaviour. It is based on Flanagan's technique of defining jobs in terms of the typical behaviour of job holders.[3] The method asks managers familiar with a job to record critical incidents of successful or less successful job behaviour. After a large number of such incidents have been collected, they are categorized to form an overall picture of the typical types of behaviour that indicate either effective or ineffective performance. Ideally, this analysis should be carried out with the managers who are going to conduct the appraisals. They can then become familiar with the approach and recognize how it can help them to make more objective assessments by comparing the actual behaviour of their staff with the realistic examples they have contributed.

In a scheme developed by the writer for agricultural salesmen, this technique was used to collect a wide range of critical incidents, such as, for product knowledge: 'Makes a point of talking to technical liaison staff about special features of products', 'Is sometimes caught out on technical points by a customer.' From these incidents, definitions were made of different levels of behaviour; for example, the definition of above standard behaviour for product knowledge: 'Carries out an analysis of the selling points of each of his products on the basis of regular contacts with research and development staff, careful study of relevant technical literature, comparative assessments of the strengths and weaknesses of competitors' products and recorded observations of the needs and reactions of customers.'

The advantage of this approach is that it is firmly rooted in observations about actual job behaviour. The disadvantages are the time and effort required to develop a scheme and its limitations to large groups of people in fairly homogeneous jobs. It is for this reason that it has never been adopted on a large scale, but the principles on which it is based are sound and the technique can be useful in defining standards of performance.

RESULTS-ORIENTATED SCHEMES. Results-orientated schemes embody the principles developed by McGregor and the management by objectives philosophy based on Drucker's writings. The aim is to relate assessments to a review of performance against specific targets and standards of performance agreed jointly by superior and subordinate. This procedure has three advantages:

1. The subordinate is given the opportunity to make his own evaluation of the results he obtains. When he is discussing results and the actions that produced those results, he is actually appraising himself and gaining insight on how he can improve his own methods and behaviour.
2. The job of the manager shifts from that of criticizing the subordinate to that of helping him to improve his own performance.
3. It is consistent with the belief that people work better when they have definite goals which they must meet in specified periods.

The difficulty most people meet is that of defining realistic and specific targets and standards, and it is still necessary when reviewing performance to analyse why the result was a relative success or failure as well as measuring what the result was.

### Counselling

Counselling is a vital part of performance reviews if they are to achieve their prime purpose of helping people to improve and develop. But it is difficult to do well and many managers are reluctant to do it at all. In one brief study conducted by the writer it was found that more people were dissatisfied after their counselling session than they were before. Even where a results-orientated approach is adopted, a clumsy interviewer can allow the discussion to degenerate into pointless arguments about where blame should be attached for something that has gone wrong.

Three types of appraisal interview have been identified by Maier:[4]

1. *The tell and sell method* in which the manager seeks first to let the employee know how he is doing, then to gain his acceptance of the evaluation, and finally to get him to follow the plan outlined for his improvement. The problem with this method is that considerable and unusual skill is required to get people to accept criticisms and to change in the required manner. There are occasions when people have to be told, but it may not always be possible to provide the movitation required for change, unless resort is made to crude threats or inducements.

2. *The tell and listen method* in which the evaluation is communicated to the employee who is then allowed to respond to it. Instead of the interviewer dominating the discussion he sits back and becomes a non-directive counsellor during the second part of the interview. The employee is encouraged to think things out for himself and to decide on what needs to be done, and the assumption is that he is more likely to change in these circumstances than if he had been told what to do. A further advantage of this approach is that the interviewer will profit more from the interview by receiving feedback from the employee on how the job may be improved with regard to supervision, work methods and job assignments. But the method requires considerable skill on the part of the interviewer in listening, reflecting feelings and summarizing opinions.
3. *The problem-solving approach* in which the interviewer abandons the role of judge and becomes a helper. The appraisal is not communicated to the employee. Instead a discussion takes place of the work problems of the employee, who is encouraged to think through his own solutions to them, including the changes he has to make to his behaviour to achieve improvement. According to Maier, this approach motivates original thinking because it stimulates curiosity. It also provides the intrinsic motivation that can be derived from work itself and the process of tackling work problems. Job satisfaction can be improved by reorganizing or enlarging the job, by changing the employee's perception of his role and by increasing the superior's ability to provide guidance and help in the form it is needed. Again, this approach needs skill, but it is the most fruitful method and it is one which can clearly be linked to results-orientated review techniques.

Effective counselling requires the use of skills which few managers are likely to acquire in the normal course of their work. It is essential, therefore, that training should be given in conducting interviews. Without such training, managers may do more harm than good. They can be helped by the issue of checklists, such as those illustrated at the end of this chapter, but skill can only be developed by practice, and the opportunity to get practice under guidance is a requisite part of any performance review scheme.

## Potential reviews

The review of potential is concerned with forecasting the direction in which an individual's career should go and the rate at which he is expected to develop. It provides information to the company on which it can base management succession plans, and to the individual on his future with the company which may encourage him to stay and to improve his abilities still further.

The assessment of potential requires the analysis of existing skills, qualities and how they can be developed to the mutual advantage of the company and the employee, as well as the identification of any weaknesses which must be overcome if the employee's full potential is to be achieved. There is also an important counselling aspect to the review of potential which consists of discussions with the individual about his aspirations and how these can best be matched to the future foreseen for him. These discussions are, in fact, a vital part of the procedure because they can provide the manager with information about his employee's feelings on this subject, which may have a marked effect on plans for development, including training and job rotation. They can also provide employees with

with additional motivation and the encouragement they may need to remain with the company.

Assessing potential, however, is not easy. It has to start with a review by the immediate manager who can only base his judgement on what he can observe about performance on the present job. This will not necessarily indicate that the individual is going to be capable to carrying greater responsibility in the future when the demands may be quite different. Hence the 'Peter Principle', invented by L.J. Peter,[5] which advances the somewhat pessimistic view that managers tend to be promoted to the level of their own incompetence. Checklists such as those shown at the end of this chapter may help, but are seldom enough.

To avoid this difficulty, some companies insist on evaluations of potential being made by managers at one level higher than the immediate manager on the grounds that they can take a more detached and knowledgeable view on the basis of some direct knowledge of the individual as well as the views of the latter's boss. This approach, which is a valuable safeguard against prejudice or partial judgements, is a necessary part of any performance appraisal procedure.

### Assessment centres

An alternative method, which has been developed to overcome these problems, is the use of assessment centres where the aim is to provide a broad approach to the identification of executive or supervisory potential. In an assessment centre, the multiple assessment of several individuals is carried out by a group of trained assessors using a variety of techniques such as games, simulations, tests and group discussions.

Assessment centres use the group selection techniques described in chapter 11. A programme may last anything from one to four days, although the longer programmes are also used as management development activities in themselves.

The characteristics assessed in a typical programme include assertiveness, persuasive ability, communicating ability, planning and organizing ability, self-confidence, resistance to stress, energy level, decision-making, sensitivity to the feelings of others, administrative ability, creativity and mental alertness. It is a formidable list and one cannot help wondering how accurately such factors can be measured even over four days and with lots of trained observers and psychologists.

The programme may consist of such activities as questionnaires filled in by participants about their attitudes to their work and the company and their aspirations, written tests, video taped ten-minute speeches, role playing exercises requiring leadership and group participation, in-basket exercises requiring participants to handle typical problems in a supervisor's in-tray, various interview simulations, management decision games, self-appraisal and peer rating, and depth interviews. Everything is observed and assessed by trained assessors.

A review by Ungerson[6] of the research findings on assessment centres concluded that there is good reason to believe that well-conducted assessment centres can and do achieve better forecasts of future performance and progress than judgments made by line managers in the normal unskilled way. Face-validity is high — everyone is impressed by the proceedings. So is reliability. He emphasized, however, that these favourable findings arose from centres run by highly trained full-time professional members using paper and pencil tests as well as subjective judgemental procedures.

The problem with assessment centres is their cost. They are not worth doing unless they are done well, and this means that amateur efforts or the use of packaged systems without proper training are to be avoided. In all but the largest organizations they are unlikely to be cost-effective. Most companies will have to rely on their normal assessment procedures, although these should ensure that judgements about potential are checked by trained managers who are aware of the qualities needed for advancement and how these can be assessed by measuring performance in the current job.

## Reward reviews

In any company where rewards such as salary increments or bonuses are related to performance there has to be some method of linking the two together. In some procedures the rate of progression through a salary bracket or the size of the increments is derived from an overall assessment of performance, so that a top 'A' rating may result in a 10% merit increment while a middling 'C' rating may result in an average increment of 5%, or whatever inflationary conditions, the financial position of the company and current pay regulations allow.

It is undesirable, however, to have a direct link of this nature between the performance review and the reward review. The former must aim primarily at improving performance and, possibly, assessing potential. If this is confused with a salary review, everyone becomes over-concerned about the impact of the assessment on the increment. Managers falsify their assessments to get their favoured staff the increment they feel they deserve. Subordinates worry more about how much money is coming out of the process than about what they must do to improve performance for a more doubtful long term reward.

It is better to separate the two. The performance review should take place at least three months before the salary review. For the latter, managers should simply be asked to provide an overall rating or indicate whether they feel their subordinates merit an average, above average, or below average increment or bonus. Clearly, their views on increments will be dependent on their assessment of performance *and* potential, but the two processes should not be conducted simultaneously so that the counselling and guidance procedures can be carried out without everyone looking over their shoulders at their cash implications.

## Performance appraisal procedures

Performance appraisal procedures should be based on the results-orientated approach, as long as this allows for a review of why the result was achieved as a basis for agreeing what needs to be done in the future. The procedure should be as simple as possible — the use of a multiplicity of elaborate forms should be avoided. It should require managers to see their subordinates to discuss and agree targets and standards, to review performance, and to provide guidance and encouragement which will enable the individual to take action himself to develop his strengths or overcome his weaknesses. It should identify for managers what they as individuals, and the company, should do to help in the process of training and development. The procedure must ensure that all concerned are properly briefed and trained. Finally, provision must be made for assessments to be reviewed by the assessor's own superior, so that the individual being appraised does not feel he is at the mercy of a prejudiced boss. It may be desirable to allow for formal appeals against assessments, or at least to let people know that they have the right to discuss their assessment informally with a higher authority if they feel it is unfair.

A performance appraisal procedure can operate without any standard forms at all, as long as managers know what to do and are motivated to do it. Targets and action plans can be jotted down and agreed on blank sheets of paper. Management development activities and training needs can be based on follow-up discussions between whoever is responsible for these functions and the departmental managers. If the company is large or complex, it might be necessary to ask for a brief report on training and development needs and an indication of who has potential for promotion, but this does not need an elaborate form.

Where it is felt that judgements must be recorded for posterity a fairly simple form such as the one illustrated in figure 12.1 can be used. A more spacious version of this form is shown in figure 12.2.

Although the aim should be to keep the procedure simple, it may be necessary in large companies to produce guidance notes on how the review should be conducted. The following is an example of the guidance notes issued in association with the form shown in figure 12.2.

## Performance review – notes for guidance

1. The performance review and meetings should be carried out well in advance of the time that salary reviews are undertaken (at least three months). Experience has shown that interviews to discuss performance are more constructive if pay is not discussed at the same time.
2. Before interviewing the job holder, the reviewing manager should:
   (a) give adequate notice of the discussion to the job holder and brief him on the purpose of the meeting;
   (b) refer to the list of main tasks and objectives that was agreed at the last meeting (or if this is the first meeting, produce an initial list of tasks for discussion) and consider the performance of the job holder on each task. The analysis should compare the results achieved with agreed targets and standards;
   (c) record any factors that might have affected results, especially those outside the control of the job holder;
   (d) consider the targets and priorities that will need to be set out in the coming period.
3. During the interview:
   (a) the analysis referred to above should be frankly discussed with the job holder who should be given an opportunity to comment on how he sees his performance and how he could do better;
   (b) targets, priorities and action for improvement in the coming period should then be discussed and agreed. A memorandum should be sent to the job holder after the discussion stating these targets and priorities. Any later amendments should also be discussed and recorded;
   (c) the reviewing manager should take particular note of the job holder's work interests and career aspirations and consider what action should be taken by the job holder, himself or the company to improve performance and develop potential;
   (d) any queries raised by the job holder about his future prospects should be answered as openly as possible. The information given should be factual and not speculative as it is easy to say things that can give rise unnecessarily to disappointments later on;
   (e) the first page of the performance review form should be filled in by the

| MERIT ASSESSMENT FORM | |
|---|---|
| Name Mr/Mrs/Miss | Job title |
| Department or office | Period covered by review |
| Age | Date started present job |

**1. Overall Assessment** (tick appropriate box)

A = Outstanding ☐

B = Better than the required standard ☐

C = Performs the job to required standard ☐

D = Falls short of the required standard in some respects ☐

E = Performance does not meet required standard ☐

X = He has not worked long enough with me to say ☐

Comment on overall performance during period

**2. Factors Affecting Performance**
Comment only on those areas where you think he/she has particular strengths or weaknesses in relation to the factors listed below.

| Factors | Comments |
|---|---|
| (a) Job knowledge — understanding of all aspects of the work | |
| (b) Effective output | |
| (c) Co-operation and willingness | |
| (d) Time-keeping | |
| (e) Additional comments | |

**3. Potential** (tick appropriate box)

A = Overdue for promotion

B = Ready for promotion

C = Has promotion potential ☐

D = No evidence of promotion potential at present

X = Has not worked long enough with me to say ☐

Positions to where he/she could be promoted if you have answered A, B or C (in the case of C state when)

**4. Proposals for Training** (what further training, if any, is needed?)

**5.** Have you discussed the assessment with him/her? YES ☐ NO ☐
If 'YES' state outcome, if 'NO' state why.

Signed . . . . . . . . . . . . . . . . . . . . . . . Date . . . . . . . . . . . . . . . . . . . .

**6. Comments of Confirming Authority**

Signed . . . . . . . . . . . . . . . . . . . . . . . Date . . . . . . . . . . . . . . . . . . . .

**Figure 12.1 Merit assessment form**

CONFIDENTIAL

## PERFORMANCE REVIEW

Sheet 1

| Name | Job title |
|---|---|
| Department | Section |
| Period covered by review — from: | to: |

**Performance Analysis**
(a) Refer to agreed main tasks/objectives for period and summarize in the first column.
(b) In the second column, comment on achievements during the period by reference to agreed indicators/measures

| Main tasks/objectives | Comments on achievement |
|---|---|
| 1 | |
| 2 | |
| 3 | |
| 4 | |
| 5 | |
| 6 | |

**Performance Review Meeting: strengths and weaknesses**
Summarize conclusions on strengths and weaknesses arising from review meeting

**Reaction of job holder**
Summarize comments of job holder on current job and career aspirations

**Main Tasks/Objectives for Next Review Meeting**
Summarize main tasks/objectives for next review meeting on attached sheet

### Figure 12.2(a) Performance review form

<table>
<tr><td colspan="2" align="center">PERFORMANCE REVIEW<br>To be completed after the performance review meeting</td><td>Sheet 2</td></tr>
</table>

**Overall Assessment:**
Indicate your opinion of overall performance by means of a tick against the appropriate heading

| A | Outstanding | An exceptionally valuable member of the staff; performance is consistently well above the required standards for the job |
|---|---|---|
| B | Very effective | Displays good all round level of effectiveness; performance meets or exceeds requirements in all important tasks |
| C | Satisfactory | A competent member of the staff; generally achieves the standards required |
| D | Barely satisfactory | Performance does not always reach the required standards; room for improvement |
| E | Unsatisfactory | Performance does not meet the required standards |

**Potential**
Indicate your opinion of potential by means of a tick against the appropriate heading

A Considerable potential for promotion to at least two grades above his present level

B Definite potential for promotion to one or two grades above his present level

C Some potential for promotion to one grade above his present level

D Unlikely to be promoted above his present level

Indicate positions to which the job holder might be promoted and when:

**Action to be Taken**
What action should be taken to improve performance in his present job and/or develop him in his career?

**Additional Comments**
By reviewer and/or countersigning manager; to include job holder's reaction:

Prepared by . . . . . . . . . . . . . . . . . . . . . .     Countersigned by . . . . . . . . . . . . . . . . .

Signature . . . . . . . . . . . . . . . . . . . . . . . .     Signature . . . . . . . . . . . . . . . . . . . . . . . ..

Date . . . . . . . . . . . . . . . . . . . . . . . . . . .     Date . . . . . . . . . . . . . . . . . . . . . . . . . . .

**Figure 12.2(b) Performance review form**

manager and agreed by the job holder.

4. After the interview, the reviewing manager should complete the second sheet of the review form covering his overall assessment of the job holder, an estimate of potential, and recommendations on action to be taken. Any problems in completing these sections should be discussed with the countersigning manager.

5. The countersigning manager should:
   (a) discuss the report with the reviewing manager, resolve any differences of opinion about his assessment, and approve the action to be taken with regard to the individual under review;
   (b) enter any comments he wants to make on the form. It is particularly important for him to comment on the job holder's potential and how this should be developed;
   (c) return the form to the management development adviser and discuss with him any points arising.

6. Steps should then be taken to implement any actions agreed by the reviewing and countersigning managers. It is essential that the reviewing manager implements all the necessary action resulting from the review and keeps in touch with his subordinate on any matters concerning his development and training to provide whatever coaching and encouragement is necessary.

## Following up

Performance appraisal procedures are useless if they are not followed up. Action must be planned and taken to exploit strengths and overcome weaknesses. Hence the validity of the results-orientated or management by objectives approach, which emphasizes joint agreement of what needs to be done.

### Revealing results

One of the most difficult problems facing those who introduce appraisal schemes and those who carry out appraisals is how to convey the results of the appraisal to the individual concerned. Clearly, unless something is passed on from the manager to his subordinate, the prime objective of appraisal — that of improving performance — will have been frustrated.

But many managers do not like doing this and, if they do it at all, do not do it well. In fact, many managers argue that appraisals should be confidential because this enables them to be frank in their assessment and to express views in their own way. They fear that if they were asked to show the report to their subordinate the latter would react negatively. It is claimed by those who oppose openness that it only results in bland, meaningless judgements.

Those who support open assessments say that as long as they are based on evidence of achievements against targets or standards no one should have any problems in presenting or receiving the report. It is, they say, when appraisers indulge in judgements on personality that they get into trouble. They also claim that the way to overcome weak assessments is to train managers in techniques of appraisal and counselling.

On the whole the 'ayes' — those in favour of open appraisals — have it. The argument that there is no point in appraising if you do not discuss the results is a compelling one. But it is dangerous to underestimate the problems of running an open scheme. Unless managers believe in it and are trained in how to do it, the scheme can do more harm than good.

## Performance appraisal checklist

### I. PERFORMANCE REVIEW CHECKLIST

**Objectives**
1. Are objectives mutually understood?
2. Is progress towards achievement of objectives being maintained?
3. What objectives have been achieved and can be eliminated?
4. What new objectives should be evolved?

**Management control**
5. Did he do what he was required to do?

**Improvement of performance**
6. What constraints or restrictions exist that prevent effective performance taking place?
7. What action can be jointly taken to bring about an improvement in the results that are being achieved?

**Effectiveness**
8. Is the job holder capable of carrying the workload that has currently been assigned to him?
9. What sort of tasks can he be relied upon to perform effectively and at what level?
10. What skills, strengths and qualities does he have?
11. Are his skills being used to mutual advantage?

**Training**
12. Does the job holder's present performance suggest that he requires training to acquire certain additional skills or knowledge to perform even better?

**Reward**
13. Does his performance justify an additional or different sort of reward?

**Motivation**
14. Does he know when he is doing well or only when he has done something wrong?
15. Is he committed to the objectives of his role?
16. What parts of his job does he like doing and what parts of his job does he find irksome or difficult?

**Feedback**
17. Were the forecasts of improvement made at the last appraisal interview reasonably accurate?
18. Was my forecast of potential accurate?
19. How did my plans for carrying out the interview work out?
20. What can I do to improve the way the next interview is carried out?

### II. ASSESSMENT OF POTENTIAL CHECKLIST

**Personal data**
1. *Physical Make-up:* Has he any defects of health or physique that may be of occupational importance? How agreeable are his appearance, his bearing and his speech?

2. *Attainments:*
    (a) How well has he done educationally?
    (b) How well has he done in each position he has held?
    (c) What salary progression and rate of promotion has he achieved? Is he likely to maintain this rate of progress?
    (d) In what sorts of activities has he been particularly successful? What tasks has he found difficult?

3. *General Intelligence:*
    (a) How much general intelligence can he display?
    (b) How much intelligence does he ordinarily display?
    (c) What is his ability to grasp details quickly and ability to analyse complex data?

4. *Special Aptitudes:* Has he any marked special aptitudes, such as a facility in the use of words or figures, or drawing ability?

5. *Interests:* What sorts of tasks does he enjoy doing? What aspects of his job does he find distasteful?

6. *Disposition:*
    (a) How acceptable does he make himself to others?
    (b) Is he steady and dependable?
    (c) Is he self-reliant?
    (d) Can he work under pressure?
    (e) Can he lead a team?

7. *Circumstances:*
    (a) What chances have come his way?
    (b) What use has he made of his chances?
    (c) What are his domestic circumstances? Do these limit his choice of job or location?

## Job training data

8. *Present Job:*
    (a) How long should he continue in his present job?
    (b) Has he been in it long enough to form an assessment?
    (c) Will the job itself grow or change?
    (d) What are his views?

9. *Future Jobs:*
    (a) What job could he move to next?
    (b) What sorts of things can he do well?
    (c) What are his interests, circumstances and ambitions?

10. *Training and Development:* What further training and experience will he need to do in his next job?
    (a) Can he get this in his present job?
    (b) Do special arrangements need to be made?

## III. APPRAISAL INTERVIEW CHECKLIST

### Preparation
1. Obtain the essential facts about the person to be interviewed.
2. Identify strengths and weaknesses for each of his main tasks.
3. Refresh your mind on the objectives the interviewee has been and is still pursuing.
4. Explain the purpose of the interview beforehand.

## Conducting the interview
5. Choose a suitable place.
6. Set a natural, easy atmosphere.
7. Start with open, general questions.
8. Refer to facts — avoid premature value judgements.
9. Let the interviewee talk.
10. Discuss each activity sympathetically.
11. Agree future actions jointly.
12. Close in a positive, friendly manner.
13. Record the outcome of the interview.

## Follow-up
14. Carry out your agreed actions.
15. Check if interviewee has carried out his agreed actions.
16. Check whether there is anything you need to do to help the interviewee achieve the agreed objective.

## References
1. McGregor, D. 'An Uneasy Look at Performance Appraisal', *Harvard Business Review*, Vol. 35, No. 3, May-June 1957, pp. 89-94.
2. Rowe, K.H. 'An Appraisal of Appraisals', *Journal of Management Studies*, Vol. 1, No. 1, March 1964, pp. 1-25.
3. Flanagan, J.C. 'The Critical Incident Technique', *Psychological Bulletin*, Vol. 51, 1954, pp. 237-58.
4. Maier, N.R.F. *The Appraisal Interview*, John Wiley & Sons, New York, 1958.
5. Peter, L.J. *The Peter Principle*, William Morrow & Co., New York, 1972.
6. Ungerson, B. 'Assessment Centres: A Review of Research Findings', *Personnel Review*, Vol. 3, No. 3, Summer 1974, pp. 5-13.

<table>
<tr><td>

*13*

</td><td>

# Employment Practices and Procedures

</td></tr>
</table>

Employee resourcing is not just about organizing, obtaining, appraising and training people. It is also about dealing with specific issues and problems concerning their employment, often on a day-to-day basis. Practices and procedures should be developed in the following areas:

1. Grievances.
2. Discipline.
3. Redundancy.
4. Transfers.
5. Promotions.

This chapter considers the basic principles which should be taken into account in each area. The precise practice to be followed will, of course, depend on the circumstances in the organization. For example, a large bureaucratic-type organization is likely to adopt a fairly rigid procedure for promotions, involving internal advertisements, formal reviews and appointment boards, all of which may be related to a career planning system. In a smaller, informal organization the procedures will be much more flexible. But the principles of giving people equal opportunity for promotion and assessing their capabilities fairly will be the same in each case.

## Grievances

It is often said that the best way to settle grievances is to get the facts and then settle on an equitable solution. This is easier said than done. The problem is frequently hedged around with matters of opinion, and it is essential to attempt to penetrate the facade — the ostensible problem or grievance — and reach the real feelings. In any case facts are always subject to interpretation and feelings are, by definition, subjective. It will not be possible to reach behind the facade or achieve the co-operation of the individual in solving the problem if an autocratic or directive approach is adopted — i.e. *telling* him what is wrong and how to improve. More co-operation and more information will be obtained if the following non-directive approach is used:

1. *Listen with intelligence and sympathy.* Someone in difficulty cannot fail to benefit if he is allowed to discuss his problem with a sympathetic listener. The interviewer's attentive silence is often his best contribution.
2. *Define the problem.* Ideally, the interviewee defines the problem for himself with the aid of sympathetic listening and brief, well-directed questions. It is essential to get the problem clearly stated and accepted as a problem by the interviewee as well as the interviewer. A considerable amount of listening and questioning may be necessary before the point becomes clear since strong

181

emotions and clarity of expression seldom go together. When you think you understand his viewpoint it is often helpful to ask a summarizing question — 'is that what you mean?' — without passing any moral judgement at this stage.

3. *Stay alert and flexible.* Plan the interview in advance to decide broadly how you will tackle it, but be prepared to change direction in the light of new information.

4. *Observe behaviour.* While listening to the words being spoken, take note of gestures, manner, tone and inflexion, pauses and others ways of responding.

5. *Conclude the interview.* Try to get the interviewee to summarize his problem and suggest a possible solution. If this response is not forthcoming, help him either by a summarizing question or a crystallizing statement, such as 'Am I right in thinking that your problem boils down to this...?'

The aim should be to get to the root of the matter and, if there is no justification for being aggrieved, let the individual work it out for himself, with prompting from the interviewer as necessary. If there is something in the complaint, time and trouble should be taken to identify causes rather than just dwelling on symptoms.

Individuals should be given the right to appeal if they feel that their complaint has not been adequately dealt with. A grievance procedure should allow people to take their case through higher levels of authority to the chief executive of the organization if they want. An example of a grievance procedure is given in Appendix D.

## Discipline

In the U.K. the way in which disciplinary problems are handled is very much influenced by the statute law on unfair dismissal as interpreted by case law and backed up by the code of disciplinary practice and procedures in employment. Although only applicable in the U.K., the regulations are based on principles of natural justice which are, or should be, universal.

When handling disciplinary problems it is advisable to be aware of what these accepted principles of natural justice are and, building on this foundation, understand:

☐ the basic provisions of the law, such as the law of unfair dismissal;
☐ the general approach that should be used to deal with disciplinary matters as set out in the code of practice;
☐ the particular approaches to be used in dealing with specific branches of discipline or with cases of unsuitability, especially incapability, misconduct, absenteeism and lateness.

### Natural justice
There are three basic principles which should govern the way in which you handle potential discipline problems:

1. The individual should know the standards of performance he is expected to achieve and the rules to which he is expected to conform.
2. He should be given a clear indication of where he is failing or the rules he has broken.
3. Except in cases of gross misconduct, he should be given an opportunity to improve before disciplinary action is taken.

Four further principles governing how disciplinary cases should be dealt with have been defined in case law:

1. The person should know the nature of the accusation against him.
2. He should be given the opportunity to state his case.
3. The disciplinary tribunal should act in good faith.
4. The employee should be allowed to appeal.

### The law of unfair dismissal

The law of unfair dismissal in the U.K. applies generally to employees with more than one year's service. Under this law, dismissals are fair if the principal reason was one of the following:

☐ incapability, which covers the employee's skill, aptitude, health and physical or mental condition;
☐ misconduct;
☐ failure to have qualifications relevant to the job;
☐ a legal factor which prevents the employee continuing work;
☐ refusal to join a trade union where a closed shop exists and it cannot be shown that the employee objects on grounds of deeply held personal conviction to joining the union;
☐ redundancy, where this has taken place in accordance with a customary or agreed procedure;
☐ the employee broke or repudiated his contract by going on strike (as long as he was not singled out for this treatment).

Dismissals are unfair in the following circumstances:

1. The employer fails to show that he has good reasons to dismiss the employee (one of the admissible reasons listed above).
2. The employer has not acted reasonably in the circumstances. This can arise when he has not followed the principles of natural justice set out earlier, especially those concerning proper warnings, the opportunity for the employee to state his case and the right to appeal. But this requirement to follow a fair procedure is modified under case law if it can be shown that adherence to the agreed procedure would have made no difference to the employer's decision.
3. 'Constructive' dismissal takes place, i.e. the employer's conduct is such that the employee would be entitled to regard his contract of employment as having been repudiated by his employer. But the employee is only entitled to leave and claim constructive dismissal if his employer is in breach of some express or implied term of the contract and the breach is so serious that it goes to the root of the contract.

Examples of constructive dismissal are:

☐ giving unjustified warnings;
☐ using extremely provocative or denigratory language;
☐ forcing the employee to resign;
☐ failing to provide a safe system and place of work;
☐ forcing an employee to do work clearly outside his contract.

When assessing whether or not a dismissal is fair, an industrial tribunal asks itself the following questions:

1. Was the manner of the dismissal correct, i.e. did the employer follow a proper

procedure, giving fair warning of the consequences of continued misconduct or incapability?
2. Was the employer's decision to dismiss based on sufficient evidence?
3. Did the employee's offence or misbehaviour merit the penalty of dismissal or would a lesser penalty have been appropriate in the circumstances?
4. Were there any mitigating circumstances which the employer should have taken into account?

## Approach to handling disciplinary cases

The approach should be clearly governed by the principles of natural justice and the legal considerations set out above. There should be a disciplinary procedure (one is, in fact, required by law in the U.K.) which is understood and applied by all managers and supervisors.

A disciplinary procedure should provide for a three-stage approach before action is taken.

1. Informal oral warnings.
2. Formal oral warnings which, in serious cases, may also be made in writing. These warnings should set out the nature of the offence and the likely consequences of further offences.
3. Final written warnings which should contain a statement that any recurrence would lead to suspension, dismissal or some other penalty.

The procedure should provide for employees to be accompanied by a colleague or shop steward at any hearing. There should also be an appeal system and a list of offences which constitute gross misconduct and may therefore lead to instant dismissal. An example of a disciplinary procedure is given in Appendix E.

Managers and supervisors should be told what authority they have to take disciplinary action. It is advisable to have all final warnings and actions approved by a higher authority. In cases of gross misconduct, supervisors and junior managers should be given the right to suspend, if higher authority is not immediately available, but not to dismiss. The importance of obtaining and recording the facts should be emphasized. The manager should always have a colleague with him when issuing a formal warning and should make a note for file of what was said on the spot.

## Incapability

Incompetence can be shown to exist by comparing actual against expected performance. But where measurement is difficult, as in managerial jobs, it can still be shown if a responsible employer has come to the conclusion over a reasonable period of time that a manager is incompetent. Employees should normally be given a reasonable period to improve. But, if there is clear evidence of inherent and irredeemable incapability such that an opportunity to improve is most unlikely to have any effect, the employer can fairly and lawfully dismiss the employee without going through the whole procedure, although the complaint should have been brought to the attention of the employee over a period of time.

It is often not possible to judge performance against clearly defined standards. A gradual decline in overall competence is particularly difficult, and, if someone has been allowed to get away with it in the past, it becomes progressively more difficult to do anything. That is why it is better for everyone's sake to take action at the time, if only to give a warning, rather than to let things slide. A soft approach now can lead to real problems in the future.

Those problems which are hardest to solve arise when 'the face doesn't fit' or attitudes to work are incompatible. Who is to blame if the boss cannot get on with his subordinates or *vice versa*? How is it possible to substantiate accusations that someone is unco-operative or upsets colleagues? What is the point of warning someone that things must improve or else, when the problem is one of an inherent personality characteristic which the individual may not accept as being a defect and, even if he did, could not do much about changing? In any case, people who are vaguely accused of being unco-operative frequently respond with remarks like 'everyone is out of step but me'.

Criticisms of behaviour are difficult to make and even more difficult to back up. The only way to do it is to produce evidence of the effects of such behaviour on performance — of the individual or of other people — and make him recognize the fault and work out for himself how to overcome it. And it is no good making blunt accusations. The best approach is to spot unsatisfactory behaviour when it starts and discuss it informally, using the non-directive interviewing techniques mentioned earlier.

## Redundancy

Redundancy is the saddest and often the most difficult problem concerning people personnel managers ever have to deal with. There are four things which can be done to make it less painful:

1. Plan ahead to avoid redundancy.
2. Use other methods of reducing numbers or man hours to avoid or minimize the effects of redundancy.
3. Call for voluntary redundancy.
4. Develop and apply a proper redundancy procedure.

### Plan ahead
Planning ahead means anticipating future reductions in manpower needs and allowing natural wastage to take effect. A forecast is needed of the amount by which the labour force has to be reduced and the likely losses through labour turnover. Recruitment can then be frozen at the right moment to allow the surplus to be absorbed by wastage.

The problem is that forecasts are often difficult to make, and in periods of high unemployment natural wastage rates are likely to be reduced. It is possible therefore to overestimate the extent to which they will take up the slack. It is best to be pessimistic about the time it will take to absorb future losses and apply the freeze earlier rather than later.

Ideally, steps should be taken to transfer people to other safer jobs and re-train them where possible.

### Use other methods
The other methods which can be used to avoid or at lease minimize redundancy include, in order of severity:

☐ calling in outside work;
☐ withdrawing all sub-contracted labour;
☐ reducing or preferably eliminating overtime;
☐ developing work-sharing: two people doing one job on alternate days or splitting the day between them;

☐ dismissing part-timers;
☐ temporary lay-offs.

**Voluntary redundancy**
Asking for volunteers − with a suitable pay-off − is one way of relieving the number of compulsory redundancies. The amount needed to persuade people to go is a matter of judgement. It clearly has to be more than the statutory minimum, although one inducement for employees to leave early may be the belief that they will get another job more easily than if they hang on until the last moment. Help can be provided to place them elsewhere.

One of the disadvantages of voluntary redundancy is that the wrong people might go, i.e. good workers who are best able to find other work. It is sometimes necessary to go into reverse and offer them a special loyalty bonus if they agree to stay on.

**Redundancy procedure**
If forced into redundancy the problems will be reduced if there is an established procedure to follow. This procedure should have three aims:

☒ to treat employees as fairly as possible;
☐ to reduce suffering as much as possible;
☐ to protect management's ability to run the business effectively.

These aims are not always compatible. Management will want to retain their key workers. Trade unions, on the other hand, will want to adopt the principle of last in, first out, irrespective of the value of each employee to the company.

The following points should be included in any redundancy procedure:

1. Early warnings and consultation with unions and staff: in the U.K. firms are required by law to inform the union and the Department of Employment if 10 or more employees are to be made redundant, giving at least 30 days' notice.
2. Means to be adopted to avoid or reduce redundancies, e.g. cutting back overtime and the use of temporary staff, short-time working, transfers to other jobs with an appropriate trial period (four weeks required in law).
3. The basis of selection for redundancy. The starting point may be the principle of last in, first out, but the right has to be reserved to deviate from this principle where selection on the basis of service would prejudice operational efficiency.
4. The basis of compensating for redundancy, i.e. payments made by the company which are additional to the statutory minimum.
5. The help the company will give to redundant employees to find other work.

An example of a redundancy procedure is given in Appendix F.

## Transfer procedures

Re-deployment in response to changing or seasonal demands for labour is a necessary feature in any large enterprise. The clumsy handling of transfers by management, however, can do as much long-lasting harm to the climate of employee relations as ill-considered managerial actions in any other sphere of personnel practice.

Management may be compelled to move people in the interests of production.

But in making the move, managers should be aware of the fears of those affected so that they can be alleviated as much as possible.

The basic fear will be of change itself — a fear of the unknown and of the disruption of a well-established situation: work, environment, colleagues, and workmates, travelling arrangements. There will be immediate fears that the new work will make additional and unpalatable demands for extra skill or effort. There will be concern about loss of earnings because new jobs have to be tackled or because of different pay scales or bonus systems. Loss of overtime opportunities or the danger of shift or night work may also arouse concern.

Transfer policies should establish the circumstances when employees can be transferred and the arrangements for pay, resettlement and re-training. If the transfer is at the company's request and to suit the convenience of the company it is normal to pay the employee's present rate or the rate for the new job, whichever is higher. This policy is easiest to apply in temporary transfers. It may have to be modified in the case of longer term or permanent transfers to eliminate the possibility of a multi-tiered pay structure emerging in the new location, which must cause serious dissatisfaction amongst those already employed there.

When transfers are made to avoid redundancy in the present location the rate for the job in the new department should be paid. Employees affected in this way would, of course, be given the choice between being made redundant or accepting a lower paid job.

The policies should also provide guidelines on how requests from employees for transfer should be treated. The normal approach should be to give sympathetic hearing to such requests from longer serving employees, especially if the transfer is wanted for health or family reasons. But the transferred employee would have to accept the rate for the job in his new department.

The procedures for handling transfers may have to include joint consultation or discussions with workers' representatives on any major transfer programme. If regular transfers take place because of seasonal changes it is best to establish a standard procedure for making transfers which would include payment arrangements. Individual transfers would be managed by departmental supervisors, but they should be made aware of company policies and procedures and the need to treat the human problems involved with care and consideration.

## Promotion procedures

The aims of the promotion procedures of a company should be, first, to enable management to obtain the best talent available within the company to fill more senior posts and, second, to provide employees with the opportunity to advance their careers within the company, in accordance with the opportunities available and their own abilities.

In any organization where there are frequent promotional moves and where promotion arrangements cause problems, it is advisable to have a promotion policy and procedure which is known to all management and staff. The basic points that should be included in such a procedure are:

☐ promotion vacancies should be notified to the personnel department;
☐ specified vacancies should be advertised internally unless there is a recognized successor or, because of unusual requirements, there is no suitable candidate within the company;
☐ departmental managers should not be allowed to refuse promotions within a

reasonable time unless the individual has been in the department for less than, say, one year, or the department has recently suffered heavy losses through promotions or transfers;
☐ promotion opportunities open to all, irrespective of race, creed, sex or marital status.

An example of a promotion procedure is given in Appendix G.

| 14 | Job Evaluation |
|----|----------------|

## What is job evaluation?

Job evaluation is the process of establishing the value of jobs in a job hierarchy. Job values may be determined by negotiation or fixed on the basis of broad assumptions about market rates and internal relativities. The job analysis techniques and evaluation schemes discussed in this chapter will establish internal relativities. But before a pay structure can be designed or amended (see chapters 15 and 16), it is necessary to make external comparisons to establish market rates and the degree to which the structure is competitive.

This chapter deals with job evaluation under the following headings:

1. The aims of job evaluation schemes and pay surveys.
2. The basis of job evaluation.
3. Benefits of job evaluation.
4. The factors affecting job values as a background against which job analysis and evaluation takes place.
5. Job analysis techniques.
6. Job evaluation schemes.
7. Pay comparisons.
8. Introducing job evaluation − the preparation of programmes and the vital process of communicating and consulting with employees.

## Aims

Job evaluation schemes aim to:

☐ establish the rank order of jobs within an organization, measure the difference in value between them and group them into an appropriate grade in a pay structure;
☐ ensure that so far as possible, judgements about job values are made on objective rather than subjective grounds − judgements are based on analytical studies of the content of the jobs irrespective of the particular contributions made by job holders;
☐ provide a continuing basis for assessing the value of jobs which is easy to understand, administer and control, and is accepted by employees as fair.

### The basis of job evaluation

Job evaluation is a comparative process. It compares jobs by using common criteria to define the relationship of one job to another. This provides the basis for grading jobs and developing a pay structure. Job evaluation, however, is about relationships, not absolutes. It cannot be the sole determinant of what pay levels should be. Jobs may have intrinsic value − the labourer is worthy of his hire — but it is impossible to determine what that value is in monetary terms without taking account of the pressures of supply and demand, the comparative strengths of union and management, and internal differentials and feelings about equity.

### Benefits of job evaluation
The obvious benefit of adopting a systematic approach to job evaluation is that it can help to overcome the problems arising from a confused pay structure. Many organizations have a bewildering array of wage or salary rates and other pay components bearing no explicable relationship to one another. Such structures breed discontent and conflict because of the inequities built into them. Job evaluation can reduce, if not eliminate, this conflict by providing a consistent and agreed framework within which defensible differentials can be maintained.

## Factors affecting job values
The main factors affecting job values are first, market rates, second, negotiated pay scales, and third, internal relativities and feelings about equity.

### Market rates
It can be said that a job is worth what the market says it is worth. Certainly, firms will have difficulty in obtaining or retaining people if their rates of pay get out of line with those prevailing in the local and national labour markets from which they recruit employees.

Market rates will have most influence on those occupations in which there is a well-marked pattern of supply and demand in the open market. It may not be possible to compare the rates for specialized jobs within the company with those paid elsewhere. In these cases the rates will be governed more by internal than external comparisons, although it is likely that those jobs for which market rates can be ascertained will serve as 'bench-marks' against which the pay of other jobs will be measured. Market rates provide data on differentials between jobs as well as actual levels of pay. The main problem with market rates is finding out what they are. The market rate can be an inexact concept for some jobs.

### Negotiated pay scales
Clearly, many pay structures are built up around pay scales negotiated either at plant level, locally or nationally. The negotiated rates will be influenced by market rates (supply and demand), the relative strength of employers and unions, the economic situation (inflation and unemployment), legislation (equal pay) and government anti-inflationary pay regulations. The negotiations may embrace the whole pay structure and lay down job grades and differentials; or they may only fix minimum rates. Companies will often pay more than the local or nationally negotiated minima to keep ahead of market rates or in response to trade union pressures. Wage drift, which takes place when earnings float upwards because of the erosion of the piecework system, will distort a negotiated pay structure, as will the differences between piecework and day work earnings, and the incidence of overtime and shift work.

### Internal relativities and equity
Pay structures are expected to reflect differences in the relative skill and responsibility of jobs. They should aim to achieve equity in the sense that individuals

should feel that their rewards are in balance both with their own output in the shape of effort, skill and contribution, and with the rewards received by others in relation to their output. In other words, it is the feeling that justice and fairness are only achieved when equal pay is received for equal work, when pay differentials can be related to finite differences in degrees of responsibility, and when pay matches individual capacity and the level of work carried out.

Equity is primarily a matter of feelings and perceptions, and this was emphasized by Wilfred Brown when he defined equitable payment as: 'The level of earnings for people in different occupations which is felt by society to be reasonably consistent with the importance of the work which is done and which seems relatively fair to the individual.'[1]

The best-known theory of equitable payment is that advanced by Jaques. He wrote that:

(a) There exists an unrecognized system of norms of fair payment for any given level of work, unconscious knowledge of these norms being shared among the population engaged in employment work.

(b) An individual is unconsciously aware of his own capacity for work, as well as the equitable pay level for that work.[2]

To be equitable, pay must be felt to match the level of work and the capacity of the individual to do it. This 'felt-fair' principle, Jaques suggests, is important to organizations when formulating pay policies.

## Job analysis

Job analysis is the foundation of job evaluation. The better it is done, the more valid the final results, irrespective of the type of scheme used. The process of job analysis can be divided into three stages:

1. Information is collected about job content and responsibilities.
2. The information is recorded in the form of a job description.
3. The content and responsibilities of the job are further analysed in terms of the factors to be used for job evaluation.

### Collecting information

Information about jobs can be collected by means of questionnaires and interviews. Observation is a possible method, but it is too time consuming to be of much practical value.

QUESTIONNAIRES. Questionnaires to be completed by job holders and approved by the job holder's superior are useful when a large number of jobs are to be covered. They can also save interviewing time by recording purely factual information and by helping the analyst to structure his questions in advance to cover areas which need to be explored in greater depth.

Questionnaires should provide the following basic information:

☐ the job title of the job holder;
☐ the job title of the job holder's superior;
☐ the job titles and numbers of staff reporting to the job holder (best recorded by means of an organization chart);
☐ a brief description (one or two sentences) of the overall role or purpose of the job;
☐ a list of the main tasks or duties that the job holder has to carry out; as

appropriate, these should specify the resources controlled, the equipment used, the contacts made and the frequency with which the tasks are carried out.

These basic details can be supplemented by questions designed to elicit from the job holder some information about the level of his responsibilities and the demands made upon him by the job. Such questions are difficult to phrase and answer in a meaningful way. The replies may be too vague or misleading and usually have to be checked with the job holder's superior and in subsequent interviews. But they at least give the job holder an opportunity to express his feelings about the job and they can provide useful leads for development in discussion. These questions can cover such aspects of the job as:

☐ the amount of supervision received and the degree of discretion allowed in making decisions;
☐ the typical problems to be solved and the amount of guidance available when solving the problems;
☐ the relative difficulty of the tasks to be performed;
☐ the qualifications and skills required to carry out the work.

An example of a questionnaire is shown in Appendix H.

INTERVIEWING. To obtain the full flavour of a job it is necessary to interview job holders and to check the findings with their superiors. The aim of the interview should be to obtain all the relevant facts about the job, covering the areas listed above in the section on questionnaires.

To achieve this aim job analysts follow these guidelines:

1. Work to a logical sequence of questions which help the interviewee to order his thoughts about the job.
2. Pin people down on what they actually do. Answers to questions are often vague and information is given by means of untypical instances.
3. Ensure that the job holder is not allowed to get away with vague or inflated descriptions of his work. He will know that the interview is part of a job evaluation exercise and he would not be human if he did not present the job in the best possible light.
4. Sort out the wheat from the chaff: answers to questions may produce a lot of irrelevant data which must be sifted before preparing the job description.
5. Obtain a clear statement from the job holder about his authority to make decisions and the amount of guidance he receives from his superior. This is not easy. If asked what decisions they are authorized to make most people look blank because they think about their job in terms of duties and tasks rather than abstract decisions.
6. Avoid asking leading questions which make the expected answer obvious.
7. Allow the job holder ample opportunity to talk by creating at atmosphere of trust.

## Writing job descriptions

Job descriptions should be based on a detailed job analysis and should be as brief and as factual as possible. The headings under which the job description should be written and notes for guidance on completing each section are set out below.

JOB TITLE. The existing or proposed job title should indicate as clearly as possible the function in which the job is carried out and the level of the job within that function. The use of terms such as 'manager', 'assistant manager' or 'senior' to describe job levels should be reasonably consistent between functions with regard to gradings of the jobs. But this does not mean that all posts described, say, as manager, should be in the same grade. It is quite possible for someone correctly described as a manager in one function to have a less responsible job than a manager in another function.

REPORTING TO. The job title of the manager or supervisor to whom the job holder is directly responsible should be given under this heading. No attempt should be made to indicate here any functional relationships the job holder might have to other managers.

REPORTING TO HIM. The job titles of all the posts directly reporting to the job holder should be given under this heading. Again, no attempt should be made here to indicate any functional relationships that might exist between the job holder and other staff.

OVERALL RESPONSIBILITIES. This section should describe as concisely as possible the overall purpose of the job. The aim should be to convey in no more than two or three sentences a broad picture of the job which will clearly identify it from other jobs and establish the role of the job holder and the contribution he should make towards achieving the objectives of the company and his own function or unit.

No attempt should be made to describe the activities carried out under this heading, but the overall summary should lead naturally to the analysis of activities in the next section.

When preparing the job description, it is often better to defer writing down the definition of overall responsibilities until the activities have been analysed and described.

MAIN TASKS. The steps required to define the main tasks of the job are as follows:

1. Identify and list the tasks that have to be carried out. No attempt should be made to describe how they are carried out, but some indication should be given of the purpose or objectives of each task.
2. Analyse the initial list of tasks and, so far as possible, simplify the list by grouping related tasks together so that no more than, say, seven or eight main activity areas remain.
3. Decide on the order in which tasks should be described. The alternatives include:
   □ frequency with which they are carried out (continually, hourly, daily, weekly, monthly, intermittently);
   □ chronological order;
   □ order of importance
   □ the main processes of management that are carried out; for example, setting objectives, planning, organizing, co-ordinating, operating, directing and motivating staff, and controlling
4. Describe each main task separately in short numbered paragraphs. No more than one or at most two sentences should be used for the description, but, if

necessary, any separate tasks carried out within the task should be tabulated (a, b, c, etc) under the overall description of the activity. A typical sentence describing a task should:

☐ start with an active verb to eliminate all unnecessary wording. Use verbs which express the actual responsibility to recommend, to do, to ensure that someone else does something, or to collaborate with someone, for example, prepares, completes, recommends, supervises, ensures that, liaises with.
☐ state what is done as succinctly as possible;
☐ state why it is done: this indicates the purpose of the job and gives a lead to setting targets or performance standards.

5. Amplify as appropriate with examples and details of any quantitative measures of the amount of work involved. The frequency with which the work is carried out and, when it can be estimated, the proportion of time involved should also be stated wherever possible.
6. Group related tasks under descriptive headings to enable a quick appreciation to be obtained of the range of activities. For example, all the work a manager does in connection with manpower and facilities planning could be placed under the heading 'planning'.

### Factor analysis

The final step is to analyse the job in terms of the factors that will be used to evaluate it. For example, in an analytical scheme, the factors and the points to be covered under each heading may be any of those listed below.

RESOURCES CONTROLLED. The resources controlled should include details of any aspect of the job which will indicate its relative size, importance and contribution. For example:

☐ total number of staff analysed into managerial, higher grade and other staff
☐ annual budget
☐ value of assets
☐ floor space
☐ turnover
☐ throughput.

DECISIONS. The job should be analysed and described in the following terms:

1. The amount of authority the job holder has to make decisions.
2. The importance of decisions with regard to their impact on the results achieved by the company and function or unit.
3. The difficulty of making decisions taking account of:
   ☐ The amount of guidance received from superiors
   ☐ The existence of clearly defined procedures or precedents
   ☐ Problems in obtaining the information required to make the decisions
   ☐ Problems in forecasting the outcome of decisions.
4. The extent to which originality or creativity is required in solving problems or making decisions.
5. The time-span over which the decisions are made, i.e. the length of time that will elapse between making a decision and obtaining information on the results achieved.

194

COMPLEXITY. The complexity of the job should be analysed in the following terms:

1. The number of units, functions or separate management positions directly controlled by the job holder.
2. The variety of tasks that have to be carried out or problems that have to be solved.

So far as possible, supporting details should be given to indicate the degree of complexity.

KNOWLEDGE AND SKILLS. The knowledge and skills required by the job holder should be analysed with regard to:

☐ professional or technical aspects of the work
☐ man management
☐ administration
☐ commercial activities
☐ contacts with other people
☐ communications − written or spoken
☐ the analytical requirements of the work.

Where appropriate indicate the level of professional or technical skill required or the type of experience or training needed to meet the demands of the job.

Even if a whole job ranking or classification scheme is used it may still be useful to analyse the job under the sort of headings listed above. The discipline of having to write down these comments ensures that the job is subjected to suitably rigorous analysis.

Again, the aim should be to be as succinct as possible. No one is going to absorb or even read lengthy and discursive narratives, But it is not easy to summarize impressions about jobs. However detailed the analytical process has been up to this stage, subjectivity inevitably creeps in. Job analysis is still more art than science and there is always a danger of the job evaluation structure being built on sand. Job descriptions can too easily set out what is supposed to be happening or what people think is happening rather than what actually happens, and an analysis based on an interpretation of doubtful facts cannot be reliable. An example of a job description is given in Appendix I.

## Job evaluation techniques

The need to evaluate does not present a choice. There has to be some basis upon which pay levels and differentials are fixed. But there is plenty of choice in selecting the method to be used or in not using any formal method at all. At one end of the scale rule of thumb methods apply. Decisions on pay are made on hearsay evidence and adjustments are made at whim or in response to pressure. At the other end of the scale there are complex points evaluation schemes where jobs are scored against a dozen or more criteria or factors whose relative importance or weighting has been worked out by elaborate statistical techniques.

Between these two extremes there is a host of systems of various degrees of formality and complexity. The basic schemes are:

☐ non-analytical schemes − ranking and job classification − where comparisons are made between 'whole jobs', i.e. the jobs are not broken down into different

characteristics or factors;
☐ analytical schemes – points rating – where the jobs are analysed and
  compared by reference to distinct factors.

## Ranking

The simplest form of job evaluation is job ranking. This is a non-analytical
approach which aims to judge each job as a whole and determine its relative
place in a hierarchy by comparing one job with another and arranging them in
order of importance. The jobs may be compared by reference to a single criterion
or factor. This could be responsibility, which might be defined as the particular
obligations that have to be assumed by any person who carries out the job; or
skill, which might be defined as what the worker is required to do, in terms of
applying knowledge and experience to the completion of tasks, exercising manual
dexterity, operating machines, or controlling processes.

In some ranking procedures, evaluators are asked to consider several facets of
the job, for example:

☐ decisions – difficulty, judgement required, extent to which the tasks are
  prescribed (amount of discretion allowed);
☐ complexity – range of tasks to be carried out or skills to be used;
☐ knowledge and skills – what the job holder is required to know and be able
  to do;
☐ physical effort required to carry out the job.

A list of factors to be considered is helpful in that it steers thinking towards
definable aspects of the content of the job rather than dealing with over-
generalized concepts such as responsibility. But there are dangers. Rankings may
be distorted because evaluators will attach different weights to the factors,
emphasizing some and not others.

The ranking procedure is as follows:

1. Analyse and describe the jobs, bringing out in the description those aspects
   which are to be used for comparison purposes.
2. Identify key or bench-mark jobs: the most and least important jobs, a job
   midway between the two extremes, and others at the higher or lower intermediate points.
3. Rank the other jobs round the bench-mark jobs until all jobs are placed in
   their rank order of importance.
4. Divide the ranked jobs into grades by grouping jobs together with common
   features such as similar duties, skills or training requirements. In effect, this
   means that the grades are now defined by the jobs that have been placed in
   them. In future, new jobs can be graded or existing jobs re-graded by reference
   to the established gradings on a job-to-job basis.

There are no fixed rules for determining grade boundaries or the number of
grades required and, at this stage in the proceedings, job evaluation becomes even
less objective than it has been before. Some guidance on the division of jobs into
grades may be provided by a natural promotion ladder, junior clerk to clerk, to
section leader to group leader and so on. The danger of this approach is that the
existing hierarchy may simply be reproduced, which would defeat the purpose
of the scheme. The promotion ladder should therefore only be used as a broad
guide. This also applies when an existing skills hierarchy is the basis for grading.
There is no point in a job evaluation exercise which simply confirms the present

arrangements, irrespective of the levels of skills involved. But it would be possible to start by grading manual jobs into skilled, semi-skilled and unskilled categories and then sub-divide each category into not more than two or three sub-grades where there are clear differences between the levels of skill required. In an engineering company, for example, it would be quite obvious that a tool room turner capable of operating several machines and working to sketch plans is working at a different level to the skilled machinist operating one machine and following relatively detailed drawings and job instructions.

The problem with this method of ranking is that the judgements become multi-dimensional when a number of jobs have to be placed in order of importance. Inconsistencies in judgement arise between people because they give more weight to one aspect of jobs than to others; while an individual carrying out a ranking exercise can be inconsistent because he does not know what complex or balance of factors is operating at any moment. Moreover, while it is easy to establish the extremes in a rank order, it may be difficult to distinguish between the middling jobs.

To overcome this problem it may be better to use the statistical technique of paired comparisons on the assumption that it is always easier to compare one job with another than to consider a number of jobs and attempt to build up a rank order by multiple comparisons. The technique requires the comparison of each job separately with every other job. If a job is considered to be more important than the one with which it is being compared, it receives two points; if it is thought to be equally important, it receives one point; if it is regarded as less important, no points are awarded. A matrix is built up showing the scores for each job against all the other jobs being ranked and the scores are then totalled as shown in the following example.

| Job | A | B | C | D | E | Total score |
|-----|---|---|---|---|---|-------------|
| A | — | 0 | 0 | 1 | 2 | 3 |
| B | 2 | — | 0 | 2 | 2 | 6 |
| C | 2 | 2 | — | 2 | 2 | 8 |
| D | 1 | 0 | 0 | — | 1 | 2 |
| E | 0 | 0 | 0 | 1 | — | 1 |

In this example, job A is compared with jobs B to E. It is considered to be less important than jobs B and C and is scored no points in both cases; equally important to job D and is scored one point; and more important than job E and is scored two points. The total score is three. The same procedure is adopted for jobs B to E. The higher the score the higher the rank, and the rank order is therefore:

| 1 | 2 | 3 | 4 | 5 |
|---|---|---|---|---|
| C | B | A | D | E |

Job ranking is the simplest type of job evaluation. It is easily understood and does not take up much time. It is, of course, based on largely subjective impressions of the value of each job, although these should be derived from a detailed analysis of responsibilities and duties. Ranking is a natural process and will at least iron out inconsistencies. The arrangement of a miscellaneous collection of jobs into grades is a useful exercise, even if a somewhat rough and ready one.

The main disadvantages are that there are no definite standards of judgement and there is no way of measuring the differences between jobs.

### Job classification

The job classification system of evaluation is an attempt to overcome the problems of providing standards of judgements by starting off with a definition of the number and characteristics of the grades into which the jobs will be placed.

The steps required to introduce a job classification scheme are:

1. Select a representative sample of bench-mark jobs covering all the occupations to be included in the scheme.
2. Analyse the jobs and prepare job descriptions.
3. Decide on the number of grades required. This will depend on the range of responsibility or skills in the jobs to be covered by the scheme. For manual workers it is not likely to be more than six to eight, and the clerical staff in most firms can be fitted into four to six grades. The number of managerial grades will vary according to the size of the firm and the level of salaries at the top. There could be any number up to about twelve grades, although this depends on a variety of considerations, including the width of the salary brackets, which are discussed in the section on salary structures in chapter 15.
4. Define each grade in terms of discernible differences in skill and responsibility. The lowest grade, for instance, may cover simple work done under close supervision, and each succeeding grade will recognize a higher level of difficulty, complexity, or the amount of discretion allowed to make independent decisions.
5. Slot each bench-mark job into a grade by reference to the job and grade descriptions.
6. Grade the other jobs by reference to the bench-mark jobs and the grade descriptions.

Alternatively, a job classification exercise can start from a predetermined grading scheme. In this case, it is simply necessary to prepare job descriptions and place the jobs into the grade.

There are some published job classification schemes which can also be used for inter-firm comparisons. In Britain the best-known scheme is the one produced by the Institute of Administrative Management for clerical workers.

The advantages of this system are that first, it is simple to operate and secondly, standards of judgement are provided in the form of the grade definitions. The process of grading new jobs or re-grading existing jobs is facilitated if comparisons are made on a job-to-job basis between the job descriptions prepared for the new job and those available for the bench-mark jobs that have already been allocated into the grades.

A job classification scheme can usefully be developed after a ranking exercise when the grade definitions are prepared by reference to the descriptions of the jobs placed in each grade. It is also possible to do without grade descriptions altogether and rely simply on comparisons between the job descriptions for the jobs to be graded and those already in existence for the bench-mark posts placed in each grade. This is a simpler approach than trying to produce grade descriptions which often turn out to be little more than broad abstractions, only meaningful when they can be related to real live bench-mark jobs.

The main criticism that can be made of job classification systems is that they cannot deal with complex jobs which will not fit neatly into one grade. They are less useful for more senior jobs where the grade descriptions have to be so generalized that they do not provide much help in evaluating borderline cases. In practice, it is better to compare jobs with jobs rather than to compare jobs with grade descriptions. The latter are helpful in directing attention to the most probable grade. Thereafter, evaluation has to be carried out on a job comparison basis.

## Points rating

Points rating schemes are based on an analysis of separately defined characteristics or factors which are assumed to be common to all the jobs. It is further assumed that differences in the extent to which the characteristics are found in the jobs will measure differences between the levels of the job. The factors selected in points schemes are therefore those that are considered to be most important in determining the relative degrees of difficulty or responsibility. Typical factors include knowledge and skills, decisions, complexity, responsibility for the work of others, resources controlled (managerial and supervisory jobs), contacts (managerial and clerical jobs) and physical effort (manual jobs).

Each factor has a range of points allocated to it so that a maximum number of points is available. The relative importance or 'weighting' of a factor is determined by the maximum number of points given to it. For each factor, the total range of points is divided into degrees according to the level at which the factor is present in the job. The characteristics of each degree in terms of, for instance, level of complexity, are defined as yardsticks for comparison purposes and each degree is given a points value or range.

Jobs are evaluated by comparing job descriptions containing analyses of the extent to which the factor is present in the job with the factor degree definitions. The jobs are thereby graded for each factor and are given a factor score in accordance with the points value attached to each factor degree. The scores for each factor are then added to produce a total score and allocated into job grades according to the points range determined for each grade.

The steps required to develop a points rating scheme are:

1. Select a representative sample of bench-mark jobs — this should cover all the major occupations and levels of responsibility to be covered by the scheme.
2. Decide on the factors to be used in analysing and evaluating the jobs. The aim should be to restrict the number to no more than eight or so. The use of too many factors results in an over-complex scheme with overlap and duplication between factors. The ideal number to produce a manageable scheme is five or six, covering at least knowledge and skills, decisions, complexity, and responsibility for the work of others. One or two additional factors can be selected to suit the particular occupations for which the scheme is to be used; for example, physical effort for manual workers.
3. Prepare a preliminary definition of each factor and divide it into degrees of levels each of which is also defined. It is usual to restrict the number of levels to five or six.
4. Analyse each bench-mark job in terms of the factors and decide on the degree to which each factor is present by reference to the preliminary definitions of the factor degrees.
5. Decide on the weights to be attached to the factors (the total points value). This is a critical decision and should always be made in accordance with company circumstances. It is dangerous to accept the weightings given in a

packaged scheme as these may produce quite misleading results. There are two approaches to weighting factors:

(a)*Trial and error.* An initial assumption is made about the overall score for each factor and this total is divided between the factor degrees to produce the points score for each degree. Thus, if the total is 100 points and there are five grades, grade one might be given a range of from 0 to 20 points, grade two, 21 to 40 and so on. The jobs are then scored and ranked according to their total score. A separate whole job overall ranking exercise is also carried out, preferably using the paired comparison method. This overall ranking is compared with the ranking produced by the points scheme to determine the degree of correlation between them. If, as a result, the paired comparison ranking list is more or less replicated by the points score ranking list, it could be assumed that the factor values are probably right. If there is little correlation between the lists, the values are probably wrong. In statistical terms, a coefficient of correlation of +0.75 is acceptable. If this exercise shows that the weightings are wrong, they should be adjusted until there is a reasonable match between the two lists.

(b)*Multiple regression analysis.* A much more sophisticated approach is to use the multiple regression analysis technique. This is a method of investigating the relationships between independent and dependent variables and obtaining a 'regression equation' for predicting the latter in terms of the former. In a factor weighting exercise the different factors are the independent variables for which points are assessed and added up to produce the dependent variable of the overall rank order. This procedure is carried out with the help of a computer and starts by a ranking of the jobs overall and for each factor by means of paired comparisons. The multiple regression analysis computer programme then, (i) establishes the degree of correlation between each factor and the overall rank order; (ii) ranks each factor in turn and works out the weighting required for each of the separate factor rankings in order to reproduce the overall rank order; (iii) tests the individual factors by measuring the correlations between them to establish the degree to which they separately contribute to produce the overall rank order (a very high correlation between two factors would suggest a high degree of overlap and might result in one of the factors being eliminated).

6. Re-define the factor definitions and points scores in the light of the results of steps 4. and 5. to produce the final scheme.

The advantages claimed for points schemes are that first, evaluators are forced to consider a range of factors which, as long as they are present in all the jobs and affect them in different ways, will avoid the over-simplified judgements made when using non-analytical methods; and secondly, that evaluators are provided with defined yardsticks which should help them to achieve a greater degree of objectivity and consistency in making their judgements. There is no doubt that many people like them because they look scientific and give a strong impression that at least everyone is trying to be fair.

There are three objections to such schemes:

1. They are complex and expensive to develop, install and maintain.
2. They give a specious impression of scientific accuracy but it is still necessary to use largely subjective judgement in selecting factors, deciding on weightings, defining levels within factors, and interpreting information about the job in relation to the often rather generalized definitions of factors and factor levels.

3. They assume that it is possible to quantify different aspects of jobs on the same scale of values and then add them together. But skills are not summable in this way — it is not possible to make a meaningful comparison in quantitative terms between the skills used by, say, a management accountant spending his time manipulating figures and a sales manager spending his time manipulating people.

These are formidable objections, and indicate that points schemes should be used with caution, if at all. Their only real justification is that the paraphernalia of factor definitions and quantifications impress people and make them feel that the system is fair. And achieving satisfaction with an evaluated pay structure is very much dependent on the 'felt-fair' principle of Professor Jaques.

### Choice of job evaluation scheme
The choice of scheme will depend on a number of factors such as the size and complexity of the company, the types of jobs to be evaluated, the views of employees and unions, the time and manpower resources available to introduce the scheme, and the likely costs. All job evaluation schemes initially cost money, both in the development and in the application. They produce adjustments to the existing pay structure which result in some upgradings and some downgradings. But no one ever suffers a reduction in pay after a scheme is installed, while it is difficult to hold back increases, although they may be phased over a period of time. As a result, job evaluation can often put up pay-roll costs by 10% to 15% which has to be weighed against the benefits of having a logical structure and, it is hoped, minimizing discontent and conflict.

The characteristics and advantages and disadvantages of each type of scheme are summarized in table 14.1.

| Scheme | Characteristics | Advantages | Disadvantages |
|---|---|---|---|
| 1. Ranking | Whole job comparisons are made to place them in order of importance. | Easy to apply and understand. | No defined standards of judgement — differences between jobs are not measured. |
| 2. Job classification | Job grades are defined and jobs are slotted into the grades by comparing the whole job description with the grade definition. | Simple to operate and standards of judgement are provided in the shape of the grade definition. | Difficult to fit complex jobs into one grade without using excessively elaborate definitions. |
| 3. Points rating | Separate factors are scored to produce an overall points score for the job. | The analytical process of considering separate defined factors provides for objectivity and consistency in making judgements. | Complex to install and maintain — judgement is still required to rate jobs in respect of different factors. |

**Table 14.1 Summary of job evaluation schemes**

The golden rule in choosing a scheme is to go for the simplest approach first and reject it only if the complexity of the situation or the need to impress everyone demands a more complicated method. All job evaluation is largely subjective when it comes to making final judgements. The main value of any of the methods described above lies in the detailed analysis of the jobs prior to making comparisons between them. It should always be remembered that job evaluation is a systematic art rather than an applied science. Many perfectly effective and acceptable schemes have been based on no more than a simple job ranking exercise, followed by drawing up a grade structure in which each grade is defined by the bench-mark jobs that have been allocated into them. In these schemes, comparisons on a job-to-job basis have produced quite satisfactory results and an elaborate points scheme would only have added an expensive gloss to the process.

## Pay comparisons

Job evaluation schemes can be used to determine internal relativities, but in themselves they cannot put a price to the job. To a large extent pay levels are subject to market forces which have to be taken into account in negotiations and in fixing the rates for particular jobs. Some specialized jobs may not be subjected to the same external pressures as others, but it is still necessary to know what effect market rates are likely to have on the pay structure as a whole before deciding on internal pay differentials which properly reflect levels of skill and responsibility. It has also to be accepted that market pressures and negotiations will affect differentials within the firm. An employer may be unwilling to submit to individual pressure because of the danger that it will distort the structure. But it may sometimes be necessary to recognize the compelling force of market or union demands in one area and adjust rates accordingly. Wherever possible such adjustments should be regarded as special measures and an attempt should be made to contain their influence on other scales by isolating them as exceptions ('red-circling').

The concept of the market rate, even in the local labour market, is an inexact one. It is noticeable that for identical jobs there is always a range of rates paid by different employers. This is particularly so in managerial jobs and other occupations where duties can vary considerably between companies, even if the job title is the same. It is therefore only possible to use pay surveys to provide a broad indication of market rates. Judgement has to be used in interpreting the results of special inquiries or the data from published surveys. There is usually plenty of scope for selecting evidence which supports whatever case is being advanced.

Information on the rates paid by other firms can come from the following sources:

☐ company surveys
☐ local surveys conducted by employers, unions or other bodies
☐ general published surveys
☐ analyses of job advertisements.

### Company surveys

Company surveys are conducted when specific information is required of the pay and benefits provided by comparable companies for similar jobs. The steps required to conduct a company survey are to:

1. Draw up a list of suitable companies which are compatible with regard to

industry, size and the sort of jobs they are likely to have.
2. Approach each company. It is clearly best to maintain a list of friendly contacts who from experience are known to give reliable information. These may develop into a 'club' which can operate at various levels of formality in exchanging information on a regular or an as-required basis. If such contacts or a club are not readily available it may be necessary to approach a company out of the blue and ask them for information. This has obviously to be provided on a reciprocal basis and it may sometimes be possible to offer the *quid pro quo* of an anonymous summary of the results. In making such contacts the messages that have to be got across are that:
☐ a responsible individual is conducting the survey;
☐ the survey will be carried out competently and in confidence;
☐ the reciprocal information provided will be relevant and useful;
☐ the company being approached will not be put to too much trouble.
3. Prepare job data and, if necessary, survey forms. It may be possible to obtain the information required over the telephone, but it is necessary to have information about the jobs ready to ensure that like is being compared with like. If a postal survey is being conducted it is even more necessary to provide basic data about the duties and responsibilities of the jobs to assist in making valid comparisons. A pro forma may be prepared by the surveying company for completion by the participating company to save time and trouble and to help in the subsequent analysis. The form should provide spaces for the information required on pay scales, actual salaries paid, overtime earnings and, for wage earners, details of basic rates, regular total earnings, variations in earnings, the make up of total earnings (base rates, bonuses, overtime, shift payments, etc.) and hours worked.
4. Where it is difficult to make valid comparisons by telephone or post by reference to outline job descriptions it may be possible to carry out on-the-spot inquiries, if other companies are willing to participate. Much more can be got out of a face-to-face discussion which will clarify any differences in responsibilities that may affect comparisons. The best results will be obtained if the parties agree to bench-mark jobs being analysed and compared using a system such as that suggested by Bowey and Lupton,[3] which is based on a factor comparison type evaluation scheme and aims to ensure that like is being compared with like.
5. Analyse the information obtained from the survey, ensuring that so far as possible like jobs are being compared and that the details provided on pay distinguish between basic rates and piecework, overtime, and shiftwork earnings. It is also important to establish that the earnings are regular and not distorted by special circumstances. If, when comparing earnings, they are brought down to an hourly rate to eliminate the effect of overtime, it is worth remembering that a simple division of the total earnings by the hours will not remove the impact of overtime if the effect of overtime premiums is not discounted.
6. Present the analysis in a form which can be easily assimilated and reveals the range of rates of pay or earnings for the jobs covered by the survey. The presentation may show the range of pay or earnings from highest and lowest, the median rate and the upper and lower quartile. The median is the middle item in the distribution of salaries or wage rates — 50% of the jobs will be paid more than the median and 50% of the jobs will be paid less. The upper quartile is the rate above which 25% of the jobs are paid more, the lower quartile is the

rate below which 25% of the jobs are paid less.

## Local surveys

Local surveys may be conducted by employers' associations or other bodies by obtaining information on the pay and earnings for certain jobs from employers in the district. They provide useful additional data but the results have to be treated with caution because of the dangers of not comparing like with like.

## National surveys and information on pay

The general salary surveys published by organizations such as the British Institute of Management or the British Institute of Administrative Management are based on information collected from firms about the salaries paid for management, administrative and clerical jobs. The survey information may be related to standard job or grade descriptions or it may simply rely upon job titles with a broad indication of the levels of the jobs within the company. To assist in making comparisons, the survey data may be grouped according to the size of the company measured by turnover or number of employees. The data is usually presented in a way which gives the average pay and an indication of the dispersion around the average, often the upper and lower quartiles.

The value of published surveys depends on a number of factors; including the size of the sample, the extent to which the sample is representative, and whether or not it is possible to relate the job titles in the survey to the job titles in the company. The range of pay rates or salaries quoted in the surveys indicates the variations that can exist in 'market rates' but is also a reflection of the differences between the jobs included in the published data. The biggest problem, however, is that of matching jobs within the company to survey jobs. The data with which comparisons are being made may be for similar job titles and companies of a similar size, but the match between jobs must be approximate. Published surveys can only give a very broad indication of market rates.

Information on national earnings and movements in pay and wage rates can be obtained from government publications such as, in Britain, the *Department of Employment Gazette*. This data is mainly useful in revealing trends which can be used to assess what increases may be required in rates of pay to keep pace with other employers. The official price and wage rate indices also provide a guide on the inflationary pressures that may have to be taken into account in deciding on an across the board pay increase, or in conducting negotiations with unions.

For negotiating purposes it is essential to keep a close look at negotiated increases in the same industry or in comparable firms. In Britain publications such as the *Department of Employment Gazette* and *Incomes Data Services* provide this information. If they are studied with care, trends can be analysed which will indicate when pay claims are likely to be made and the size of the settlement that may have to be conceded on the grounds of comparability.

## Advertisements

Advertisements are often used to give information on salary or wage levels. But they should be treated with caution. The rates quoted may be inflated to attract candidates and the information about the job may be too imprecise to permit useful comparisons to be made.

## Using pay survey data

Except in highly defined local labour markets the main difficulties in using market rate data to fix pay levels are the variety of information that can come from different sources, and the inexact nature of the details usually available about the jobs covered by the surveys. In these circumstances judgement is required in deciding which market rate to take. The judgement will be governed by estimates of the relative reliability of the data, but ultimately it becomes a subjective process of extracting a derived market rate which seems to offer a reasonable balance between the competing claims of the various rates available.

When conducting negotiations, pay survey data may, of course, be used differently. The aim is to obtain the data required to estimate what the unions are likely to ask for and accept and what the company should offer or, finally, may have to concede. The data needs to be available in a form which will help the employer to support his offer and, to a reasonable degree, withstand the union's claims.

## Introducing job evaluation

The steps required to introduce job evaluation are to:

☐ inform staff and agree on how they should be involved;
☐ clarify trade union attitudes, where appropriate;
☐ select bench-mark jobs;
☐ plan the job evaluation programme.

### Informing and involving staff

Staff must obviously be informed about the exercise. It affects them deeply and their help will be required in analysing jobs. The objectives and potential benefits should be discussed and it should be made absolutely clear that it is the jobs which are to be evaluated and not the people carrying out the jobs. The way in which staff are consulted will depend on the company's normal policies for consultation and negotiation.

There is much to be said for involving staff in the job evaluation programme. They can assist in selecting, analysing and evaluating bench-mark jobs. It is becoming increasingly common to set up job evaluation committees to establish and maintain the scheme and to hear appeals.

### Trade union attitudes

If the company is unionized, the form in which consultation and participation takes place will be strongly influenced by union attitudes. Staff unions may insist on being involved in the job evaluation programme, although they might not be prepared to commit themselves in advance to accept its findings. The guidelines on job evaluation issued by one major union are as follows:

1. A preliminary meeting should be held between management and union to establish the need for job evaluation and the method to be used.
2. A job evaluation committee should be set up to define the scheme's terms of reference and the extent and method of communication between management and union.
3. A decision should be made as to which union members should take an active part in the scheme.
4. An appeals procedure should be set up.
5. Revision of the scheme should be carried out at regular intervals in order to identify changes both in individual jobs and in company objectives.

One union has stated very firmly that no job evaluation scheme should be allowed to undermine the traditional role of collective bargaining in determining pay. The function of job evaluation, according to this union, is to deal with the job structure. The pay structure is a matter for negotiation.

Another union produced the following list of reservations about job evaluation:

1. Error-prone management judgements will replace negotiations and weaken the joint determination of wage rates and structures.
2. The wage system arrived at can be rigid, whereas wage systems should be dynamic and part of a continuous process.
3. Job evaluation can emphasize 'the rate for the job' and overlook the importance of 'the rate for the ability to do the job'.
4. At the time of introduction there is the possibility that the new pay structure will involve no more than a rearrangement of the old structure and not include any increase or benefit for employees as a whole.

These guidelines and attitudes are typical. They should be taken into account in any organization where staff are represented by unions or by staff associations with negotiating rights.

### Select bench-mark jobs
In any exercise where there are more than 30 or 40 jobs to be evaluated it is necessary to identify and select a sample of bench-mark jobs which can be used for comparisons inside and outside the organization. The bench-mark jobs should be selected to achieve a representative sample of each of the main levels of jobs in each of the principal occupations, functions and departments.

The size of the sample depends on the number of different jobs to be covered. It is unlikely to be less than about 5 per cent of the total number of employees in the organization and it would be difficult to produce a balanced sample unless at least 25 per cent of the distinct jobs at each level of the organization were included. The higher the proportion the better, bearing in mind the time required to analyse jobs (seldom less than one man day for each job).

### Draw up job evaluation programme
The following points should be covered in a job evaluation programme:

1. *Staffing:* who is responsible for analysis, evaluation, pay comparisons and the design of the salary structure.
2. *Briefing:* of management, staff and unions on the objects of the exercise and how they are to be achieved.
3. *Procedures:* the terms of reference, membership and methods of working of any job evaluation committee.
4. *Training:* the training to be given to full and part-time analysts and evaluators. This is a vital part of the programme. If training is carried out thoroughly, many of the limitations of job evaluation referred to earlier can be minimized.
5. *Job analysis:* the methods to be used in job analysis, the jobs to be covered and the timetable for completing the programme.
6. *Job evaluation:* methods and procedures, including appeals, and the timetable for completing the programme.
7. *Pay comparison:* methods of conducting market rate surveys and the timetable for completing them.

8. *Salary structure:* the methods to be used and the timetable for completing the design.
9. *Communication and negotiation:* the approach to communicating the results of the exercise to staff and for negotiating the structure with unions. It is highly desirable to produce a booklet explaining the scheme.
10. *Maintenance:* the procedures for maintaining the scheme, including regradings and appeals.

## Staffing the job evaluation exercise

Responsibility for the overall co-ordination of the introduction of job evaluation should be in the hands of a senior executive who can then report on progress to the board and advise it on ensuing salary policy developments.

Where there is a developed personnel function the personnel manager will take control. In larger organizations with a salary administration department the executive in charge of this function will normally take responsibility for the introduction and maintenance of the scheme. Provided adequate training is given at the outset, job analysis is an excellent way for new personnel or other company trainees to familiarize themselves with the company and the work done in its different departments. Many large organizations expect their personnel trainees to spend a year or more working on job analysis as an essential addition to their background experience. Analysts will need to be taught the basic skills of interviewing and the elements of a concise descriptive style for writing job descriptions.

The use of analysts either to write job descriptions or check on those written by job holders and their supervisors often greatly improves the quality of job descriptions submitted for evaluation.

Staffing the job evaluation committee is a fairly delicate exercise. A balance has to be struck between the different divisions or departments in the organization and the different levels of staff covered by the scheme. Again the process of job evaluation is an excellent training ground because it exposes committee members to a detailed analysis of the kinds of work done elsewhere in the organization and to an extended period of discussion and negotiation with other staff of different levels. Where trade unions are involved it is usual for them to nominate an agreed number of representatives balanced by management nominees and a mutually acceptable chairman, often the personnel manager.

### Briefing for job evaulation

Effective briefing of all staff involved at the introduction stage of a job evaluation scheme is usually crucial to its success. This can be done at a meeting or series of meetings at which the executive responsible for the introduction of the scheme outlines its aims and emphasizes the long-term benefits for both company and staff of a properly evaluated basis for the new salary structure. A simple question and answer sheet given out at the meeting and covering the common, if basic, questions employees normally ask will also help remove any misgivings that may arise. Some of the most common questions are:

☐ What is job evaluation?
☐ Why does this company need job evaluation?
☐ How will it work?
☐ How does it affect promotion policy?
☐ How will the system be kept up to date?

☐ Does job evaluation mean that everyone whose job is in the same grade gets the same rate of pay?
☐ How does the publication of job grades and salary bands affect confidentiality
☐ How does the system cater for additions to or alterations in jobs?
☐ What happens if an individual disagrees with his grading?
☐ How quickly will appeals on grading be dealt with?
☐ How will the company go about grading new jobs created as the result of change or expansion?

Answers should be tailored to proposed company practice.

### Briefing the job evaluation committee

Much of the success of a job evaluation committee depends on how it is briefed and the way in which an *esprit de corps* is developed. The first meeting should discuss the collective responsibilities of the committee, answer members' questions and perhaps try a few 'practice runs' before formal grading gets under way.

Briefing is usually the chairman's responsibility or that of the personnel manager if he is not chairman. The main points that need to be covered at the first meeting are:

☐ restatement of the purpose of job evaluation;
☐ detailed briefing on every aspect of the company's own scheme;
☐ reminders that the committee has the right to go back to the individual or supervisor for further details and clarification as often as necessary and the right not to evaluate any job until they are completely satisfied that the job description is adequate.

Committee proceedings are usually confidential but minutes summarizing the reasons for grading each job should be kept.

### How much time is involved?

However much the company may want to get the scheme fully implemented it is unwise to rush job evaluation. Even the keenest evaluation committee can only grade a limited number of jobs in a day: eight is probably a realistic average maximum. After this the quality of evaluation tends to drop and more time has to be spent later in checking and assessing the validity of grading. The final review of all the grades allocated to check that no inconsistencies have occurred should be done meticulously and with enough time allowed for re-evaluation if necessary. Extra time devoted at this stage will help reduce appeals to the inevitable few. Careful preparation for the communication of job grades and of the handbooks or other documents describing the scheme and its operation will also assist acceptance.

### Appeals procedure

Even the most committed and highly trained job evaluation committees make mistakes. Add to this 'political' considerations such as managers who expect the people they supervise to be more highly graded as a reflection of departmental status and individuals who feel the importance of their job has been undervalued, and the need for an appeals procedure is inevitable. Unions will want to negotiate the basis for appeals when the introduction of job evaluation is agreed. A fairly typical appeal sequence covering unionized and non-unionized staff would be:

1. Appeal goes to supervisor.
2. Supervisor and employee appeal to grading committee.
3. If the decision is not acceptable:
   (a) unionized staff involve branch officials
   (b) non-unionized staff go through their own grievance procedure to higher authority.
4. The appeal goes to a top management committee for final decision.

### References
1. Brown, W. *The Earnings Conflict*. Heinemann, London, 1973.
2. Jaques, E. *Equitable Payments*. Heinemann, London, 1961.
3. Bowey, A. and Lupton, T. *Job and Pay Comparisons*. Gower Press, London, 1972.

# 15 | Salary Administration

## The fundamentals of salary administration

Salary administration is concerned with deciding how and what staff should be paid and with the techniques and procedures for designing and maintaining salary structures, rewarding staff and exercising salary control.

### Aims of salary administration

The basic aims of salary administration are to attract, retain and motivate staff by developing and maintaining a competitive and equitable salary structure. These aims should be defined more fully to include the control aspects of salary administrations as follows:

☐ to ensure that a sufficient number of suitable staff is attracted to join the undertaking;
☐ to encourage suitable staff to remain with the organization;
☐ to develop and maintain a logical salary structure which achieves equity in the pay for jobs of similar responsibility and consistency in the differentials between jobs in accordance with their relative value;
☐ to ensure that salary levels match market rates;
☐ to keep the salary levels adjusted in line with increases in the cost of living, so far as government anti-inflationary policy allows;
☐ to maintain consistency in methods used to fix and review salary levels and differentials;
☐ to provide for progression within the salary structure in accordance with performance and level of responsibility;
☐ to operate the salary system fairly and convince the staff that the system is fair;
☐ to maintain a flexible salary system which will accommodate changes in the market rates for different skills and in the company's organization structure;
☐ to achieve simplicity in operations as an aid to staff understanding and to minimize administrative effort;
☐ to operate effective systems of controlling salary costs and the administrative procedures required to achieve the above aims at the least cost to the organization.

### Components of salary administration

The starting point of salary administration is the determination of salary levels by job evaluation, as described in chapter 14. Thereafter, salary administration is concerned with:

☐ the design and maintenance of salary structures;
☐ the operation of salary progression systems;

210

☐ the administration and control of salary reviews;
☐ the design and operation of bonus schemes;
☐ the provision of employee benefits and other allowances;
☐ the development of a total remuneration policy.

These components are discussed in turn in this chapter.

## Salary structures

A salary structure consists of a company's salary grades or ranges and its salary levels for single jobs or groups of jobs. The ultimate aim of a job evaluation exercise (as discussed in chapter 14) is to design a salary structure into which jobs can be correctly graded on the basis of an assessment of their relative value to the company. It is also necessary to ensure that salaries are in line with market rates.

In some firms there is no salary structure in the accepted sense of the word, only rates for the jobs, with no defined minimum or maximum salaries. These structures are particularly subject to external and internal pressures which distort the system and result in inequities. The main objectives in designing a salary structure are to provide for internal equity in grading and paying staff and to maintain competitive rates of pay. Neither of those objectives can be achieved if a chaotic set of rates exists which has evolved over the years and is altered at whim or because of a panic reaction to difficulties in recruitment or retention. To avoid the discontent and losses that result from this approach it is necessary to have a formal salary structure which can be one of the following three types or, quite often, a combination of two or more of them:

1. Graded salary structures.
2. Salary progression curves.
3. Rate for age scales.

### Graded salary structures

A typical graded structure consists of a sequence of salary grades or ranges, each of which has a defined minimum and maximum. It is assumed that all the jobs allocated into a grade are broadly of the same value, although actual salaries earned by individuals will depend on their performance or length of service. Across the board cost of living or market rate increases will usually result in an increase to the minima and maxima of each grade. All the jobs in an organization may be covered by the same structure of salary ranges or there may be different structures for different levels or categories of jobs.

BASIC FEATURES OF A SALARY STRUCTURE. The basic features of a salary structure should be as follows:

☐ All jobs are allocated into a salary grade within the structure on the basis of an assessment of their internal and external value to the organization.
☐ Each salary grade consists of a salary grade or range. No individual holding a job in the grade can go beyond the maximum of the salary grade unless he or she is promoted.
☐ Jobs can be re-graded within the structure when it is decided that their value has altered because of a change in responsibilities or a pronounced movement in market rates. In the latter case, it is necessary to note that this is a special market rate for the job imposed by external circumstances and that this does

not imply that jobs previously placed by job evaluation at the same level should also be re-graded.

☐ General increases in the cost of living or in market rates are dealt with by proportionate increases to the minima and maxima of salary grades.

☐ The salary grades are wide enough to provide room to recognize that people in jobs graded at the same level can perform differently and should be rewarded in accordance with their performance. To allow room for progression, the ranges at junior clerical level need be no wider than 15% to 20% of the minima for the grade. At senior levels, however, where there is more scope for improvement and variations in performance, the grades could be between 35% and 60%, although the most typical width is about 50%.

☐ There is a differential between the mid-points of each salary grade which provides adequate scope for rewarding increased responsibility on promotion to the next higher grade but does not create too wide a gap between adjacent grades and thus reduce the amount of flexibility available for grading jobs. This differential should normally be between 15% and 25%, but 20% of the mid-point of the lower grade is a typical differential.

☐ The mid-point of each grade is the 'target salary' for the grade and it is assumed that if there is a fairly steady movement of staff through the grade, the average salary of the staff in the grade will correspond with the target salary.

☐ There is an overlap between salary grades which acknowledges that an experienced person doing a good job can be of more value to the company than a newcomer to a job in the grade above. Overlap, as measured by the proportion of a grade which is simultaneously covered by the next lower grade, can be between 25% and 50%. A large overlap of between 40% and 50% is typical in companies with a wide variety of jobs where a reasonable degree of flexibility is required in grading them. It results in a larger number of grades than is required for a typical promotion ladder within a department, and implies that in some circumstances a grade can be jumped following promotion.

☐ All jobs allocated into a salary grade are assumed to be broadly of the same level. In other words, they normally have the same minimum and maximum rates which correspond with the grade boundaries.

☐ Progression within a grade depends on the performance of the individual. It would generally be assumed that all fully competent individuals in any jobs in a grade would eventually reach the normal maximum for a grade, if they are not promoted out of it. Less competent individuals may stop progressing at some point below the grade maximum. In some circumstances, provision may be made for exceptional individuals to receive more than the grade maximum if there are no immediate opportunities for promotion but the company wishes to retain their services and maintain their motivation.

☐ The number of salary grades or ranges will depend on, (i) the number of distinct levels of jobs in the hierarchy, (ii) the width of each salary grade, (iii) the extent of the overlap, if any, between grades and (iv) the salary levels appropriate for the most senior and most junior jobs − this gives the overall range of salaries within which the individual salary grades have to be fitted. A structure designed according to the principles defined above and extending from £3,000 to £23,000 would have ten grades, which is fairly typical in large organizations.

MAKE-UP OF A SALARY GRADE. A basic principle of a salary structure is that individuals advance through the structure either by progressing within the salary grade for the job as they improve their performance, or by promotion.

In the simplest structure, people move more or less steadily from the entry point of the grade (which might be above the minimum if they have already gained relevant experience elsewhere or within the firm) to the upper limit, unless they move to a higher grade. It is possible, however, to distinguish three stages into which this progression is divided, and for salary administration purposes it is helpful to divide the grade into three zones which correspond to these stages.

The three zones are:

1. *The learning zone,* which covers the period when a person is on his 'learning curve', familiarizing himself with the knowledge and skills required if he is to become fully competent. The length of time to go through this zone will vary according to the individual's experience, competence and ability to learn. It would be accepted that someone might enter the range at any point in this zone, from bottom to top, depending on experience.

2. *The qualified zone,* which covers the period when the job holder continues to increase his capacity to do the work and to improve his performance. The minimum salary in this zone should be the market rate for the job, so far as this can be ascertained, the assumption being that the market rate is the salary level required to attract a competent individual from another job to join the company. The mid-point in this zone, which is also the mid-point of the grade, is the salary level which all competent employees would be expected to achieve. This is above the market rate in order to retain these individuals. An employee who is no more than competent could stop at this point, but most would continue to advance until they reach the top of the qualified zone, which would be regarded as the normal maximum for the job. Many such employees would in any case be promoted to a higher grade before they reach the upper limit of this zone.

3. *The premium zone,* which is reserved for those employees, especially in the higher grade jobs, who achieve exceptional results but for whom suitable promotion opportunities do not exist. This zone enables outstanding staff to be given additional rewards and encouragement. In some salary structures, the published salary grades for each job only cover the learning and qualified zones, the premium zone being reserved for use in special cases. Progression through that zone would not be regarded as normal by management or staff.

A 50% salary grade made up according to these principles is illustrated in figure 15.1.

RELATIONSHIPS BETWEEN GRADES. Figure 15.2 illustrates the relationships between grades if a differential of 20% is established between them. Promotion could take place between grades one and two or between grades one and three. In the former case, the existence of the new job in the next higher grade implies some overlap in the knowledge and skills required and it might be appropriate to promote someone to the starting point of the qualified zone, or even in exceptional cases, into the qualified zone, as long as there is still reasonable scope for salary progression within the grade. A jump in grades implies that the promoted employee would have quite a lot to learn in his new job and is likely to start at the minimum salary, which still allows a reasonable promotion increase even if he is some way through the qualified zone in the lower grade. An example of a

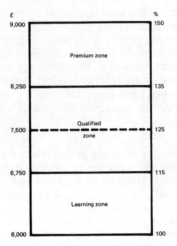

**Figure 15.1 Make-up of a salary range**

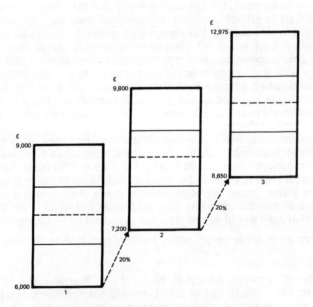

**Figure 15.2 Relationships between grades**

a salary structure designed in accordance with these principles is shown in figure 15.3.

### Designing the salary structure
The simplest and therefore the best way to design a salary structure is to take the following steps:

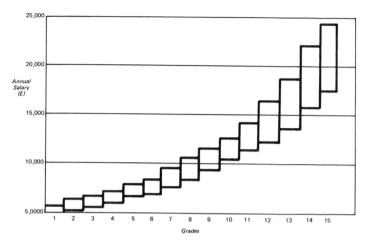

**Figure 15.3 Salary structure**

*Step 1:* Establish by market rate surveys and studies of existing structures and differentials the salary levels of the most senior and most junior jobs to be covered by the structure.

*Step 2:* Draw up a salary grade structure between the upper and lower limits, as established in step 1, according to policies for differentials, the width of salary grades and the size of overlap between grades.

*Step 3:* Conduct a job evaluation exercise, preferably by means of a simple ranking scheme, although this could be refined by using paired comparisons.

*Step 4:* Obtain market rate data, bearing in mind that there is likely to be a range of market rates rather than a precise figure.

*Step 5:* Slot the jobs into the grade structure in accordance with the results of both the job evaluations and the market rate surveys. It is here that judgement is required. While some decisions on grades will be obvious, others will be more difficult. If in doubt, re-evaluate the borderline cases to help make the final marginal decision. One advantage of an overlapping structure is that such decisions are less critical.

**Salary progression curves**
Salary progression curves, sometimes called maturity curves or career curves, aim to link increases in salary over a fairly long period to increased maturity or experience. They are best used for professional, scientific or other highly qualified staff who are carrying out work in which their contribution is almost entirely related to their professional capacity rather than to a more or less fixed set of duties that enable their job to be firmly placed in a rigid hierarchy.

Progression curves are mostly used for professional or scientific staff whose starting salary is linked to the market rate for their degree or to a professional qualification. The system assumes that they will develop within their discipline at some standard rate or rates as a result of their experience.

A single progression curve is illustrated in figure 15.4. This is almost a rate for age curve except that progression is not inevitable — the curve is only a guideline

215

and some may advance more rapidly than others. Another difference is that progression curves are, or should be, determined by reference to a salary survey which indicates the salaries people carrying out professional or scientific work can expect to get at certain ages. A scatter-graph of market rates, as shown in figure 15.5 can indicate the appropriate rate of progression if a 'line of best fit' is drawn which represents the trend between the two variables of salary and age.

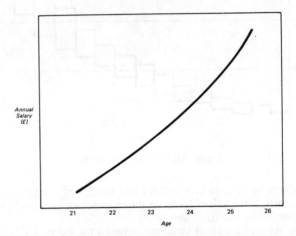

**Figure 15.4 Salary progression curve**

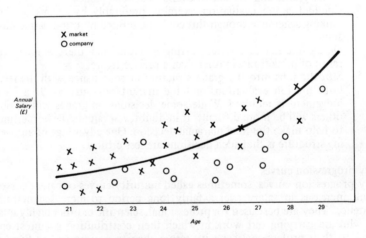

**Figure 15.5 Salary survey and progression curve**

More than one rate of progression may be provided where it is felt that there should be some scope to reward and encourage individuals according to their performance and potential. The approach is illustrated in figure 15.6 where there are three different starting rates, A, B and C, which might be related to level of qualification; for example, post-graduate qualification, first or upper second degrees, lower second or pass degree. Thereafter, the curves A, B and C represent the expected rate at which an individual with the relevant starting qualifications may be presumed to progress with increased experience. Of course, the initial qualification does not guarantee that performance will be maintained at the same level. People with lower qualifications may rapidly catch up or overtake those with higher qualifications and would be moved towards or on to a higher scale than that on which they started.

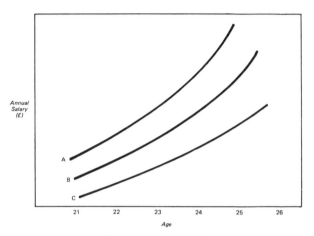

**Figure 15.6 Graded progression curves**

A progression curve system designed along these lines must be used flexibly or it will defeat its purpose. The aim is to allow plenty of scope to advance people according to their contribution. The curves should only be used as guidelines to assist in salary planning — ensuring that individuals advance in salary at a rate appropriate to their performance and potential.

### Rate for age
A rate for age system is an incremental scale in which a specific rate of pay or a defined pay bracket is linked to each age for staff in certain jobs. Rate for age scales are usually reserved for young employees under training or for junior clerical or laboratory staff carrying out routine work. The assumption behind rate for age scales is that the staff are on a learning curve which means that their value to the company is directly linked to increased experience and maturity.

The simplest structure consists of one rate for each age as shown in figure 15.7.

A more complex structure to accommodate three different job grades is shown in figure 15.8.

It may be thought desirable to allow some scope for merit at each age and figure 15.9 shows how merit can be catered for in a rate for age scale.

Rate for age scales of the basic type illustrated in figure 15.7 are inflexible but they may have to be used because they are a tradition in the local labour market and with a highly mobile form of labour it is essential to keep pace with market rates. Their great advantage is that they are easy to administer — invidious decisions about the relative merit of people under training do not have to be

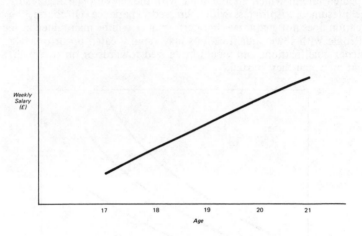

**Figure 15.7 Rate for age structure**

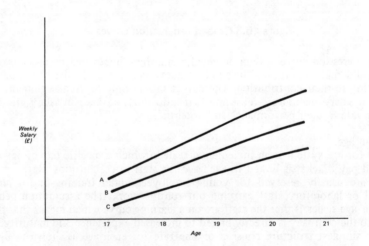

**Figure 15.8 Rate for age structure for three job grades**

made and the scales achieve complete equity. They may be worth retaining for these reasons, but there is a lot to be said for relating pay to age *and* performance as in figure 15.9, rather than to the arbitrary criterion of age.

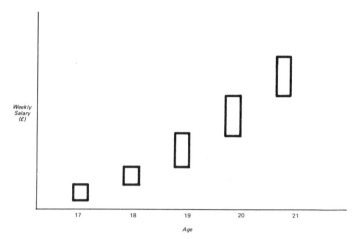

Weekly
Salary
(£)

17  18  19  20  21

Age

**Figure 15.9 Rate for age structure with merit bands**

## Salary progression

Salary progression policies and procedures relate increases in salary to merit, as shown by current and recent performance, as well as providing motivation for improved performance in the future, or encouragement for those with high potential to remain within the company. The aim should be to relate such rewards to performance consistently and equitably while retaining an adequate degree of control over salary costs.

### Salary progression procedures
The essential features of a systematic procedure for salary progression are as follows:

☐ The salary ranges are divided into defined areas or zones, as described earlier in this chapter, through which an individual progresses.
☐ Incremental systems, as described below, exist which indicate the rates at which individuals can progress through the various zones according to merit or experience.
☐ Guidelines exist for determining merit increments and planning salary progression. These are also discussed below.

### Incremental systems
Incremental systems vary from rigid procedures with fixed and predetermined movements through a scale related to age, service in the company or service in the job, to flexible systems where management exercises complete discretion over the award and size of increments without any guidelines. Between the two extremes there is a middle ground of semi-flexible systems.

The main types of systems are:

1. *Fixed scales with automatic progression* where individuals move through jobs or grades by predetermined steps related to age or service; these could be rate for age scales. They are widely used in the British Civil Service and other parts

219

of the public sector where there is similar emphasis on service and experience. Fixed scales are criticized because they do not give enough incentive to effort and the improvement of performance – promotion might only be an award in the longer term, if at all. They are defended because they can be operated with complete impartiality – many people, especially civil servants, question the possibility of determining a fair relationship between merit and reward where the only method of measurement is the subjective opinion of someone's boss.

2. *Fixed scales with limited flexibility* where it is possible to give double or even triple increments to high flyers and withhold increments for poor performers.
3. *Semi-fixed scales* which allow automatic progression to a 'merit bar' at which progression for some people may stop while others can advance at different rates according to performance.
4. *Fixed parallel scales* which allow for the exercise of more managerial discretion by providing different patterns of incremental progression for different levels of performance, as shown in figure 15.10.

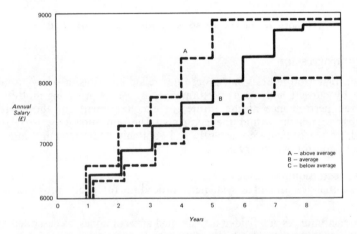

**Figure 15.10 Incremental system with fixed parallel scale**

5. *Variable progression with guidelines* where there are no fixed incremental points, but managers are given more or less mandatory instructions on how they should exercise their discretion. The minimum guidelines in this system may consist of the annual increments that can be awarded for different levels of performance. These may be extended in more rigid systems to give the proportion of staff who should receive a given increment.
6. *Variable progression in a range without guidelines* where management discretion in the award of increments and the determination of their size tends to be restricted only by the maximum of the salary range and the budget they are allowed for salary increases.

The choice of approach will depend largely on the organization climate and managerial style of the company. A bureaucratic or mechanistic organization might believe in strict control over managerial judgements by using a fixed or semi-fixed system. If such an organization decided to recognize the need to

220

reward and encourage good performance it might adopt a variable progression system but impose very strict controls on the amount and the distribution of merit awards. On the other hand, a less autocratic organization, which accepts that line managers should have scope to exercise discretion, would adopt a variable progression system incorporating only the broadest of guidelines. The latter approach is to be preferred in any organization which has to operate flexibly, but it is obviously necessary to exercise control over the amount of the increments, and some guidance on distribution may still be required to reduce inequities between departments (methods of exercising control are discussed later in this chapter).

### Salary planning

The aim of salary planning is to ensure that individuals are correctly placed in their salary range in relation to their performance and that they move through and between salary grades at a rate appropriate to their progress and potential. Most salary planning decisions are short term ones in that they are concerned with deciding on the next increment to be paid because of merit or promotion. Longer term salary plans are closely linked with career planning procedures (see chapter 9), and the advantage of a formal salary structure is that it is possible to forecast future salary progression in the event of promotion.

Salary planning in the short term can be carried out by means of a variable increment system with guidelines which show the various rates at which people can progress through a zoned salary range. It is then possible to take a view on the likely or desirable rate at which someone's salary should advance by reference to an assessment of performance and an estimate of potential.

There are no fixed principles for doing this. The approach should be, first, to compare what an individual is being paid with what his level of performance suggests he should be paid. This will indicate what his immediate increase should be, although if his salary is considerably below what he should be getting it may be necessary to phase his increases. Secondly, consideration should be given to his potential and the salary progression that would be appropriate if he is to be given further encouragement to develop and remain with the company. There is no question of predetermining future increases at this stage, but it may be necessary to adjust the current increase to which he would normally be entitled. This could be higher than usual if it is thought that potential should be recognized now before it is too late and the individual has left the company. It could be lower than usual if it is felt that the increments to which he is entitled in his present salary range should be spread over an extra year or two so that he does not come to a grinding halt too soon.

Salary planning is greatly assisted if salary progression curves can be used to compare where the individual has got to with the standard curves and with his contemporaries. In the simplified example in figure 15.11 the fact that Mr Y has fallen behind is clearly revealed and steps can be taken to find out if this is deserved or whether he should be given a higher increment or increments to restore him to his rightful place.

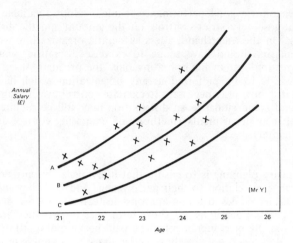

Figure 15.11 Progression curves and salary planning

## Salary administration procedures

Salary administration procedures are concerned with the implementation and control of salary policies and with the control of salary costs against budgets. Control is an essential element of salary administration, and this section will therefore begin with a general discussion of the desirable features of a control system. It will then deal more specifically with the following procedures:

☐ salary budgets
☐ cost of living or general reviews of salary levels
☐ individual salary reviews
☐ fixing salary levels on joining the company or on promotion.

### Desirable features of control

To achieve effective salary control the salary administration procedures should have the following features:

1. Defined ranges with minima and maxima to which all jobs are allocated on the basis of their value, with all employees paid within the ranges for the jobs performed.
2. Defined methods of progress within the range based on specific criteria.
3. A detailed salary budget based on the number of staff required to carry out the forecast volume of work; forecast salary levels taking into account the effects of general and incremental increases; forecasts of promotions and promotional increases and numbers joining and leaving the organization; and forecasts of the likely effect on salary costs of changes in the numbers employed and of differences between the salary levels of those joining or leaving.
4. Clear statements of the degree of authority at each management level to award or to confirm increments with arrangements for authorizing proposed salary changes and checking their consistency with policy.
5. Clear salary review guidelines defining the limit to which the pay-roll costs of

each department can increase as a result of merit awards, together with other instructions on, for example, the maximum awards that can be given and the distribution of awards according to performance and between the population in each salary grade.

6. Procedures for auditing increases and salary levels to ensure that they are in accordance with salary policies, and for monitoring actual salary costs against budgeted costs.

## Salary budget

A salary budget is a statement in quantitative and usually financial terms of the planned allocation and use of resources to meet the operational needs of the company. All budgets are based on a planned level of activity or volume of output which determines the resources required. In the case of the salary budget, the forecast levels of activity indicate the number of different categories of staff that are needed for the budget period. The annual salary budget is a product of the numbers of staff to be employed and the rates at which they will be paid.

The salary budget has to take account of the financial resources available to the company. This will affect the ability to pay general or individual merit increases, or the numbers employed, or both. Salary budgets in large organizations are prepared by departmental managers in accordance with instructions issued by the accounts department. They are often based on current salary levels and are inflated at a later stage when decisions are made about how much money can be allocated for individual and general salary increases. An example of a budget form is shown in figure 15.12.

| Salary budget for year ending . . . . | | | | | | | | | |
|---|---|---|---|---|---|---|---|---|---|
| Department: | | | Proposed by: | | | Approved by: | | | |
| Actual — previous year........... | | | | Forecast — forthcoming year.......... | | | | | |
| No. | Salary cost | Overtime cost | Total cost | Category of staff | No. | Salary cost | Overtime cost | Total cost | Increase or decrease in total cost |
| | | | | Managers | | | | | |
| | | | | Supervisors | | | | | |
| | | | | Clerical staff | | | | | |
| | | | | Temporary staff | | | | | |
| | | | | Total | | | | | |
| Reasons for forecast increase/decrease over previous year: | | | | | | | | | |

**Figure 15.12 Salary budget form**

Historical control over salary costs is achieved by comparing budgeted costs with actuals, analysing any variances, and deciding on corrective action; which could take the form of a reduction in manning levels or in the budget for merit increases if salary costs are over the budget. A cost comparison form is illustrated in figure 15.13.

| Department | | | | COST COMPARISON STATEMENT | | | Quarter ending: | | |
|---|---|---|---|---|---|---|---|---|---|
| This quarter | | | | Category of staff | Year to date | | Forecast for year | | |
| Number | | Pay-roll cost | | | Pay-roll cost | | Pay-roll cost | | |
| Actual | Variance | Actual | Variance | | Actual | Variance | Actual | Variance | |
| | | | | Managers | | | | | |
| | | | | Supervisors | | | | | |
| | | | | Clerical staff | | | | | |
| | | | | Temporary staff | | | | | |
| | | | | Total | | | | | |
| Reasons for variance and proposed actions: | | | | | | | | | |

**Figure 15.13 Salary cost comparison form**

But backward looking controls are not enough. It is also necessary to ensure that the salary policies and guidelines laid down by management are implemented, and the procedures required for this purpose are described below.

### General salary reviews

General salary reviews take place when it is necessary to increase all or most salaries in response to increases in the cost of living or in market rates, or as a result of settlements affecting either staff or hourly paid employees.

In an inflationary period, general reviews are at least an annual event, government regulations permitting, and external pressures may mean that they have to take place at different times of the year to individual merit reviews. There is no reason why they should be separated, except that when general and merit reviews are combined it may be easier to control costs by cutting down on merit increases if a large cost of living increase has to be given. In fact, in times of galloping inflation, many companies with cash flow problems have had to reconcile themselves to eliminating merit payments in order to finance general increases.

Companies without staff unions who operate a secret salary policy often try to differentiate between a general and a merit increase. Their staff receive their annual award and do not know how much is general or how much is particular to them. Companies pursue secrecy in salary policies because it enables them to exercise complete control until, that is, the staff lose patience and move into the ever-welcoming arms of the trade unions. Companies are frightened of divulging their salary structure or review policies to staff because they feel that this may open the door to recognition claims and pay negotiations. The other reason for not publishing salary scales, which is not admitted to so freely, is that the structure is so illogical that it would be impossible to explain or to justify it to the staff.

It is difficult to reconcile this point of view, especially with regard to merit increments, with the equally prevalent view that money is the great motivator. How can money motivate effectively if everyone is kept in the dark about the relationship between effort and reward?

The best approach is to distinguish between general and individual increases, even if they are paid at the same time. The general increase is paid to everyone, although some companies reserve the right to withhold general increases or give smaller increments to staff whose performance is below average or overpaid. At the same time, the salary brackets are adjusted, usually at both ends, by the same amount. It is equally important to keep individuals informed of how they stand in the salary structure and the rewards they are getting or can obtain.

### Individual salary reviews

The purpose of an individual salary review is to decide on the merit increments that should be given to staff. The usual practice is to have one annual review for all staff, with the possibility of a half-yearly review for younger staff with high potential who need encouragement more than once a year. Some companies phase increases throughout the year on birthdays or on the anniversary of staff joining the company. This, they say, enables more individual attention to be paid to staff and removes the emotional atmosphere that surrounds the annual review. But phased reviews are more difficult to administer and control except where a fixed increment system is in use, and most organizations prefer one or two fixed dates for a review. Individual salary reviews require the preparation of budgets and guidelines for management.

SALARY REVIEW BUDGET. The best way of planning and controlling the individual or merit review is to determine the increase to the pay-roll that can be allocated for merit payments. The review budget can then be expressed as, say, 50% of pay-roll costs, and this is the limit given to each manager for increasing the pay-roll. The following factors influence the size of the budget:

☐ The salary policies of the company on the rates at which staff of different levels of ability should progress through their salary ranges.
☐ The extent to which the actual salaries in each grade differ from the target salary, which is usually the mid-point in the grade and, ideally, should correspond to the average salaries of the job holders in the grade. The information used for this purpose is the compa-ratio as described below.
☐ The potential effect of what is termed salary attrition on average salaries over the year. Attrition is the reduction in salary costs which can take place over a period of time as a result of staff joining the company at a lower salary than those who leave. This process is also discussed below.
☐ The amount the company thinks it can afford to pay on the basis of forecasts of revenue, profits and pay-roll costs and an analysis of the effects of salary attrition on costs.
☐ The effect of government regulations on pay increases.

*Compa-Ratios.* A compa-ratio (short for comparative ratio) is a measure of the extent to which the average salaries in a grade deviate from the target salary. It is used to compare actual averages with the target salary to indicate the extent to which salary levels are high or low, and thus suggest where action may have to be taken to limit increases or to adopt a more generous policy. The formula for calculating a compa-ratio is:

$$\frac{\text{Average of all salaries in the grade}}{\text{Mid-point of the salary range}} \times 100$$

A compa-ratio of 100 would indicate that the average salary is aligned to the mid-point of the salary grade and that no corrective steps need to be taken. An average salary of £4800 compared with a mid-point of £6000 would produce a compa-ratio of 80 and would indicate the need to investigate why average salaries were low and possibly no longer competitive. This could have arisen because of an influx of new staff or those promoted into a salary grade.

A compa-ratio of 120 arising if average salaries were £7200 in a grade where the mid-point was £6000 would suggest either there were a lot of long-service staff in the grade(which could be a cause of congratulation|or alarm)|or that staff were being overpaid and increases needed to be modified. Compa-ratio analysis can therefore reveal a situation where earnings drift has taken place — the natural but not necessarily appropriate tendency for salaries to drift towards the upper range or top of a salary range irrespective of the merits of the individuals concerned.

Information on compa-ratios and changes in the average salaries can be recorded on a form such as the one illustrated in figure 15.14 and used for annual comparisons and to provide guidance on the likely effects of salary attrition.

| | | Number in grade | | Average salary | | Compa-ratio | |
|---|---|---|---|---|---|---|---|
| Grade | Salary range | Last year | This year | Last year | This year | Last year | This year |
| | | | | | | | |
| | | | | | | | |
| | | | | | | | |
| | | | | | | | |
| | | | | | | | |
| | | | | | | | |

**Figure 15.14 Compa-ratio summary form**

*Salary Attrition.* Attrition to the costs of awarding merit increments takes place when the average salary of leavers in a company exceeds the average salary of joiners. This is the normal situation and it means that an increase in the salary bill of, say, 3% at the beginning of a year could be steadily eroded during the year as a result of the inflows and outflows of staff.

In practice, the difference between the salaries of leavers and joiners is not likely to correspond exactly with the cost of the merit increase. But if there are movements in and out of a company or a salary grade and if the salaries of leavers are higher than joiners, which is highly probable, then there must be some attrition.

The importance of attrition for salary control purposes is that it is possible to assume that it will finance the cost of merit increases wholly or in part during the year. Alternatively, it can be assumed that merit increases in a fixed incremental system, where people are likely to be moving steadily into, out of and through grades, are not inflationary.

Some companies have developed attrition models which they use to determine in advance the cost of merit awards. Other companies adopt the less sophisticated approach of calculating attrition as the residual figure which remains after general and merit increases, expressed as a percentage of pay-roll, have been subtracted from the percentage increase in average salaries.

SALARY REVIEW GUIDELINES. Salary review guidelines are necessary to inform managers of what they can pay and how they should distribute it amongst their staff. The aim should be to give managers the maximum amount of authority to determine merit increments within a budget as long as this freedom does not result in unacceptable inconsistencies in the awards given to staff. It has to be faced that any merit review system which relates rewards to performance and not to a time-scale will result in inconsistencies. Even if rigid guidelines are laid down on the amount and distribution of awards, the ultimate decision on who gets what will depend on the largely subjective judgement of someone. It is best, however, for this judgement to be exercised by people in direct charge of staff rather than by remote control.

The various types of guidelines available are:

1. *Overall cost guidelines* where a budget of, say, 4% of pay-roll is imposed for merit reviews. This is the essential guideline and managers may be left to distribute the pool as they please, or they may be subjected to various degrees of control on the grounds that they might otherwise make eccentric awards such as giving everyone exactly the same small amount or giving a limited number of people excessively high increases.
2. *Guidelines on maximum and minimum increases* where managers are told that they cannot give an increase of more than, say, 10% or less than, say, 3% on the grounds that too high an increase could produce inequities and too low an increase is meaningless — 3% or 4% is generally regarded as the minimum worthwhile increase. These limiting guidelines are not too restrictive and can easily be added to the basic budget figure to produce a reasonable balance between excessive control and excessive freedom.
3. *Guidelines on the relationship between performance and reward* where it is laid down that awards should be related to an overall assessment of performance on a scale like this:

| Assessment | Increment % |
|---|---|
| A — outstanding | 9 – 10 |
| B — very satisfactory | 7 – 8 |
| C — satisfactory | 4 – 6 |
| D — barely satisfactory | 3* |
| E — unsatisfactory | 0 |

* but only if there is hope of improvement and the individual needs encouragement.

The problem with this approach is that the assessments are entirely subjective. There will be no common standards of judgement between departments and the distribution of awards will be as inconsistent as ever. All that such guidelines can do is to provide some indication to managers about how they might distribute the pool of money made available to them amongst their staff.

4. *Guidelines on the distribution of increments* where, in an attempt to over-come the varying standards of judgement leading to an 'all my geese are swans' approach to rewarding staff, managers are required to conform to a forced distribution of merit increases. For example, they are not allowed to give an increase of 9% to more than 10% of their staff. The distribution scale may be related to the guidelines on increments like this:

| Assessment | Increment % | Distribution % |
| --- | --- | --- |
| A – outstanding | 9 – 10 | 10 |
| B – very satisfactory | 7 – 8 | 20 |
| C – satisfactory | 4 – 6 | 40 |
| D – barely satisfactory | 3 | 20 |
| E – unsatisfactory | 0 | 10 |

In this example a normal distribution is followed, but this may be rejected, quite rightly, by managers as an entirely arbitrary device. They will claim that their departments are exceptional and will refuse to accept any contention that the abilities of their staff conform to the normal distribution of the population as a whole. They will claim, and they might even be right, that they have trained and developed a body of exceptional men and women and that they have taken great care both to avoid selecting duds and to remove anyone who has slipped through the net. Distributions can, of course, be altered to conform to this viewpoint by increasing the proportion of higher increments, thus conceding that the normal distribution of abilities does not apply. But this is still an entirely arbitrary process.

5. *Guidelines on rates of progression* where managers are helped to plan salary progression by being given an indication of the number of years it should take staff at different levels of performance to reach the top of the grade and, in a zoned salary range, the limits within the range which can be reached according to their performance. For example:

| Assessment | Limit in grade | Years to limit from grade minimum |
| --- | --- | --- |
| A | Grade maximum | 7 – 8 |
| B | Qualified zone maximum | 7 – 8 |
| C | Mid-point | 8 – 9 |
| D | Learning zone maximum | 5 or more |
| E | Not normally retained | – |

Again, such guidelines may be helpful in salary planning but it would be wrong to apply them too rigidly.

There is a danger of going too far with guidelines and imposing so much rigidity on the system that it collapses under the strain. There is a limit to the extent to which it is appropriate or possible to direct increments in any situation where decisions are not all made centrally. Constraints in the form of budgets and upper and lower limits can and should be applied, but the other guidelines on amounts and distribution should never be used as mandatory controls. They can be helpful in showing managers how the system can work but as examples only.

The best form of guideline, other than the essential budget limits, is the briefing and training that should be given to managers who are recommending increments. Thereafter, guidance should be based on an analysis of recommendations from the centre so that managers who adopt a seemingly eccentric approach can be asked to justify it. If they cannot, they must be persuaded to think again and to do better next time.

CONTROL INFORMATION. In a smaller or even medium sized organization, control over the implementation of individual salary reviews is easily achieved by checking through recommendations and ensuring that they appear to be reasonable and that the total increase to the pay-roll does not exceed the budget.

In a larger organization it may be advisable to exercise control by means of a salary review form for each department such as the one illustrated in figure 15.15.

Overall control can be maintained quite simply by requiring each department to produce a summary of the individual recommendations which shows the percentage increase to the pay-roll and the distribution of merit awards of different amounts. A more elaborate approach, suitable only for organizations which want to exercise close central control, is to use a summary sheet showing details of average salaries and increments in each grade as illustrated in figure 15.16.

## Procedures for grading jobs
The procedures for grading or re-grading jobs should lay down that new jobs or jobs where the responsibilities have changed can only be graded or re-graded when a job evaluation has taken place. This should require the preparation of job descriptions which can be matched with other jobs and grade definitions, or can be used as a basis for an analytical job evaluation.

Managers who wish to re-grade a job or increase a salary because of market rate pressures or because a member of staff is 'holding a pistol at their heads' by threatening to leave for a higher salary, should be required to produce evidence to support their case. The evidence should be positive. It is not enough to refer to one or two carefully selected advertisements. And it is always dangerous to succumb to blackmail, however valuable the individual appears to be. Panic measures should be avoided by keeping a careful watch on market rate trends and taking any necessary action in good time.

## Fixing salaries on appointment or promotion
Control over starting salaries should be exercised by providing guidelines on the policies to be followed and by defining who has the authority to approve salaries. The guidelines should state that the normal practice is to start inexperienced staff at the bottom of the range, but salaries up to, say, 15% above the minimum can be offered if this would not cause embarrassment by appointing an outsider at a higher salary than existing staff. Appointments at a salary above this level would only be made with the approval of a higher authority.

Promotions should be dealt with as they arise rather than being left to the annual review. The increase should be meaningful, say, 10% or more, and the starting point in the new salary grade should provide adequate scope to reward performance in the new job. Ideally, therefore, the starting point should not be

| FUNCTION/DEPARTMENT | | | | | PROPOSED BY | | | | DATE | | APPROVED BY | | | DATE | |
|---|---|---|---|---|---|---|---|---|---|---|---|---|---|---|---|
| Name | Job title | Date | | | Job grade | Last increase | | | Present salary | Assessment (2) | Proposed increase | | Approved increase | | Comments |
| | | of birth | of joining present job | started present job | | Amount | Date | Reason (1) | | | Amount | New salary | Amount | New salary | |
| (1) | (2) | (3) | (4) | (5) | (6) | (7) | (8) | (9) | (10) | (11) | (12) | (13) | (14) | (15) | (16) |
| | | | | | | | | | | | | | | | |
| Total number | | | | | | | Total | | | Totals | | | | | |

NOTES

1. Reasons for last increase:
   M = merit
   P = promotion

2. Assessment
   A — Outstanding
   B — Very satisfactory
   C — Satisfactory
   D — Barely satisfactory
   E — Unsatisfactory

Figure 15.15 Individual salary review form

DEPARTMENT    PROPOSED BY    DATE    APPROVED BY    DATE

| Grade | Present | | Proposed | | | | | | | | | | | |
| | No. in grade | Salary bill £ | Average salary £ | Distribution of merit increments (number) | | | Number not receiving increment | | | Distribution in grade (number) | | | Salary bill £ | Average salary £ | % Increase |
| | | | | A | B | C | Assessed D/E | On maximum | On mid-point | Premium zone | Qualified zone | Learning zone | | | |
| | (1) | (2) | (3) | (4) | (5) | (6) | (7) | (8) | (9) | (10) | (11) | (12) | (13) | (14) | (15) |
| 1 | | | | | | | | | | | | | | | |
| 2 | | | | | | | | | | | | | | | |
| 3 | | | | | | | | | | | | | | | |
| 4 | | | | | | | | | | | | | | | |
| 5 | | | | | | | | | | | | | | | |
| 6 | | | | | | | | | | | | | | | |
| 7 | | | | | | | | | | | | | | | |
| 8 | | | | | | | | | | | | | | | |
| 9 | | | | | | | | | | | | | | | |
| 10 | | | | | | | | | | | | | | | |
| 11 | | | | | | | | | | | | | | | |
| 12 | | | | | | | | | | | | | | | |
| 13 | | | | | | | | | | | | | | | |
| 14 | | | | | | | | | | | | | | | |
| 15 | | | | | | | | | | | | | | | |
| 16 | | | | | | | | | | | | | | | |
| 17 | | | | | | | | | | | | | | | |
| 18 | | | | | | | | | | | | | | | |
| Total | | | | | | | | | | | | | | | |
| Approved total | | | | | | | | | | | | | | | |

Figure 15.16 Salary review summary sheet

231

higher than 15% or so above the minimum rate for the grade.

## Salary administration problems

Salary structures, job evaluation schemes, progression policies and salary review procedures all aim to make salary administration a scientific process. But they cannot entirely succeed. Salary administration is as much art as science and, inevitably, there are problems which can only be solved by exercising judgement in the light of circumstances. Some of the more typical problems are discussed below.

### Market rates

The policy may be to match market rates, but the application of this policy can produce a number of practical difficulties. First, there is the problem of finding out what the market rate is. For some specialized jobs there may be no market rates at all; for others, the range of market rates may be so large that it is impossible to fix a firm rate for comparison purposes. Secondly, there are the problems that result from attempting to reconcile market rate pressures with the need to preserve equity and appropriate differentials within the firm. A job grade structure may have been carefully designed as a result of a job evaluation exercise, but the salaries attached to the job grades must reflect market rates — where they exist. In order to attract and retain particular categories of staff who are in short supply it may be necessary to offer them salaries which place them in a higher salary bracket than would be justified on the basis of the internal evaluation alone. This can seriously upset differentials and result in frustration and dissatisfaction amongst those who see their colleagues earning more for doing a job which they feel is no more important than their own.

A similar situation arises when salary levels generally lag behind increases in market rates. This results in staff being recruited into the same grade as those colleagues in similar jobs, but at a higher salary. It is often easier for managers to offer higher starting salaries than to get the administration to accept that the salaries of existing staff should keep pace with market rates. This situation is endemic when government anti-inflation measures succeed in controlling pay increases within a firm but fail to control the salaries offered to individual recruits.

It is easy to say that internal equity considerations should prevail, but it is difficult to apply them in practice. Companies may vigorously pursue policies of promotion from within but they will be forced to recruit from outside sometimes. If the market, and therefore the company, are subject to rapid change there will be a recurring need to compete for talent on the open market. Where the situation is fluid it is even more difficult to maintain a completely equitable salary structure. It has to be accepted that some people will be paid more because they cannot be obtained or held otherwise. But these jobs should be noted as exceptions and, as it were, starred in the salary structure to show that they are being paid more than the internally equitable rate. This 'red-circling' process, as it is sometimes called, ensures that adjustments can later be made to the rates for the job if the market rates are no longer inflated. This may mean that some existing staff are overpaid but these anomalies should disappear in time if they are noted and salary increments adjusted accordingly.

To avoid the danger of bringing in staff at a higher salary than existing employees it is necessary to carry out a regular audit of market rates and adjust internal structures accordingly. The problem here is that this can be an expensive process, and a management decision would have to be made on whether the benefits of overcoming the dissatisfaction caused by the situation justify the costs.

### Erosion of the salary structure

Appropriate differentials can be established by job evaluation but they can easily be eroded, either because of market rate pressures or because of what may be termed 'grade drift' — the tendency for upgradings to take place as a means of providing more money, even where there has been no increase in responsibilities.

Erosion is best controlled by establishing procedures for grading and re-grading jobs which require an analysis and evaluation to take place before the change is authorized. It is essential, of course, to monitor and control the implementation of the procedures.

### Squeezed differentials

In many organizations the differentials between first line supervisors and the people they supervise are being continuously squeezed, either because employees of the rank and file are benefiting from a negotiated increase which is not extended to their supervisors, or because supervisors are not paid overtime or do not receive bonus earnings.

This sort of pressure from below can result in considerable dissatisfaction amongst supervision. It can only be dealt with by making frequent comparisons of earnings and rates of pay. The aim should be to maintain a reasonable differential of, say, 20% between the mid-point of the salary range for supervisors and the average earnings, including normal overtime, of the employees they supervise. Less experienced supervisors may find that the earnings of some operators receiving exceptionally high bonuses or working long hours surpass their own, but this has to be accepted on the grounds that the high pay of the operators is a reflection of their extra efforts and longer working hours. It is possible to reduce these differential problems in some circumstances by paying supervisors for overtime, but the practice is not encouraged in most companies, especially where supervisors can control the amount of overtime worked.

The biggest danger of pressure from below is that it sets off a chain reaction which affects all other salary brackets. But if the salary levels for senior staff can be reviewed regularly to counter the effect of inflation and market rate increases, it is unlikely that they will get seriously out of line with the pay of hourly paid workers or junior clerical staff. What should be avoided are panic measures, introduced because of a temporary surge in operators' pay arising from high bonus earnings or overtime.

Differentials can also be squeezed higher up the scale if the salaries of senior management are insufficiently high to provide head room. The aim should be to ensure that the span of salary levels between the lowest grade of staff and the chief executive is sufficiently wide to enable a differential of between 15% and 20% to be maintained between each clear step in the hierarchy of jobs. This aim can be frustrated by government anti-inflation policies or by chief executives who, laudably, do not want to appear to be too greedy. In the former case, there is little that the company can do about it except go in for such tax planning devices as are available to reduce the incidence of taxation and maintain differentials in real terms. In the latter case, it is necessary to impress on those concerned that lack of head room can result in a squeeze at lower levels.

### Staff reaching their salary limits

A graded salary structure implies that there is a limit to the salary progression anyone can make in a job. If there are no promotion prospects, this means that an individual who reaches the top of his bracket can go no further. How, in these circumstances, can he be motivated? This question assumes that people are only motivated by salary increases, which is not necessarily the case. But this situation does present a problem which cannot be resolved except by telling the individual quite frankly that unless he is promoted he will receive no further increases, except those resulting from across the board cost of living reviews.

The existence of this problem is used by some companies to support their policy of secrecy about the salary structure. They claim that if people do not know what their upper limits are they will keep on being motivated in the hope that they can still earn increases. This seems to be a fundamentally dishonest approach and it ignores the basic concept of the expectancy theory of motivation, which states that people are only motivated if there is a defined goal for them to achieve and if they feel that they have a reasonable chance of attaining the goal.

One way of alleviating this impasse is to provide for the payment of special bonuses to reward exceptional work. But these should not be paid automatically for the obvious reason that they will in effect be no more than an extension to the salary scale and will thus fail to provide extra motivation.

### Salary structure audits

The approaches suggested above combined with the salary administration procedures described earlier should help to keep the salary structure up-to-date and relatively undistorted by external or internal pressures. But it is also necessary to review the gradings by carrying out a periodical spot check of bench-mark jobs. These should be re-evaluated to ensure that inevitable changes in responsibility have not made them less appropriate as reference points in the structure. A check should be made at the same time on market rates to assess the degree to which the structure is competitive.

The job evaluation scheme itself should be reviewed from time to time. The original factor definitions and weightings can easily become out-of-date. The evaluators themselves should also be checked to ensure that they are carrying out their work properly.

## Bonus schemes

Bonus schemes provide an award, usually in the form of a lump sum payment, which is additional to basic salary and is related in some way to the performance of the individual or group of individuals receiving the bonus. Bonus schemes should be distinguished from profit-sharing schemes, as described in chapter 16, which share out a proportion of profits to all or most staff on the basis of a formula or management decision which is seldom related to individual performance, although the profit share is usually paid in proportion to salary.

### Aims of bonus schemes

The principal aim of a bonus scheme is to provide an incentive and a reward for effort and achievement. Executive bonus schemes linked to company profits can also aim to make senior managers feel that their personal prosperity is linked to the performance of their company or unit.

Bonus schemes are supplementary to basic salary and are most appropriate where they apply to entrepreneurial types such as chief executives, marketing men and sales staff who, it is assumed, will strive for material reward, and whose results upon which their bonus depends can be clearly linked to their personal efforts and achievements.

### Bonus schemes criteria

When assessing whether or not a bonus scheme is appropriate, the following criteria should be used:

☐ The amount of the award received after tax should be sufficiently high to encourage staff to accept exacting targets and standards of performance. Standard bonuses should not be less than 10% of the basic salary and, if an effective incentive is wanted, the standard bonus should be around 20% to 30% of salary.

☐ The incentive should be related to quantitative criteria over which the individual has a substantial measure of control.

☐ The scheme should be sensitive enough to ensure that rewards are proportionate to achievements.

☐ The individual should be able to calculate the reward he can get for a given level of achievement.

☐ The formula for calculating the bonus and the conditions under which it is paid should be clearly defined.

☐ Constraints should be built into the scheme which ensure that staff cannot receive inflated bonuses which may not reflect their own efforts.

☐ The scheme should contain provisions for a regular review, say, every two or three years, which could result in its being changed or discontinued.

☐ The scheme should be easy to administer and understand, and it should be tailored to meet the requirements of the company.

### Executive bonus schemes

There are innumerable formulae for executive bonus schemes, and each company must adopt one which suits its own circumstances. The simplest formula is for a percentage out of net profits before tax to be paid *pro rata* to the executive's basic salary. In some schemes, dividend payments and provisions for reserves are deducted from net profits before the distribution of bonuses and there is usually an upper limit to the amount of bonus that can be paid. These schemes are crude but provide a direct incentive as long as results are directly influenced by the actions of the executives in the scheme. They can get out of hand unless an upper limit is strictly applied, and their emphasis on profits may make some executives seek short term gains at the expense of the longer term development of the company.

Other schemes are based on a formula which measures company performance. Bonuses are paid when a target figure is attained and increased further as the target figure is exceeded. The increase of bonus may be on a straight-line basis, i.e. directly proportionate to the improvement in results. Alternatively, it may be geared either by decreasing the rate of bonus the more the target is exceeded, which is generally regarded as poor practice, or by increasing the rate, which could be an expensive device. A straight-line progression is to be preferred.

The formula in some schemes is directly applied to the executive's salary. In other schemes, a percentage of profits on an increasing scale is released into a bonus pool which is distributed in proportion to salary.

### Incentive schemes for sales staff

Where it is felt that sales staff need to be motivated by an incentive commission scheme the majority of companies find that the best approach is a basic commission on sales volume or, in more sophisticated firms, on the contribution to fixed costs and profits of the sales of each product group or product. The standard commission is typically set at about one-third of salary to provide a noticeable incentive without adversely affecting feelings of security.

A successful sales commission plan should satisfy all the criteria listed above for bonus schemes. But it is particularly necessary to ensure that:

(a) the reward is fair in relation to the efforts of the sales representative. This means that attention has to be paid to setting and agreeing realistic and equitable targets, making allowances for special circumstances outside the control of the sales representative which might affect sales, and splitting commission fairly when more than one person has contributed to the sale;

(b) the scheme directs sales effort in accordance with management's policy on the product mix and does not encourage the representative to concentrate on what is easiest to sell;

(c) the scheme does not encourage high pressure selling which results in an unacceptable level of returns, cancellations and complaints;

(d) the scheme does not encourage representatives to neglect their indirect selling activities, such as servicing customers.

These criteria are not always easy to satisfy and a cautious approach is therefore needed before introducing an incentive scheme. A straight salary may be more appropriate where there is a wide range of products, a highly technical product, a high proportion of non-selling activities such as merchandizing to be carried out, or when flexibility is required in allocating salesmen to customers, territories or products.

## Employee benefits

Employee benefits consist of any items or rewards that are provided by employers for the benefit of their employees which are not part of normal pay. They are sometimes called 'fringe' benefits, but some benefits are so essential that the use of the word 'fringe' seems quite inappropriate. These include pensions, sick pay, and holidays. Others, such as cars, housing benefits, medical benefits and the range of benefits that can be made available to executives can be regarded as optional extras.

### Pension schemes

Pension schemes are designed to provide employees with security by currently building up rights which will give a guaranteed income to the employee or his dependants on retirement or death. Pensions are essentially deferred pay and they are financed by contributions from the company and in most, but not all, cases the employee.

Pensions are generally regarded as the most important employee benefit after basic pay, although many employees, especially younger ones, express little

236

interest in their pension arrangements until in many cases it is too late.

The need to ensure that the pension arrangements are the best the company can afford arises for three reasons:

1. A company has a moral obligation to do the best it can to provide a reasonable degree of security for its employees, especially its longer-service employees.
2. A good pension scheme demonstrates that the company has the long term interests of its employees at heart.
3. A good scheme will help to attract and retain high quality staff, especially older staff employed at senior levels who are likely to be most interested in pension rights.

MAIN FEATURES OF PENSION SCHEMES. Pension schemes are usually complex affairs and their provisions can vary considerably. Professional advice from pensions specialists is always required when reviewing pension arrangements to assess what the company needs, what it can afford and all the legal and tax considerations surrounding pension schemes. The following is a list of the main features that have to be dealt with when reviewing pension schemes.

*Pension Formulae.* There are four main types of formulae for determining pensions on retirement:

1. Final salary (salary service), where the pension is calculated as a fraction of the salary at retirement or as an average over the closing years or months of service. If the arrangement is to pay one sixtieth of final salary for every year's service the formula would be described as n/60ths. In this case, someone on retirement with 40 years' service would obtain 40/60ths of his final salary as a pension, the maximum allowed in the U.K. under the Inland Revenue code of approval for pension schemes.
2. Average salary (salary graded), where fixed amounts of pension are given for each year spent in a salary bracket.
3. Flat rate, where a flat rate payment is made which is quoted as a given rate for each year of service.
4. Money purchase, where contributions are fixed and accumulate in a 'pool' for each employee.

A final salary scheme is clearly preferable for the employee because the pension will be based on earnings just before retirement, which should keep pace with increases in the cost of living. But in inflationary times, which are always with us, a final salary scheme can be very costly.

*Contributions.* Schemes can be either contributory — requiring contributions from both the employer and the employee — or non-contributory, in which case only the employer makes the contribution. The contributions of employees tend to average about 5% to 6% of basic salary.

The arguments advanced in favour of a contributory scheme are that sharing the cost means that more money is available to buy better benefits, and that employees appreciate benefits more when they have had to pay for them. The arguments in favour of non-contributory schemes are that they are an attraction to employees, are more flexible in response to change and cost less to run.

*Entry Age.* The entry age can be fixed at 25 or, preferably, 21. There is usually a qualifying period of six months to a year.

*Post-Retirement Pension Increases.* Pension schemes can be more or less inflation-proofed by the process of escalation — allowing for increases in pensions in response to changes in the cost of living. This is a highly desirable but potentially expensive feature.

*Lump Sum on Retirement.* Pension schemes can offer the right of commutation of pension on retirement which allows the exchange of part of the pension for a tax free lump sum. This provides a useful aid to those wanting to buy a retirement home, or it can be used for special purchases or investment.

*Widows' Benefits.* Pension schemes support a widow whose husband has died in service either by providing a lump sum, a reduced widows' pension or a combination of the two. If wisely invested, a lump sum can often provide a better income than a pension. During his working life a man should know that there will be adequate provision for his dependants.

Arrangements for paying a widow's pension after the husband's death in retirement vary widely. The best method is to provide a pension of up to two-thirds of the husband's pension.

*Early and Late Retirement.* Early retirement pensions are usually calculated at a reduced rate and schemes may define the reduction that will apply for each year between the year of early retirement and the normal retiring age. If an employee retires early through ill-health he or she should at least be entitled to the pension earned up to retirement age. A more favourable arrangement would be to pay an improved pension which would take account of potential service up to normal retirement age.

There may be situations in which the company wants employees to stay on after normal retiring age, but their continued service should be reviewed regularly from the point of view of their health. Pension schemes should always provide for a 'late retirement increment' under which an employee who continues to work after his normal retirement date can receive an enhanced pension without any further contributions from himself or his employer.

*'Top Hat' Arrangement.* A 'top hat' arrangement is one in which a pension scheme for directors or senior staff is topped up by means of an additional non-contributory scheme. A 'top hat' scheme is offered when a company wishes to provide a greater benefit to individuals over and above that supplied under its main fund. Such benefits could usually be provided by augmentation within the fund but there are sometimes internal company reasons for requiring a separate policy.

*Funding.* All schemes have to be funded so that the money is available to pay the promised benefits. The usual arrangement is to build up funds by contributions which are invested in securities or in an insurance policy or both. The basic choice is between running a private self-administered fund through trustees or operating a scheme through an insurance company. Private schemes require considerable investment expertise and administrative effort to organize, although some large companies feel they can run a better and less costly scheme if they go it alone with specialist actuarial advice. The majority of schemes are designed and administered for their clients by insurance companies who have the actuarial, investment and administrative skills required.

CHOICE OF SCHEME. Pension schemes are complicated affairs and are subject to a number of legal and fiscal considerations. The choice of what goes into the scheme in the shape of alternative types and levels of benefits will depend largely on what the company can afford to pay. It may be necessary to trade off one benefit against another by, for example, reducing the pensions formula from n/60ths to n/80ths in order to introduce a 50% widows' pension. If there is any choice within a budget, employees should be consulted about their preferences.

The cost of pension schemes can be anything up to 25% of pay-roll, so it is worth taking care in setting them up and maintaining them. They should be reviewed regularly with the help of expert advice to ensure that they are properly funded (although in periods of high inflation this is difficult) and that a reasonable mix of benefits is being provided for the money subscribed by the company and its employees.

### Sick pay

For junior staff most companies provide sick pay on a sliding scale according to service. A reasonably generous but not untypical arrangement would be:

Up to 1 year's service    — 4 weeks' full pay
1 to 5 years' service    — 13 weeks' full pay
5 years plus    — 13 weeks' full pay plus 1 week for each year of service.

For managerial staff, the majority of companies in the U.K. give full pay for six months or more.

Many companies seem to adopt an ungenerous approach to sick pay because they feel it could be costly with large numbers of staff and because they are unlikely to get much credit for their generosity. These arguments are not usually advanced on firm grounds and perhaps more credit at small cost could be obtained from an increase in sick pay allowance than most companies realize.

### Holidays

Most staff in the U.K. now receive at least three weeks' paid annual holiday and, for management, four to five weeks is increasingly becoming the rule. There has traditionally been a differential between staff holidays and those given to manual workers and this has been maintained in a certain degree as manual worker holidays have increased. In the E.E.C. countries, holidays tend to be longer than in the U.K. but in North America, executives' holidays lag behind — many still have only two weeks a year.

### Cars

After pensions and holidays, which are usually taken for granted, cars have been the most highly regarded fringe benefit in the U.K. The provision of a company car saves the executives both the capital costs of acquisition and, usually, the heavy running costs, but this advantage has been reduced by recent U.K. legislation. From the company's point of view, the provision of a car can still be less costly than paying the extra salary needed to compensate the executives for not having a car when allowance is made for tax. And in the U.K. at least, where over 90% of top management have company cars, it has been almost impossible to be competitive without giving a car or the equivalent net salary.

But there are some disadvantages. A car is a very visible sort of benefit and great care has to be taken to ensure that the size or cost of cars accurately reflects differentials. It is also costly to administer a car fleet. A further point to consider is that not all people like to have a company car imposed upon them. Many would prefer to spend the equivalent money as they wish.

### Housing assistance
Housing assistance falls into three categories:

1. Allowances to transferred staff, including removal expenses, travelling expenses for visits, lodging allowances, settling in grants or disturbance allowances, and assistance with conveyancing and estate agents' fees.
2. Allowances to new employees which may include assistance with removal, travelling and lodgings.
3. Assistance with house purchase which can include arrangements with a building society or insurance company to obtain a mortgage on preferential terms and to reserve funds for company employees, or various forms of long term or bridging loans at reduced interest rates.

### Medical benefits
The most popular form of medical benefit is medical insurance, and a large number of U.K. companies participate in schemes such as B.U.P.A. or Private Patients' Plan.

### Other benefits
There is a long list of other benefits that can be provided, many of them being reserved for executives as special rewards. These benefits include:

☐ low interest loans
☐ help with education
☐ payment of professional subscriptions
☐ free or heavily subsidized meals
☐ subsidized accommodation
☐ service agreements for executives.

The danger of an over-liberal approach to executive benefits is that they enlarge the gap between the 'haves' and the 'have nots' and can therefore be divisive, and the material advantages conferred by these benefits can be considerably reduced if they are taxed at the full rate.

### Other allowances
The main allowance that can be paid to staff is for overtime. Normally this is reserved for junior staff although union pressures have extended its application in some companies. Where normal overtime is worked it is usual to pay for overtime at a flat rate, adding a premium of, say, an extra 50% if excessive overtime is worked. The approach differs considerably between companies and some organizations have adopted premium payments for all overtime. Other premiums may be given to employees who work unsocial hours or on regular shifts.

## Total remuneration

The total remuneration concept is based on the belief that all aspects of pay and employee benefits should be treated as a whole, the different parts of which can be adjusted according to the needs of the company and the individual. This means that, in setting levels of remuneration, account is taken of the value to employees and the cost to the company of each of the benefits to which job holders are entitled as well as their basic salary and bonus payments. Remuneration is thereby treated as a total package so that employees can be told about the complete value of what they are getting, valid comparisons can be made with other companies and an appropriate balance is achieved between the different components of remuneration.

The concept applies to all levels of staff, but it is of more importance at higher levels because of the tax advantages that may be achieved by providing certain benefits as an alternative to basic salary. Although, as tax authorities tighten up on their regulations, the scope for tax planning to reduce the incidence of income tax on higher earnings is becoming increasingly restricted.

### Total remuneration and the company

The approach to total remuneration should be to decide on the mix of basic pay, bonuses and other employee benefits that should be provided at different levels by reference to company policies on differentials and external comparisons. Ideally, the value of each element should be assessed in terms of the benefit received by individuals — gross and net of tax — at different salary levels and the cost to the company, also gross and net of tax. By comparing remuneration on both a gross and net basis the scope for using fringe benefits to reduce the effect of progressive taxation can be identified. It is unlikely that benefits other than basic salary, especially pensions, will take up an increasing proportion of total remuneration as responsibility increases.

### Total remuneration and the individual

Everyone starts off with wanting a good basic salary to provide for the necessities of life and satisfy the basic needs in Maslow's hierarchy of human needs — to survive and to achieve security. Thereafter other needs become more important, and these are the ones that can best be satisfied by the intrinsic motivators present in the work itself.

At the same time people begin to seek alternative means of providing for their needs and, particularly at higher levels, may not find the package offered by the company fully acceptable. This is why what has been termed the 'cafeteria' system has been devised whereby people can choose from the benefits on display as long as they are within their budget. In its simplest and most readily applicable form, the 'cafeteria' system might offer a straight choice between an improved benefit such as a bigger car or an augmented pension, and the equivalent increase in gross salary. More elaborate versions will give a range of benefits to choose from, and one method works out the value of the benefits, expresses them in points terms and allocates so many points to an executive to deploy as he wishes. Such approaches have only limited application, but the least a company can do is to avoid the mistake of forcing benefits on people who may not appreciate them. If money is to motivate, it should satisfy needs that the individual actually possesses rather than those he is assumed to have.

# 16 | Wage Payment Systems

## The basis of wage payment systems

Wage payment systems consist of the pay structure and the methods used to motivate and reward workers for their efforts.

### Objectives of management

The objectives of management in developing and maintaining wage payment systems are to achieve the purposes of the organization by attracting, retaining and motivating workers so that maximum productivity and quality are obtained at minimum cost. The assumption behind most payment systems is that pay is the key motivating factor. This is not necessarily completely valid. But it is certainly reasonable to assume that pay is a major factor in obtaining and retaining workers and can be an important cause of dissatisfaction, even if it is not by any means the only motivator.

Management's job is, therefore, to assess what level and type of inducements it is able to offer in return for the contributions it requires from its work force.

### The effort bargain

The worker's objective is to strike a bargain with management about the relation between what he regards as a reasonable contribution, and what the employer is prepared to offer to elicit that contribution. This is termed the 'effort bargain' and is, in effect, an agreement between managers and unions which lays down the amount of work to be done for the agreed wage, not just the hours to be worked. Explicitly or implicitly all employers are in a bargaining situation with regard to payment systems. A system will not be effective or workable until it is agreed as being fair and equitable by both sides.

### Developing and maintaining wage payment systems

To develop and maintain wage payment systems it is necessary to:

☐ understand the basic principles governing the design of pay structures;
☐ appreciate the uses, advantages and disadvantages of the various payment systems available: individual schemes, group incentive schemes, and factory-wide incentive schemes;
☐ adopt a systematic approach in evaluating the different schemes and selecting the system which is most appropriate;
☐ introduce any changes to the system with great care;
☐ establish means of monitoring the effectiveness of the payment systems.

These aspects of wage payment systems are discussed in the following sections of this chapter.

## Pay structures

A pay structure consists of the rates paid for the jobs within a factory. The structure will incorporate pay differentials between the various jobs which reflect real or assumed differences in skill and responsibility but are strongly influenced by pressures from the local labour market, by custom and practice, and by the respective bargaining strengths of management and workers.

The pay differentials may be expressed in a formal structure consisting of a hierarchy of grades into which jobs are allocated according to their relative value. Each grade may consist of a pay bracket to allow scope for individual merit payments to be made above a minimum time rate. Alternatively, there is a fixed rate for each job in the grade. Relativities may be determined by bargaining, tradition, or a formal system of job evaluation. Frequently, however, there is no formal structure, or the structure is limited to a crude division of jobs into skilled, semi-skilled or unskilled categories. In these cases, differentials within or between categories may be haphazard; dictated by custom and practice or by the way in which a payment by results scheme rewards particular classes of employees.

Unplanned structures may easily result in a mass of overlapping and confused grades without any acceptable pattern of rational differentials between jobs. Such structures offer endless scope for argument and conflict over grading and upgrading issues.

The case for a planned and rational pay structure is overwhelming, although achieving order from chaos is usually a formidable task. Differentials which have been built into the system over a number of years are hard to change. This is where a job evaluation programme which involves the full participation of both management and unions can be so valuable (job evaluation schemes are dealt with in chapter 14).

The ideal structure should have the minimum number of grades required to accommodate the clearly differentiated levels of skill and responsibility that exist in the organization. The more straightforward the production process, the less reason to have numerous grades. Current practice is to aim for five to seven grades covering all factory personnel. It is important to have adequate pay differentials between each grade so that a significantly increased reward results from an upgrading, and to avoid the arguments about re-gradings which result if the increases between grades are too small.

The pay levels within the structure will be determined in various ways. They may be imposed by national, local or plant negotiations, or they may be fixed by management by reference to the national minimum rates, the local going rates, as established by pay surveys and, possibly, job evaluation.

The structure will have to take account of any payment by results schemes in operation. Pay rates may, therefore, be divided into a basic time rate for the job which is paid according to the hours worked, and a piecework rate which varies according to the amount earned under the piecework system. Traditionally, the ratio of basic rate to incentive has been $2 : 1$, but the current trend is nearer $4 : 1$ to minimize fluctuations in earnings and to control wage drift (increases in piecework earnings which have not resulted from specific pay increases achieved by negotiated settlements or granted by an employer). There might also be a guaranteed or 'fall-back' rate for pieceworkers which could be equivalent to the consolidated rate for timeworkers carrying out a similar job. Additionally, the pay structure will incorporate overtime and shift premium rates and allowances for dangerous or dirty work or for special responsibility.

## Individual payment systems

Individual payment systems can be divided into three main categories: time rate, payment by results and measured day work. Each category includes a number of variants, and in most organizations there is a measure of choice about which system to adopt.

### Time rate systems

Time rate, also known as day rate, day work, flat rate or hourly rate, is the system under which operators are simply paid a predetermined rate per week, day or hour for the actual time they have worked. The basic rate for the job is fixed by negotiation, by reference to local rates, or by job evaluation, and only varies with time, never with output or performance.

In some circumstances, what are termed high day rates are paid which are higher than the agreed minimum rates. The high day rate may include a consolidated bonus element and is probably higher than the local going rate in order to attract and retain labour. High day rates have been a feature in some parts of the British motor industry where above minimum earnings are expected because of a history of payment by results, and where there is a high proportion of machine control of output. They are most appropriate in assembly lines where workers can be trained to produce work of a specified standard and to maintain a fixed working pace determined by work study.

Time rates are most commonly used where it is thought that it is impossible or undesirable to apply a payment by results system, for example, in maintenance work. But they may also be adopted as an alternative to an unsatisfactory piecework system. From the point of view of operators, the advantages of time rates are that earnings are predictable and steady and they do not have to engage in endless arguments with supervision and ratefixers about piece rate or time allowances.

The obvious accusation made against time rates is that they do not provide the motivation of a direct incentive relating the reward to the effort. The logical point is that people want money and will work harder to get more of it. The argument is a powerful one, and explains the high proportion of workers on payment by results schemes — for example, one half of manual workers in the British engineering industry. But it ignores all the problems associated with piecework, which are discussed below, and pays insufficient attention to the other motivating factors intrinsic to the job or provided by management. It is true, however, that time rate systems, especially high day rates, make greater demands on management and supervision.

One way of getting over this problem of incentive is to adopt a system of measured day work, as described below. Alternatively, some form of merit award system can be used. In their crudest form, merit awards are administered by management or supervision and consist of additions to the base rate of so much per hour, usually with an upper limit. They may be awarded on the basis of the purely subjective judgement of a superior, or they may be determined by reference to a systematic merit assessment procedure which will review the worker's performance under such headings as effective output, skill, versatility and timekeeping. Such procedures seldom succeed in removing the subjectivity which is the major drawback to merit assessment schemes and explains why unions tend to dislike them.

## Payment by results systems

Payment by results systems relate the pay or part of the pay received by the worker to the number of items he produces or the time he takes to do a certain amount of work.

STRAIGHT PIECEWORK. The most common of the schemes of payment by results which are purely individual in character is what is called straight piecework. This means payment of a uniform price per unit of production and it is most appropriate where production is repetitive in character and can easily be divided into similar units.

Straight piecework rates can be expressed in one of two main forms, 'money piecework' or 'time piecework'. In the case of money piecework, the employee is paid a flat money price for each piece or operation completed. In the case of time piecework, instead of a price being paid for operation, a time is allowed (this is often called a time-allowed system). The worker is paid at his basic piecework rate for the time allowed, but if he completes the job in less time he gains the advantage of the time saved, as he is still paid for the original time allowed. Thus, an operator who completes a job timed at 60 hours in 40 hours would receive a bonus of 50% of his piecework rate, i.e. $[(60\text{-}40)/40)] \times 100$.

Piece rates may be determined by work study using the technique known as effort rating to determine standard times for jobs. In situations where work is not repetitive, especially in the engineering industry, times may be determined on a much less analytical basis by ratefixers using their judgement. This often involves prolonged haggles with operators.

DIFFERENTIAL PIECEWORK SYSTEMS. Straight piecework systems result in a constant wage cost per unit of output, and management objections to this feature led to the development of differential systems where the wage cost per unit is adjusted in relation to output. The most familiar applications of this approach have been the premium bonus systems such as the Halsey/Weir or Rowan schemes. Both these systems are based on a standard time allowance and not a money piece rate, and the bonus depends on the time saved. Unlike straight piecework, the wages cost per unit of production falls as output increases, but the hourly rate of workers' earnings still increases, although not in proportion to the increased output. For obvious reasons, these systems are viewed with suspicion by unions and workers and many variations to the basic approach have been developed, some of which involve sharing the increments of higher productivity between employers and workers. For a fuller description of the various types of individual and group incentive schemes reference should be made to *Incentive Payment Systems* by R. Marriott.[1]

ARGUMENTS IN FAVOUR OF PIECEWORK. The main argument in favour of any payment by results system is, of course, that people work to make money – the more money they make the happier they are and they will work harder if, and only if, they are paid more money. Higher output becomes what both management and workers want and everyone is happy. Underlying this argument is the assumption that the piecework operator has the power to control the amount of effort he puts into the job, and that he adjusts his effort solely or mainly in relation to the monetary return he gets from it.

ARGUMENTS AGAINST PIECEWORK. Arguments against the 'economic man' philosophy of piecework and its practical effects have been gaining ground over a number of years, especially since a number of research projects into what actually happens on the shop floor have exposed the inadequacies of the system – for example, those carried out by Tom Lupton.[2]

The argument against the 'economic man' rationale for payment by results schemes is that it is a naive view of motivation. People at work have much more complicated goals than the simple pursuit of money and are not so many donkeys as to react as required to the carrot or the stick. One of the earlier formulations of this argument came from Douglas McGregor who wrote:

> The practical logic of incentives is that people want money, and that they will work harder to get more of it. Incentive plans do not, however, take account of several other well-demonstrated characteristics of behaviour in the organizational setting: (1) that most people also want the approval of their fellow workers and that if necessary they will forego increased pay to obtain this approval; (2) that no managerial assurances can persuade workers that incentive rates will remain inviolate regardless of how much they produce; (3) that the ingenuity of the average worker is sufficient to outwit any system of controls devised by management.[3]

The more specific arguments against payment by results systems are that they:

(a) are not effective in themselves – they do not increase effort or output;
(b) cause more trouble than they are worth in the shape of conflict between management and men, arguments about rates, jealousies between those on piecework and those on lower time rates, damage to pay structures where carefully calculated relativities are upset because one group of workers is fortunate enough to benefit from a loose rate, and frustrations to workers who suffer from unstable and unpredictable earnings;
(c) are a major cause of wage drift – the inflation of earnings outside the normal pattern of negotiated pay settlements.

## Measured day work

In measured day work the pay of the employee is fixed on the understanding that he will maintain a specified level of performance, but the pay does not fluctuate in the short term with his performance. The arrangement relies on work measurement to define the required level of performance and to monitor the actual level. Fundamental to measured day work is the concept of an incentive level of performance, and this distinguishes it clearly from time rate systems. Measured day work guarantees the incentive payment in advance thereby putting the employee under an obligation to perform at the effort level required. Payment by results, on the other hand, allows the employee discretion as to his effort level but relates his pay directly to the output he has achieved. Between these two systems are a variety of alternatives that seek to marry the different characteristics of payment by results and measured day work, including banded incentives, stepped schemes and special forms of high day rate.

Measured day work seeks to produce an effort-reward bargain in which enhanced and stable earnings are exchanged for an incentive level of performance. The criteria for success in operating it are:

☐ total commitment of management, employees and their unions, which can only be achieved by careful planning, joint consultation, training, and a staged introduction of the system;
☐ an effective work measurement system, and efficient production planning and

control and inventory control procedures;
- ☐ the establishment of a logical pay structure with appropriate differentials from the beginning of the scheme's operation — the structure should be developed by the use of job evaluation and in consultation with employees;
- ☐ the maintenance of good control systems to ensure that corrective action is taken quickly if there is any shortfall on targets.

## Group incentive schemes

Group or area incentive schemes provide for the payment of a bonus either equally or proportionately to individuals within a group or area. The bonus is related to the output achieved over an agreed standard or to the time saved on a job — the difference between allowed time and actual time.

Group bonus schemes are in some respects individual incentive schemes written large — they have the same basic advantages and disadvantages as any payment by results system. The particular advantages of a group scheme are that it encourages team spirit, breaks down demarcation lines and enables the group to discipline itself in achieving targets. In addition, job satisfaction may be achieved through relating the group more closely to the complete operation. Group bonuses may be particularly useful where groups of workers are carrying out interdependent tasks and when individual bonus schemes might be invidious because workers will have only limited scope to control the level of their own output and will be expected to support others, to the detriment of their personal bonus.

The potential disadvantages of group bonus schemes are that management is less in control of production — the group can decide what earnings are to be achieved and can restrict output. Furthermore, the bonus can eventually cease to be an incentive. Some opponents of group schemes object to the elimination of personal incentive, but this objection would only be valid if it were possible to operate a satisfactory individual incentive scheme, which is not always the case.

Group schemes may be most appropriate where people have to work together and teamwork has to be encouraged. They are probably most effective if they are based on a system of measured or controlled day work where targets and standards are agreed by the group, which is provided with the control information it needs to monitor its own performance.

## Factory-wide incentive schemes

Factory-wide incentive schemes provide a bonus for all factory workers which is related to an overall measure of performance. They are sometimes referred to as share of production plans. The basic type of scheme links the bonus to output or added value (the value added to the cost of raw materials and bought out parts by the process of production). Other schemes such as the Scanlon and Rucker plans have more elaborate formulae for calculating bonus and built-in arrangements for joint consultation.

In their simplest form these schemes provide for a direct link between the bonus and output or added value. Alternatively, a target for output or added value may be set and the bonus paid on a scale related to achievements above the target level.

In many ways, these schemes resemble profit-sharing plans, except in the choice of the factor governing the size of the bonus. As in the case of profit sharing, the main advantage claimed for schemes of this nature is that they increase the identification of employees with the company and create interest in increasing productivity. To make any impact at all, the scheme should provide employees with a reasonable chance of earning at least 10% bonus on their basic pay.

The main argument against any type of factory-wide incentive scheme is that it does not provide a direct incentive because the link between individual effort and the eventual reward is so tenuous. There is also the problem of establishing a suitable relationship between bonuses and the performance indicator. It may be difficult to devise a consistent method of measuring results, and even if a reliable and understandable measure is available, it may not be easy to work out a formula which provides an acceptable basis for calculating the bonus. A factory-wide bonus scheme, however, can be more effective in improving motivation and performance if it includes arrangements for participation in the planning of changes to production methods along the lines of the Scanlon and Rucker plans.

## Profit-sharing schemes

Profit sharing is a plan under which an employer pays to eligible employees, as an addition to their normal pay, special sums related to the profits of the business. Shares are distributed at regular intervals and the amount is determined either on the basis of an established formula, which may be published, or entirely at the discretion of management.

### Objectives of profit sharing

The objectives of most profit-sharing schemes are to increase motivation and commitment. They aim to encourage employees to identify themselves more closely with the company by developing a common concern for its progress.

The better schemes are based on the principle that everyone can make a contribution to increasing productivity and should share in the beneficial results of their activities. Such schemes serve primarily as a means for initiating joint action on improving results. They provide a focal point for discussions which relate improvements in output to the increased profit share for employees that should result from them.

It is generally accepted that profit-sharing plans cannot provide a direct incentive because of the difficulty of linking effort and reward. A further problem is that of calculating the profit formula — profit levels are strongly influenced by accounting conventions and it is often difficult to show how they have been calculated. Workers can easily suspect that the figures are being 'fiddled' by management. But if the formula is not published, the shares become no more than a management hand-out, which is nice for those who get it, but defeats the main purpose of the exercise, which is to increase commitment. Too many profit-sharing schemes are regarded as just another fringe benefit.

### Criteria for profit-sharing schemes

The two basic criteria that a profit-sharing scheme should satisfy are, first, a meaningful sum should be distributed to employees, consistent with providing an appropriate return on the shareholders' investment. Secondly, the links between effort and reward should be as well-defined as possible and should not be too extended. This implies positive action by management to point out and discuss with employees how improved performance can result in increased profit shares. It also implies the reasonably frequent distribution of profit shares.

Profit-sharing schemes have to be tailored for individual companies. There are no standard schemes. The following factors should be taken into account when designing and operating schemes:

☐ The money that an employee can reasonably expect to receive if profit targets are met should be significant, say, 10% of basic pay.

☐ The basic share of, say, 10% should be paid when a suitable target figure for profitability is achieved (the usual basis is return on capital employed). An alternative approach is to set aside a percentage of profits before tax to finance dividend payments and then to split the remaining profits between the company and its employees. In some schemes this is done on a 50/50 basis.

☐ If the scheme is based on a target for return on capital employed, some incentive should be provided even before the target return is achieved. Thereafter, the rate at which profit shares increase relative to increases in the return on capital employed should accelerate after the target return has been achieved. There should, however, be a maximum share of, say, 25% of basic pay.

☐ The financial implications of the scheme in relation to profit forecasts, allowing for inflation, should be thoroughly explored in advance. The scheme should only be introduced if the profit forecasts show that there is a reasonable chance of meeting the basic criteria of the scheme for the distribution of profits.

☐ The basis for calculating profits and valuing assets should be carefully determined in advance.

☐ The profit share for employees should be paid on top of the market rate for the job.

☐ Profit shares should be distributed as frequently as possible, consistent with the need to have reliable financial information and to distribute a meaningful sum of money to individual recipients.

☐ Profit sharing is most effective when it is used as a talking point with employees. It is essential to communicate as much information as possible to them, and by meetings and discussions relate the results achieved to their performance so that they can identify for themselves areas for improvement which will increase their share of profits.

☐ Profit sharing is most likely to be effective in compact organizations whose management believe in the scheme, are prepared to work hard to put it into practice and are absolutely open to their employees about the scheme.

☐ Profit sharing as a means of increasing motivation and commitment is not a substitute for good management.

☐ It will be difficult to assign any certain benefits to the company arising from a profit-sharing scheme. It may be appreciated by employees as extra cash but it may have no direct effect on productivity unless used as a talking point.

## Selecting a wage payment system

The steps required to select a wage payment system are:

1. Define objectives and assumptions.
2. Analyse existing situation.
3. Evaluate alternative systems.

### Defining objectives and assumptions

Everyone starts by wanting a system which will help with the recruitment of good quality employees and which will reduce labour turnover. Managements also want the system to provide direct incentives to increase output, although some may recognize the limits to which this can be done in their environment and attach importance to one or more of the following objectives:

☐ obtaining consistency in performance
☐ containing labour costs
☐ reducing pay disputes
☐ improving product quality
☐ improving delivery times
☐ improving equipment utilization
☐ obtaining a lower level of rejects
☐ reducing the level of work in progress
☐ gaining control over the pay structure to reduce wage drift and problems of differentials
☐ improving methods, planning, work loading and labour flexibility.

The analysis of objectives should define priorities and assess how far they are being achieved by the present payment system. But it is also necessary to examine and if necessary challenge the assumptions that management holds about payment systems. Rightly or wrongly it may be assumed that 'the workers in this plant are only interested in money', or that 'the existing system is the best one we've got, so why change it?', or 'all we need to do is to tighten up the loose rates' (rather than find out why the rates are loose in the first place), or 'that's the way the men want it', and so on.

### Analysing the existing situation and evaluating alternatives

Decisions on payment systems are critical ones and can have far-reaching effects. The existing arrangements need to be analysed with great care to establish the extent to which the objectives are being achieved and to compare the systems in use or available with the circumstances in the firm. The points to be covered when assessing alternatives are set out below.

INDIVIDUAL PIECEWORK. This may be appropriate when individual effort clearly determines output and:

(a)  the job cycle is short;
(b)  the number of modifications is small;
(c)  the work requires purely manual skills and/or only single purpose hand tools or simple machine tools are used;
(d)  product changes and modifications are limited;
(e)  job stoppages are small;
(f)  a high proportion of tasks is specified;
(g)  effective work measurement techniques are in use;
(h)  good quality work study and rate fixing staff are available;
(i)  reasonably stable industrial relations are maintained on the shop floor.

GROUP PIECEWORK. Group piecework systems may be suitable if collective effort clearly determines output and the other features necessary for individual piecework systems are present.

MEASURED DAY WORK. Measured day work may be appropriate where individual effort largely determines output and:

(a) conditions are inappropriate for individual piecework;
(b) operations are of the process type or assembly line;
(c) the job cycle is long;
(d) accurate work measurement of operations is possible so that acceptable standards can be agreed;
(e) high quality work study staff are available;
(f) high quality management negotiators are available;
(g) the unions are responsive to the advantages of measured day work and there is a reasonable chance of reaching agreement on the system and the standards adopted.

TIME RATES. Time rates with, possibly, some system of merit rating are more appropriate where the conditions do not meet the criteria for a payment by results system mentioned earlier, especially in circumstances where:

(a) individual or group effort does not determine output;
(b) it is difficult to determine accurate standards by means of work measurement;
(c) there are many modifications or design changes;
(d) product changes are numerous;
(e) job stoppages may be numerous;
(f) there is a tradition of unsatisfactory shop floor relations.

## Installing a wage payment system

The process of installing a wage payment system, whether it consists of the modification of an existing scheme or a radical change to the whole basis upon which payments are made for work done, is primarily a matter of evaluation, consultation, negotiation and, possibly, productivity bargaining after the initial studies have been completed.

The main installation steps are as follows:

1. Define the objectives of the payment system and list and, if necessary, challenge the assumptions held about the purpose of the system and how it should operate.
2. Collect facts about the existing system: the pay structure, the types of payment schemes in use, the number of people paid under each arrangement, the levels of earnings in different occupations, and the make up of earnings, including overtime payments.
3. Analyse the circumstances in which the payment system operates.
4. Compare the existing or proposed arrangements against the criteria for evaluating systems listed above.
5. Analyse the effectiveness of the pay structure and payment systems by:
   (a) comparing the results achieved with the objectives of the system under such headings as ability to attract and retain staff, effect of productivity, effect on management/employee relationship;
   (b) identifying particular problem areas where the system is producing anomalies in pay or earnings between occupations or units, where the

requirements of equal pay legislation are not met or where rates of pay are not competitive with local going rates.

6. Consider conducting an attitude survey to obtain the views of workers, rate fixers and supervisors about the present system and what changes need to be made.
7. Consult as required with unions and employees on the present arrangements and what needs to be done about them.
8. Conduct pay surveys as required to establish local market rates (see chapter 14).
9. Conduct job evaluation studies as required in consultation with unions to establish correct relativities and to provide the basic data for designing a logical pay structure (see chapter 14).
10. Develop pilot tests and install any revised or new individual, group or measured day work payment systems that may be required in consultation with unions.
11. Revise the pay structure as necessary in the light of the actions taken in steps 8. to 10. and in consultation with the unions or employee representatives. In a unionized concern, revisions to the pay structure would, of course, have to be negotiated with the unions.
12. Ensure that information is available which will enable the effectiveness of a revised pay system or structure to be monitored.

### Consultation and negotiation

In any unionized concern, changes to the payment system can only be made following consultation and negotiation. In non-union firms it is highly desirable that employees should be consulted on their views about the payment arrangements.

There is everything to be said for involving workers in job evaluation exercises and in reviews of the payment system. Some unions are suspicious about job evaluation either because they feel it is an essentially spurious device for determining relativities, or because they think it cuts the ground from beneath their negotiating feet (or both). They may not wish to commit themselves in advance to accepting the results of the evaluation but they are much more likely to feel that it is fair and, therefore, acceptable if they have had the chance to take part in the planning and execution of the job evaluation study.

## Productivity agreements

A productivity agreement can be defined as one in which workers agree to make a change, or a number of changes, in working practice that will lead to more economical working, while in return the employer agrees to a higher level of pay or other benefits. Productivity bargaining produces a 'package deal' in which the agreement covers a number of issues and points, providing a comprehensive package in which the different parties make concessions on particular aspects in order to achieve a total agreement considered to be of overall advantage to all concerned. The main characteristics of a productivity agreement are as follows:

1. It is usually related to one plant and covers all the manual employees in that plant.
2. It records agreement on the means by which improved efficiency is to be achieved, e.g. through greater labour flexibility by the relaxation of demarcation rules, reducing unnecessary overtime, relaxing restrictions on output.

3. It incorporates either, (i) buying out on the basis of *quid pro quo*, offering immediate wage increases in exchange for concessions such as the relaxation of rigid demarcation rules, elimination of tea breaks, forfeiture of 'mates' (e.g. electricians' mates), reduction in the total labour force or, (ii) an agreement for allowing savings to be accumulated over a period of, say, six to twelve months when they are then split on a 50/50 or some other proportionate basis between workers and the company. A higher proportion would go to employees in a labour intensive concern than in a capital intensive company. The savings may be worked out as in the Scanlon scheme by computing the savings in labour cost resulting from a reduction in the ratio of labour cost to sales value or added value.
4. It may provide for the introduction of a new job evaluated pay structure or a new payment system such as the replacement of piecework by measured day work.

Employers have engaged in productivity bargaining for various reasons, including increasing productivity and getting a revised pay structure or payment system accepted. Less justifiably, they have used productivity bargaining techniques to buy themselves out of industrial relations trouble. Too often, pay has gone up but not productivity. Consequently, productivity bargaining fell into some disrepute when the honeymoon period after the Esso Petroleum Farley agreements in the 1960s had ended. The possibility of productivity bargains on the scale negotiated then also diminished in the periods of increasing unemployment and government pay restrictions in the 1970s. In particular, agreements of the buying out type requiring reductions in manning are not going to be entered into by unions when unemployment is high. A situation in which there is short time working and mounting redundancies is not conducive to worker/management co-operation in increasing productivity.

But there are other ways of increasing productivity besides a reduction in the labour force; and even if old-style productivity agreements are not feasible there is still much to be said for the principle of management and unions getting together to discuss how productivity can be improved and how the benefits of such improvements should be shared between the company and its employees. As Turner wrote:

> Perhaps the most important achievement of productivity bargaining is that it is helping to undermine the iron curtain which for nearly half a century has restricted negotiations between managements and employees over a large area of British industry, setting off 'managerial functions' on the one hand and 'craft regulations' on the other as areas which are not subject to bargaining.[4]

The approach to productivity bargaining should be based on a recognition by both sides of a mutual interest in cost-reduction based upon a rational study of the situation in the company. Management must be prepared with its estimates of the changes in manpower utilization and methods of working which are to be brought about once the agreement is put into operation. Estimates should also be prepared of the net benefits which should derive from those changes in reduced costs per unit of output, having allowed for increases in costs arising from changes in the wage structure. The bargaining element in a productivity agreement relates to how these benefits should be shared.

Productivity agreements can help to modify attitudes about the effort-reward bargaining process and gain acceptance of a more explicit link between performance and pay. Any change to a payment system will be regarded with suspicion by the employees concerned. A move from piecework to measured day work will produce a major upheaval in the way in which people work. Changes on this scale cannot be entered into lightly. Even if a full productivity bargain, old style, is not entered into, there is still plenty of scope and potential benefit for mutual discussions in shaping the future payment system and deciding the way in which management and employees should work together in implementing it.

## Maintaining the payment system

Any payment system can erode or decay, however carefully its installation was managed. It is essential to review the system in operation regularly to ensure that it continues to achieve its objectives. The review should consider labour unit costs and performance as well as measuring earnings in different sections and jobs in order to spot anomalies. It may be particularly important to analyse overtime earnings as these are often responsible for creating semi-permanent distortions in the earnings structure when overtime is not controlled properly. Attention might also be directed towards shift premiums and other special allowances for dirty or dangerous work or unsocial hours, to ensure that they are reasonable and in tune with market rates. Finally, a review should consider the equal pay situation to ensure that the arrangements conform with equal pay legislation – in Britain, that separate male and female rates should not exist and women should be paid the same as men if they are employed on the same or broadly similar work as men.

A review of the payment system could include an analysis of present arrangements as described earlier in this chapter. The other matters that could be looked at specifically include:

☐ labour cost per unit of output;
☐ output figures and performance levels;
☐ the proportion of bonus to total pay;
☐ levels of earnings in different departments and jobs;
☐ percentage of time paid on average bonus when normal bonus work was available;
☐ percentage overtime worked;
☐ percentage shift premium in total pay;
☐ average earnings compared with the salary levels of first line supervisors.

The aim of the review should be to ensure that management is prepared to take corrective action in good time when the payment system is not operating effectively.

### References
1. Marriott, R. *Incentive Payment Systems*. Staples Press, London, 1969.
2. Lupton, T. *On the Shop Floor*. Pergamon Press, Oxford, 1963.
3. McGregor, D. *The Human Side of Enterprise*. McGraw-Hill Book Company, New York, 1960.
4. Turner, H.A. 'Collective bargaining and the eclipse of incomes policy', *British Journal of Industrial Relations*, July 1970, p. 207.

<table>
<tr><td>*17*</td><td># Health and Safety</td></tr>
</table>

| *17* | # Health and Safety |
| --- | --- |

Health and safety policies and programmes are concerned with protecting employees — and any other people affected by what the company produces or does — against the hazards arising from their employment or their links with the company.

Occupational health programmes deal with the reactions of work people to their working environment and with the prevention of ill-health arising from working conditions and circumstances. They consist of two main elements — occupational medicine, which is a specialized branch of preventive medicine concerned with the diagnosis and assessment of health hazards and stresses at work; and occupational hygiene which is the province of the chemist and the engineer engaged in the measurement and physical control of environmental hazards.

Safety programmes deal with the prevention of accidents and with minimizing the resulting loss and damage to persons and to property. They relate more to systems of work than to the working environment, but both health and safety programmes are concerned with protection against hazards and their aims and methods are closely interlinked.

This chapter therefore treats health and safety as two aspects of the same problem, although the particular considerations affecting occupational hygiene or accident prevention are treated separately, as are special areas of the subject such as fire precautions.

Health and safety programmes need to be considered against the background of the factors that affect health and safety at work, and the chapter begins with an analysis of these factors and a discussion of the basic principles that influence policies and procedures. This is followed by a description of the elements of the overall health and safety programme, and the chapter then deals with each of these elements, namely:

☐ the identification and analysis of health and safety hazards and problems;
☐ health and safety policies;
☐ the organization of health and safety;
☐ occupational health programmes and procedures;
☐ accident-prevention programmes and procedures;
☐ the prevention of fire and explosions;
☐ education and training in health and safety precautions;
☐ the measurement and control of health and safety performance.

## Factors affecting health and safety

The work and writings of a number of distinguished practitioners and researchers in health and safety have resulted in a range of basic principles, concepts and approaches which need to be understood by anyone concerned with the development and implementation of health and safety programmes.

The first and most influential of the practitioners was H.W. Heinrich[1] who developed his axioms of industrial safety to underline his thesis that the conventional approach to prevention, by concentrating on injuries that had happened rather than on accidental occurrences that might be predicted, looked at only a fraction of the total problem and looked at it backwards. From this analysis a considerable body of literature has developed advocating the techniques of 'damage control' and 'total loss control'. The basic message of these approaches, which were mainly North American in origin, is that the employer who wants to prevent injuries in the future, to reduce loss and damage, and to increase efficiency, must look systematically at the total pattern of accidental happenings — whether or not they caused injury or damage. He must then plan a comprehensive system of prevention rather than rely on the *ad hoc* patching-up of deficiencies which injury accidents have brought to light.

### Principles of health and safety management

An analysis of the contributions of various schools of thought on health and safety matters suggests that there are five basic principles which should determine the approach to be used in health and safety management.

1. Industrial disease and accidents result from a multiplicity of factors, but these have to be traced to their root causes, which are usually faults in the management system arising from poor leadership from the top, inadequate supervision, insufficient attention to the design of health and safety into the system, an unsystematic approach to the identification, analysis and elimination of hazards, and poor education and training facilities.
2. The most important function of health and safety programmes is to identify potential hazards, provide effective safety facilities and equipment, and to take prompt remedial action. This is only possible if there are:
    □ comprehensive and effective systems for reporting all accidents causing damage or injury;
    □ adequate accident records and statistics;
    □ systematic procedures for carrying out safety checks, inspections and investigations;
    □ methods of ensuring that safety equipment is maintained and used;
    □ proper means available for persuading managers, supervisors and workpeople to pay more attention to health and safety matters.
3. The health and safety policies of the organization should be determined by top management who must be continuously involved in monitoring health and safety performance and in ensuring that corrective action is taken when necessary.
4. Management and supervision must be made fully accountable for health and safety performance in the working areas they control.
5. All employees should be given thorough training in safe methods of work and should receive continuing education and guidance on eliminating health and safety hazards and on the prevention of accidents.

## Health and safety programmes

The essential elements of a health and safety programme are:

□ analysis — of health and safety performance, problems and potential hazards;
□ development — of policies, organization, procedures and training systems;

☐ implementation – of the programme by means of training schemes, inspections, investigations and audits;

☐ evaluation – of control information and reports and of the effectiveness of the organization and training systems. This evaluation should provide feedback to be used for improving performance.

The constituents of the health and safety programme are shown in figure 17.1.

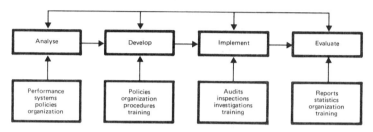

**Figure 17.1 Health and safety programme**

Health and safety programmes are the responsibility of top management but they should enlist the support of middle management, supervisors and workpeople in conducting the initial analysis and in developing and implementing the programme. Assistance and guidance can be provided internally by specialist health and safety advisers and externally by the government inspectorate (in the U.K. the Health and Safety Executive), bodies concerned with health and safety such as, in the U.K., the Royal Society for the Prevention of Accidents, or employers' associations, some of whom have strong safety departments. But advisory services do not detract from the ultimate responsibility of management for health and safety performance.

## Analysis of health and safety performance

Health and safety programmes must be based on an analysis of the facts on the organization of health and safety as it exists, on the procedures used and results obtained.

The facts should be analysed under the following headings:

☐ policies – the extent to which health and safety policies are defined and implemented;

☐ the organization – the role and effectiveness of management, supervision and workpeople, health and safety staff and satefy committees;

☐ systems and procedures – for carrying out inspections and investigations, reporting and recording accidents, ensuring at the design or development stage that equipment, facilities, plant, processes or substances are not dangerous, providing safety equipment, educating and training employees;

☐ performance – the health and safety record of the company as shown by statistics, reports, special investigations and sample checks.

Such an analysis will involve discussions with managers, supervisors, workpeople, shop stewards, factory inspectors and insurers, as well as a review of standard procedures and an examination of safety records.

## Health and safety policies

Written health and safety policies are required to demonstrate that top management is concerned about the protection of their employees from hazards at work and to indicate how this protection will be provided. These are therefore: first, a declaration of intent; secondly, a definition of the means by which that intent is to be realized; and, thirdly, a statement of the guidelines that should be followed by management and workpeople in implementing the policy. The policies should provide a base for organization, action and control as shown in figure 17.2.

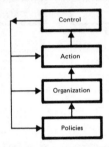

**Figure 17.2 The role of health and safety policies**

The policy statement should consist of three parts:

1. The general policy statement.
2. The description of the organization for health and safety.
3. Details of the arrangements for implementing the policy.

**The general policy statement**
The general policy statement should be a declaration of the intention of the employer to safeguard the health and safety of his employees. It should emphasize four fundamental points: first, that the safety of employees and the public is of paramount importance; second, that safety will take precedence over expediency; third, that every effort will be made to involve all managers, supervisors and employees in the development and implementation of health and safety procedures; and fourth, that health and safety legislation will be complied with in the spirit as well as the letter of the law. (See Appendix C.)

**Organization**
This section of the policy statement should describe the health and safety organization of the company through which high performance standards are set and achieved by people employed at all levels in the organization.

The statement should underline the ultimate responsibility of top management for the health and safety performance of the company. It should then indicate how key management personnel are to be held accountable for performance in their areas. The role of safety committees and safety representatives should be defined and the duties of the specialists who advise on health and safety matters, such as the safety adviser and the medical officer, should be summarized.

### Health and safety arrangements

The description of health and safety arrangements should indicate how the general policy statement is to be put into effect. It should cover:

☐ procedures for reporting accidents, illness and safety and health hazards, fire precautions; first aid;
☐ arrangements for monitoring the atmosphere and maintaining high standards of hygiene with regard to potentially harmful substances;
☐ arrangements for instructing workpeople in safe working methods and for training employees in health and safety matters;
☐ good housekeeping requirements covering storage facilities, adequate space for machinery and plant, the provision of gangways, and welfare arrangements;
☐ special rules for work done at a height, in confined spaces, on certain electrical equipment or unguarded machinery;
☐ the maintenance of equipment and the provision of proper inspection and testing arrangements;
☐ general rules on safe working habits;
☐ special rules for internal transport drivers;
☐ arrangements for checking new machinery and materials;
☐ safety inspections;
☐ the provision of personal protective equipment, and rules as to its use;
☐ suggestions on safety matters.

## Health and safety organization

Health and safety concerns everyone in an establishment, although the main responsibility lies with management and supervision for formulating and implementing safety policies and procedures.

### The role of management

The role of management is to develop health and safety policies and procedures with the help of its medical and safety advisers. Management must then ensure that the procedures are implemented by making supervisors accountable for health and safety performance in their areas and by providing them with the help, guidance and training they need to carry out their responsibilities. Management must also set up information and control systems so that the health and safety performance can be monitored and corrective action initiated when required.

It is essential to have a director with specific responsibility for health and safety matters. His job is to advise the board on policies, to ensure that the agreed policies are implemented and to report back to the board on health and safety performance. He should also be responsible for the overall management of the health and safety organization.

### The role of supervision

Supervisors can exert the greatest influence on health and safety. They are in immediate control of employees and work processes and it is up to them to keep a constant watch to reveal potentially unsafe practices or conditions. But they need all the support and encouragement they can get from higher management to fulfil these responsibilities. If the emphasis from above is purely on output and cost reduction, supervisors can hardly be blamed if they neglect safety precautions. Exhortations on safety from management or safety advisers are useless unless it can be demonstrated that health and safety considerations will be given priority if there is any conflict between them and the output and cost budgets.

Supervisors need training and guidance on their safety functions. This can be provided by the safety and training departments, if any, but the existence of well-defined safety rules and procedures should also help.

### The role of the medical adviser

Medical advisers have two functions: preventive and clinical. The preventive function is the most important, and this covers advising on health precautions, conducting inspections and inquiries, establishing health standards and holding medical examinations. Their clinical function is to deal with industrial accidents and diseases and to advise on the steps necessary to recover from injury or illness. It is not their job to usurp the role of the family doctor, but their special knowledge of the factory should enable them to give more relevant advice on matters concerning health at work.

Only larger companies can afford full-time medical officers, but any company with more than 100 employees should be able to call on the part-time advice of a local doctor who is interested and able to help.

### The role of the safety adviser

The main functions of the safety adviser should be to:

☐ advise on health and safety policies and standards, rules and procedures;
☐ advise on the health and safety aspects of the design and use of plant and equipment;
☐ advise on the use of safety equipment and protective clothing;
☐ plan and carry out safety audits and inspections;
☐ conduct investigations into accidents;
☐ maintain safety records and statistics;
☐ liaise continually with management, supervision and safety representatives;
☐ liaise with the health and safety inspectorate.

### The role of the safety committee

Safety committees should be concerned with reviewing unsafe practices and conditions and making suggestions on methods of improving health and safety performance. Like all such committees, they are most effective when they can be involved in real issues and can see their recommendations put into effect. That is why they should take part in formulating health and safety policies, procedures and rules, carrying out safety audits and inspections, investigating accidents and analysing accident reports and statistics.

## Occupational health programmes

Occupational health programmes are concerned with the identification and control of health hazards arising from toxic substances, radiation, noise, fatigue and the stresses imposed upon body and mind at work.

### Basic approach

In each of these areas the same basic approach is necessary. The first stage is to identify the substances, conditions or processes which are actually or potentially dangerous. The second stage is to evaluate how the hazard arises by studying the nature of the substance or condition and the circumstances in which the danger occurs. This means establishing the point at which a substance or an environmental condition is in danger of becoming harmful in terms of the intensity of exposure and the duration of exposure. It also means that the effect of working methods and processes on the human body and mind has to be examined. Industrial hygiene research into these matters should be carried out by specialist medical advisers working closely with process engineers and chemists. In particularly hazardous environments, research and advice may be required from members of the growing profession of occupational hygienists.

The final stage is to develop methods for minimizing the risk by exercising control over the use of dangerous substances or over the environment in which the hazard occurs. Control of occupational health and hygiene problems can be achieved by:

- eliminating the hazard at the source by means of design and process engineering which may, for example, ensure that harmful concentrations of toxic substances are not allowed to contaminate the worker;
- isolating hazardous operations or substances so that workers do not come into contact with them;
- changing the process or substances used to promote better protection or to remove the risk;
- providing protective equipment, but only if changes to the design, process or specification cannot completely remove the hazard;
- training workers to avoid risk by eliminating dangerous practices or by using the protective equipment provided;
- maintaining plant and equipment to minimize the possibility of harmful emissions;
- good housekeeping to keep premises and machinery clean and free from toxic substances;
- regular inspections to ensure that potential health risks are identified in good time. (Procedures for conducting safety inspections which also cover occupational health hazards are discussed below.)
- pre-employment medical examinations and regular checks on those exposed to risk.

### Toxic substances

Many toxic substances are present in working environments in the form of dusts (e.g. lead oxide), liquids (e.g. carbon disulphide) and gases (e.g. chlorine) and can be absorbed into the body through the lungs, mouth or skin. The increasing use in industry of potentially harmful chemical substances is producing new and more subtle hazards against which constant vigilance is necessary.

The work of environmental hygienists in the control of toxic substances must be firmly based on medical intelligence. But chemists, engineers and doctors should be part of one team working on the scientific assessment of the risks and the precise quantification of preventive standards in the form of agreed maximum levels of exposure expressed in threshold limit values (in the U.K. these are published by the Health and Safety Executive for a wide variety of substances used in industry).

It is the job of line management in a factory to ensure that they get information and advice from their own specialists or those who can be made available from government agencies. This should enable the company to identify and list hazards from toxic substances and decide on the control actions required. These could be any combination of the control steps listed above but, in addition, specific instructions and training should be made available for each operator exposed to risk on what should be done to avoid contamination and disease.

Environmental controls need to cover dust, fumes, gases, smoke and vapour in addition to the materials used in manufacturing processes. These create health risks, but they also result in pollution to the atmosphere, and control over pollution is a legal requirement as well as a social responsibility.

### Radiation
Radiation hazards are familiar enough to have generated an ultra-cautious attitude to the use of radioactive substances, resulting in the imposition of elaborate controls. This is an area where expert advice is essential for any employer who is not familiar with the subject so that protection can be provided by monitors, remote control systems, special clothing, and rigid control over the doses of radiation any person is allowed to receive.

### Noise
Noise is an aspect of occupational health which is probably more neglected than any other. Yet excessive noise can cause fatigue, speech interference, loss of hearing and emotional stress. Any of these could be instrumental in producing lasting physical damage or in increasing the likelihood of an accident.

A noise control programme should be based on a survey of the factory to identify the areas of noise and determine the abatement methods that can be used. The main problem is that noise reduction is something which should be catered for at the design stage — once the plant has been installed it becomes an expensive business to attack noise.

### Fatigue
Fatigue is the inevitable result of continued exertion — either mental or muscular. The factors that increase fatigue are badly designed machines, high temperature or humidity, excessive noise, inadequate lighting or glare, the nature of the floor upon which workers have to stand, and the absence of training in how to perform tasks with the least amount of exertion.

Fatigue induces carelessness and is therefore a potential cause of accidents. It can be attacked by paying attention to all the factors listed above when designing plant and fitting out factories or offices, carrying out work study exercises and designing training programmes.

### Physical and mental stress
Physical and mental stress can result from fatigue or from the strains and pressures built into the system of work. This problem also needs to be tackled at the design stage so that the machine (or office procedure) can be designed to fit the man rather than the man made to fit the machine. This is the science of ergonomics and some large companies such as Pilkingtons Glass employ full-time ergonomists who join teams in the design stages of factory programmes and advise on the mental factors that should be heeded when developing office systems and procedures. It is a highly technical and important discipline and it is sad that so little attention is paid to it when training design or system engineers.

The avoidance of strain from lifting heavy objects or from bad posture is also a matter of designing a safe work system. But this is an area where intensive training and constant propaganda are required to reduce risks.

### Medical checks

The importance of preventive medicine in industry can hardly be over-emphasized. It is the role of the medical adviser in co-operation with occupational hygienists, engineers, chemists and ergonomists to identify health risks and establish general threshold limits for exposure to the risks and individual standards of health and physique for employees.

The aim should be to develop health standards for each occupation and use these as selection and placement criteria when carrying out pre-employment medical examinations, which are a must in any situation where there are health risks.

A continuing programme of preventive medicine is required which should include checks on the extent to which employees are being exposed to health hazards, inspections to review and revise exposure threshold limits and health standards, and regular medical examinations for anyone at risk. It is essential to produce a detailed programme for this purpose, and the medical adviser should be required to keep top management informed of his programme and the results of his work.

## Accident prevention

The prevention of accidents is achieved by:

☐ identifying the causes of accidents and the conditions under which they are most likely to occur;
☐ taking account of safety factors at the design stage – building safety into the system;
☐ designing safety equipment and protective devices and providing protective clothing;
☐ carrying out regular inspections and checks and taking action to eliminate risks;
☐ investigating all incidents resulting in damage to establish the cause and to initiate corrective action;
☐ developing an effective health and safety organization;
☐ maintaining good records and statistics which will identify problem areas and unsatisfactory trends;
☐ conducting a continuous programme of education and training on safe working habits and methods of avoiding accidents.

### Identifying the causes of accidents

The process of identifying causes is mainly one of conducting inspections, checks and investigations, as described below. Some consideration should be given, however, to the general factors that induce accidents, as these will indicate the approach that should be used at the design and inspection stages.

Fundamentally it is the system of work to which human beings are exposed that is the cause of accidents. Carelessness, fatigue, lack of knowledge, inexperience, inadequate training or poor supervision may, in different degrees, be the immediate causes, but all these factors are related to the basic system of work.

The causes of accidents can therefore be divided into two main areas:

263

1. Those related to the system at work which are the basic reason for most accidents.
2. Those related to immediate individual factors, which in most cases arise from the system of work, but which might not have happened if there had been no human failure at or near the point of time when the accident occurred.

SYSTEM OF WORK FACTORS. The main factors in the system of work which induce accidents are:

☐ unsafely designed machinery, plant and processes;
☐ congested layouts;
☐ unguarded or inadequately guarded machinery;
☐ defective plant, materials or working conditions; rough, sharp or obstructive objects; slippery or greasy conditions; decayed, corroded, frayed or cracked containers, wires, conveyor belts or piping; badly maintained machinery;
☐ poor housekeeping – congestion; blocked gangways or exits; inadequate disposal arrangements for swarf or other waste products; lack of storage facilities; unclean working conditions;
☐ overloading of machines, transport vehicles or conveyor belts;
☐ inadequate lighting, glare;
☐ inadequate ventilation or systems for removing toxic fumes from the working environment;
☐ lack of protective clothing or devices.

It should be noted that although these factors are all connected with the system of work they all result from a human failure at some time.

IMMEDIATE FACTORS. The immediate, direct and personal factors causing accidents are:

☐ using unsafe equipment;
☐ using equipment unsafely – deliberately or through fatigue;
☐ unsafe loading and placing of materials or parts on machines or transport systems;
☐ operating without sufficient clearance;
☐ operating at an unsafe speed;
☐ making safety devices inoperative to reduce interference and speed up work;
☐ distractions from other people, noise or events taking place in the workshop;
☐ failure to use protective clothing or devices.

Any of these factors may result from personal failures such as carelessness, recklessness, laziness, impatience, lack of consideration, or inadequate knowledge, training, skill or supervision.

### Building safety into the system
The hazards to employees who operate and maintain machines arise from the belts and pulleys, gears, projecting parts, shaft ends, clutches and other moving parts used to stamp, to press, to cut or to shape materials. Transmission and transportation arrangements and the layout of plant and processes are also hazardous areas.

The prevention of accidents should be a major factor when designing plant or work processes. It is much more effective and economical to build safety into the system at the design stage rather than try to add makeshift safety devices later. It is equally important to specify the procedures and methods to be used in operating machines safely.

Designers should obtain feedback on accidents that may have been caused by a design fault, so that accidents can be eliminated by modification to existing and future designs.

## Safety inspections

The purpose of safety inspections is to locate and define the faults in the system and the operational errors that allow accidents to occur. It is essential to develop a systematic and thorough programme of inspections and spot-checks which will cover all parts of the factory at regular intervals. The five steps required are described below:

☐ *The first step* is to define the general points that should be covered in any area in which an inspection takes place. These are included in question 19. of the checklist at the end of this chapter.

☐ *The second step* is to divide the plant into areas (which may or may not follow existing departmental boundaries) and list the specific points to which attention should be given.

☐ *The third step* is to determine methods of inspection. These can take four forms.

1. Checklists are prepared of the points to be covered and a programme is planned to deal with them at regular intervals or over a series of inspections covering particular areas or safety points. This may be described as the audit approach, and the aim is to carry out a comprehensive review of all aspects of health and safety. Figure 17.3 is an example of the layout of a form that can be used for this purpose.

| Audit area | | Audited by | | Date | |
|---|---|---|---|---|---|
| Check points | Symptoms | Causes | Action recommended | Responsibility for action | Date for completion |
| | | | | | |

**Figure 17.3 Safety audit form**

2. Spot-checks can be made in each area on a random sample basis or to cover special problems, such as the inadequate use of protective clothing. In their simplest form these may simply enumerate the unsafe acts or conditions observed by the inspector or inspection team and thus identify areas where more detailed investigations are required. A numerical count of this nature can also be done on a comprehensive basis prior to a thorough inspection. An example of the layout of a sample inspection form is shown in figure 17.4.
3. Supervisors can be required to make daily checks of safety points in the areas under their control which should list the problem conditions and indicate the

| Area | Check carried out by | | | Date |
|---|---|---|---|---|
| | Number of observations | | | |
| Unsafe act or condition | Department A | Department B | Department C | Department D |
| | | | | |

**Figure 17.4 Safety sample inspection form**

action to be taken either by the supervisor himself, management, or the safety adviser. An example of a supervisor's checklist is shown in figure 17.5.

| Department | Supervisor | Date | |
|---|---|---|---|
| Item | Condition | Immediate action taken | Future action proposed |
| | | | |

**Figure 17.5 Supervisor's daily checklist**

4. Regular inspections, as required by legislation or by insurance companies, of boilers, pressure vessels, pipe-lines, dangerous processes, lifts, hoists, etc.

The best approach is to use all four methods. The comprehensive audit can be a continuous Forth Bridge-type operation, but spot-checks should be used to supplement the audit and keep supervisors and workpeople alert. The supervisor's checklist is also required to formalize the inspection procedures and this should be regarded as one of his key responsibilities. Statutory or insurance company inspections are obligatory, of course.

□ *The fourth step* is to define the responsibility for planning, conducting and acting on safety inspections. A safety adviser or the manager responsible for health and safety can prepare the checklists and programmes, although this should be done in consultation with managers, supervisors and workpeople. The inspections themselves should involve everyone concerned with safety; they should not be left to the safety adviser. This means that managers and supervisors and safety representatives should physically check conditions in their working areas. They may do this individually, but it is best done by a joint team working under the aegis of a health and safety committee. The safety adviser will still, of course, carry out his own investigations, but the prime responsibility for completing the pre-planned programme and taking action should rest with line management and the people working in the factory.

☐ *The fifth step* should be to set up systems of reporting on the results of inspections and on the action taken or proposed. It is essential that top management should take a direct interest in the inspection programme and that control procedures should be installed to ensure that audits, spot-checks and inspections do take place. The safety adviser can help top management to exercise control, but the ultimate responsibility is theirs.

### Accident reports and investigations

A standard system for reporting accidents should be used which will classify all incidents under appropriate headings, indicate the likely cause of the accident and suggest any remedial action that should be taken. It is necessary to have a standard classification system for accidents under headings such as those listed below:

1. *Type of accident*
   - falls of persons
   - falls of material
   - flying material
   - handling (manual)
   - handling (mechanical)
   - stepping on or striking against stationary objects
   - hand tools
   - railways and vehicles
   - escapes of gas, fumes, etc.
   - escapes of steam, hot water, liquids, etc.
   - machinery in motion
   - electricity
   - welding, brazing, burning, etc.
   - fires
   - explosions
2. *Location of the injury*
   - head and neck
   - eyes
   - back
   - upper limb
   - lower limb
   - hand
   - fingers
   - foot and toes
   - body system
3. *Severity of the injury*
   - fatal injury
   - permanent injury, total disablement
   - permanent injury, partial disablement
   - temporary injury, total incapacity for work
   - temporary injury, capable of carrying out alternative work
   - temporary injury, able to continue work.

An example of a simple report form is shown in figure 17.6.

Accident-reporting systems can only work if supervisors and medical or first-aid staff are trained in how to prepare reports. It is also necessary to emphasize, and to keep on emphasizing, the importance of the reports as a means of

267

| Department | | |
|---|---|---|
| Name of injured | Date of injury | |
| | Date/time of return to work | |
| Where and how did the accident occur? | | |
| Nature of injury | | |
| Name(s) of witnesses | | |
| Classification of accident | | |
| Type of accident | Location of accident | Severity of injury |
| | | |
| Measures taken and proposed to avoid repetition | | |
| Signed _____  Date _____ | | |

**Figure 17.6 Accident report form**

identifying causes and preventing the recurrence of accidents in order to ensure that they are completed accurately, comprehensively and in good time.

A report is useless unless it can contribute to increased understanding of health and safety problems and to the formulation of action programmes. In the case of minor and isolated incidents, it may not be necessary to follow up every report, although statistical trends should be kept under review to reveal areas where accidents are increasing and thus show the need for a special investigation.

More serious incidents must, of course, be investigated by the safety adviser or manager responsible for safety. Line management and supervisors should also be involved in the investigation of accidents in their areas, and safety representatives should be included in major investigations. The aim of the investigation should be to decide what needs to be done to avoid future incidents. It should not simply be a matter of apportioning blame. The results of the investigation, however, may well be used as evidence in later inquiries or court actions and it is essential to document all the circumstances, record the observations of eye witnesses, take photographs and ensure that defective machines or parts are isolated.

## Prevention of fire and explosion

The prevention of fire and explosions is achieved by adopting the same basic procedures as those used in preventing accidents. The steps required are to appraise the risks and to develop the basic precautionary measures.

### Appraising the risks
The appraisal should be carried out in conjunction with the local fire brigade, the Health and Safety Inspectorate, insurers, architects and process engineers.

### Developing precautionary measures
After the initial survey of the premises and plant, it is necessary to list the precautions required to minimize risk. These precautions can be classified under these headings:

☐ preventive maintenance programme
☐ regular inspections to identify potential risks
☐ safety rules
☐ detection and warning devices
☐ procedures and devices for dealing with fires and explosions, for evacuating the premises and for calling in outside help.

In each of these areas expert advice from specialists in the prevention of fires and explosions should be obtained.

## Education and training

Healthy and safe conditions at work do not simply happen. They have to be planned for and managed, and an essential part of this process is the education and training of managers, supervisors and workpeople.

### Educational programmes
The aim of educational programmes should be to ensure that everyone is fully aware of the hazards they meet at work and the potential consequences of hasty or thoughtless actions. They should be designed to create and maintain interest, using all the formal and informal means of communication available – safety bulletins, posters and notices, films and slides, talks and discussions.

Educational programmes should be continuous – they should not rely on intermittent spurts of activity, although they can include campaigns to deal with specific problems such as strains from lifting heavy objects. The message should be delivered straight to the people who need to hear and learn from it. This is why generalized campaigns are less effective than those aimed at people in their own workshop by the supervisors with whom they are in contact every day.

This can be done informally, but it is better to have an organized programme which supervisors can be trained to administer. Such a programme is the 'Safety Contact Scheme' developed by the Distillers Company, the essential elements of which are as follows:

☐ Supervisors are required to contact each employee in their section at least once in every four-week period to discuss with them a safety topic which has been selected for them by management.
☐ The supervisors are trained in how to run the contact sessions and given carefully prepared notes for guidance on the subject matter which summarize the

main points to be made and provide illustrations which help to get the message across.

☐ After each contact the supervisor records it on a record card which is inspected regularly by his manager to ensure that the programme is being followed.

### Safety training

Safety training programmes should be derived from an analysis of training needs. This should refer to the hazards generally present in the company as well as the specific hazards associated with individual jobs.

Managers, supervisors, safety advisers and safety representatives should be trained in such techniques as conducting inspections and investigations, collecting and analysing statistical data and communicating with people on health and safety matters.

Employees should be provided with general induction training as well as training in the hazards present in specific occupations.

INDUCTION TRAINING. Induction training should aim to give new employees a general understanding of what they must do to avoid risks and how the safety policies and facilities of the company will help them to avoid occupational illnesses and accidents. The points that should be covered include:

(a) the health and safety policies of the company, with particular reference to the duties of employees to work safely;
(b) the organization of the safety function;
(c) the arrangements for safety training;
(d) the main hazards that the employee is likely to face and what he should do about them;
(e) the unsafe practices that he should avoid;
(f) the use of protective clothing and safety equipment;
(g) the safety rules and procedures of the company;
(h) the procedure for reporting accidents;
(i) evacuation procedures in case of fire or explosion;
(j) first-aid facilities.

JOB TRAINING. Job safety training should be based on an analysis of the special hazards presented by a job. The job should then be broken down into its constituent parts, and the safety points to which the operator must pay attention should be defined for each part.

## Measurement and control of health and safety performance

Effective measurement and control is primarily a matter for action by management and supervision with the help of health and safety advisers. The procedure for carrying out surveys and inspections and for investigating incidents referred to earlier in this chapter provides the best means of monitoring performance and identifying where preventive or corrective action needs to be taken.

These measures, however, should be supplemented by safety statistics – not as an end to themselves (which they too often are) but as a basis for comparisons, inside and outside the company, and as a means of identifying undesirable trends which may not be revealed so clearly by the normal inspection procedures.

## Statistical measures

The most commonly used measure in the U.K. is the 'incidence rate', which is the number of reportable injuries (involving absence for over three days) per 1000 manual workers employed, thus:

$$\text{Incidence rate} = \frac{\text{Number of reportable injuries in period}}{\text{Average number of manual employees in period}} \times 1000$$

Other measures include the 'frequency rate', which is the number of disabling injuries per 1,000,000 man-hours and the 'severity rate', which is the days lost through accidents per 1,000,000 hours worked.

The problem with these indices is that they only deal with reportable accidents, and in smaller companies the number of such accidents may be so small that the statistics will not provide a reliable indication of trends. It may be better in these circumstances to measure the incidence of all accidental injuries, or even of all accidents causing damage.

## Measuring the cost

These statistics also ignore the cost of accidents and those who advocate the 'total loss control' approach emphasize the need to look at accidents from the point of view of their cost to the company as a whole as well as their effect on the individuals who sustain them. This approach, they claim, will provide a much greater incentive for commercially minded managements to take action.

The costs of accidents, other than the cost of insurance and special medical and safety facilities, can be allocated under the following headings:

1. Wages paid to injured workers who are off work.
2. Wages paid to workers who are not personally involved in the accident but lose time as a result of it.
3. Damage to machines, equipment, materials and buildings.
4. Loss of production because of damage or because workers are less effective when they return to work after an accident.
5. Salaries paid to managers, supervisors and other staff concerned in dealing with the accident and investigating its cause.
6. Other costs, including public liability claims, additional overtime, and the cost of renting equipment.

If these costs can be analysed (which could prove difficult) it is possible to work out a 'cost severity rate', which is the total cost of accidents per 1,000,000 man-hours worked, thus:

$$\text{Cost severity rate} = \frac{\text{Total cost of accidents over a period}}{\substack{\text{Total man-hours of production and} \\ \text{maintenance during the period}}} \times 1,000,000$$

# Conclusion

Inspection, investigations, reports and statistics are all necessary to the improvement of health and safety performance. But they depend for their effectiveness entirely upon the will power of the managers and supervisors concerned, who in turn will depend upon the leadership exercised by top management. That is why the Robens Committee report on Safety and Health at Work emphasized that:

Promotion of safety and health at work is an essential function of good management. We are not talking about legal responsibilities. The job of a director or senior manager is to manage. The boardroom has the influence, power and resources to take initiatives and to set the pattern.[2]

## References

1. Heinrich, H.W. *Industrial Accident Prevention*. McGraw-Hill Book Company, New York, 1959.
2. *Safety and health at work: report of the Committee 1970-72*, Cmnd. 5034, Her Majesty's Stationery Office, London, 1972.

<table>
<tr><td>*18*</td><td>**Welfare**</td></tr>
</table>

## Why welfare?

Welfare includes such activities as private advice on any type of personal problem; assistance with problems of health or sickness; special responsibilities for young people, elderly and retired staff and the provision of sports and social facilities. The first question to be answered is why any organization should be concerned with these matters.

### The case against welfare

The arguments against are obvious. Welfare implies 'do-gooding'; the personnel management fraternity have spent many years trying to shake off their association with what they, and others, like to think of as at best peripheral and at worst redundant welfare activities. Welfare is provided for by the state services — why should industrial, commercial or public sector organizations duplicate what is already there? The private affairs of employees and their out of work interests should not be the concern of their employers. It is selfish to maintain large playing fields and erect huge sports pavilions if they are going to be used by a minute proportion of staff for a very limited period of time — the space and facilities could be better used by the community. The argument that the provision of welfare services increases the loyalty and motivation of employees has long been exploded. If welfare services are used at all, they are taken for granted. Gratitude is not a prime motivating factor.

### The case for welfare

The case against welfare is formidable; the last point is particularly telling and there is some validity in each of the others — although there are limitations to their validity. Welfare state services are in theory available to all, but the ability of social workers to give individual advice, especially on problems arising from work, is limited in terms both of time and knowledge. It is all too easy for people to fall into the cracks existing in the edifice of the welfare state.

The case for welfare has to rely mainly on the abstract grounds of the social responsibility of organizations for those who work in them. This is not paternalism in the Victorian sense — turkeys at Christmas — or in the Japanese sense, where the worker's whole life centres around his employer. Rather, it is simply the realization that in exchange for offering his services, an employee is entitled to rather more than his pay, his statutory fringe benefits and healthy and safe systems of work. He is also entitled to consideration as a human being, especially when it is remembered that many of his personal problems will arise in the context of work and are best dealt with there. People's worries arise from work — about security, pay, health, relationships with others. But they also bring their personal problems to work; and many of these cannot be solved without reference to the situation there — they may require time off to deal with aged parents or sick wives, or advice on how to solve their problems and so minimize interference with their work.

The argument for welfare services at work was well put by A.O. Martin when he wrote:

Staff spend at least half their waking time at work or in getting to it or leaving it. They know they contribute *to* the organization when they are reasonably free from worry, and they feel, perhaps inarticulately, that when they are in trouble they are due to get something *back* from the organization. People are entitled to be treated as full human beings with personal needs, hopes and anxieties; they are employed as *people;* they bring themselves to work, not just their hands, and they cannot readily leave their troubles at home.[1]

The social argument for welfare is the most compelling one, but there is also an economic argument. Increases in morale or loyalty may not result in commensurate or, indeed, in any increases in productivity, but undue anxiety can result in reduced effectiveness. Even if welfare services cannot increase individual productivity, they can help to minimize decreases. Herzberg's two factor model in effect placed welfare amongst the hygiene factors, but he did not underestimate the importance of 'hygiene' as a means of eliminating or at least reducing causes of anxiety or dissatisfaction.

A further practical argument in favour of welfare is that a reputation for showing concern helps to improve the local image of the firm as a good employer and thus assists in recruitment. Welfare may not directly increase productivity but it may add to general feelings of satisfaction with the firm and cut down labour turnover.

A case for welfare therefore exists and the real question is not 'why welfare?' but 'what sort of welfare?'. This question needs to be answered in general terms before discussing the type of welfare services that can be provided and how they should be organized.

## What sort of welfare?

Welfare services fall into two categories:

1. Individual or personal services in connection with sickness, bereavement, domestic problems, employment problems, elderly and retired employees.
2. Group services, which consist of sports and social activities, clubs for retired staff and benevolent organizations.

### Principles of personal casework

Individual services require personal casework and the most important principle to adopt is that this work should aim to help the individual to solve his own problems. The employer, manager or welfare officer should not try to stand between the individual and his problem by taking it out of his hands. Emergency action may sometimes have to be taken on behalf of the individual, but if so, it should be taken in such a way that he can later cope with his own difficulties. Welfare action must start on the basis that disengagement will take place at the earliest possible moment when the individual can, figuratively, stand on his own two feet. This does not mean that follow-up action is unnecessary, but this is only to check that things are going according to plan, not to provide additional help unless something is seriously wrong.

Personal services should be provided when a welfare need is established, and a welfare need exists where it is clear that help is required, that it cannot be given more effectively from another source, and that the individual is likely to benefit from the services that can be offered.

In an organizational setting, an essential element in personnel casework services is confidentiality. There is no point in offering help or advice to someone if he thinks that his personal problems are going to be revealed to others, possibly to the detriment of his future career. This is the argument for having specialized welfare officers in organizations large enough to be able to afford them. They can be detached in a way that line managers and even personnel managers cannot be.

### Principles for providing group services

Group services, such as sports or social clubs, should not be laid on because they are 'good for morale'. There is no evidence that they are. They are costly and should only be provided if there is a real need and demand for them, arising from a very strong community spirit in a company or lack of local facilities. In the latter case, the facilities should be shared in an agreed and controlled way with the local community.

## Individual welfare services

### Sickness

These services aim to provide help and advice to employees absent from work for long periods because of illness. The practical reason for providing them is that they should help to speed the return of the employee to work, although it is no part of the welfare function to check up on possible malingerers. The social reason is to provide employees with support and counsel where a welfare need exists. In this context, a welfare need will exist where the employee cannot help himself without support and where such aid is not forthcoming from the state medical or welfare services or the employee's own family.

Welfare needs can be established by keeping in touch with an absent employee. This should not be done by rushing round as soon as anyone has been absent for more than, say, ten days or has exhausted his sickness benefit from work. It is generally better to write to sick absentees, expressing general concern and good wishes for a speedy recovery and reminding them that the firm can provide help if they wish, or simply asking them if they would like someone to visit them — with a stamped addressed envelope for their reply. Such letters should preferably be sent by the employee's line manager.

There will be some cases where the employee is reluctant to request help or a visit and the company may have to decide whether a visit should be made to establish if help is required. This will be a matter of judgement based on the known facts about the employee and his circumstances.

Visits can be made by the line manager, a personnel officer or a specialized full- or part-time welfare officer. Alternatively, arrangements can be made for a colleague to pay the visit. The aims of the visit should be first, to show the employee that his company and colleagues are concerned about his welfare; second, to alleviate any loneliness he may feel; and third, to provide practical advice or help. The latter may consist of putting him in touch with suitable organizations or ensuring that they are informed and take action. Or more immediate help may be provided to deal with pressing domestic problems.

## Bereavement

Bereavement is a time when many people need all the help and advice they can get. The state welfare services may not be able to assist and families are often non-existent or unhelpful. Established welfare organizations in industry, commerce or the public sector attach a lot of importance to this service. The advice may often be no more than putting the bereaved employee or the widow or widower of an employee in touch with the right organizations, but it is often extended to help with funeral arrangements and dealing with will and probate matters.

## Domestic problems

Domestic problems seem the least likely area for welfare services. Why should the company intervene, even when asked, in purely private matters? If, for example, an employee gets into debt, that is surely his affair. What business is it of the company?

These are fair questions. But an employer who has any real interest in the welfare of his staff cannot ignore appeals for help. The assistance should not consist of bailing people out of debt whenever they get into trouble or acting as an amateur marriage guidance or family casework officer. But, in accordance with the basic principle of personal casework already mentioned, employees can be counselled on how to help themselves or where to go for expert advice. A counselling service at work, whether operated by full-time welfare officers or by others on a part-time basis, can do an immense amount of good simply by providing an opportunity for employees to talk through their problems with a disinterested person. There is a limit to how much can or should be done in the way of allowing employees to pour out their troubles on willing shoulders but, used with discretion, it is a valuable service.

## Employment problems

Employment problems should normally be solved by discussion between the individual and his boss or through the company's grievance procedure. There may be times, however, when employees have problems over interpersonal relations, or feelings of inadequacy, about which they want to talk to a third party. Such counselling talks, as a means of relieving feelings and helping people to work through their problems for themselves, can do a lot of good, but extreme caution must be displayed by the company official who is involved. He must not cut across line management authority but, at the same time, he must preserve the confidentiality of the discussion. It is a delicate business and where it affects superior/subordinate relationships, it is one in which the giving of advice can be dangerous. The most that can be done is to provide a counselling service which gives employees an opportunity to talk about their problems and allows the counsellor to suggest actions the employee can take to put things right. The counsellor must not comment on the actions of anyone else who is involved. He can only comment on what the employee who seeks his help is doing or might do.

## Elderly and retired employees

Welfare for elderly employees is primarily a matter of preparing them for retirement and dealing with any problems they have in coping with their work. Preparation for retirement is a valuable service that many firms offer. This may be limited to advising on the classes and facilities local authorities provide for people prior to retirement, or when they have retired, or it may be extended to sponsoring special classes held during working hours. Some companies have made special provision for elderly employees by setting aside jobs or work areas for them. This has its dangers. Treating someone as a special case ahead of his time may make him over-aware of his condition or over-dependent on the services provided for him. There is everything to be said for treating elderly employees as normal workers, even though the health and safety services may take particular care to ensure that the age of the worker does not increase the danger of accident or industrial disease.

Retired employees, particularly those with long service, deserve the continuing interest of their late employer. The interest need not be oppressive, but continuing sick visiting can be carried out and social occasions can be provided for them.

## Group welfare services

Group welfare services mainly consist of sports and social clubs, although some companies still support various benevolent societies which provide additional help and finance in times of need.

A massive investment in sports facilities is usually of doubtful value unless there is nothing else in the neighbourhood and, in accordance with the principles mentioned earlier, the company is prepared to share its facilities with the local community. In a large company in a large town it is very difficult to develop feelings of loyalty towards the company teams or to encourage people to use the sports club. Why should they support an obscure side when their loyalties have always been directed to the local club? Why should they travel miles when they have perfectly adequate facilities near at hand? In the writer's experience, such clubs are usually supported by small cliques who have little or no influence over the feelings of other employees, who leave the enthusiasts to get on with whatever they are doing.

The same argument applies to social clubs, especially those forced on to employees by paternalistically minded companies. It is different when they arise spontaneously from the needs of employees. If they want to club together then the company should say good luck to them and provide them with a reasonable amount of support. The subsidy, however, should not be complete. The clubs should generate their own funds as well as their own enthusiasm. Facilities can be provided within the firm's premises if they are needed and readily available. An investment in special facilities should only be made if there is a real likelihood of their being used regularly by a large proportion of employees. This is an area where prior consultation, before setting up the facility, and self-government, when it has been established, are essential.

## Organization of welfare

It can be argued that the prime responsibility for welfare should rest with line managers on the principle that an officer's first concern should be the well-being of his troops. This is correct up to a point but the military analogy is not really valid. The basic unit in an army, the platoon, has a quite dissimilar function to that of the basic unit in an office or section, and the relationships between officers and their men have traditionally been quite different from those between a supervisor and his subordinate. Managers must be aware of personal problems and if people come to them for help and advice, so much the better. But this is a bonus and should not be relied upon. Line management may not be qualified to give advice or even direct people to where advice can be obtained, and employees may be reluctant to reveal personal problems which may prejudice their boss against them.

The obvious alternative is the personnel manager or local personnel officer. These people should be knowledgeable about how help can be provided and capable of exercising counselling skills. In smaller organizations it is inevitable that they should have a welfare role in addition to their normal personnel functions. But the welfare role is not necessarily consistent with their other responsibilities. Personnel managers are there to provide a service to management. This will involve providing certain services to employees, including welfare, but the interests of the company as a whole may have to prevail over the interests of an individual employee. A personnel officer is not therefore always in a position to give disinterested advice. In any case, he may not have the time to provide both the advice and the other personnel services.

In larger organizations the case for specialized welfare officers is that they should have the expertise and time to deal with individual casework and should be in a position to provide a sufficiently detailed counselling service. Clearly, they have to be aware of the fact that they only exist because the company exists. The advice and help they give cannot be contrary to the interests of the company as a whole, which will include the interests of colleagues or the individuals they have dealings with. But they can listen to people's problems and help them to help themselves without suffering from the conflicts of interest and shortages of time to which line and even personnel managers are prone. Their role is a delicate one, for reasons that have already been discussed, but they can have an important part to play in ensuring that the organization is able to meet its social responsibilities towards its employees.

### Reference
1. Martin, A. *Welfare at Work*. Batsford, London, 1967.

# 19 Personnel Records and Information Systems

## The need

Personnel record and information systems are required for three main purposes:

1. To store for reference the personal details of individual employees.
2. To provide a basis for decision-making in every area of personnel work, especially:
   □ manpower forecasting and planning;
   □ recruitment and selection;
   □ employment, including promotion, transfers, disciplinary procedures, termination and redundancy;
   □ education and training;
   □ pay administration;
   □ health and safety.
3. To provide data for returns to government departments and agencies.

Personnel records and information procedures can be based on an entirely manual system but, increasingly, they are being computerized to a greater or lesser degree. The advent of micro-computers is accelerating this process. There are, however, certain basic principles and practices which apply to any system and these are considered in the first three sections of the chapter: requirements of a good record system, identifying information requirements and designing the system. The next section deals with basic forms and returns which may exist only as a manual system or may be linked to a computer. Finally, the use of computers is considered in some detail.

## Requirements of a good record system

Personnel records, like any other records, must be simple, easy to maintain, comprehensive and relevant to the needs of the undertaking.

Simplicity and ease of maintenance are vital; records can be expensive to set up and maintain. A universal hatred of form filling and paper work generally will be enhanced to the total detriment of accuracy and utility if forms and records are complex, difficult to complete or hard to understand. This means designing forms so that entries can be made in logical and convenient sequence, left to right across the paper and from top to bottom. So far as possible, the method of completing the form should be self-explanatory — elaborate notes for guidance should be avoided. Plenty of space should be provided for each item; if different units of information are 'boxed' in, the form will be easier to complete and to read. Particularly vital pieces of information should be given prominence and may be placed in a more heavily defined box. Space should be provided for alterations and additions. One side of one sheet of paper is the ideal size although

279

clearly, some records such as application forms may have to be longer.

It is also important to ensure that records are not unduly duplicated, and this may mean taking care when assessing the degree to which records should be centralized or decentralized (discussed below).

Accuracy partly depends upon ensuring that clear definitions are made of the information that has to be entered on the form. If there is any ambiguity about, for example, a job title, the resulting entry may produce misleading information later for manpower planning or training surveys. It is important to place accurate information on the record. It is equally important to remove redundant information from the card or dossier. Many employee dossiers are full of useless documents which take up unnecessary space and increase the difficulty of getting at essential information. A regular review of records is required to clear out useless data.

A comprehensive system of records covers all the information required about individual employees or needed for personnel decision-making. But the information must be relevant. Every piece of information must be challenged with the questions 'what purpose will this serve?', 'to what use will it be put?'. The first point to clear when setting up a record system is the objective of each item in terms of the decisions it will help to make, its contribution to the assembly of essential statistical information, or its importance as a reference point in dealing with matters affecting individual employees.

It is necessary to avoid gaps in information essential to decision-making. It is equally necessary to avoid gathering useless data or maintaining elaborate statistics to which no one ever refers. Too often, a 'one-off' request for information leads to the setting up of a permanent record or data collection system, although the information may never be requested again. Regular reviews should be made of all records and returns to ensure that they are serving a useful purpose and that they are generally cost-effective. It may be cheaper in some circumstances to maintain manual records rather than to computerize. It may be less time-consuming and costly to carry out a special exercise rather than to maintain a permanent record, just in case.

## Identifying information requirements

The starting point should be an analysis of the decisions that the company makes or may need to make about individuals or groups of employees or the work force as a whole. This should be followed up by an analysis of the information required by government departments and agencies and by employers' associations.

### Personnel decisions requiring statistical data
The main decisions for which statistical information or individual data may be required include:

☐ forecasting the future supply of manpower by analysing, for each category of staff, labour turnover, age distribution, absenteeism and promotions;

☐ forecasting the future demand for manpower by ratio-trend analysis (calculating current ratios of manpower to activity levels and forecasting future ratios by reference to projected activity levels) and other statistical means;

☐ the introduction of productivity improvement or cost reduction campaigns based upon analyses of present manpower productivity levels and costs (e.g. manpower cost per unit of output, or the ratio of manpower costs to sales turnover or profit);

☐ planning recruitment campaigns on the basis of analyses of the results of previous campaigns, especially sources of recruits, media costs and success rates, and the relative pulling power of different inducements and recruitment methods;

☐ introducing new or improved interviewing and testing techniques on the basis of comparisons between interview and test assessments and subsequent performance;

☐ identifying people with particular skills or potential for new appointments or promotion;

☐ improving disciplinary procedures or amending works rules by analysing disciplinary cases,

☐ introducing new or improved time-keeping methods or considering the introduction of flexi-time by reference to time-keeping records;

☐ planning redundancies – consulting unions, transferring or re-training employees, selecting employees for redundancy, helping to place redundant employees;

☐ planning training programmes – subjects to be covered, types of courses and numbers of courses – by reference to analyses of future changes in manpower (numbers and skills), performance review records and job and training specifications;

☐ taking steps to improve job satisfaction and morale by reference to statistics on labour turnover, absenteeism, sickness, accidents, discipline cases and grievances;

☐ changing pay systems on the basis of statistics of wage drift, fluctuations in earnings, the proportion of employees on average earnings rather than payment – by results, cost per unit of output, fluctuations in earnings, the number and consequences of arguments over job rates;

☐ reviewing pay structures and levels of pay by reference to statistics of earnings in the company, rates of pay elsewhere, and the distribution of rates in each pay grade (e.g. compa-ratios for salary structure analysis as described in chapter 15);

☐ controlling merit reviews by analysing the distribution of merit awards in relation to budgets and guidelines and by assessing the implications of salary attrition (see chapter 15);

☐ taking steps to improve employee relations by analysing the causes of disputes;

☐ determining the information that should be communicated to unions and employees about the company or to assist in negotiations and joint consultation;

☐ improving health, safety and fire precautions by analysing reports on industrial disease, accidents and dangerous occurrences, monitoring returns on exposure to health hazards in relation to predetermined threshold limits, and studying reports on health, safety and fire inspection, spot-checks and audits.

## Personnel returns

The personnel returns required may include (in Great Britain):

☐ manpower and earnings statistics to the Department of Employment or employers' associations;

☐ training statistics to industrial training boards;

☐ health and safety statistics to the Health and Safety Executive.

### Individual data

Individual information should include:

- [ ] the application form giving personal particulars;
- [ ] interview and test record;
- [ ] job history after joining the firm including details of transfers, promotions and changes in occupation;
- [ ] current pay details and changes in salary or pay;
- [ ] education and training record with details of courses attended and results obtained;
- [ ] details of performance assessments and reports from appraisal or counselling sessions;
- [ ] absence, lateness, accident, medical and disciplinary records with details of formal warnings and suspensions;
- [ ] holiday entitlement;
- [ ] pensions data;
- [ ] termination record, with details of exit interview and suitablity for re-engagement.

### Collective data

Collective information may include:

- [ ] numbers, grades and occupations of employees;
- [ ] absenteeism, labour turnover and lateness statistics;
- [ ] accident rates;
- [ ] age and length of service distributions;
- [ ] total wage and salary bill;
- [ ] wage rates and salary levels;
- [ ] employee costs;
- [ ] overtime statistics;
- [ ] records of grievances and disputes;
- [ ] training records.

## Designing the system

The type and complexity of the personnel records and information system must obviously depend upon the company and its needs. Small companies may only need a basic card index system for individual employees and a simple set of forms for recording information on numbers employed, labour turnover and absenteeism. But a larger company will almost certainly need a more complex system because more information has to be handled, many more decisions have to be made, and the data changes more often. Card indexes are not enough, because supplementary records may be needed to give more detailed information about individual employees.

The key decisions to be made when designing the system concern:

- [ ] the design of the basic records, forms and input material;
- [ ] the use of computers;
- [ ] the extent to which records should be centralized or decentralized;
- [ ] the procedures and programme for collecting, recording, updating and disseminating information.

### The design of basic records and forms

The basic records and forms must be designed in accordance with the principles of simplicity, clarity, cost-effectiveness and relevance discussed earlier. Examples of typical forms and statistical returns are given at the end of this chapter and can be found elsewhere in this book.

## The use of computers

Advances in computer technology mean that relatively small firms can use computers, not only to store data but also to generate information for decision making purposes. When thinking about converting manual records to a computer system or updating an existing system, the points to consider are:

1. Why computerize?
2. To what uses can a computer be put?
3. What systems should be selected and how?
4. How should the system be operated?

### Why computerize?

Computers will hold records in a more compact and accessible way, and they can be justified for this reason alone. They can generate information for decision making more flexibly, more quickly and more comprehensively than any manual system.

### Uses of computers in personnel management

The main uses to which computers can be put in personnel departments are:

1. *Keeping records* — replacing card indexes and filing cabinets by magnetic discs.
2. *Listings* — providing quickly listings of employees by department, occupation, grade, pay level, length of service, age, sex, qualifications, skills, etc.
3. *Automatic letter writing* — producing standard letters and forms for recruitment, promotion, transfer, upgrading, appraisal, pay review and new contracts of employment.
4. *Manpower planning* — using manpower data to forecast the future demand for and supply of people. Manpower models can be used, such as the following developed by the Institute of Manpower Studies:
   *Prospect* — a forecasting model for examining a hierarcy of grades by age. Useful for gaining a general understanding of future movement of staff and changes in age/grade structure.
   *Prospect 2* — similar to Prospect but much more flexible in the manpower structure it can represent, the types and combinations of flows modelled and the variety of output which can be obtained.
   *Expro* — a simple model which looks at individuals rather than groups.
5. *Labour turnover analysis* — providing labour turnover statistics such as wastage or survival rates, by occupation or department. Analyses by reason for leaving, age and service can be produced. This data can be incorporated in the manpower planning model to forecast future losses and replacement needs.
6. *Career development* — as a development of manpower planning models, computerized personnel information can be used to improve succession planning.
7. *Recruitment* — the computer can, in effect, be used as a filing cabinet to store details of each applicant, date of receipt of application, when called for interview and the outcome. If an applicant contacts the company, he can rapidly

be told the progress of his application. Managers can be given details of the number of applicants and how many have been interviewed. Lists and automatic letters can be produced when calling for interview, rejecting applicants or making offers.

8. *Training* — records can be kept to check on who has received training or on progress through apprenticeship or other training schemes. Listings of skills and qualifications by department or occupation can be produced to identify gaps and training needs.

9. *Pay* — information can be drawn from both personnel and pay-roll systems to analyse pay-roll costs and ratios and to assess the impact of various pay increase options on the pay structure and on total pay-roll costs. Budgetary control systems can be computerized to show actual pay-roll costs against budget and to project future costs.

10. *Salary administration* — salary analysis reports can be produced which give information by employee on occupation, salary, position in salary range, total and percentage increases over previous years and appraisal codes. Individual forms and departmental schedules can be generated for salary reviews and analyses can be made of the salary structure (e.g. compa-ratios), actual and percentage increases in pay-roll costs against budget, distribution of staff in salary ranges (e.g. number at each point in an incremental scale), and salary attrition (i.e. the extent to which the cost of merit increases is eroded over the year because of movements of leavers and joiners into the salary system). IBM has produced the PERSIS personnel information system (personnel, administration, services and salary policy) which they use in conjunction with their own personnel data system (PDS) to assist in the implementation of the key points of IBM's salary policy which are:
    □ all jobs evaluated into levels to which salary ranges apply;
    □ salary ranges based on surveys;
    □ progress through range over time;
    □ different ceilings for different performances;
    □ increases awarded on a rolling basis.

11. *Job evaluation* — databases can be created to hold and process information on job evaluation, such as grades and points scores. Weightings of job evaluation factors can be determined by multiple regression analysis and the recording and analysis of paired comparisons can be computerized. In a job evaluation exercise, the information system can be used to print out the names of those whose jobs are to be evaluated. Details of job, grade, function, location, sample size and current point ratings can be programmed in. The data base can link together similar posts in different parts of the organization. Listings of all gradings, re-gradings and points scores can be produced.

12. *Absence and sickness* — absences can be recorded by employee, with reasons, and analyses produced of absenteeism and sickness. In the U.K. the introduction of the Statutory Sick Pay Scheme (SSP) with all the recording which it entails has accelerated the use of computers as a database for sickness records.

13. *Health and safety* — records can be maintained on accidents and absence due to health hazards. Trends can be analysed and information produced on who has worked in certain areas, or who has used certain processes and for how long.

## Selecting the system

The extent to which an organization will want to use any of the facilities provided by a computer, apart from the basic record keeping and listing functions, will vary according to its size, complexity and the importance it attaches to basing decisions on accurate and quickly provided information. Before selecting the system a cost/benefit analysis is required. Some savings in staff time and in space for storing records will be obvious. Others will be more subjective. It is best to start in a fairly small way and add extra facilities as experience is gained. This implies, however, that the basic system must be flexible and can be extended.

A flexible and not too ambitious approach is desirable. Control of the project should be vested in the personnel department – the user should always head the study, although he will have to accept technical advice on systems, feasibilities and costs. Advice from internal systems analysts or, if they are not available, external consultants is obviously essential. The development should be staged, starting with a fairly modest record keeping facility and extending to the more sophisticated applications as experience is gained. It is unwise to try to do too much too quickly. In designing the system, ease of operation, clarity of presentation, economy in use and flexibility are all important considerations.

Clearly, the choice of system is strongly influenced by the uses to which it will be put. For example, if the system will need to answer questions rapidly, it is desirable to have an on-line (i.e. immediate access) facility to the data held in it. If it is to be used in modelling and in posing 'what if?' questions, then the system will require sizeable computing power, particularly if large amounts of data are involved. This may rule out micro-computers and it will be necessary to use a main-frame or at least a mini-computer.

A decision will have to be made on whether the personnel and pay-roll systems should be integrated. Much common data is held on these two systems and it seems to make sense to combine them. Many companies operate a 'pay-roll driven' system in which the basic pay-roll data is augmented by personnel information. Such systems are usually cheaper to introduce and operate than completely separate ones.

Finance departments often want to keep control over pay transactions and there is a danger of losing flexibility if the systems are too closely linked. A strong case can be made for a separate system doing what the personnel department wants it to do. But such systems can be costly to develop and use.

The choice of basic system lies between:

1. *Bureau*, which uses its own software (i.e. programs) on its own hardware (i.e. computer and peripheral equipment). Bureaux are used because they have the software and computer resources available and therefore relieve the client company of pressure on its own system development and hardware resources. It is usually cheaper to develop a system at a bureau than in-house, but a standard package has to be accepted which may not fit the company's needs.
2. *Internal development software run on in-house hardware*. Given the time, money and resources needed, this approach should provide the most appropriate and flexible system. The initial choice lies between using an existing 'main-frame' or mini-computer or installing a micro-computer for the personnel department's exclusive use. The latter alternative has some attractions on the grounds of accessibility and control but restricts the amount of dates and facilities available. There is, however, considerable cost and always some risk in developing new software, which is why alternative 3 below is sometimes

adopted. And there is also the risk that an internal main-frame or even a mini-computer might become overloaded, making access difficult. It is possible to avoid this problem by installing a micro-computer within the personnel department.
3. *Externally developed software run on in-house hardware.* This alternative reduces the cost and risk of developing special programs, but the result may not be so relevant to the company's needs.

**Operating the system**
The system needs to provide for the following operational requirements:

1. *Updating* — in a paper-driven system changes are originated on forms and either transcribed ready for punching or used to 'key in' the information directly (i.e. 'on-line'). Changes are often processed in batches. With most mini- or micro-based systems the updating is carried out not only on-line but also in 'real-time'. This means that changes are immediately made to the record being updated rather than being processed some time later.
2. *Enquiries* — the ideal method is to have an on-line system, which means that enquiries can be answered immediately, using a terminal.
3. *Reports* — reports will be produced either on a routine or an *ad hoc* basis depending on requirements and the programs available.
4. *Security* — a system has to be introduced to protect information and to prevent unauthorized changes being made to salaries, pay grades or other personal data. Access to the computer must be restricted to authorized individuals who will have to use 'blind' (i.e. secret) passwords before updating records or asking for information. Different levels of authority will have to be allocated.

# Centralization and decentralization of records

In a small company, or one in which operations are concentrated on one site, the issue of centralization and decentralization may not be an important one. Although, even in the latter case, there may be problems of duplication if departments insist on keeping records of their own employees in addition to those maintained centrally.

The advantages of centralization are that there is less expenditure on space and equipment, company statistical analyses can more easily be prepared and duplication is avoided. The disadvantages are that local departments or units may not have ready access to the information they need while there may be delays in obtaining the data required by central records.

The advantages of decentralization are that departments have the information they need on the spot, and delays in transmitting data are reduced. The disadvantages are additional costs because of space requirements and duplicated efforts and possible loss in effectiveness at the centre because of difficulties in analysing the total situation in the company.

In a divisionalized company, where these problems are likely to be most pressing, the answer is usually a compromise. Divisions maintain all their own personnel records but a standardized set of returns is devised for transmission to the central personnel information office to be processed by the computer or manually so that the group statistical analyses and returns can be prepared. In this situation, the aim should be to keep the central returns to a minimum, possibly only covering basic data on manpower numbers and trends, and earnings.

## Procedures

The procedures to be used in collecting, analysing, disseminating and updating information should be laid down at the design stage so that everyone knows what to do and when to do it. Decisions should be made at this stage as to whether data should be *event triggered* or *time triggered.*

*Event triggered* data are recorded when pre-specified events occur, giving information about the occurrence or non-occurrence of a particular event, e.g. an accident, or someone leaving, which is important for control purposes. *Time triggered* recordings are generated at pre-specified intervals of time, e.g. earnings surveys.

The procedures for disseminating information should list who initiates the report, to whom it goes and, where appropriate, what action should be taken. Updating procedures may include reviews of the relevance and accuracy of data as well as systems to ensure that changes in data are recorded quickly and accurately.

## Examples of forms and statistical returns

The examples of forms and statistical returns illustrated in this chapter and elsewhere in the book are listed below.

| Area | Type of Form | Figure No. |
|---|---|---|
| General | Basic personnel record card | 19.1 |
| | Quarterly return — employment, labour turnover and earnings | 19.2 |
| | Monthly analysis of leavers | 19.3 |
| | Monthly/annual summary of absence | 19.4 |
| Manpower Planning | Staff forecast form | 10.2 |
| Recruitment | Staff requisition form | 11.3 |
| | Job specification form | 11.4 |
| | Retirement control sheet | 11.5 |
| | General application form | 11.6 |
| | Senior staff application form | 11.7 |
| | Interview assessment form | 11.8 |
| Management Development | Management succession schedule | 21.2 |
| Performance Appraisal | Merit assessment form | 12.1 |
| | Performance review form | 12.2 |
| Salary Administration | Salary budget form | 15.12 |
| | Salary cost comparison form | 15.13 |
| | Compa-ratio summary form | 15.14 |
| | Individual salary review form | 15.15 |
| | Salary review summary sheet | 15.16 |
| Health and Safety | Safety audit form | 17.3 |
| | Safety sample inspection form | 17.4 |
| | Supervisor's daily checklist | 17.5 |
| | Accident report form | 17.6 |

| Name | | Date joined |
|---|---|---|
| Date of birth | Marital status | No. of children |
| Address | | Home telephone no. |
| | | |
| Qualifications | | |
| Languages | | |

| Previous employment | | |
|---|---|---|
| Company | Position | Dates |
| | | |

| Present employment | | |
|---|---|---|
| Department | Position | Dates |
| | | |
| Date left | Reason for leaving | |

*Front*

| Salary — Performance — Potential Record | | | |
|---|---|---|---|
| Date | Salary | Performance rating | Potential rating |
| | | | |

| Training received | |
|---|---|
| Date | Course |
| | |

*Reverse*

**Figure 19.1 Basic personnel record card**

| QUARTERLY RETURN – EMPLOYMENT, LABOUR TURNOVER AND EARNINGS | | | | | | | | *Quarter ending* | |
|---|---|---|---|---|---|---|---|---|---|
| | Number on pay-roll | | | Labour turnover annual rate % | | | Average weekly earnings | | |
| | | Increase(+) or decrease(-) since: | | | Increase(+) or decrease(-) since: | | | Increase(+) or decrease(-) since: | |
| **Occupation** | This quarter | Last quarter | Same quarter last year | This quarter | Last quarter | Same quarter last year | This quarter | Last quarter | Same quarter last year |
| | | | | | | | | | |
| *Total* | | | | | | | | | |

Figure 19.2 Quarterly return – employment, labour turnover and earnings

## MONTHLY ANALYSIS OF LEAVERS

| Month of | 19 | | Department | | | | | | Occupation(s) | | | | | | |

| Length of service | Sex | Discharge | | Redundancy | Personal betterment | Reasons for Leaving | | | | | | Domestic reasons | Retirement | Death | Unknown | Total |
|---|---|---|---|---|---|---|---|---|---|---|---|---|---|---|---|---|
| | | Unsuitable | Discipline | | | Pay | Work | Dissatisfaction with: | | | | | | | | |
| | | | | | | | | Working conditions | Hours | Management | Other factors | | | | | |
| Less than 1 month | M | | | | | | | | | | | | | | | |
| | F | | | | | | | | | | | | | | | |
| 1 - 3 months | M | | | | | | | | | | | | | | | |
| | F | | | | | | | | | | | | | | | |
| 4 - 12 months | M | | | | | | | | | | | | | | | |
| | F | | | | | | | | | | | | | | | |
| 1 - 5 years | M | | | | | | | | | | | | | | | |
| | F | | | | | | | | | | | | | | | |
| Over 6 years | M | | | | | | | | | | | | | | | |
| | F | | | | | | | | | | | | | | | |
| Total | M | | | | | | | | | | | | | | | |
| | F | | | | | | | | | | | | | | | |

**Labour turnover rate expressed as an annual rate%***

| | This month | Last month | Same month last year |
|---|---|---|---|
| Male | | | |
| Female | | | |
| **Total** | | | |

* Monthly labour turnover rate expressed as an annual rate% = $\left[\dfrac{\text{Number of leavers during month}}{\text{Average number employed during month}}\right] \times 100 \times 12$

**Figure 19.3 Monthly analysis of leavers**

## MONTHLY/ANNUAL SUMMARY OF ABSENCE

| Year | | Department/company | | Occupation(s) | | | | |
|---|---|---|---|---|---|---|---|---|
| Month | Hours of absence | | | | | Total planned hours (including overtime) | % lost of planned hours (including overtime) |
| | Sickness or accident | | Other absence | | Total absence (including lateness) | | |
| | Certified | Uncertified | Authorized | Unauthorized (inc. lateness) | | | |
| January | | | | | | | |
| February | | | | | | | |
| March | | | | | | | |
| April | | | | | | | |
| May | | | | | | | |
| June | | | | | | | |
| July | | | | | | | |
| August | | | | | | | |
| September | | | | | | | |
| October | | | | | | | |
| November | | | | | | | |
| December | | | | | | | |
| Total for year | | | | | | | |

Figure 19.4 Monthly/annual summary of absence

## Part IV
# Employee Development

This part considers how organizations should train and develop their staff. Chapter 20 covers training techniques and procedures, starting from an analysis of learning theory and going on to a discussion of how systematic training procedures should be developed and implemented. The importance of developing managers to improve corporate performance and provide for the future is emphasized in chapter 21 which considers the various procedures available for increasing the effectiveness of managers and developing their potential.

# 20 | Training

## Aims

The aims of training are to:

☐ shorten learning time so that new recruits reach their peak of efficiency as quickly and economically as possible;
☐ improve the performance of existing employees;
☐ help people to develop their capacities so that the company can meet most, if not all, its future requirements for managers, supervisors and higher grade professional, technical, sales or production staff from within the organization.

These aims can be achieved by adopting a systematic approach, as suggested below, concentrating mainly on 'on the job' and 'do-it-yourself'. For detailed descriptions of these types of training, see Appendix J.

## The process of training

Training is the systematic development of the knowledge, skills and attitudes required by an individual to perform adequately a given task or job. The key word in this definition is 'systematic'. Systematic training is training which is specifically designed to meet defined needs. It is planned and provided by people who know how to train. Training programmes can all too easily be irrelevant. It is easy to fall into the trap of training for training's sake. It is necessary to adopt a systematic approach, which need not be elaborate or costly and which involves:

☐ defining training needs;
☐ deciding what sort of training is required to satisfy these needs;
☐ using experienced trainers to plan and implement training;
☐ following up and evaluating training to ensure that it is effective.

Training involves learning, of various kinds and in various situations. Learning may be something that the trainee wants to do for himself or it may be necessary to provide it for him. If training is provided, the individual may need to be given an incentive − to be motivated − to learn and to apply his learning. Even if no incentive is required − if the trainee is self-motivated − it may still be necessary to provide the guidance and training facilities which will help him to channel his enthusiasm towards a worthwhile end.

Training can take place in various situations: on the job or off the job; in the company or outside the company. It can involve the use of many techniques: demonstration, practice, coaching, guided reading, lectures, talks, discussions, case studies, role playing, assignments, projects, group exercises, programmed learning, the discovery method, and so on. And these techniques can be deployed by many people: specialist company trainers, managers, supervisors, colleagues or external trainers and educationists.

Therefore training is, or at least can seem to be, a complex process and the techniques used can vary almost infinitely according to the situation. There are, however, certain fundamental concepts and principles upon which all training should be based and, in this chapter, these will be reviewed before consideration is given to their application to the training for different occupations.

The first area that will be covered is learning theory, because all training is, or should be, based upon an understanding of how people learn.

The essential components of the sequence of training as shown in figure 20.1 will then be dealt with. These consist of:

☐ the identification and analysis of training needs – all training must be directed towards the satisfaction of defined needs; for the company as a whole, for specific functions or groups of employees, or for individuals;

☐ the definition of training objectives – training must aim to achieve measurable goals expressed in terms of the improvements or changes expected in corporate, functional, departmental or individual performance;

☐ the preparation of training plans – these must describe the overall scheme of training and its costs and benefits. The overall scheme should further provide for the development of training programmes and facilities, the selection and use of appropriate training methods and the selection and training of trainers;

☐ the implementation of training plans, including the maintenance of training records;

☐ the measurement and analysis of results, which require the *validation* of the

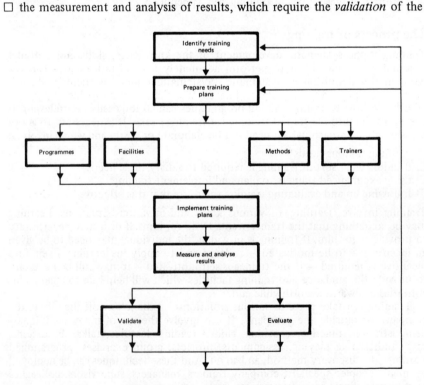

**Figure 20.1 The sequence of training**

achievements of each training programme against its objectives and the *evaluation* of the effect of the whole training scheme on company or departmental performance;
☐ the feedback of the results of validations and evaluations so that training plans, programmes and techniques can be improved.

## Learning theory

Learning theory provides the background against which training programmes and techniques should be developed and used. A knowledge of the basic concepts of how people learn is essential to anyone who plans or conducts training. Even during the initial phase of the training sequence — when training needs are being identified — it is still necessary to be aware of learning theory as this will help to direct inquiries towards those areas where training is most likely to be effective.

Learning theory suggests that there are ten main conditions required for learning to be effective:

1. *The individual must be motivated to learn.* He should be aware that his present level of knowledge or skill, or his existing attitude or behaviour, needs to be improved if he is to perform his work to his own and to others' satisfaction. He must, therefore, have a clear picture of the behaviour he should adopt.
2. *Standards of performance should be set for the learner.* Learners must have clearly defined targets and standards which they find acceptable and can use to judge their own progress.
3. *The learner should have guidance.* The learner needs a sense of direction and 'feedback' on how he is doing. A self-motivated individual may provide much of this for himself, but the trainer should still be available to encourage and help him when necessary.
4. *The learner must gain satisfaction from learning.* Learners are capable of learning under the most difficult circumstances if the learning is satisfying to one or more of their needs. Conversely, the best training schemes can fail if they are not seen as useful by the trainee.
5. *Learning is an active not a passive process.* The learner needs to be actively involved with his trainer, his fellow trainees and the subject matter of the training programme.
6. *Appropriate techniques should be used.* The trainer has a large repertory of training tools and materials. But he must use these with discrimination in accordance with the needs of the job, the individual and the group.
7. *Learning methods should be varied.* The use of a variety of techniques, as long as they are equally appropriate, helps learning by maintaining the interest of the trainee.
8. *Time must be allowed to absorb the learning.* Learning requires time to assimilate, test and accept. This time should be provided in the training programme. Too many trainers try to cram too much into their programmes and allow insufficient scope for practice and familiarization.
9. *The learner must receive reinforcement of correct behaviour.* Learners usually need to know quickly that they are doing well. In a prolonged training programme, intermediate steps are required in which learning can be reinforced.
10. *The need to recognize that there are different levels of learning and that these need different methods and take different times.* At the simplest level,

learning requires direct physical responses, memorization and basic conditioning. At a higher level, learning involves adapting existing knowledge or skill to a new task or environment. At the next level, learning becomes a complex process when principles are identified in a range of practices or actions, when a series of isolated tasks have to be integrated or when the training deals with inter-personal skills. The most complex form of learning takes place when training is concerned with the values and attitudes of people and groups. This is not only the most complex area, it is also the most difficult and dangerous.

### Applying learning theory

Each of the ten conditions mentioned above needs to be applied to make training work. Particular attention should be given to motivation, providing satisfaction from learning, making training an active process, and reinforcement. Training is about changing behaviour and all these factors are important if change for the better is to take place. Hence the importance of what has been termed the behaviour modelling approach to training.

### Behaviour modelling

The behaviour modelling approach is based on the logic that training begins with the learning of new behaviour. Contrary to the opinion of many trainers, Campbell[1] has shown that attempts to change behaviour by verbal persuasion or logic do not always succeed. The main block to attitude change is the existence of defence mechanisms which come into action when customary beliefs or attitudes are threatened. Under pressure, temporary changes in attitudes may result from training. But it may not be transferred to successful changes in behaviour on the job after training has been completed. And one of the main problems in training is achieving 'transfer'. It is too easy for trainees at the end of the course to be full of knowledge and enthusiasm following their classroom or training centre experiences. Unfortunately, it is even easier for them to come up against obstacles (sometimes self-induced) and indifference back at work which make it difficult to apply what they have learned. Action learning, do-it-yourself training and training on the job may help to overcome the problem, but off the job training must still take place, and where it involves changes in attitudes as well as behaviour, the technique of behaviour modelling has a part to play.

The training theory incorporated in behaviour modelling is based on reinforcement to obtain retention of learning and the transfer of behaviour. Reinforcement as a principle developed by behaviourists such as Skinner[2] is defined as any consequence which strengthens or increases a behaviour which it follows. From this basic concept Bandura[3] developed his social learning theory. Social learning is based on observing the behaviour of other people. In a sense it is vicarious reinforcement. A model is formed of desirable behaviour by observation and this is reinforced by practising the new behaviour with other members of the training group. Behaviour modelling procedures are quite different from many other traditional training approaches in that they do not rely on changing attitudes first and then hoping that behaviour will fall into line with these new attitudes. Instead, these procedures are aimed at directly changing behaviour without relying on the tactics of attitude change.

The foundation of behaviour modelling is the modelling of a set of desirable behaviour patterns live, on video tape or on film. Steps are taken to ensure that the trainee can retain sufficient knowledge of the model behaviour to be able to tackle the next stage, in which he practises or rehearses the desired behaviour. The final stage, which is the key to success, is to achieve social reinforcement by getting the trainee involved with other trainees in practising the new behaviour. This active and joint process enables trainees to observe the other participants and learn from their behaviour. To ease transfer from the classroom to the job, the model and the rehearsals are made to look as much like the job as possible.

Social modelling uses existing techniques of role playing and simulation but places these methods in the context of a much more structured attempt to ensure reinforcement from the behaviour of other trainees and to relate what is being learned off the job to the behaviour required on the job.

## Identifying training needs

Training will not be effective unless it is based on an understanding of learning theory. But training must have a purpose and that purpose can only be defined if the training needs of the organization and the groups and individuals within it have been identified and analysed. Put like that, this seems a trite and obvious statement. Too much training in industry and commerce, however, has been training for training's sake. In effect, people have said: 'Training is a good thing, let there be training.' Perhaps the major contribution of the industrial training boards in Great Britain has been to emphasize the importance of an analytical and systematic approach to training. And analysis starts at the beginning, with the study of training needs.

### Training needs analysis – aims
The analysis of training needs aims to define the gap between what *is* happening and what *should* happen. This is what has to be filled by training (see figure 20.2).

**Figure 20.2 The training gap**

The gap may consist of the difference between:

☐ how the company or a function within the company is performing and how it should perform;
☐ what people know and can do and what they should know and do;
☐ what people actually do and what they should do.

### Training needs analysis – areas
Training needs should be analysed first for the company as a whole – corporate needs; secondly for departments, functions or occupations within the company – group needs; and thirdly for individual employees – individual needs. These

three areas are inter-connected, as shown in figure 20.3. The analysis of corporate needs will lead to the identification of training needs in different departments or occupations, while these in turn will indicate the training required for individual employees. The process also operates in reverse. As the needs of individual employees are analysed separately, common needs emerge which can be dealt with on a group basis. The sum of group and individual needs will define corporate needs, although there may be some super-ordinate training requirements which can only be related to the company as a whole — the whole training plan may be greater than the sum of its parts.

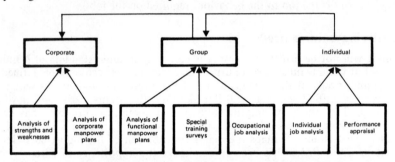

**Figure 20.3 Training needs — areas and methods**

*Corporate needs* can be determined by analysing company strengths and weaknesses — a procedure that should normally be part of the corporate planning process. These should be examined in each of the main activity areas: for example, development, production, marketing, finance, personnel, and management services. The aim should be to identify those problems that can be attributed to weaknesses or gaps in the knowledge, skill and capacities of managerial, technical, clerical and production staff. This is necessarily a broad brush approach. It may do no more than highlight areas within functions or departments where further study is required.

Corporate training needs should also be recorded by the manpower plan, which will indicate the numbers and types of people required in the future. In fact, the manpower planning process, as described in chapter 10, should provide a major source of information on longer term training requirements.

*Group needs* can be identified by analysing functional or departmental manpower plans or by conducting special surveys using questionnaires and interviews, as discussed below. Job analysis can be used to determine the knowledge and skills required in specific jobs and this information can be supplemented by analysing the results obtained from the assessment of individual needs.

*Individual needs* can be assessed by the use of job analysis and by analysing the information obtained from performance reviews, as discussed below.

### Training needs analysis — methods
Surveys to identify training needs can be conducted by questionnaire or by interview or preferably by a combination of these two methods. They may use job analysis on a comprehensive or sample basis, or they may rely upon broader questions designed to reveal problem areas. Training surveys may complement more analytical investigations by seeking to identify general training needs which might not be revealed, except with a great deal of effort, by looking at individual

jobs. They may also provide a framework for the training plan and the more detailed studies that follow. Their aim should be to define manpower problems that can be solved by training. Training is always more relevant, and therefore more effective, if it ensures that trainees understand and take the action required to overcome the actual problems they meet when carrying out their work. Training should be problem-based and action-orientated.

The simplest method of conducting training surveys is to go round asking managers and supervisors what they think are the training priorities in their departments. The results obtained may be subjective but, as long as the surveys are comprehensive and the answers are analysed carefully, they will provide a useful starting point for more detailed analysis. They will also ensure that management and supervision feel involved from the beginning – they are more likely to help with job analysis and to support the training programme if they have been consulted about their requirements.

If a general survey is being carried out for the first time and in the absence of any other information, it should obtain details of:

☐ numbers and types of employees;
☐ future manpower requirements;
☐ any difficulties experienced or anticipated in obtaining adequate staff in sufficient quantities;
☐ any operating problems which can be attributed to shortages of manpower or poor quality performance;
☐ specific jobs or occupations where gaps in knowledge or lack of skill are producing unsatisfactory results;
☐ high labour turnover, absenteeism or grievance rates which may indicate that employees have not been properly trained or that additional training for managers and supervisors is required;
☐ present training arrangements and their adequacy;
☐ the priorities for improving or instituting training schemes.

Follow-up surveys, which aim to audit training arrangements, should concentrate on analysing the effectiveness of training schemes in solving management's problems, and on up-dating the information on manpower plans and training priorities.

The results of the training surveys should be used to define objectives, priorities and the likely pay-off of any proposed schemes.

## Job analysis
Of all the stages in the systematic training process, job analysis is probably the most important. Good training is synonymous with relevant training. By defining the duties, responsibilities, tasks, knowledge and skills which make up a job – and specifying training accordingly – relevance must result.

Job analysis is the process of examining a job in order to identify its component parts and the circumstances in which it is performed. It can be a highly detailed and expensive procedure, or it can embrace no more than a broad study of duties and training requirements. The stages required in a detailed study are:

☐ *a broad analysis* of the requirements of the job and any special problems surrounding it as seen by the job holder, his superior and, possibly, his colleagues;
☐ a detailed study of the responsibilities, duties and tasks carried out which

forms the basis for a *job description;*
- [ ] an analysis of the knowledge and skills required by the job holder which forms the basis for a *job specification;*
- [ ] a description of the training requirements for the job – the *training specification.*

THE BROAD ANALYSIS. The aim of the broad analysis is to get an overall picture of the demands of the job and the problems job holders meet in doing their work which will provide a basis for the subsequent more detailed study. It should also place the job in its organizational setting and establish relationships with other jobs so that linked training schemes can be planned and priorities determined.

The broad analysis should provide information on:

- [ ] the overall purpose of the job – a brief summary of what the job holder does and how the job fits in with other functions;
- [ ] the main knowledge and skills required;
- [ ] how training is carried out at present – and how effective it is;
- [ ] the problems facing the job holders – in learning the job, in carrying it out, in relating to other people;
- [ ] any weaknesses in performance – general, or particular to individual employees;
- [ ] action required.

JOB DESCRIPTION. The material for job descriptions can be assembled by questionnaires, interviews, observation, activity sampling or diary sheets. The choice of methods will depend on the type of job, the circumstances in which the information has to be obtained, and the amount of time and money available.

For training purposes the job description should contain information on:

- [ ] the job title;
- [ ] organization position – immediate superior and subordinates;
- [ ] the main role – the overall purpose of the job;
- [ ] the main activities and tasks carried out;
- [ ] the standard or measures of performance for each activity;
- [ ] the contacts made with other given departments;
- [ ] the limits of authority given to the job holder.

JOB SPECIFICATION. A job specification is a product of job analysis. It breaks down the broad duties contained in the job description into the detailed tasks that must be carried out. In then sets out the characteristics that the worker should have in order to perform these tasks successfully. These characteristics are:

- [ ] *Knowledge* – what the worker needs to know. It may be professional, technical or commercial knowledge; or it may be about the commercial, economic or market environment, the machines to be operated, the materials or equipment to be used or the procedures to be followed, the customers, clients, colleagues and subordinates he or she is in contact with and the factors that affect their behaviour; or it may refer to the problems that will occur and how they should be dealt with.
- [ ] *Skills* – what the worker needs to be able to do if results are to be achieved and knowledge is to be used effectively. Skills are built gradually by repeated

training or other experience. They may be manual, intellectual or mental, perceptual or social.

☐ *Attitudes* – the disposition to behave or to perform in a way which is in accordance with the requirements of the work.

TRAINING SPECIFICATION. The training specification is a detailed statement of what the trainee needs to learn based on a comparison between the job specification and the trainee's present level of performance. For inexperienced recruits, the job specification is, in effect, the training specification, although it might have to be presented in a different form to be of use as the base of a training programme. For more experienced people, the training specification should describe what training is required to fill the gaps between what they should know and do know, and between what they should do and can do.

General training specifications for new starters or for workers transferred to new jobs normally assume no previous knowledge or experience. Individual training programmes would then have to be modified to take account of existing skills.

## Planning training programmes

Training plans derive directly from the process of analysis that has just been described. The steps required are as follows:

1. Summarize training needs.
2. Formulate training policies.
3. Decide where training should take place.
4. Decide on the training methods to be used.
5. Set objectives.
6. Determine methods of evaluating training.

### Summarizing training needs
The summary of training needs should establish the main areas and priorities for training. The summary should be supported by the detailed training specifications for each occupation.

Where large numbers of apprentices or other trainees are to be trained, the summary should show the numbers to be trained and the expected output of the training schemes. Similarly, an indication should be given of the numbers to be trained in any of the more specialized areas, including supervisor and management training. The summary may list individual requirements for training or present them on a departmental or functional basis.

The overall summary should set out for each category of employee:

☐ the number employed at present;
☐ the number of those requiring training;
☐ the number of new entrants expected;
☐ training required (cross referenced to detailed training specifications);
☐ a broad indication of priorities.

### Training policies
Training policies should be developed which will provide guidelines on the detailed planning of training by defining the scope and aims of the training schemes, the basis of training plans, the procedure for developing formal training schemes, and methods of evaluating and controlling training.

**Where should training take place?**
There are three places where training can take place: in company, on the job, off the job; and external, off the job. Each has its uses, its advantages and disadvantages.

IN COMPANY, ON THE JOB. In company, on the job training may consist of teaching or coaching by managers, supervisors or trainers at the desk or at the bench. It may also consist of individual or group assignments and projects. It is the only way to develop and practise managerial, supervisory, technical, selling, manual, and clerical skills. It has the advantage of actuality and immediacy. The trainee works, learns and develops expertise at the same time. Theory is put into practice immediately and its relevance is obvious. The disadvantages are that the effectiveness of the learning is strongly influenced by the quality of the guidance and coaching provided on the job. Many managers and supervisors are unskilled at training and disinclined to carry it out or to encourage it. Relying on fellow employees − 'sit by me' or 'sitting by Nellie' training − has equally obvious disadvantages. The instruction may be inadequate and the training may perpetuate bad habits. Above all, the trainee may be distracted by the environment and find it difficult to acquire the basic skills quickly.

IN COMPANY, OFF THE JOB. In company, off the job training can take place on special courses or in training areas or centres which have been specially equipped and staffed for training. It is the best way to acquire advanced manual and clerical skills and to learn about company procedures and products. It helps to increase the identification of the trainee with the company as a whole, and the use of systematic training techniques, special equipment and trained trainers means that the basic skills and knowledge can be acquired quickly and often economically. The main disadvantage arises when trainees are transferred from the training course to a job to apply their knowledge and skills in practice. On a full-time manual skills course in a training centre, they will have been sheltered from the realities of the rough and tumble in most workshops, especially in batch production factories. At manager and supervisor level the problem of transferring from the 'training situation' to 'real life' may be even more difficult.

EXTERNAL TRAINING. External training is useful for the development of managerial, supervisory, technical and social knowledge and skills, especially if the courses cover standard theory and practice which can easily be translated from the general to the particular. External training should be able to supply the quality of instruction which it might be uneconomic to provide from internal resources. It can be used to implant highly specialized knowledge or advanced skills and has the added advantage of broadening the horizons of those exposed to it. The main disadvantage is that of transferring learning into practice − even more acute with external courses. However effective the training, the knowledge and skills acquired may be quickly dissipated unless they are used immediately. It may also be difficult to select relevant courses from the bewildering variety available.
The art of designing training programmes is to select the right blend of on the job and off the job training. There are no rules for doing this. Each programme has to be considered individually. But the emphasis should always be towards putting learning into practice and, therefore, first consideration has to be given to what happens on the job. Off the job courses, whether internal or external,

should be regarded as complementary and supplementary activities which may stimulate learning or provide knowledge and skills that cannot be obtained internally; but they are always subsidiary to what an individual does and learns in his normal place of work.

### Training techniques

There are many training techniques, and the choice of technique will depend on the training situation in which it is to be deployed. The techniques available are analysed in Appendix J.

## Setting objectives

It is essential to define the objectives of the training programme. Objectives can be defined as 'criterion behaviour', i.e. the standards or changes of behaviour *on the job* to be achieved if training is to be regarded as successful. This should be a definition of what the trainee will be able to *do* when he goes back to work on completing the course, in other words, terminal behaviour. Transfer of training is what counts and behaviour on the job is what matters. Training objectives are best expressed as follows:

> On completing the training (or this part of the course) the trainee will be able to ... (read a balance sheet, program a micro-computer, operate a work processor, work to a high degree of accuracy, etc.).

## Evaluation of training

It is at the planning stage that the basis upon which each category of training is to be evaluated should be determined. At the same time, it is necessary to consider how the information required to evaluate courses should be obtained and analysed.

The process of evaluating training has been defined by Hamblin as: 'Any attempt to obtain information (feedback) on the effects of a training programme, and to assess the value of the training in the light of that information.'[4] Evaluation leads to control which means deciding whether or not the training was worthwhile (preferably in cost/benefit terms) and what improvements are required to make it even more cost-effective.

Evaluation is an integral feature of training. In its crudest form it is the comparison of objectives (criterion behaviour) with effects (terminal behaviour) to answer the question of how far training has achieved its purpose. The setting of objectives and the establishment of methods of measuring results are, or should be, an essential part of the planning stage of any training programme.

Evaluation is difficult because it is often hard to set measurable objectives and even harder to collect the information on the results or to decide on the level at which the evaluation should be made.

### Evaluation levels

Hamblin, whose book on *Evaluation and Control of Training*[4] is the definitive work in this field, has suggested that there are five levels at which evaluation can take place:

1. *Reactions.* The reactions of trainees to the training experience itself: how useful or even how enjoyable they feel the training is, what they think of

individual sessions and speakers, what they would like put in or taken out, and so on.

2. *Learning.* Evaluation at the learning level requires the measurement of what trainees have learned as a result of their training – the new knowledge and skills they have acquired or the changes in attitude that have taken place. This is the terminal behaviour that occurs immediately after the training has finished.

3. *Job behaviour.* At this level, evaluation attempts to measure the extent to which trainees have applied their learning on the job. This constitutes an assessment of the amount of transfer of learning that has taken place from an off the job training course to the job itself. If the training is carried out on the job there should be little difference between learning and job behaviour.

4. *Organization.* Evaluation at this level attempts to measure the effect of changes in the job behaviour of trainees on the functioning of the organization in which they are employed. The measurement might be in such terms as improvements in output, productivity, quality, morale (if that can be measured), contribution, or sales turnover. In effect, the question answered by this type of evaluation is not simply what behavioural changes have taken place, but what good have those changes been for the unit or department in which the employee works.

5. *Ultimate value.* This is a measure of how the organization as a whole has benefited from the training in terms of greater profitability, survival or growth. But it might also be defined in terms of the trainee's personal goals rather than those of the organization which sponsored him. This could be a legitimate company goal for training if it is believed that what is good for the individual is good for the organization, or if the company feels that it has a social duty to educate and train its employees to the maximum of their capacity. Fundamentally, however, evaluation at this level is related to the criteria by which the organization judges its efficiency and its success or failure. The difficulty is assessing how far training has contributed to the ultimate results.

As Hamblin points out, the five levels are links in a chain: training leads to reactions, which lead to learning, which leads to changes in job behaviour, which lead to changes in the organization, which lead to changes in the achievement of ultimate goals. But the chain can be snapped at any link. A trainee can react favourably to a course – he can 'enjoy it' – but learn nothing. He can learn something, but he cannot, or will not, or is not allowed to, apply it. He applies it, but it does no good within his own area. It does some good in his function, but does not further the objectives of the organization.

Evaluation can start at any level. Ideally, some people might say, it starts and finishes at levels four and five; organizational and ultimate value. This is all that really matters, they claim. But it may be difficult, if not impossible, to measure the effect of training in these respects. In any case, it may be desirable to work backwards to find out what went wrong at earlier levels if the ultimate benefits arising from training are inadequate.

## Conducting training programmes

The only general rule for conducting training programmes is that the courses should continually be monitored to ensure that they are proceeding according to plan and within the agreed budget. This is the job of the head of training who should be required to report on progress against plan at regular intervals.

There are, however, a number of considerations which affect the conduct of training for specific occupations, and those concerning managers and supervisors (these are considered jointly because the basic principles are similar), sales staff, craftsmen and clerical staff are discussed briefly below. Industrial relations training is dealt with in chapter 22 and communications training in chapter 24.

## Management and supervisory training

As the old saying goes, managers learn to manage by managing under the guidance of a good manager. The emphasis should therefore always be towards on the job training, by planned experience, coaching or assignments. This can be supplemented — but never replaced — by off the job training to extend knowledge, fill in gaps, develop skills or modify attitudes.

In his report on the experienced manager, Alastair Mant[5] said, on the basis of extensive research, that:

☐ the majority of managers do not benefit greatly from external management courses;
☐ managers benefit more from well designed and well conducted internal courses variously termed 'in-company', 'in-plant' or 'in-house', which are linked to the job and involve problem-orientated project work;
☐ the organization and not the individual should be regarded as the main consumer of management training, the aim of which is to secure better results for the company.

Professor Revans[6] has taken the same standpoint consistently over many years in developing his concept of 'action learning'. Action learning is based on the conviction that, valuable though specialist knowledge may be as a tool, the most effective resources available to those who want to improve performance are their own talents and experience. Action learning aims to help individuals and groups to recognize and develop these natural resources and put them to good use. It is described in more detail in Appendix J.

Project training is a particularly valuable method of providing managers and supervisors with new experience and the opportunity to extend their knowledge over a wider range of problems and to exercise their analytical skills in solving them.

Courses should be used judicially. They can provide:

☐ concentrated knowledge;
☐ an opportunity to acquire new skills or to develop and practice existing skills;
☐ a framework for analysing past experience;
☐ the chance to reflect on ways in which better use can be made of future experience;
☐ a means of having new ideas accepted and changing attitudes through group activities which is not available on the job.

INTERNAL COURSES. An important spin-off from internal courses, especially resident ones, is that the participants get to know more about their company and their colleagues. Their sense of identification with the organization is thereby increased.

The essential characteristics of an effective formal internal course are threefold.

First, it should be problem-based. It must help participants to overcome the actual problems that have been identified as those most likely to prevent good performance. Secondly, it should be action-orientated. It must result in positive action which produces improvements in performance. The effectiveness of the course is primarily measured by the extent to which the desired action has resulted from it. Thirdly, senior management should be involved in the course, thus demonstrating their support of the manager or supervisor and their recognition of his responsibilities and importance.

It goes without saying that the course should be highly participative, making the maximum use of discussion, case studies and group exercises. Throughout the programme participants should be compelled to list the action points to which they will give attention when they return to their jobs. The course may aim to impart knowledge, but the emphasis should be on the skills required to make effective use of the knowledge the participants have or acquire on the course.

EXTERNAL COURSES. External general management courses should be used with caution. They can broaden the knowledge and skills of those attending and they can serve as a sort of accolade to demonstrate that someone has 'arrived' or is about to 'arrive'. But the problem of transferring learning back to work can be a formidable one.

The purpose of an external general management course should be to develop the natural ability of managers and to build upon their experience by helping them to:

☐ think more clearly and critically about all aspects of their jobs;
☐ understand more about the management techniques that are available so that they can appreciate the ways in which these techniques overlap and are interdependent and how they can be used to get results;
☐ obtain a broader understanding of business and organizational problems, thus overcoming any tendency towards insularity or a narrow departmental viewpoint.

CONTINUITY. Whatever form of training is used, management and supervisory training should be seen as a continuous process. One of the greatest fallacies of the typical one-week internal management course, as described above, is that this is sufficient. This applies equally to longer external courses. The management and supervisory training programme should therefore be established as a continuing activity at all levels of management to avoid the dissipation of interest and enthusiasm that follows an isolated course, and to promote the progressive development of managerial and supervisory skills as new experiences are encountered and as conditions change.

### Sales training
The aim of sales training should be to equip the salesman with the knowledge, skills, attitudes and habits required to meet or exceed his sales targets.

The first requirement is knowledge of the company and its products, customers, competitors and sales administration procedures.

Secondly, he has to acquire and develop skills: prospecting, making the approach, making presentations, handling objections, closing the sale, and handling complaints. Perhaps the most important skill to be developed, however, is analytical ability. The salesman must be taught how to analyse his product into its technical characteristics and, most important, its selling points – those aspects of the product that are likely to appeal to particular customers. He must also be taught how to analyse his customers from the point of view of their buying habits and the features of the product that are most likely to appeal to them. In addition, he must be able to analyse himself – his own strengths and weaknesses as a salesman so that he can exploit his strengths and overcome his weaknesses.

Thirdly, training should aim to develop attitudes: of loyalty to the company and belief in its products, and of understanding and tolerance with regard to potential and existing customers. The salesman has to believe in himself, he must be given confidence and provided with the motivation to go out and sell – a task which requires courage, determination and persistence.

The fourth requirement is to develop sound work habits: organizing time, planning activities, following up leads, maintaining records and submitting reports.

Sales training, like any other form of training, should be based on an analysis of the salesman's job and the problems he is likely to meet. The training programme should be continuous; there can never be a time in any salesman's career when he would not benefit from training. Use should be made of classroom training to provide basic knowledge and an opportunity to practise skills. But most training should be carried out on the job by sales managers or supervisors who can demonstrate sales techniques and observe and comment on the efforts of the salesman.

Classroom training should be highly participative and involve the trainees in practising every aspect of selling. The members of the course should be made to carry out detailed analyses of the selling points of the company's products in comparison with those of competitors. They should also be asked to work out for themselves the sort of sales resistance they will meet and how they should handle objections. Above all, role playing exercises should be used to give each trainee experience in every aspect of selling, and closed circuit television is invaluable as a training aid for this type of exercise. Sales training films are helpful, but they should not be relied upon too much. If one of the main aims of a classroom course is to increase the identification of the salesman with the company and its products, then it is essential for the message to be given by company sales executives and sales training managers.

Field training should be complementary to classroom training. It should be carefully programmed so that area or district sales managers know exactly what sort of training every salesman under their control should be receiving at any point in time. Field sales managers and supervisors therefore need to be thoroughly trained themselves in coaching techniques and in running local sales meetings.

The field training programme should consist of an appropriate mix of live demonstrations with customers, of observations of the salesman at work by the manager followed immediately by 'kerbside' coaching sessions, and of more formal off the job counselling or training sessions. The latter may be restricted to the manager and an individual salesman, or may consist of sales meetings which follow a programme of sales topics laid down by headquarters and supplemented by sessions dealing with local problems. It is essential for the field sales training programme to be monitored from headquarters by the sales training manager. Some field managers recognize the importance of training and are good at it. Others neglect it to pursue sales, or are not particularly effective trainers. These individuals need encouragement, stimulation and help.

Selling is a highly personal business and it is therefore important to recognize and meet individual training needs. A performance review system is required for this purpose which focuses attention on the results achieved and the areas where performance needs to be improved by training to obtain better results. The scheme should be linked to informal counselling and coaching sessions as well as more formal training activities.

### Apprentice training
Apprenticeship schemes can be divided into four main types:

☐ *Graduate* — post-graduate training usually lasting two years, leading to a professional qualification.

☐ *Student* — a course of education and practical training leading to a degree or some other qualification as a technologist. In the U.K. the course may include 'block' release to college for periods of, say, four weeks. Or, more commonly, it is a 'thin sandwich' — periods of up to six months in college and at the works, or a 'thick sandwich' — one year's basic training, three or four years at university and one year's post-graduate training.

☐ *Technician* — a four- to five-year course of education and training leading to employment as a technician or draughtsman and an appropriate technician's qualification.

☐ *Craft* — a three- to four-year course which will consist of practical training and education leading to a craft certificate. Not all schemes have an educational element.

PHASES OF TRAINING. In the major craft industries — engineering, construction and shipbuilding — the practical training for all types of apprentices consists of the following three phases:

1. *Basic Training* — in which the apprentice receives training in basic skills in a basic training workshop. This training should consist of a series of modules such as those drawn up by the Engineering Industry Training Board in Great Britain. Clearly, the standard modules should be chosen on the basis of an analysis of the knowledge and skills required, and additional modules should be specially developed if necessary. A basic course for an engineering craft apprentice may last a full year, by which time he should be fully equipped with all the basic skills.

   Each module should have defined objectives — criterion behaviour. There should also be predetermined methods of measuring terminal behaviour by tests or observations after the module has been completed.

   The training should be given by trained instructors in a space set aside for training.

2. *General Training* — in which the apprentice is given experience in a number of different shops, processes or operations to consolidate his training. If it is already decided that he is to become, say, a tool room turner, he would be given an extended period of familiarization in the tool room. But he would also spend some time in related areas; for example, the jig and tool drawing office, the foundry, the machine shop and various fitting and assembly shops.

   Technician, student and graduate apprentices in engineering would also spend a general period of training 'round the shops' but would then move into the engineering, design or development departments, depending on their speciality. A production specialist, for example, would spend time in the planning, jig and tool, production control, work study, rate fixing and quality control departments.

During the period, graduate and student apprentices should be given special projects which will test their understanding of the design, development, engineering and manufacturing functions. Craft and technician apprentices may return to the training school for advanced skill courses in machine operation, draughting or any other speciality.

The biggest danger to avoid in this period of general training is that apprentices aimlessly wander from shop to shop and find themselves relegated to a tedious job out of harm's way because no one wants to know about them. The burr bench in a machine shop is a favourite dumping ground for unwanted apprentices. To avoid this danger, it is essential to have a syllabus of training in every workshop which is based on an analysis of knowledge and skill requirements. There should be one trained supervisor responsible for training in each workshop and in a large department, such as a machine shop, there may be more than one full-time training supervisor. The training department should also monitor the progress of apprentices carefully to ensure that they are following the syllabus and are acquiring the knowledge and skill they need. In a large organization there may be one or more full-time apprentice supervisors who spend all their time in the shops chasing shop supervisors and checking on the progress of apprentices.

The apprentices themselves should know what they are expected to learn at each stage so that they can request a move if they feel they are wasting their time or are not covering the syllabus. They should also be required to keep log-books to record what they have done. These should be seen regularly by their training officer as a check on their progress.

3. *Final Training* – in which the apprentice settles down in the department of his choice, or the department for which he is best fitted. During this period he will probably be doing the same work as experienced craftsmen, technicians or technologists. The aim is to ensure that he is equipped to apply his learning in normal working conditions and at the pace and level of quality expected from a fully experienced and competent individual.

Throughout these three stages the training department has to work closely with the educationists to ensure that, so far as possible, the theory is complementary to the practice.

The length of the period of training at each stage will obviously depend on the level and complexity of the knowledge and skills that have to be acquired and on the type of apprenticeship. Tradition or union agreements may lay down the length of apprenticeship in some cases. The experience of any company conducting apprenticeship training along the lines described above, however, has shown that if the basic training is sufficiently comprehensive and the period of experience is adequately planned and monitored, the length of time to reach a fully experienced worker's standard may be considerably less than the traditional period.

Apprentices training for other skilled crafts should follow the same pattern of basic training: familiarization with the application of different aspects of the craft, and final consolidation of knowledge and skills. The basic training period, however, may not be so elaborate and may well be carried out in a local technical college which is better equipped to provide the skilled instruction required.

311

INTEGRATING EDUCATION AND TRAINING. One of the main problems faced in running apprenticeship training schemes is that of integrating education and training: that is, ensuring that the theoretical instruction provided by a university, polytechnic or technical college is of practical use. This particularly applies to graduate, student and technician apprentices.

It is, of course, impossible to ensure that all college instruction is directly relevant. And it would be undesirable to make the attempt. The aim of technical education should be to train the mind of the apprentice and to equip him with understanding of general principles and concepts which he can put to use. But some parts of the course will deal with applications, and it is in these areas that integration is desirable.

Integration can be achieved by maintaining good liaison with the college, which should have industrial liaison officers for this purpose. It is also a good idea to keep in touch with lecturers and instructors and give them a chance to look at the work carried out by apprentices in the company.

Members of the training department should see apprentices regularly to discuss progress in their studies and how they can make the best use of what they have learned. In some companies it may be helpful to have qualified engineers in the design, development, production engineering and manufacturing departments to act as tutors for groups of graduate, student or technician apprentices. They can arrange individual or collective meetings regularly to discuss practical applications and to provide advice on the course of studies.

## Clerical training

Clerical training is the most neglected form of training. Perhaps this is because both line and training managers often despise or at least underestimate the skill content of most clerical work. This feeling has been intensified because of the tendency of O & M analysts to de-skill clerical jobs.

But inefficiency in clerical work can be an important factor in reducing the efficiency of the organization as a whole. A company cannot afford to neglect training in clerical skills and departmental procedures.

Clerical training should be divided into three areas: basic training, further education, and continuation training. During the basic training stage, when the clerk is being taught how to carry out his or her first job, a foundation is being laid for the employee's career. During this period, young clerks and trainees should obtain background knowledge of the company and acquire the basic knowledge and skills they need.

Clerical trainees should be encouraged to follow a further course of studies leading to a professional or commercial qualification. The course of studies should be decided by agreement between the employee, his departmental manager and the training department.

The third area is continuation training. Training and development should be a continuous process. When each trainee has completed his basic training programme and, preferably, has obtained a qualification, his abilities should be developed by providing broader experience within the company and by short technical courses. The aim at this stage should be to ensure that staff with potential are not allowed to stagnate within a department and that they are prepared for greater responsibility.

## References

1. Campbell, J.P. 'Personnel Training and Development', *Annual Review of Psychology*, Palo Alto, California, 1971.
2. Skinner, B.F. *Science and Human Behaviour*. Free Press, New York, 1953.
3. Bandura, A. *Social Learning Theory*. Prentice Hall, Englewood Cliffs, NJ, 1977.
4. Hamblin, A.C. *Evaluation and Control of Training*. McGraw-Hill, Maidenhead, 1974.
5. Mant, A. *The Experienced Manager*. British Institute of Management, 1970.
6. Revans, R.W. *Developing Effective Managers*. Longman, Harlow, 1971.

# Management Development

## What is management development?

### Objectives

Management development is a systematic process which aims to ensure that the organization has the effective managers it requires to meet its present and future needs. It is concerned with improving the performance of existing managers, giving them opportunities for growth and development, and ensuring, so far as possible, that management succession within the organization is provided for.

The objectives of a typical management development programme are to improve the financial performance and long term growth of the company by:

☐ improving the performance of managers by seeing that they are clearly informed of their responsibilities and by agreeing with them specific key objectives against which their performance will be regularly assessed;

☐ identifying managers with further potential and ensuring that they receive the required development, training and experience to equip them for more senior posts within their own locations and divisions within the company;

☐ assisting chief executives and managers throughout the company to provide adequate succession and to create a system whereby this is kept under regular review.

### Role of the organization

The traditional view is that the organization need not concern itself with management development. The natural process of selection and the pressure of competition will ensure the survival of the fittest. Managers, in fact, are born not made. Cream rises to the top (but then so does scum).

The reaction to this can be summed up in John Humble's phrase, 'programmitis and crown princes'.[1] Management development is seen mainly as a mechanical process using management inventories, multi-coloured replacement charts, 'Cook's tours' for newly recruited graduates, detailed job rotation programmes, elaborate points schemes to appraise personal characteristics, and endless series of formal courses.

The true role of the organization in management development lies somewhere between these two extremes. On the one hand, it is not enough, in conditions of rapid growth (when they exist) and change, to leave everything to chance — to trial and error. On the other hand, elaborate management development programmes cannot successfully be imposed on the organization. Because, as Drucker says: 'Development is always self-development. Nothing could be more absurd than for the enterprise to assume responsibility for the development of a man. The responsibility rests with the individual, his abilities, his efforts.'[2] But he goes on to say:

Every manager in a business has the opportunity to encourage individual self-development or to stifle it, to direct it or to misdirect it. He should be specifically assigned the responsibility for helping all men working with him to focus, direct and apply their self-development efforts productively. And every company can provide systematic development challenges to its managers.

Executive ability is eventually something which the individual must develop for himself on the job. But he will do this much better if he is given encouragement, guidance and opportunities by his company and his manager. In Douglas McGregor's phrase: managers are grown — they are neither born nor made. The role of the company is to provide conditions favourable to faster growth. And these conditions are very much part of the environment and organization climate of the company and the management style of the chief executive who has the ultimate responsibility for management development. As McGregor wrote:

The job environment of the individual is the most important variable affecting his development. Unless that environment is conducive to his growth, none of the other things we do to him or for him will be effective. This is why the 'agricultural' approach to management development is preferable to the 'manufacturing' approach. The latter leads, among other things, to the unrealistic expectation that we can create and develop managers in the classroom.[3]

### Responsibility for management development
Management development is not a separate activity to be handed over to a specialist and forgotten or ignored. The success of a management development programme depends upon the degree to which all levels of management are committed to it. The development of subordinates must be recognized as a natural and essential part of any manager's job. But the lead must come from the top.

### The approach to management development
Management development should be regarded as a range of related activities rather than an all-embracing programme. The use of the word 'programme' to describe the process smacks too much of a mechanistic approach.

This does not imply that some systematization is not necessary. First, because many managers have to operate in more or less routine situations and have to be developed accordingly; and secondly, because organizations will not continue to thrive if they simply react to events. There must be an understanding of the approaches that can be used to develop managers and means of assessing the existing managerial resources and how they measure to the needs of the enterprise. And plans must be made for the development of those resources by selecting the best of the methods available. But this should not be seen as a 'programme' consisting of a comprehensive, highly integrated and rigidly applied range of management training and development techniques.

The management development activities required will depend on the organization: its technology, its environment and its philosophy. A bureaucratic, mechanistic type of organization, such as a large government department, a nationalized industry, a major insurance firm or a large process manufacturing company, will be inclined to adopt the programmed routine approach, complete with a wide range of courses, inventories, replacement charts, career plans and management by objectives based review systems. An innovative and organic type of organization may rightly dispense with all these mechanisms. Its approach should be to provide its managers with the opportunities, challenge and guidance they require, relying mainly on seizing the chance to give people extra responsibilities, and ensuring that they receive the coaching and encouragement they need. There

315

may be no replacement charts, inventories or formal appraisal schemes, but people know how they stand, where they can go and how to get there.

## Management development activities

Management development activities can be divided into seven areas:

1. Organization review.
2. Manpower review.
3. Performance review.
4. Management by objectives.
5. Training.
6. Succession planning.
7. Career planning.

These activities are interrelated, as shown in figure 21.1 and, in this sense, it would be possible to talk about a 'programme' of management development

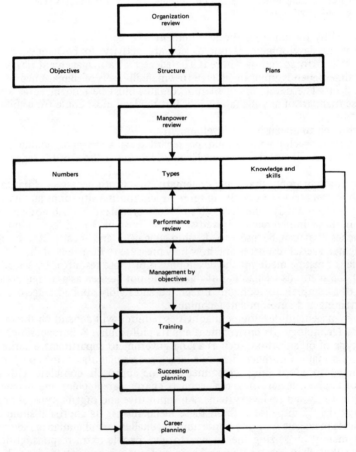

**Figure 21.1 The process of management development**

where the process consists of education and training, career planning and succession planning activities which are derived from the outcome of the organization, manpower and performance reviews.

## Organization review

Management development is closely related to organization development, which focuses attention on people and the social system in which they work – individuals, working groups and the relationships between them – and uses various educational activities which may aim primarily to develop teamwork but also provide training for the individuals concerned. Management development appears to focus attention more on individuals than on groups and relationships, but it must do this within the context of the needs of the organization as a whole.

Management development activities should therefore be founded upon a review of the objectives, plans and structure of the organization and the implications of present weaknesses and future demands on managerial requirements.

## Manpower review

The organization review leads naturally into a review of manpower resources. This is the manpower planning aspect of management development and, where the circumstances permit, it implies an analysis of the present resources and future requirements in terms of numbers, types and knowledge and skills. This is a general review, and individual and management succession needs would be analysed separately, although performance reviews will provide information on strengths and weaknesses that affect the overall plan.

It may be impossible to prepare precise forecasts of future requirements, but it is still desirable to give some thought to the general considerations that will affect education and training, career planning and succession planning.

## Performance review

Performance review systems are used to identify development needs by highlighting strengths and wealnesses and, so far as this is possible, potential for promotion. They are also a basis for the counselling and coaching activities which should form the most important part of an individual's development within a company. The general approaches available are considered in chapter 12 but a particular approach – management by objectives – which incorporates a performance review element as well as a number of other features concerned with management development is discussed below.

## Management by objectives

Management by objectives has in some quarters been regarded as the key activity in a management development programme. Perhaps it has been oversold as the universal panacea for all management development problems, but it can have a part to play in an integrated programme and its basic philosophy is relevant to anyone concerned with the management of people.

Management by objectives has been defined by John Humble as 'A dynamic system which seeks to integrate the company's need to clarify and achieve its profit and growth goals with the manager's need to contribute and develop himself. It is a demanding and rewarding style of managing a business.'[4]

Management by objectives is essentially a method of managing organizations and people and of improving the performance of managers. The basic processes are as follows:

☐ Subordinates agree with their managers the objectives of their job – expressed as targets or standards of performance for each key result area. The individual objectives are in line with unit and organizational objectives, and are defined in a way which emphasizes the contribution they make to achieving departmental and corporate plans. So far as possible, the objectives are quantified, 'job improvement' plans (in Humble's phrase) are jointly developed to indicate what the manager should contribute to the unit's and the company's plans for better performance.

☐ Performance is reviewed jointly by the manager and the subordinate to compare results with the defined objectives and standards.

☐ The manager and subordinate agree where improvements are required and how better results can be achieved and, as necessary, re-define targets and standards.

Management by objectives has often developed into a range of elaborate systems and techniques – too elaborate many people say – but it is based upon a fundamental philosophy with which it is difficult to quarrel.

### Philosophy of management by objectives

If, irreverently, Odiorne in America and Humble in Britain can be described as the high priests of the management objectives movement, then the messiah must be recognized as Drucker, although McGregor, who followed Drucker in time, cannot be regarded as a mere disciple – he had more of a Pauline role, interpreting and reinterpreting the gospel: in his case, in behavioural science terms.

Drucker coined the phrase in *The Practice of Management*, in which he wrote:

> An effective management must direct the vision and efforts of all managers towards a common goal. It must ensure that the individual manager understands what results are demanded of him. It must ensure that the superior understands what to expect of each of his subordinate managers. It must motivate each manager to maximum efforts in the right direction. And while encouraging high standards of workmanship, it must make them the means to the end of business performance rather than the ends in themselves.[2]

In Drucker's view, this approach would first ensure that individual and corporate objectives would be integrated. Secondly, it would eliminate the ineffectiveness and misdirection that result from management by 'crisis' and 'drives'. Finally, and most important, it would make it possible for managers to control their own performance: 'Self-control means stronger motivation: a desire to do the best rather than just enough to get by. It means higher performance goals and broader vision.'

McGregor's contribution arose from his Theory Y and Theory X concept. He said that:

> The central principle which derives from Theory Y is that of integration: the creation of conditions such that the members of the organization can achieve their own goals *best* by directing their efforts towards the success of the enterprise.[3]

McGregor, however, emphasized that the aim should be to achieve 'management by integration and self-control'. He criticized some interpretations of management by objectives which have led to no more than a new set of tactics within a strategy of management by direction and control. He also stressed that his concept of management by integration and self-control is a strategy – a way of managing people:

> The tactics are worked out in the light of the circumstances. Forms and procedures are of relatively little value... 'Selling' management a programme of target setting and providing standardized forms and procedures is the surest way to *prevent* the development of management by integration and self-control.[3]

It is a pity that these words of wisdom in 1960 have been largely ignored by the academics, management consultants and civil servants who have since erected great edifices of forms and systems. All too often these have come crashing down on the heads of those who have tried to live with them because managers rightly revolt against the reduction of their skills to a series of mechanical processes.

But these criticisms are levelled at some applications of management by objectives, rather than the basic concept. It can still play an important part in management development as long as it avoids infecting itself with the disease of 'programmitis' that Humble suggested was endemic in traditional management development schemes.

### Using management by objectives

Management by objectives should have the active support of top management. It should not be seen by line managers as yet another form-filling exercise imposed upon them by the personnel department or outside consultants. Their commitment to it as a means of helping them to manage more effectively and thereby helping themselves must be obtained. Management by objectives is most effective when managers recognize for themselves – with or without encouragement – that it is something they can use to their own advantage. It is even more effective if they are allowed the maximum amount of freedom to apply it in their departments in their own way – let them develop their own forms, if they want to use them. If not, let them do without. The agreed objectives can be written out on the back of an envelope if they prefer it that way – as long as they can find the envelope when it comes to a review.

### Implications of management by objectives

Management by objectives in practice has been criticized because it has over-emphasized ends expressed in quantifiable terms. This has led to the pursuit of short term goals at the expense of longer term results. Attempts to quantify the unquantifiable have also led managers to reject M by O as unrealistic.

It can also be argued that it is impossible to divorce ends from means. Management by objectives purists say that it is only the results that count. But if managers are to improve their performance they must improve the way in which they get results. They should indeed be encouraged to think this out for themselves – and M by O, if conducted properly should help – but they will also need the guidance of their managers about the means they use as well as the ends they should aim to achieve.

Management by objectives in its ripest form is probably best applied in large bureaucratic organizations where its routines fit in with the prevailing climate and management style. In other organizations it provides a basic philosophy of 'management by integration and self-control' which should be a part of any management system. For management development purposes the concept of

M by O is useful, not for the procedures that surround it, but because it does focus attention of the needs of the individual manager in his job and on the role of his manager in helping him to identify and meet these needs.

## Management training

Management development is sometimes seen as primarily a matter of providing a series of appropriate courses at various points in a manager's career. But, as Hawdon Hague[5] suggests, the best definition of training is the 'modification of behaviour through experience', which means that managers will develop best if they receive their training in the 'real' situation, i.e. in the normal course of their work through coaching, projects and guided self-analysis.

The principal method by which managers can be equipped is by ensuring that they have the right variety of experience, in good time, in the course of their careers. This experience can and should be supplemented, but never replaced, by courses carefully timed and designed to meet particular needs.

The various approaches to management training on the job and on formal courses are discussed more thoroughly in Appendix J. It is sufficient to state now that while training is an important part of management development, it should not be allowed to degenerate into no more than a series of formal courses, even when these are based on elaborate job descriptions, job analyses and performance review systems. This guarantees a static and increasingly irrelevant approach. Formal training courses should only be used when it is essential to supplement what managers are learning on the job. The key management development activity is therefore ensuring that managers are given the chance to learn; and this is primarily a matter of encouraging and stimulating on the job training and providing career opportunities to broaden experience.

## Management succession planning

The aim of management succession planning is to ensure that as far as possible suitable managers are available to fill vacancies created by promotion, retirement, death, leaving or transfer. It also aims to ensure that a cadre of managers is available to fill the new appointments that may be established in the future.

The information for management succession planning comes from organization and manpower reviews and assessments of performance and potential. This information needs to be recorded so that decisions can be made on promotions and replacements, and training or additional experience arranged for those with potential or who are earmarked for promotion.

The records need not be elaborate. In practice, complex inventories and detailed succession charts replete with colour codes and other symbols are a waste of time, except in the largest and most bureaucratic organizations. All the information required can be recorded on a simple management succession schedule such as the one illustrated in figure 21.2.

## Career planning

Career planning has two aims: first, to ensure that men and women of promise are given a sequence of experience that will equip them for whatever level of responsibility they have the ability to reach; secondly, to provide individuals with potential with the guidance and encouragement they may need if they are to

| MANAGEMENT SUCCESSION SCHEDULE | | | | | | | Department | Director/Manager | | |
|---|---|---|---|---|---|---|---|---|---|---|
| **Present Managerial and Supervisory Staff** | | | | | | | | **Possible successors** | | |
| Name | Position | Age | Date due for replacement | Rating | | If promotable, indicate what position and when | | Names (1st & 2nd choice) | Positions | When ready |
| | | | | Performance | Potential | | | | | |
| | | | | | | | | | | |
| | | | | | | | | | | |
| | | | | | | | | | | |
| | | | | | | | | | | |
| | | | | | | | | | | |

Figure 21.2 Management succession schedule

321

fulfil their potential and remain with the organization.

Career planning is most effective when it is linked to management succession planning, so that the experience and training provided is leading towards a job that has to be filled. The extent to which careers can be planned, however, is limited if it is difficult to forecast replacement needs, assess long term potential or provide an appropriate sequence of experience. These difficulties exist in most organizations and it is usually only possible to plan the next step towards promotion. But even that is better than leaving everything to chance.

Career planning may involve counselling individuals on their possible career paths and what they must do to achieve promotion. This does not mean that a long range plan consisting of a number of predetermined steps can be revealed. It is seldom, if ever, possible to be precise about long term career prospects. Even if it were possible, it would be dangerous either to raise expectations which might not be fulfilled or to induce a feeling of complacency about the future. It may be feasible to talk about the next step but, beyond that, the wisest approach is to do no more than provide – in planning jargon – a scenario of the opportunities that might become available. Career counselling should not be concerned with making what might turn out to be empty promises. Its main aim should be to help the individual concerned to develop himself by giving him some idea of the direction in which he ought to be heading.

## Conclusion

The activities that have just been described are all potentially useful. But they should not allow the organization to be distracted from the prime objective of management development, which is to ensure that managers and potential managers get the most out of the experience they acquire in their day-to-day jobs. The emphasis must be on the clarification of the roles and objectives of managers and their subordinates so that the latter can receive the direction and guidance they need to develop their knowledge and skills.

## Reference

1. Humble, J. 'Programmitis and Crown Princes', *The Manager*, December 1963.
2. Drucker, P.F. *The Practice of Management*. Heinemann, London, 1955.
3. McGregor, D. *The Human Side of Enterprise*. McGraw-Hill Book Company, New York, 1960.
4. Humble, J. *Management by Objectives in Action*. McGraw-Hill Publishing Company, Maidenhead, 1970.
5. Hague, H. *Management Training for Real*. Institute of Personnel Management, London, 1973.

## Part V
# Employee Relations

Employee relations consists of all those aspects of personnel management where employees are dealt with collectively. The primary aims of employee relations policies and procedures are to improve co-operation to minimize unnecessary conflict, to enable employees to play an appropriate part in decision-making and to keep them informed on matters that concern them.

Wherever there are trade unions, industrial relations will be a major preoccupation of personnel management. Industrial relations policies and procedures need to be developed and operated in the light of an understanding of the processes at work in collective bargaining, where the 'web of rules' is developed by formal and informal negotiations and by discussions between management and the trade unions. Chapter 22 therefore starts with an analysis of industrial relations as a system of rules developed by formal and informal processes of collective bargaining. It goes on to discuss the framework of industrial relations and the roles of the various parties involved before considering industrial relations strategies, procedural agreements and negotiating techniques.

The remaining chapters in this part then examine the important subjects of participation, consultation and communications and the means available to develop procedures and techniques which will create a climate of employee relations which is more conducive to co-operation and trust.

# 22 | Industrial Relations

Industrial relations is concerned with the systems, rules and procedures used by unions and employers to determine the reward for effort and other conditions of employment, to protect the interests of the employed and their employers, and to regulate the ways in which employers treat their employees. The systems and procedures will include the processes of collective bargaining as well as formal procedure agreements. It is concerned also with the roles of the parties involved in the system – management, union officials, shop stewards and employees – and the relationships between them. It covers the industrial relations strategies adopted by management and unions, the procedure agreements evolved to enable the system to operate, and, of course, the processes of negotiating.

Industrial relations is dealt with here under the following headings:

1. *Industrial relations as a system of rules* – the basis upon which industrial relations operates.
2. *Collective bargaining* – the process of industrial relations which concludes agreements and handles disputes.
3. *The framework of industrial relations* – the roles of the government, the trade unions and the employers' associations.
4. *The role of management.*
5. *The role of shop stewards.*
6. *Industrial relations strategy* – especially for union recognition.
7. *Procedural agreements* – their purpose and content.
8. *Procedures for non-unionized companies.*
9. *Negotiating* – bargaining strategies and techniques.
10. *Industrial relations training.*

## Industrial relations as a system of rules

Industrial relations can be regarded as a system or web of rules regulating employment relations. The essence of the system is that the rules are jointly agreed by the representatives of the parties to employment relations, which makes for readier acceptance than if they are imposed by a third party, such as the state.

The system of rules is not necessarily a formal system. The rules appear in many more or less formal or informal guises: in legislation and statutory orders, in trade union regulations, in collective agreements and arbitration awards, in social conventions, in managerial decisions, and in accepted 'custom and practice'. They may be defined and coherent, or ill-defined and incoherent. Within a plant the rules may mainly be concerned with doing no more than defining the *status quo* which both parties recognize as the norm from which deviations may only be made by agreement. In this sense, therefore, an industrial relations system is a normative system where a norm can be seen as a rule, a standard or a pattern for action which is generally accepted or agreed as the basis upon which the parties concerned should operate.

### Types of regulations and rules
Job regulation aims to provide a framework of minimum rights and rules. Internal regulation is concerned with procedures for dealing with grievances, redundancies or disciplinary problems and rules concerning the operation of the pay system and the rights of shop stewards. External regulation is carried out by means of employment legislation, the rules of trade unions and employers' associations, and the regulative content of national or local agreements.

The rules can be of two kinds:

1. *Procedural* which deal with such matters as the methods to be used and the rules to be followed in the settlement of disputes, and regulate the behaviour of the parties to the agreement.
2. *Substantive* which refer to working hours or to other job terms and conditions in the area of employment covered by the agreement. These rules regulate the behaviour of employers and employees as parties to individual contracts of employment.

Procedural rules are intended to regulate conflict between the parties to collective bargaining and when their importance is emphasized a premium is being placed on industrial peace, and less regard is being paid to the terms on which it may be obtained. Substantive rules settle the rights and obligations attached to jobs. It is interesting to note that in Britain the parties to collective agreements have tended to concentrate more on procedural rather than on substantive rules. In the United States, where there is greater emphasis on fixed term agreements, the tendency has been to rely more on substantive rules.

## Collective bargaining

The industrial relations system is regulated by the process of collective bargaining, defined by Flanders as a 'social process that continually turns disagreements into agreements in an orderly fashion'.[1] Collective bargaining aims to establish by negotiation and discussion agreed rules and decisions in matters of mutual concern to employers and unions as well as methods of regulating the conditions governing employment.

It therefore provides a framework within which the views of management and unions about disputed matters that lead to industrial disorder can be considered with the aim of eliminating the causes of the disorder. Collective bargaining can also be regarded as a joint regulating process, dealing with the regulation of management in its relationships with work people as well as the regulation of conditions of employment. It has a political as well as an economic basis – both sides are interested in the distribution of power between them as well as the distribution of income.

Collective bargaining takes two basic forms, as identified by Chamberlain and Kuhn:[2]

1. *Conjunctive bargaining* which 'arises from the absolute requirement that some agreement – *any* agreement – be reached so that the operations on which both are dependent may continue' and results in a 'working relationship in which each party agrees, explicitly or implicitly, to provide certain requisite

services, to recognize certain seats of authority, and to accept certain responsibilities in respect of each other'.
2. *Co-operative bargaining* in which it is recognized that each party is dependent on the other and can achieve its objectives more effectively if it wins the support of the other.

A similar distinction was made by Walton and McKersie[3] when they referred to *distributive bargaining* as the 'complex system of activities instrumental to the attainment of one party's goals when they are in basic conflict with those of the other party', and to *integrative bargaining* — 'the system of activities which are not in fundamental conflict with those of the other party and which therefore can be integrated to some degree. Such objectives are said to define an area of common concern, a purpose.'

Both forms of collective bargaining emphasize that in industrial relations the parties cannot withdraw, or not for long; they are dependent upon each other for performance of their specialist functions and for their survival (except in the isolated cases where workers' co-operatives independently keep a firm going after its financial collapse). Conjunctive or distributive bargaining is a recognition of this mutual interdependence, but it is limited and negative. Co-operative or integrative bargaining is based on both the mutual interdependence of management and employees *and* their recognition that they can achieve more for themselves by adopting this approach.

## The framework of industrial relations

The rule making and regulating processes of industrial relations take place within the framework of government, national, corporate and plant institutions which operate according to certain stated or unstated principles. These principles, and the framework within which they operate, vary substantially from country to country. In the U.K. the institutions consist of:

1. THE GOVERNMENT which, according to its political persuasion, creates a legal framework which confers rights on employees and duties on employers by such acts as the Employment Protection (Consolidation) Act (1978) and the Employment Acts of 1980 and 1982.

   The British government has established institutions such as the Advisory, Conciliation and Arbitration Service (ACAS) which, besides carrying out the functions set out in its title, has the objective of encouraging the development of collective bargaining and the development and, where necessary, reform of collective bargaining machinery. There is also a network of industrial tribunals to hear unfair dismissal, equal pay and equal opportunity cases and other matters raised where employers are failing to comply with the provisions of employment legislation.
2. THE UNIONS whose objectives can broadly be defined as being:
   (a) to redress the bargaining advantage of the individual worker *vis-a-vis* the individual employer by substituting joint or collective action for individual action;
   (b) to secure improved terms and conditions of employment for their members and the maximum degree of security to enjoy those terms and conditions;
   (c) to obtain improved status for the worker in his work;
   (d) to increase the extent to which unions can exercise democratic control

327

over decisions that affect their interests by power sharing at the national, corporate and plant level.

The union power is exerted primarily at two levels — at the industry-wide level, to establish joint regulation on basic wages and hours with an employers' association or equivalent; and at the plant level, where the shop stewards' organizations exercise joint control over some aspects of the organization of work and localized terms and conditions of employment. Unions are party to national, local and plant procedure agreements which govern their actions to a greater or lesser extent, depending on their power and on local circumstances.

Unions could be said to be in the business of managing discontent and Clive Jenkins referred to the professional union bargainer as sitting on 'a pinnacle of institutionalized indignation'.[4] But it does not follow that unions introduce conflict — Jenkins also suggested that 'a union official is vocationally a gladiator because the work of the union is basically defensive'. It can be said that the role of a union is simply to provide a highly organized and continuous form of expression for sectional interests which would exist anyway. Such conflicts of interest are inherent in working relationships and unions can contribute to their solution by bringing issues out into the open and jointly defining with employers procedures for dealing with them.

There are various types of unions in Britain, including *craft unions*, the oldest kind, which require entry by apprenticeship and try to maintain standards by the joint control of apprenticeships and by resisting 'dilution' of the craft by those who have not become full members of the union; *general unions*, the largest kind, which take in recruits without being concerned about their level of skill, occupation or industry; *industrial unions*, which contain recruitment and representation to one industry; *sectoral unions*, which cater for one sector of employment only, such as the civil service; *manual unions*, which recruit what are normally termed manual workers; and *white collar unions*, a growing field, which include workers who are removed by one or more degrees from direct production or direct service, such as clerks, supervisors, technicians, scientists and managers. These types of unions can be combined or overlap; for example, there are white collar sections in general unions, or unions catering for one sector such as banking which are exclusively for white collared workers.

Most of the unions are federated on a fairly loose basis to the Trades Union Congress which exerts political influence and tries with varying degrees of success to co-ordinate and regulate the trade union movement — a difficult task because of the jealously guarded independence of individual members.

Individual unions are run by full-time central and district officials, with local committees of members. Their organization extends into the place of work by means of shop stewards whose role is discussed later in this chapter.

3. THE EMPLOYERS' ASSOCIATIONS which vary enormously in their size and influence over their members. Some will be heavily involved at national and local level in negotiations with unions. Others are mainly advisory in character. Individual employers in manufacturing and some nationalized industries may subscribe to the Confederation of British Industry which exerts political influence and provides advice but does not negotiate, and exerts no control over employers' associations.

## The role of management

Management typically sees its function as that of directing and controlling the work force to achieve economic and growth objectives. To this end, it believes that it is the rule making authority. Management tends to view the enterprise as a unitary system with one source of authority — themselves — and one focus of loyalty — the company. It extols the virtue of team work, where everyone strives jointly to a common objective, each pulls his weight to the best of his ability, and each accepts his place and his function gladly, following the leadership of the appointed manager or supervisor. These are admirable sentiments but unrealistic, and they sometimes lead to what McClelland has referred to as an 'orgy of avuncular pontification'[5] on the part of the leaders of industry.

The realistic view, as advanced by Fox,[6] is that an industrial organization is a plural society, containing many related but separate interests and objectives which must be maintained on some kind of equilibrium. In place of a corporate unity reflected in a single focus of authority and loyalty, management has to accept the existence of rival sources of leadership and attachment. Management has to face the fact that in Drucker's phrase,[7] a business enterprise has a triple personality: it is at once an economic, a political and a social institution. In the first, it produces and distributes incomes. In the second it embodies a system of government in which managers collectively exercise authority over the managed, but are also themselves involved in an intricate pattern of political relationships. Its third personality is revealed in the plant community which evolves from below out of face-to-face relations based on shared interests, sentiments, beliefs and values among various groups of employees.

The role of management is to exercise authority as well as to build up team work and it is concerned with the development of rules for this purpose. But management has increasingly to accept that it no longer has absolute authority. To a very great extent management and unions are mutually dependent. For each, the achievement of its own function is dependent upon a working relationship with the other. And there are three factors which are important in this relationship. The first is stability — a firmly established basis for interaction between management and employees. This is why many managers deplore closed shops in theory as an infringement of liberty, but in practice accept that there is less likelihood of trouble if all employees in a job category or unit are members of one union. For the same reason, one union covering all members of the plant may be preferred as a way of reducing the fragmentation of bargaining and of avoiding inter-union rivalries and demarcation — 'who does what' — disputes, even though a monolithic union may be more powerful. The second factor is trust — a belief that when the bargaining is over and the agreement is reached, both parties will keep their word. The third factor is understanding of each other's point of view. This does not mean that the parties must always be at one about the fundamental issues that affect them. But they must know how each side sees these issues if a collective agreement is eventually to be negotiated or if a relatively stable working relationship is to be maintained.

At the highest level, management has often been too remote from the unions and their members. J.T. Winkler's interesting piece of research on this subject, published under the apt title of *The Ghost at the Bargaining Table*, revealed that: 'Most directors have no significant contact with any manual or clerical staff other than their secretaries... Non-contact was also just as much the norm for production directors and for those normally responsible for personnel matters.'[8]

According to Winkler, their withdrawal is a coping device which enables low-level compromises with unions to take place on a pragmatic basis which do not threaten any fundamental principles.

Sir Michael Edwardes when he was chairman of British Leyland took a different view from the directors interviewed by Winkler. In *Back from the Brink* Edwardes emphasized his conviction that leadership in industrial relations had to come from the top and had to include direct contact with workers. His objective in tackling the sad state of industrial relations in BL was, as he put it:

> ...not to destroy or weaken the unions. On the contrary, it was to rebalance the whole order of things so that, together with management, national union officials would be able to play a proper role without finding their authority eroded by strong stewards, weak management, and a lack of understanding of what management was trying to achieve. This mixture has led to chaos in the past.[9]

## The role of shop stewards

The role of shop stewards is to represent their members to management in all matters that affect them. They negotiate and resolve disputes, but they may also deal with a host of day-to-day issues affecting the interests of their members.

Shop stewards can help management and supervision by squashing unreasonable complaints, or by dealing with issues as they arise on the shop floor, thus preventing escalations into major disputes. Commenting on his study of industrial relations in a British car factory, Clack wrote that 'the convenors and shop steward organization at the factory did not appear as a driving force behind labour unrest, but could more validly be regarded as "shock absorbers" of the industrial relations machinery'.[10]

The popular stereotype of the difficult, aggressive, and often surly shop steward as a common feature of the British industrial scene has been largely dispelled by research such as that carried out by Marsh, Evans and Garcia[11] on workshop industrial relations in over 400 British engineering establishments. This revealed that the overwhelming proportion of the managers in the survey thought that shop stewards were helpful (80%) – 9% thought they were obstructive and the remaining 11% had no firm views on the subject. There are, of course, difficult shop stewards, just as there are difficult managers and supervisors. And shop stewards are militant when they feel they have to be; as Phillip Higgs, convenor of a Midlands engineering factory said: 'It is our job to do more damage to the enemy than he does to us. If you can get a limited objective with very few casualties, you are all the more ready to move on to the next step. With each such advance we secure a little more control, a little more of managerial function is taken from management.'[12]

A satisfactory climate of relationships with unions and shop stewards cannot be achieved either by exaggerating militancy or by underestimating it. The approach management should use is to take steps to understand why it exists and to develop strategies, rules and procedures which will enable conflict to be managed by co-operative as well as conjunctive processes of collective bargaining. These approaches are discussed in the next section.

## Industrial relations strategy

The relationships that exist between employers and those they employ usually exist in tactical situations. Events happen and management and unions react to them. Employers are disagreeably surprised when they are suddenly faced with a claim for union recognition from their white collared staff. Unions are shocked by the absence of any procedure for dealing with redundancies. Industrial relations too often involves tactics without strategy.

It could be claimed that trade unions do have a general strategy: to protect the interests of their members and to improve their conditions. Many employers could also be said to operate in accordance with a general if somewhat negative strategy: to contain the constant pressure from the trade unions. But these are attitudes not strategies. All too often, there seems to be little evidence that any considered thought has been given to longer range developments and to the plans that are required to create and exploit opportunities to improve relationships or to meet potential threats to industrial harmony.

The aim of the industrial relations strategies of an organization should be to ensure that corporate objectives can be achieved by gaining the maximum amount of co-operation from employees and by minimizing the amount of industrial unrest. The factors influencing industrial relations strategy can be divided between those operating mainly within the organization and those bringing pressure to bear from outside.

### Internal factors affecting industrial relations strategy

The main internal factors are as follows:

☐ The attitudes of management to employees – the extent to which management recognizes that it has a responsibility towards its employees as well as to its shareholders and customers.

☐ The attitudes of employees to management – the extent to which they are satisfied with the company as an employer and with their work and prospects.

☐ The attitudes of management to trade unions, which tend to fall into three categories:

    (a) negative – those who resent the existence of unions either because they feel they unnecessarily interfere with management's authority or because they feel they will damage the paternalistic climate that exists and will erode the loyalty of employees to the company;

    (b) neutral – those who accept the unions if they are there, possibly as a necessary evil, but do not believe that there is any point in management taking an active interest in promoting good relationships with them;

    (c) positive – those who believe that unions can play an important role in partnership with management in developing better relationships between the company and its employees.

☐ The attitude of employees to unions. They can also have negative, neutral or positive feelings about unions.

☐ The inevitability of differences of opinion between management and unions. The primary role of the unions is to look after the interests of their members, while management is primarily concerned with economic performance. These interests are bound to clash sometimes over how the earnings of the company should be distributed between its owners and its employees.

☐ The extent to which management can or wants to exercise absolute authority to enforce decisions affecting the interests of employees.

☐ The present and likely future strength of the unions.

☐ The extent to which there is one dominating union or the existence of a number of competing unions which may lead to inter-union and demarcation disputes.

☐ The extent to which effective and agreed procedures for discussing and resolving grievances or handling disputes exist within the company.
☐ The effectiveness of managers and supervisors in dealing with industrial relations problems and disputes.
☐ The effectiveness of shop stewards or employee representatives and the degree of authority they can exercise over their members.
☐ The prosperity of the company, the degree to which it is expanding, stagnant or running down and the extent to which technological changes are likely to affect employment conditions and opportunities.

### External factors affecting industrial relations strategy
The main external factors are as follows:

☐ The militancy of the unions – nationally or locally.
☐ The effectiveness of the union and its officials and the extent to which the officials can and do control the activities of shop stewards within the company.
☐ The authority and effectiveness of the employer's association.
☐ The extent to which bargaining is carried out at national, local or plant level.
☐ The effectiveness of any national or local procedure agreements that may exist.
☐ The employment and pay situation – nationally and locally.
☐ The legal framework within which industrial relations exists.

### Areas covered by industrial relations strategy
Industrial relations strategies cannot be developed in isolation, as an analysis of the internal and external factors affecting them clearly indicates. They must be related to overall business strategies as well as to other personnel policies concerning employment, training, pay and working conditions. The specific areas in which industrial relations strategies can be developed are as follows:

☐ The improvement of relationships with employees generally through joint consultation and communications procedures (these are considered in chapters 23 and 24).
☐ The improvement of relationships with unions or staff associations by developing better collective bargaining and other industrial relations procedures or by improving the operation of existing procedures.
☐ The improvement of the competence of managers and supervisors in dealing with industrial relations matters, including communications and joint consultations.
☐ The education and training of shop stewards or staff representatives (in conjunction with the union or staff association).

In some situations, alternative strategies may have to be considered; for example, when a non-union company is confronted with the possibility of trade unionism. Figure 22.1 is an example of how the alternatives could be set out in the form of a decision tree.

## Union recognition

One of the biggest industrial relations problems that can face a company is that of recognition, whether of any union in a non-unionized company, or of additional unions in a company which is already partly unionized. Recognition can take place in two forms: first, representative rights which simply allows the

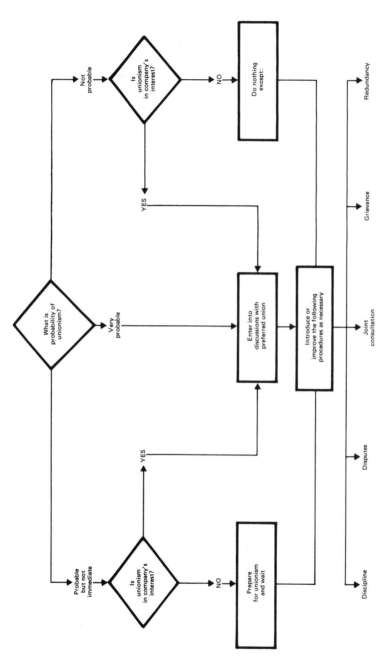

**Figure 22.1 Trade Union membership — alternative strategies**

union to represent employees on issues affecting them but does not concede that they have the right to negotiate terms and conditions of employment; second, negotiating rights, which give them full authority, within any national agreement, to negotiate terms and conditions. The unions will naturally want negotiating rights and may only accept representative rights as a second best if they are forced to do so by lack of support from employees or a particularly tough management. Clearly, they regard representative rights as a step towards full negotiating rights.

### Recognition strategy in a non-unionized company

Management in a non-unionized company may well feel that they have to resist the unions to the last ditch as a disruptive influence which will erode management's traditional prerogative — the authority to manage its own affairs. This is understandable. Unions may not be so disruptive as they fear, but they certainly reduce the absolute authority of management. And no one voluntarily likes to relinquish long-established authority.

The six main strategies for dealing with potential or actual recognition issues are shown in figure 22.2. These provide for a steadily increasing degree of formalization and loss of authority by management.

☐ *Strategy one* is the minimum that any company should do and, under British law, there have to be published grievance and disciplinary procedures.

☐ *Strategy two* is an attempt to divert interest by introducing joint consultation. It may work in the increasingly rare situations where staff are totally uninterested in unions but in most cases where there is any pressure for unionization it fails. The failure of joint consultation as a means of holding unions at bay is because too many committees are so emasculated that employees can easily become disillusioned about them.

☐ *Strategy three* is a diversion strategy for setting up a staff association which has been adopted with some success in Britain by a number of commercial companies such as building societies and insurance companies. It may sometimes only be a delaying tactic and can lead inexorably into the situation where the staff association becomes in effect a union with full negotiating rights.

☐ *Strategy four* is a stronger version of strategy three when the staff association acquires negotiating rights. In Britain a company sponsored staff union will not be recognized in law as a trade union, which opens the door for outside unions to press for recognition. Irrespective of this factor, it is advisable for management to have as little to do as possible with setting up an association apart from a few words of encouragement, and nothing to do with supporting it financially or with special facilities. If it is seen as a creature of the company, a staff association will soon lose credibility and will totally fail in its objective of keeping other unions at bay. It may, and often does, fail anyhow because the unions are too strong for it, or because the staff have acquired a taste for collective bargaining and decide that they will do better with the backing of a union. The staff association strategy is therefore one which should only be entered into deliberately and with great care when the company is confident that it will work. It should not be used as a last despairing device to keep the unions out — it will always fail in these circumstances.

☐ *Strategies five and six*, which involve recognizing the union as a representative or a negotiating body respectively, may be forced on a company if its strategies at earlier stages have failed. It is a pity when this happens, not because the

company has had to accept a union (which will always be much easier than was anticipated), but because it has been forced to capitulate. This is a bad start to the relationship. It creates initial feelings of resentment and may give the union the impression that management will always be likely to collapse if pressed fairly hard. The bargaining advantage will have moved to the union. If the climate of opinion nationally and within the firm is mainly in favour of recognition, then it is better to concentrate on getting a satisfactory procedure agreement as a basis for co-operative collective bargaining in the future rather than fighting on.

CHOICE OF STRATEGIES. The choice of strategies is a management decision in the sense that it depends initially on its assessment of three factors: first, the extent to which it approves or disapproves of unions; second, the strength of the unions inside and outside the company; and third, the consequences of resisting the union. Management's choice may, of course, be limited if the unions are already strong enough to force the company into recognizing them. The aim of the strategy should be to avoid being put under this sort of pressure either by gracefully granting recognition, on good terms, or by adopting one of the other approaches, if they seem appropriate.

The first step management should take before deciding on its strategy is to examine and if necessary revise its assumptions about unions. This could be done by talking to other employers or even by meeting a real live union official or two and finding that horns and tails are not as much in evidence as was thought. The next step should be to assess the strength of feelings of employees and to evaluate the strength of the union, if it is still felt that unionization constitutes a threat.

The strength of a possible approach from a union can be assessed informally by keeping ears close to the ground. First line supervisors should know what their groups are thinking, and it is up to higher management to ensure that any reliable information they acquire is passed upwards. There is no point in being taken completely by surprise.

It is necessary to assess at the same time which union, if any, is likely to approach and how strong its attack will be. Employers' associations and local contacts amongst employers of similar categories of staff can provide some guidance. It may be helpful to form some idea of which union would be preferable if there is more than one union on the scene. Steps can then be taken later to provide more encouragement (or less discouragement) to the preferred union.

A union, of course, may make a formal approach to talk to employees about joining them. It is normally unwise to reject such approaches. Facilities can easily be given for the union officials to meet interested employees out of working hours on the company's premises. Many firms have found that the number attending such meetings gives an indication of the feelings of their employees. Arrangements can usually be made for feedback on what went on, which can give valuable clues to the attitude of employees and the strategy being followed by the union. It is important at this stage and all subsequent stages to obtain a realistic view of the strength of the union and the reactions of employees. There is no point in fighting bloody battles if it is inevitable that the war will eventually be lost. This only stores up trouble for the future. On the other hand, it is inadvisable to give in too easily. The union must appreciate now that management can be firm when it wants to be.

The tactics of management now and later should be based on its judgement of present and future union strengths and the direction in which the loyalties of its employees may go. More reliable information on the views of employees can be obtained by conducting an attitude survey, or, as it might more appropriately be termed, a preference survey. This would ask whether or not they wish to be represented by a union, or whether they would prefer an employees' association or some other non-unionized consultative body to represent their interests. Employers often resist the approaches of unions, on the grounds that their employees might not wish to be forced to join or even live with a union. This could be true in some circumstances, where the staff are mainly white collared workers with the typical middle class suspicion of trade unions. But it could be a rationalization of management's own fears about loss of prerogative. No harm can be done by testing reactions – there is no evidence that the mere fact of conducting a survey encourages staff to think about joining a union. The value of a formal assessment is that it provides a reasonably factual basis for deciding on the strategy and tactics that the company should adopt.

At a later stage it may be decided that a ballot should be held to decide whether or not a union should be recognized. Management may feel strongly that recognition should not be given until at least 51% of the relevant employees are actually members of a union. This sounds reasonable, but it may be necessary to concede recognition with a lower percentage if it seems inevitable that more employees will join. There are no guidelines available on what is the minimum percentage for recognition. Each case has to be decided on its merits.

### Recognition strategy in a partly unionized company
A partly unionized company may be faced with a claim for recognition by a union representing employees who are not currently covered by a union agreement. Strategies in this case can be developed along the lines suggested for a non-unionized company facing unions for the first time, except that the company can presumably benefit when formulating its approach from the experience it has already gained. This situation is most likely to arise when white collar unions make an approach to clerical, technical, supervisory or management staff. Top management may feel increasingly despondent as their own kind fall into what they might regard as the maw of the unions, but most companies have learned to live with staff unions quite happily.

A more difficult situation arises when an alternative or breakaway union tries to encroach on the membership of existing unions. There are two dangers: first, of the fragmentation of bargaining units and second, inter-union strife. There is everything to be said for minimizing fragmentation. A bargaining unit, in the sense of a body of employees who are represented by one union, should preferably cover all employees of the same status or occupation in one plant. Bargaining units may be stratified according to status or divided according to occupation but they should not overlap. This causes confusion, lack of stability and difficulties in reaching agreements. It is not easy to control a move towards fragmentation when unions are taking the initiative, but management can at least resist recognition claims if they seem to be undesirable.

### Closed shop recognition
Closed shops can be pre-entry, when employees are required to join a union before starting work, or post-entry when they have to join the union within a stated period. A company may give *de facto* recognition to either sort of closed shop, or it may conclude a membership agreement with the union. Such recognition is legalized under British law and a company which has a membership agreement with a recognized union can insist on an employee joining the union and

dismiss him fairly if he refuses, as long as he does not have genuine religious objections.

Libertarians object on principle to the closed shop, but most managers who live with closed shops prefer the stability they bring to the chaos that can result if a few employees resist joining the unions. One of the most notorious failures of the 1971 Industrial Relations Act in Britain was its attempt to make closed shops illegal. Managements universally ignored the law and went on recognizing closed shops *de facto*, just as before.

Clearly, a closed shop should only be recognized if there is a very large majority of union members and it is possible to avoid serious difficulties over non-union employees who are reluctant to join. The decision may be a difficult one, as it could require balancing the interests of stable relationships with the union against the rights of the individual. The latter may have to be subordinated to the general good, but it could be an unpleasant business. The only answer is to conclude an agreement with the union that those existing employees who have genuine conscientious or religious objections to joining can be allowed to remain, possibly subscribing the normal union dues to a recognized charity. More recently in the U.K. the government has issued a code of practice on closed shops which defines the circumstances in which closed shops should be set up, provides guidelines on agreements and indicates where dismissal from a closed shop would be unfair. And the 1980 and 1982 Employment Acts provide greater protection to individuals in closed shops.

## Procedural agreements

A procedure is an established way of carrying out some piece of business. The aim of a procedural agreement is to ensure that the business conducted between management and union is carried out in an orderly, consistent and generally accepted manner.

Procedural agreements have evolved as a method of exercising joint regulation over matters that affect the interests of both the company and its employees. A procedural relationship is established between an employer and a trade union as soon as the union's right to represent the interests of its membership has been recognized. When that right includes the settlement of terms and conditions of employment by negotiation the active continuity of the relationship is maintained as adjustments are made to meet constantly changing circumstances. The procedural aspects of an act of recognition establishing negotiating rights are usually concerned with defining the area in which the union's representative capacity is acknowledged, indicating the subjects which are brought within the scope of negotiation, the steps by which agreement is to be sought and the procedure to be followed if there is failure to agree.

Procedural agreements may contain the following sections:

1. A preamble defining the objectives of the agreement.
2. A statement that the union is recognized as a representative body with negotiating rights.
3. A statement of general principles, which will include a commitment to use the procedure (a no-strike clause) and may additionally include a *status quo* clause which restricts the ability of management to introduce changes outside negotiated or customary practice.
4. A statement of the facilities granted to unions, including the rights of shop

stewards and the right to hold meetings.
5. Provision for joint negotiating committees (in some agreements).
6. The negotiating or disputes procedure.
7. Provision for terminating the agreement.

### Preamble – objectives
The objectives of the agreement should be stated in the preamble, for example:

> 'To use the processes of negotiation to achieve results beneficial to the company and the employees.'
> 'To provide a framework which will enable discussions to take place at all levels on ways of continuing the development of good industrial relations in the company.'
> 'To provide an arrangement through which matters of concern to both employers and management can be discussed and negotiated at an appropriate level.'
> 'To provide a means of negotiation and consultation on all matters directly and indirectly affecting the company's employees with the objective of achieving sound and constructive relations between the management and the employees.'

### Union recognition
The recognition section should confirm the right of the signatory union or unions to represent specific categories of employees within an agreed bargaining unit. The rights may be defined as being:

> 'To represent and to negotiate wages and conditions of employment on behalf of its members who are employed by the company.'

Reference may also be made in this section to union membership. A general phrase would be used such as:

> 'The company and the union recognize that it is in the interests of good industrial relations that all employees in agreed bargaining units should become and remain members of the union.'

This reference to union membership could be accompanied by an undertaking from the company to encourage employees to join the union. It could be further developed into a closed shop agreement, although those words would never be used, by a statement to the effect that all existing employees in the defined bargaining unit should become members of the union within, say, four weeks of the date of the agreement unless they have genuine religious objections. The agreement could go on to state that all new employees should join the unions within, say, two weeks of starting with the company. In the more extreme cases, where a pre-entry closed shop is in force, the agreement would state that the company undertakes only to engage men or women who are already members of the union, unless they have genuine religious objections. Reference might be made in these circumstances to the payment by those with religious objections of the equivalent of the union dues to a charity agreed with the union.

### General principles
The statement of general principles should indicate how the parties to the agreement are going to work together to achieve its objectives. The following points should be included:

☐ A statement of common purpose – 'The company and the union have a common objective in using the processes of negotiation and consultation to achieve results beneficial to both parties.'
☐ A definition of the role of the unions as recognized by management – 'The

company recognizes that effective industrial relations are best realized through fully representative unions capable of authoritative negotiation.'
□ A definition of the role of management as recognized by the unions – 'The unions for their part recognize that management has the prime responsibility to manage the undertaking in order to achieve its objectives efficiently.'
□ An undertaking not to take industrial action until the agreed procedures are exhausted (a commitment to use procedure or no-strike clause) – 'The company and the unions agree that mutually satisfactory conditions are best achieved through the process of negotiation. The company therefore agrees to refrain from lockout, and the union from stoppage of work or other restrictions on production until the procedure for resolving disputes prescribed in this agreement (and the national agreement) has been exhausted.'
□ An undertaking may be included not to change the *status quo* without prior consultation – 'Prior consultation will take place before any change in working practices or methods of payment is implemented. Should the change result in a dispute between the management and the unions, the practice shall revert to what it was prior to the dispute and the change shall only be made subsequently should it be agreed through the negotiating procedure.'

### Union facilities
The agreement on union facilities should cover the following three areas:

1. *Rights and duties of shop stewards* – it is necessary to define:
    □ The right of employees to elect shop stewards – 'Employees of the company who are members of the union will elect representatives to act on their behalf in accordance with this agreement.'
    □ What a shop steward is – 'For the purpose of this agreement a shop steward is an accredited representative of the union who has been recognized by the company.'
    □ Eligibility – the agreement may define a minimum length of service before becoming eligible for election as a steward. It may also state that the company will recognize shop stewards elected in accordance with the agreed procedure but reserves the right, after consultation with the district or regional union organizer, to withhold or withdraw recognition from any particular individual.
    □ The number of shop stewards – 'The company and the union will agree the number of shop stewards to be elected each year and the areas of production or groups of people whom they will represent.'
    □ Election arrangements – 'Elections by secret ballot may be held at a mutually convenient time and the company will assist in providing ballot facilities if required.'
    □ Notification arrangements – 'When a shop steward has been elected the company will be notified officially by the union.'
    □ Provision for a senior shop steward – 'The shop stewards may elect a senior shop steward.'
    □ The duties of shop stewards – 'Shop stewards will act in accordance with agreements between the union and the company, so far as these affect the relations between the company and its employees. They will be subject to the control of the union in trade union matters.'
    □ Facilities for shop stewards – 'Facilities will be afforded to shop stewards by the company to carry out their functions within the framework of this

of this agreement to deal with questions and problems in the department or section represented by the shop steward.'
☐ Arrangements for shop stewards leaving work and holding meetings and discussions − 'A shop steward wishing to leave his work to investigate a grievance, contact a union official, meet other shop stewards or carry out any other union business will first obtain the permission of his foreman or other person in authority. Should he wish to visit a department other than the one for which he is the elected representative, he will also obtain permission of the foreman or other person in authority in that department or section. Such permission will not unreasonably be withheld.'
☐ The basis upon which shop stewards are paid while carrying out their duties − 'Shop stewards will suffer no financial loss through the discharge of their duties as shop stewards.'
☐ Training arrangements − 'The parties agree on the need to provide suitable training for shop stewards to achieve the skills required to carry out their duties.'
☐ Protection of employment rights − 'Action taken by shop stewards in good faith in pursuance of their duties, shall not in any way affect their employment with the company.'
☐ Arrangements for transferring or dismissing shop stewards − 'Before a shop steward is transferred from a department or section he represents, and before he is dismissed from the company, the transfer or dismissal will be brought to the notice of the branch secretary by management.'
2. *Union meetings and communication facilities* − for which the agreement should define:
☐ Arrangements for meetings between the company and the union − 'Meetings between representatives of the company and the union will normally be held during working hours and on the company's premises.'
☐ Arrangements for union meetings − 'The company recognizes that on certain occasions union meetings can with advantage be held on the company's premises outside working hours. Permission to hold such meetings should be obtained in advance from the company.'
☐ The use of notice-boards by unions − 'The union will be allowed the reasonable use of company notice-boards for union announcements.'
3. *The collection of union dues* − the agreement may specify a 'check-off' arrangement for the company to collect union dues − 'It is agreed that a check-off system will operate whereby the company agrees to deduct union dues (but not entrance fees or special levies) from the wages of union members and to pay them to the union. This will only apply to employees who have previously authorized the deductions in writing.'

**Joint negotiating committee**
Provision for a joint negotiating committee is not a necessary part of a procedural agreement. Many, if not most, companies would prefer to avoid formalizing negotiating arrangements in this way. A joint negotiating committee, however, is sometimes set up when a large company agrees that terms and conditions of employment should be determined by collective bargaining within the company or plant, and prefers to regularize negotiating procedures rather than engage in a series of *ad hoc* trials of strength.
The terms of reference of a company joint negotiating committee should cover the following points:

1. *Objective.* To provide the means of negotiation and consultation on all matters directly and indirectly affecting the hourly paid employees in the company's establishment.
2. *Terms of reference*
   (a) To negotiate company-wide wage systems, hours of work, overtime rates and other conditions of employment.
   (b) To provide a means of joint consultation on production, safety, welfare matters and on general company problems.
   (c) To review the operation of domestic disputes and disciplinary procedures and to decide on any changes necessary.
3. *Composition*
   (a) Numbers of shop stewards and management representatives.
   (b) Constituencies of shop steward members.
   (c) Method of election of accredited shop stewards.
4. *Officers.* Chairman and secretary of management and union sides.
5. *Meetings.* Arrangements for regular ordinary meetings and extraordinary meetings (when agreed by both chairmen).
6. *Agenda.* Arrangements for placing items on the agenda and raising additional items.
7. *Minutes.* Arrangements for chairmen to agree minutes and for distributing same.
8. *Failure to agree.* Procedure to be followed if the committee fails to agree. This could include bringing in full-time union officials and employer's officials for a works conference and, if this fails, progression through the normal negotiating procedure for the industry or some form of conciliation process. In Britain this could be provided by the Advisory, Conciliation and Arbitration Service (ACAS).

### Disputes procedure

A domestic disputes procedure should describe each of the stages for dealing with disputes in the company from when an issue is first raised on the shop floor until, assuming it is not settled at an earlier stage, it is either referred to outside conciliation or is dealt with in accordance with the agreed procedure for avoiding disputes in the industry. A disputes procedure of this nature is, in effect, a grievance procedure for employees who are members of a union.

The domestic procedure should state the principle that no strike or lockout should take place until the procedure has been exhausted, unless this has already been stated as a general principle in the procedural agreement. Time limits should be given for moving from one stage to the next of the procedure in the event of a failure to agree.

The following is an example of a typical staged disputes procedure in a medium sized plant where there is no national agreement.

### Domestic disputes procedure

STAGE 1
1. All queries and grievances should in the first place be raised by the employee with his foreman. If the employee chooses to approach the shop steward in the first instance concerning the matter, they may subsequently jointly discuss it with the foreman, or the shop steward may raise the matter on the employee's behalf with the foreman. (The latter sentence goes further than

many procedures which lay down that the shop steward should only become involved on individual issues if the employee has failed to get satisfaction. In practice, however, shop stewards do become involved in the first instance and it is realistic to allow for this in the procedure.)

2. If the issue affects a group of union members in the same department or section, the shop steward raises the matter with the foreman.
3. The foreman will do his best to resolve the issue and give an answer within *three* working days of the matter being raised with him. However, if the issue is one on which he cannot give a decision he will immediately refer the matter to stage 2 of the procedure.

STAGE 2

4. If the employee or shop steward is not satisfied with the answer provided by the foreman, the latter will refer the issue to the departmental manager who will discuss the matter with the shop steward. The departmental manager may ask the personnel manager to attend this meeting and the shop steward may be accompanied by the senior shop steward of his union.
5. The departmental manager, following discussions with the personnel manager, will give his answer within *three* working days of the matter being raised with him (i.e. within six working days of the matter being raised initially).

STAGE 3

6. If the shop steward is not satisfied with the answer given by the departmental manager, the departmental manager will refer the matter to the works manager who, together with the personnel manager, will discuss the matter with the shop steward and the senior shop steward.
7. The works manager will give his answer within *three* working days of the matter being raised with him (i.e. within nine working days of the matter being raised initially).

STAGE 4

8. If the union is dissatisfied with the answer provided by the works manager a conference should be held to discuss the matter within the company at which a director of the company, other appropriate members of management, the senior shop steward and, if required, the district officer of the union will be present.

STAGE 5

9. If a mutually satisfactory agreement is not reached in stage 4 the matter will be referred to conciliation and, if that fails, arbitration. The means of conciliation or arbitration will be agreed between the company and the district officer of the union.
10. The recommendations of the conciliation body, or the decision of the arbitration body, will not be regarded as final and binding on either the company or the union. However, both parties will use these findings as a basis for further negotiation.

GENERAL

11. No lockout, stoppage of work or other unauthorized action will take place as a result of any complaint, grievance or dispute in which the company and union members are concerned. Any such action before the procedure has

been exhausted will be a breach of this agreement.

RECORDS
12. Records will be maintained by company foremen or managers of the details of the complaint and decisions made at each stage of the procedure. Copies of the records will be given to shop stewards or union officials concerned.

### Disciplinary procedure
It is normal to include a disciplinary procedure in a formal procedural agreement. The points that should be covered and an example of a procedure are given in chapter 13 and Appendix E.

### Termination of the agreement
It is usual in Britain not to specify a terminal date for the procedural agreement but to state that it would be subject to, say, six months' notice of termination from either side.

### Redundancy procedures
It is not common practice for redundancy procedures to be incorporated in a procedural agreement, mainly because it is difficult to obtain complete agreement in advance on the precise criteria for redundancy and the compensation to be offered. Such procedures are often discussed separately and informal agreement reached that they should be used as guidelines for action in the event of redundancy. The points that should be covered in redundancy procedures are considered in chapter 13 and Appendix F.

## Industrial relations procedures for non-unionized companies or employees

In non-unionized companies, or for categories of employees who are not members of a union there is, of course, no formal negotiating procedure. There may be arrangements for joint consultation (see chapter 23) and the terms of reference of joint consultative committees or works councils might possibly allow reference to conditions of employment, but it is most unlikely that such committees would be allowed to negotiate on pay matters. A company may decide to encourage an employees' association and negotiate with it, but this is tantamount to a union, especially if the company keeps at arm's length from the association.

A non-unionized company should at least have a disciplinary procedure (Appendix E) and a grievance procedure (Appendix D). Both are required in Britain under the Employment Protection Act. In addition, it may be advisable to have a redundancy procedure (Appendix F), even if this is not announced to staff.

### Grievance procedure
Grievance procedures for individual employees should aim to settle the grievance fairly and as near as possible to the point of origin. They should be simple and rapid in operation. The procedure should be in writing and state that:
(a) the grievance should normally be discussed first between the employee and his or her immediate superior;
(b) if satisfaction is not achieved at this level the employee should have the right

of appeal to the next higher level of management and, if he wishes, may be accompanied by another member of the company's staff to help him put his case;

(c) there should be a further right of appeal to the highest level in the company if satisfaction is not achieved at an earlier stage.

## Negotiations

Negotiations take place when two parties meet, one or both aiming to win as much as they can from the other while giving away as little as possible. Negotiating can be a war game. It is a battle in the sense that the bargainers are pitting their wits against each other while also bringing in the heavy artillery in the shape of sanctions or threatened sanctions. As with other battles, the negotiation process can produce a pyrrhic victory in which both sides, including the apparent winner, retire to mourn their losses and lick their wounds. It is a game in the sense that both sides are trying to win, but there are various conventions or rules which the parties tacitly adopt or recognize, although in practice they may break them in the heat of the battle.

Negotiations can normally be broken down into four stages:

1. Preparing for negotiation: setting objectives, defining strategy and assembling data.
2. Opening.
3. Bargaining.
4. Closing.

Before analysing these stages in detail it may be helpful to consider the process of bargaining and list the typical conventions that operate when bargaining takes place.

### The process of bargaining

The process of bargaining consists of three distinct, though related, functions. First, bargainers state their bargaining position to their opposite numbers. Second, they probe weaknesses in the bargaining position of their opposite numbers and try to convince them that they must move, by stages if this is inevitable, from their present position to a position closer to what the bargainer wants. Third, they adjust or confirm their original estimate of their own bargaining position in the light of information gleaned and reactions from their opposite number, so that, if the time comes to put an estimate of bargaining position to the test, the ground chosen will be as favourable as possible.

The essence of the bargaining process was well put by Peters in *Strategies and Tactics in Labour Negotiations*. He comments:

> In skilful hands the bargaining position performs a double function. It conceals and it reveals. The bargaining position is used to indicate − to unfold gradually, step by step − the maximum expectation of the negotiator, while at the same time concealing, for as long as necessary, his minimum expectation. By indirect means, such as the manner and timing of the changes in your bargaining position, you, as a negotiator, try to convince the other side that your maximum expectation is really your minimum breaking-off point... Since you have taken an appropriate bargaining position at the start of negotiations, each change in your position should give ever-clearer indications of your maximum expectation. Also, each change should be designed to encourage or pressure the other side to reciprocate with as much information as you give them, if not more.[13]

### Bargaining conventions

There are certain conventions in collective bargaining which most experienced and responsible negotiators understand and accept, although they are never stated and, indeed, may be broken in the heat of the moment or by a tyro in the bargaining game. These conventions help to create an atmosphere of trust and understanding which is essential to the maintenance of the type of stable bargaining relationship that benefits both sides. Some of the most generally accepted conventions are listed below:

1. Whatever happens during the bargaining, both parties are using the bargaining process in the hope of coming to a settlement.
2. Attacks, hard words, threats and (controlled) losses of temper are perfectly legitimate tactics to underline determination to get one's way and to shake the opponent's confidence and self-possession. But these are treated by both sides as legitimate tactics and should not be allowed to shake the basic belief in each other's integrity or desire to settle without taking drastic action.
3. Off-the-record discussions are mutually beneficial as a means of probing attitudes and intentions and smoothing the way to a settlement. But they should not be referred to specifically in formal bargaining sessions unless both sides agree in advance.
4. Each side should normally be prepared to move from its original position.
5. It is normal, although not inevitable, for the negotiation to proceed by alternate offers and counter-offers from each side which lead steadily towards a settlement.
6. Concessions, once made, cannot be withdrawn.
7. Firm offers must not be withdrawn, although it is legitimate to make and withdraw conditional offers.
8. Third parties should not be brought in until both parties are agreed that no further progress would be made without them.
9. The final agreement should mean exactly what it says. There should be no trickery, and the terms agreed should be implemented without amendment.
10. If possible, the final settlement should be framed in such a way as to reduce the extent to which the opponent obviously loses face or credibility.

### Preparing for negotiation

Negotiations take place in an atmosphere of uncertainty. You do not know how strong your employees' bargaining team is and what it really wants. The members of that team do not know how much you are prepared to concede or the strength of your convictions.

In a typical wage negotiation the union or representative body making the claim will define three things:

☐ the target it would like to achieve;
☐ the minimum it will accept;
☐ the opening claim which will be most likely to help them achieve the target.

You as the employer will define three related things:

☐ the target settlement you would like to achieve;
☐ the maximum you would be prepared to concede;
☐ the opening offer you will make which will provide you with sufficient room to manoeuvre in reaching your target.

The difference between their claim and your offer is the negotiating range. If your maximum exceeds their minimum this will indicate the settlement range. This is demonstrated in figure 22.3. In this example the chance of settlement without too much trouble is fairly high. It is when your maximum is less than their minimum, as in figure 22.4, that the trouble starts. Over a period of time a negotiation where a settlement range exists proceeds in the way demonstrated in figure 22.5.

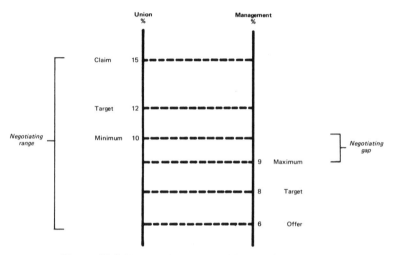

**Figure 22.3 Negotiating range with a settlement zone**

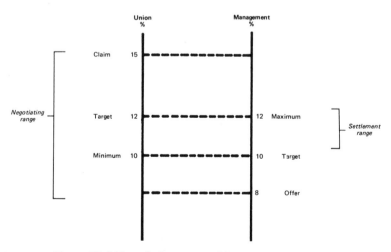

**Figure 22.4 Negotiating range without a settlement zone**

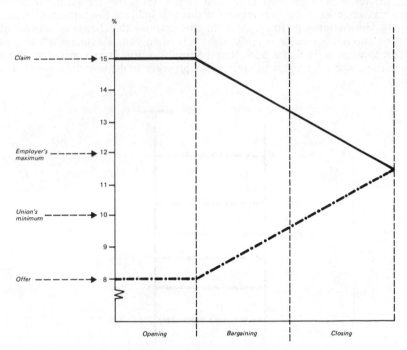

**Figure 22.5 Stages of a negotiation**

OBJECTIVES. Your objectives should be defined in the form of your target settlement and your initial and maximum offers. These will be conditioned by:

☐ the relative strengths of your case and that of the union;
☐ the relative power of the company *vis a vis* the union;
☐ the size of the union's claim and whether it is realistic;
☐ the likely target and minimum acceptable offer set by the union;
☐ the amount of room for negotiation you want to allow;
☐ your ability to pay;
☐ the going rate elsewhere;
☐ the rate of inflation. Although you should never concede that it is your job to protect your employees from inflation, the cost of living will usually be one of the chief arguments advanced by a union for an increase.

STRATEGY. Your strategy should clearly be designed to achieve your target settlement, with the maximum you are prepared to concede being your fallback position. You need to decide two things:

1. The stages you would ideally like to follow in moving from your opening to your closing offer. This is dependent on the amount of room for negotiation you have allowed.
2. The negotiating package you want to use in reply to whatever package the

union has put forward. Your aim should be to provide scope for trading concessions during the course of negotiations. There is also much to be said for having in reserve various conditions which you can ask the unions to accept in return for any concessions you may be prepared to make. You might, for example, ask for an extended period before the next settlement in return for an increase in your offer.

PREPARATION. It is essential to prepare carefully for negotiations so that you do not, in Aneurin Bevan's phrase, 'go naked to the conference table'. The following steps should be taken:

1. List the arguments to be used in supporting your own case.
2. List the likely arguments or counter-arguments that your opponent is likely to use.
3. List your own counter-arguments to the arguments of your opponent.
4. Obtain the data you need to support your case.
5. Select the negotiating team. This should never have fewer than two members, and for major negotiations should have three or more: one to take the lead and do most of the talking, one to take notes and feed the negotiator with any supporting information he requires, and the others to observe opposite numbers and play a specific part in negotiations in accordance with their brief.
6. Brief the members of the negotiating team on their roles and the negotiating strategy and tactics that are to be adopted. If appropriate, prepared statements or arguments should be issued at this stage to be used as required by the strategic plan.
7. Rehearse the members of the team in their roles. They can be asked to repeat their points to other members and deal with responses from them; or someone can act as devil's advocate and force the leader or other members of the team to handle awkward points or negotiating ploys.

At this stage it may be possible to meet the opponent informally to sound out his position, while he sounds out yours. The 'early warning' system can be used to condition the opponent to modify his likely initial demands by convincing him of the strength of your own position or your determination to resist.

## Opening

Your tactics when opening the negotiation should be as follows:

1. Open realistically and move moderately.
2. Challenge your opponent's position as it stands; do not destroy his ability to move.
3. Explore attitudes, ask questions, observe behaviour and, above all, listen in order to assess your opponent's strengths and weaknesses, his tactics and the extent to which he may be bluffing.
4. Make no concessions of any kind at this stage
5. Be non-committal about proposals and explanations (do not talk too much).

## Bargaining

After the opening moves you begin the main bargaining phase during which you narrow the gap between the initial positions and try to persuade your opponent that your case is sufficiently strong to force him to close at a less advantageous point than he had planned. Employ the following tactics:

1. Always make conditional proposals: 'If you will do this I will consider doing that.' The words to remember are: 'if ... then ...'
2. Never make one-sided concessions: always trade off against a concession from the other party: 'If I concede x then I expect you to concede y.'
3. Negotiate on the whole package: do not allow your opponent to pick you off item by item, and keep the issues open to extract the maximum benefit from your potential trade-offs.

## Closing

When and how you close is a matter of judgement, and depends on your assessment of the strength of your opponent's case and his determination to see it through. There are various closing techniques:

1. Making a concession from the package, preferably a minor one which is traded off against an agreement to settle. The concession can be offered more positively than in the bargaining stage: 'If you will agree to settle at x, I will concede y.'
2. Doing a deal: splitting the difference, or bringing in something new, such as extending the settlement time-scale, agreeing to back payments, phasing increases, making a joint declaration of intent to do something in the future (e.g. introducing a productivity plan).
3. Summarizing what has happened to date, emphasizing the concessions that have been made and the extent to which you have moved, and stating that you have reached your final position.
4. Applying pressure through a threat of the dire consequences which will follow if your offer is not accepted.
5. Giving your opponent a choice between two courses of action.

Do not make a final offer unless you mean it. If it is not really your final offer and your opponent calls your bluff, you will have to make further concessions and your credibility will be undermined. He will, of course, attempt to force you into revealing the extent to which you have reached your final position. Do not allow him to hurry you. If you want to avoid committing yourself and thus devaluing the word 'final', state as positively as you can that this is as far as you are prepared to go.

## Industrial relations training

Industrial relations training is required for four categories of people in a company: managers, supervisors, shop stewards and employees. The training should be planned along the lines suggested in chapter 20 which means that it should be based on an analysis of training needs and should include specific objectives to be achieved by the course as a whole and by each session in a course. Training for shop stewards and employees can be usefully carried out jointly with the trade union, but it is even more important to train managers and supervisors.

### Management training

Managers are often taught about 'human relations' on courses but are seldom given training in collective bargaining or education in the role of the unions. This shows up in two ways: first, at the conference table where inexperienced managers are often completely outgeneralled by well-trained and experienced union officials and, secondly, in the unco-operative attitude taken by some managers to unions because they fail to understand company policy on industrial relations or the useful part that unions can play in achieving stable industrial relations.

Negotiating skills are mainly acquired by experience and practice, but it is dangerous to allow inexperienced managers to practise negotiating techniques with experienced shop stewards or union officials. The answer is to run special company courses, or to have separate sessions on existing courses, which deal with negotiating skills and allow managers to practise them in role playing exercises. They can also be required to analyse industrial relations case studies to determine the tactics that should be used. The case studies should preferably be based on actual problems that have occurred within the company.

## References

1. Flanders, A. *Management and Unions: The Theory and Reform of Industrial Relations.* Faber and Faber, London, 1970.
2. Chamberlain, N.W. and Kuhn, J.W. *Collective Bargaining.* McGraw-Hill, New York, 1965.
3. Walton, R.E. amd McKersie, R.B. *A Behavioural Theory of Labor Negotiations.* McGraw-Hill, New York, 1965.
4. McCarthy, W.E.J. 'Restrictive Labour Practices', *Royal Commission on Trade Unions and Employers' Associations Research Paper No. 4.* Her Majesty's Stationery Office, London, 1967.
5. McClelland, G. *British Journal of Industrial Relations*, June 1963, p. 278.
6. Fox, A. 'Industrial Sociology and Industrial Relations', *Royal Commission on Trade Unions and Employers' Associations Research Paper No. 3.* Her Majesty's Stationery Office, London, 1966.
7. Drucker, P. *The New Society.* Heinemann, London, 1951.
8. Winkler, J.T. 'The Ghost at the Bargaining Table: Directors and Industrial Relations', *British Journal of Industrial Relations*, Vol. XII, No. 2, July 1974.
9. Edwardes, Sir Michael *Back from the Brink.* Collins, London, 1983.
10. Clack, G. *Industrial Relations in a British Car Factory.* Cambridge University Press, Cambridge, 1967.
11. Marsh, A.I., Evans, E.O. and Garcia, P. *Workplace Industrial Relations in Engineering.* Kogan Page, London, 1971.
12. Higgs, P. 'The Convenor', *Work 2.* Penguin Books, Harmondsworth, 1969.
13. Peters, J. *Strategies and Tactics in Labour Negotiations.*

# 23 | Participation and Joint Consultation

## What is participation?

Participation takes place when management and employees are jointly involved in making decisions on matters of mutual interest where the aim is to produce solutions to the problems which will benefit all concerned. Participation does not mean that the parties subordinate their own interests entirely. But it does mean that they aim to achieve objectives which are not in fundamental conflict with those of the other party, and which can therefore be integrated to some degree. Participation does not require total and bland agreement all the time, and bargaining about issues is not excluded. It is akin to integrative or co-operative bargaining where the parties find common or complementary interests and solve problems confronting both of them.

Participation should be distinguished from negotiation which, although it involves joint decision-making, does this by a process of distributive or conjunctive bargaining where the sole aim is to resolve pure conflicts of interests.

Participation is more than joint consultation, which is the process by which management seeks the views, feelings and ideas of employees through their representatives, prior to negotiating or making a decision. Although joint consultation may involve the discussion of mutual problems and is a necessary aspect of participation, it leaves with management the ultimate responsibility for making decisions. Participation is also more than communications, which is the process of keeping people informed about intentions, opinions, results or decisions on matters that interest them, although effective two-way communications are necessary to successful participation and joint consultation.

### The purpose of participation

The purpose of participation should be to advance the well-being of all concerned – owners and managers in addition to workpeople. It should be a means of enabling the enterprise to achieve its objectives, as long as it is understood that those objectives include acting in a socially responsible way to employees as well as the maximization of profits.

The objective of participation is not, therefore, simply to provide people with job satisfaction because they feel that they are involved. This is an important and legitimate aim, but it is not the only one. Participation should do more than help people to feel good. It should provide them with the means of identifying their own interests with those of the enterprise in which they work, so that both can flourish. Participation should therefore provide employees with the opportunity to contribute to the success of the organization by involving them in decision-making and by means of joint consultation, productivity committees, suggestion schemes and, the latest development, quality circles.

352

## Participation and industrial democracy

Are participation and industrial democracy the same thing? To some, industrial democracy is an alternative way of describing more or less traditional forms of joint consultation. To others, it comprises the joint regulation or control by unions and management of decisions and actions which affect the present and future conduct of the business. This implies trade union participation in decision-making at all levels in the enterprise, including the highest level, the board. This view, as held by trade unionists, rejects conventional joint consultative arrangements or paternalistically based profit-sharing schemes as a charade of participation which gives workpeople none of the substance of control that has been firmly based with the leading shareholders. The demand for two-tiered board structures and for union representation on the board arises from this latter viewpoint.

The debate on industrial democracy has often been concerned with means rather than with ends. It is the *form* and extent of participation that has caused most argument, not the objective. There has been a fair measure of agreement on both sides of industry with the following definition of the two basic purposes of industrial democracy prepared by the Industrial Participation Association (Great Britain) for its evidence to the Committee of Inquiry on Industrial Democracy:

(a) That it is both reasonable and just that the employees of a company should have the means to influence the major decisions that may determine the conditions of their own working lives, and thereby the lives of their families – decisions that are commonly taken at a level where at present it is not usual for employees to be directly involved or represented.
(b) That an essential purpose of industrial democracy must be to improve the efficiency and productivity of the enterprise, by enabling employees at all levels to make a more effective contribution – increased productivity being the context in which employees' interests, as well as the interests of other parties, can best be advanced.[1]

# Forms of participation

Participation can vary according to the level at which it takes place, the degree to which decision-making is shared, and the mechanisms of a greater or lesser degree of formality which are used.

## Levels of participation

Participation takes various forms at different levels in an enterprise. These levels were classified by the Industrial Society[2] as:

☐ job level;
☐ management level;
☐ policy-making level;
☐ ownership level.

Participation at the job level involves the supervisor and his immediate group, and the processes include the communication of information about the work, the delegation of authority, and the interchange of ideas about how the work should be done. These processes are essentially informal.

Participation at management level can involve sharing information and decision-taking about issues which affect the way in which work is planned, co-ordinated and controlled, and the conditions under which the work is carried out. There are limitations. Management as a whole, and individual managers, must retain authority to do what their function requires. Participation does not imply anarchy. But it does require some degree of willingness on the part of management to share their decision-making powers. At this level, participation becomes more formalized, through consultative committees, briefing groups or other joint bodies involving management and trade unionists.

At the policy-making level, where the direction in which the business is going is determined, total participation implies sharing the power to make the key decisions on investments, disinvestments, new ventures, expansions and retractions which affect the future well-being of both the company and its employees. Ultimately, it means that such decisions are made fairly by directors who represent the interests of the owners, the management, and the workpeople. The proposal to have a supervisory board upon which worker representatives have the power to veto major investment decisions, mergers or take-overs, closures or major redeployment is not full participation, but it is in accordance with the reality of the divided loyalties that worker representatives would have if they had to share the responsibility for unpopular decisions by becoming full board members in the accepted sense.

At the ownership level, participation may imply a share in the equity, which is not meaningful unless the workers have sufficient control through voting rights to determine the composition of the board. Workers' co-operatives are also participative in the sense that the workers, including managers and supervisors, *are* the management and must therefore be involved in joint decision-making at board level.

### The degree to which decision-making is shared

At the one end of the scale management can make decisions unilaterally; at the other end, much more rarely, workers decide unilaterally. Between these extremes there is a range of intermediate points which can be expressed (figure 23.1) as a scale.

The point on this scale at which participation should or is able to take place at any level in an organization will depend on the attitudes, willingness and enthusiasm of both management and employees. Management may be reluctant to give up too much of its authority except under duress from the unions, or legislation aimed at developing industrial democracy (the political term for participation). Unions may prefer not to be over-involved in decision-making so that they can shoot from the side-lines when they want to.

### Mechanisms for participation

At the job level participation should be as informal as possible. Groups may be called together on an *ad hoc* basis to consider a particular problem, but formal committees should be avoided in small departments (say, less than 250 people) or at section level. Briefing groups (see chapter 24) can be used to provide for informal two-way communications.

At the next higher level, more formality may be appropriate in larger organizations. There is scope for the use of joint consultative committees or joint negotiating committees with carefully defined terms of reference on the matters they can discuss.

At the policy-forming level, participation becomes more difficult to organize. This is when management will be most reluctant to abandon its prerogatives unless forced to by legislation. Unions, as already mentioned, do not like to be put in a position where they may have to endorse unpopular decisions. Works

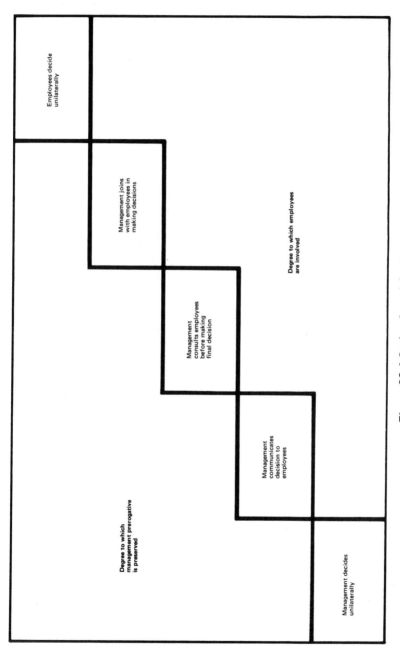

**Figure 23.1 Scale of participation**

councils may be given the chance to discuss policy issues, but if the final decision on any matter which is clearly not negotiable is made at board level, the works council may be seen as an ineffectual body.

## Arguments for and against participation

The arguments for and against participation are not evenly balanced; they cannot be. They represent totally different points of view or, to put it more plainly, prejudice. And there is prejudice on both sides. Essentially, the favourable arguments are optimistic about human nature while the unfavourable ones are pessimistic. It would be a pity if the pessimistic view prevailed in this as in other spheres. But a favourable view on participation should not be allowed to develop into idealism.

*In favour*

☐ It satisfies the individual's basic need for involvement in affairs that affect him or her.

☐ It makes better use of the skills and capacities available in the enterprise.

☐ It gives people the opportunity to influence events which will have a direct or indirect effect on their present and future prosperity and security.

☐ It recognizes the reality of life today in which traditional authoritarian patterns of behaviour are being steadily eroded.

☐ It is better to develop a participative system within an organization in a planned and orderly way rather than have it forced upon the company by the government or the unions.

*Against*

☐ The board must exercise direction and control, and management must manage — managers cannot be effective unless they are allowed to exercise their authority with the minimum of interference.

☐ Direction and management are specialized skills which are not shared amongst all employees. The extent to which workers' representatives at board level and elsewhere can make a real contribution is limited.

☐ Power-sharing implies information-sharing — the necessarily confidential nature of much top management decision-making would be seriously impaired if workpeople were involved.

☐ The unions do not want it because it might impair their negotiating power or put them in an invidious position if they have to support unpopular management decisions.

☐ Employees do not want increased participation, either because they are apathetic or because they do not see any advantage to themselves in it.

☐ Participation may drive key decisions under cover if directors or managers form secret cabals or starve workers' representatives of the information they need to make a proper contribution.

A touch of realism along the lines suggested by the pessimists is required to make participation work.

## Requirements for successful participation

Irrespective of the level at which participation takes place or the degree to which it is formalized, there are ten basic requirements for success:

1. The objectives of participation must be defined, discussed and agreed by all concerned.
2. The objectives must be related to tangible and significant aspects of the job, the process of management or the formulation of policies that affect the interests of employees. They must not relate to peripheral matters such as welfare or social amenities, i.e. in Herzberg's phrase, they should not be concerned with the 'hygiene' factors alone.
3. Management must believe and must be seen to believe in participation. Actions speak better than words and management must demonstrate that it will put into effect the joint decisions made during discussions.
4. The unions must believe in participation as a genuine means of advancing the interests of their members and not simply as a way of getting more power. They should show by their actions that they are prepared to support unpopular decisions to which they have been a party.
5. Joint consultation machinery should be in line with any existing systems of negotiation and representation. It should not be supported by management as a possible way of reducing the powers of the union. If this naive approach is taken it will fail — it always does. Joint consultation should be regarded as a complementary process of integrative bargaining to the distributive bargaining that takes place in joint negotiating committees. A separate consultative system may not be necessary in a well-organized 100% union establishment.
6. If management does introduce joint consultation as a means of keeping unions out, it should be prepared to widen the terms of reference as much as possible to cover issues which might normally be the subject of negotiation with unions. This approach can backfire if the staff representatives acquire a taste for negotiation and turn to the unions if they find they are not getting what they want. It is an approach which should be used with extreme caution. It has been known to work with white collar unions but, in Britain at least, recent legislation makes it much more difficult to resist union demands for recognition. It would be a pity in these circumstances to lose face by abandoning a management sponsored system.
7. Joint consultative committees should always relate to a defined working unit, should never meet unless there is something specific to discuss, and should always conclude their meetings with agreed points which are implemented quickly.
8. Employee and management representatives should be properly briefed and trained and have all the information they require.
9. Managers and supervisors should be kept in the picture.
10. Consultation should take place *before* decisions are made.

## Joint consultation

Joint consultation is the most obvious method of participation. It is essentially a means for management and employees to get together to discuss and, where appropriate, determine matters affecting their joint or respective interests.

In its simplest form joint consultation is the informal exchange of views between individual employees and their managers, and takes place all the time in a well-run enterprise. But where the number of employees, or a complex organization, makes access from employees to management or from management to employees difficult, then informal methods need to be systematized.

### Objectives of joint consultation

The objectives of joint consultation should be to provide a means of jointly examining and discussing problems of concern to both management and employees. It involves seeking mutually acceptable solutions through a genuine exchange of views and information. Joint consultation allows management to inform employees of proposed changes which affect them and employees to express their views about the proposed changes. It also provides a means for employees to contribute to their own views and knowledge on such matters as productivity and safety.

### Topics for joint consultation

Joint consultation does not mean power-sharing – involving employees in policy decisions on such matters as investments, marketing and product development plans, and mergers. These would only be the subject of joint decision-making if full participation at board level were to take place.

The terms of reference to joint consultative committees often exclude the discussion of basic terms and conditions of employment such as wage rates and premium payments, hours of work and holidays. These are either regarded as part of management's prerogative in a non-unionized plant or are dealt with through the normal negotiation machinery. This leaves matters such as methods of work, job evaluation, works rules and safety as usual – and important – topics for joint consultation.

### Joint consultation and negotiation

There are dangers in having two separate systems of employee representation. If the firm is strongly unionized, the unions will dominate the consultative committee, which is wasteful and often leads to the consultative committee system dealing with trivialities and falling into disrepute. It may be useful to have a place where people can argue about the quality of the sausages in the canteen, but if that is all they ever talk about (and sometimes this appears to be the case) then it would be better to abandon formal joint consultation altogether and rely on other channels. A reverse situation can sometimes occur when companies set up joint consultation as an alternative to a union negotiating committee. What may happen is that the joint consultative committee members persuade or force management to negotiate with them with the result that there are two competing negotiating bodies, which is a recipe for disaster.

The argument in favour of keeping negotiating issues outside the terms of reference of joint consultation committees is that it gives the latter more opportunity to deal calmly with non-controversial matters. Negotiating committees may get into so many conflict situations that they are no longer capable of looking dispassionately at even the least controversial issues. There is some truth in this argument, but the ideal approach in a strongly unionized plant is to have one system of representation, and for all concerned to do everything in their power to develop a co-operative climate for consultation as well as negotiation.

When a company is involved in negotiations there is no easy answer to the problem of reconciling the machinery required for that purpose with the system most appropriate to joint consultation. It is no good, however, clinging to an effete joint consultative arrangement if all the real decisions are made with union representatives through the negotiating machinery. Separate joint consultation arrangements should be maintained only if they do provide proper representation for non-unionists and a genuine opportunity for employee representatives to discuss real issues which might be neglected in the hurly-burly of negotiations.

An interesting approach to solving this problem was developed at Glacier Metal by Wilfrid Brown[3] with the help of Elliott Jaques.[4] In *The Changing Culture of a Factory* the latter described the process of working through problems in the developing representative system, while in *Exploration in Management* Brown describes how the representative, legislative and appeals system functioned. The representative system was the basic machinery through which employees could express their views, but a legislative system was established above, and not in parallel to the representative system which 'comprises councils ... in which the executive and representative systems meet and by means of which every member can participate in formulating policy and in assessing the results of the implementation of that policy'.[3]

### Constitution

Before deciding on detailed terms of reference it is necessary to determine the aims and scope of joint consultation, paying particular attention to the question of the extent to which committees can become involved in policy or negotiating issues. It is also necessary to consider who should be covered by the committee system. A choice will have to be made. It could only cover non-managerial or supervisory employees, or supervisors and even managers could be catered for separately. Finally, decisions will have to be made on the committee structure, which in a large organization often consists of separate councils for each major department or group of departments and an overall works council. It is sometimes best to start in a modest way with one or two pilot schemes in large departments before setting up too elaborate a system. Some large companies, however, have restricted the system to one works council on the grounds that departmental matters are best dealt with informally by local management.

The following points should be covered in the constitution of a consultative committee:

☐ The objectives of the committee.
☐ Its terms of reference – the matters which it can and cannot discuss.
☐ Its composition:
    – employee representatives (number, constituencies)
    – management representatives
    – co-option provisions
    – officers.
☐ The period of office of members and arrangements for their retirement.
☐ Election procedure:
    – who organizes
    – when held
    – qualifications of candidates and voters
    – nominations
    – voting arrangements.
☐ Committee meetings:
    – frequency

- where held
- procedures for placing items on the agenda
- arrangements for minutes.
☐ Facilities for committee members:
- liaising with constituents
- payment while attending meetings.

## Suggestion schemes

Suggestion schemes can provide a valuable means for employees to participate in improving the efficiency of the company. Properly organized, they can help to reduce the feelings of frustration endemic in all concerns where people think they have good ideas but cannot get them considered because there are no recognized channels of communication. Normally, only those ideas outside the usual scope of employee's duties are considered and this should be made clear, as well as the categories of those eligible for the scheme – senior management are often excluded.

The basis of a successful suggestion scheme should be an established procedure for submitting and evaluating ideas, with tangible recognition for those which have merit and an effective system for explaining to employees without discouraging them that their ideas cannot be accepted.

The most common arrangement is to use suggestion boxes with, possibly, a special form for entering a suggestion. Alternatively, or additionally, employees can be given the name of an individual or a committee to whom suggestions should be submitted. Management and supervision must be stimulated to encourage their staff to submit suggestions, and publicity in the shape of posters, leaflets and articles in the company magazine should be used to promote the scheme. The publicity should give prominence to the successful suggestions and how they are being implemented.

One person should be made responsible for administering the scheme. He should have the authority to reject facetious suggestions, but should be given clear guidance on the routing of suggestions by subject matter to departments or individuals for their comments. The administrator deals with all communications and, if necessary, may go back to the individual who submitted the suggestion to get more details of, for example, the savings in cost or improvements in output that should result from the idea.

It is desirable to have a suggestion committee consisting of management and employee representatives to review suggestions in the light of the comments of any specialist functions or executives who have evaluated them. This committee should be given the final power to accept or reject suggestions but could, if necessary, call for additional information or opinion before making its decision. The committee could also decide on the size of any award within established guidelines, such as a proportion of savings during the first year; usually not less than 10% and not more than $33^{1}/_{3}\%$. There should be a standard procedure for recording the decisions of the committee and informing those who made suggestions of the outcome – with reasons for rejection if appropriate.

## Planning for participation

The form of participation appropriate for a company will depend upon the attitudes and relative strengths of management and unions, its past experience of negotiation and consultation, and the current climate of employee relations. The form may also be affected by government legislation; but whatever method is adopted it is essential to take into account the requirements for successful participation listed earlier in this chapter and to plan its introduction or development in the following stages:

1. Analyse and evaluate the existing systems of consultation, communication and other formal and informal means of participation.
2. Identify the influences within and without the company which affect the climate of industrial relations and suggest the most appropriate form in which participation should take place.
3. Develop a plan for improving or extending participation in whatever form is appropriate to the company.
4. Discuss the plan in depth with all concerned – management, supervisors, workpeople and unions. The introduction of improved participation should itself be a participative process.
5. Brief and train those concerned with participation in their duties and how they should be carried out.
6. Introduce new schemes on a pilot-scheme basis – do not expect immediate results and be prepared to modify them in the light of experience.
7. Keep the whole system under continuous review as it develops to ensure that it is operating effectively.

## Quality circles

It can be argued that one of the greatest failings which result from the 'top-down' type of management prevailing in the U.K. and many other Western countries is that it ignores the knowledge that exists at the lowest level in the organization. Many investigators who have been trying to establish the secret of the success of Japan's industry have decided that a major ingredient is the degree to which collective or group management is practised.

One of the techniques of group involvement used successfully in Japan (although the idea originated in the United States in the 1950s) is quality circles. Quality circles grew out of Japan's great need in the early 1960s to lose its post-war reputation as a clever producer of shoddy copies of Western products and to raise the quality of its goods. The approach owes a lot to the strong attachment to working in cohesive groups which exists in Japan. The first circle was registered in 1963 within the Nippon Telegraph and Telephone Public Corporation, and now there are hundreds of thousands of circles operating in Japan. Virtually all big companies use them.

### Aim
The aim of quality circles is to improve quality and productivity by obtaining employee involvement and commitment in solving problems jointly, and getting the solutions implemented.

### Operation
As operated in Japan, quality circles are groups of workers, led by their supervisor, who meet voluntarily and in their own time to discuss the problems they face in achieving quality, or some other important target. The circle is given training in problem-solving techniques and the resources to solve the problems it identifies.

In the U.K. and other Western countries there are a number of different methods of operation but the essential ingredients are the same. The group consists of five to ten members, and attendance is voluntary. They may meet in company time. They are usually led by their immediate supervisor, although the leader is often chosen by the group. The leader has to be thoroughly trained in how to run the circle. He cannot be too directive but he must ensure that the problem is identified and defined clearly and that analytical problem solving techniques are used to solve it. He must help the group to keep its feet on the ground and come up with practical solutions. And he has to guide the circle when the agreed answer is being implemented. His role is a key one. Quality circle members are usually employees doing similar work.

The sequence of events in a typical quality circle is as follows:

1. The members identify problems in their work area, although on occasions supervisors or managers can indicate problems that need to be solved.
2. When the problem has been identified the circle agrees a realistic goal for its activities, such as to reduce defects from six to three per cent over a period of three months.
3. The circle draws up a plan for solving the problem using appropriate analytical techniques.
4. The base data are collected by members of the circle and possible solutions to the problem are reviewed. Expertise from supervision or technical personnel can be called on.
5. When a solution has been agreed the circle presents to management its analysis of the problem and its proposals for solving it.
6. The circle is responsible for implementing solutions agreed by management. It monitors results, carries out tests as necessary and reports on progress.

## Requirements for success
Quality circles will only be effective under the following conditions:

1. They must be introduced slowly and carefully. Pilot tests are essential. There is no formula which guarantees success.
2. Someone in authority must be given the responsibility for introducing the scheme. He should be thoroughly trained; outside consultants can be used to help carry out this training and to launch the initial programme. If consultants are used they should have been able to demonstrate practical and successful experience in introducing quality circles in a similar environment. If the company decided to go it alone the least it should do is to pick the brains of other organizations who have implemented quality circles effectively.
3. The scheme must have the full and continuous support of top management.
4. There must be a reasonable chance that quality circles will be able to identify and solve problems — given the right training, encouragement and support.
5. There must also be a working climate in the company which will allow quality circles to flourish. By themselves they cannot overcome a long tradition of autocratic and rigid top-down management. If the management style of the company is not conducive to involvement of the type required in quality circles then either the style should be changed or the attempt to introduce quality circles should be abandoned.
6. An organizer, sometimes called a facilitator or adviser, should be appointed to co-ordinate the programme. But his role should be to train, guide and encourage — not to direct. The aim is to get the quality circles to think for themselves,

not to get someone else to do their thinking for them.

The performance and output of the quality circles should be continually monitored by the organizer. If interest is flagging either amongst managers or within the quality circles it is his job to stimulate commitment and activity. The worst thing that can happen is for good ideas to be ignored. This is why top management as well as middle managers and supervisors must believe that the system is worthy of support. This belief will be reinforced if good ideas are forthcoming. It is the organizer's job to ensure that management is aware of the benefits resulting from quality circles.

Quality circles are hard work. They do not provide an easy answer and they are not always fruitful. Some people question them on the grounds that, while they may be successful in Japan, they will not transfer easily to Western culture. In fact they have been used effectively in many companies in the U.K. and the U.S.A., but they have usually had to make an effort to adapt their management style to the 'bottom-up' approach characteristic of quality circles. If management does not believe in group involvement and that good ideas can originate from the shop floor, especially if encouraged by quality circles, then there is little point in launching them on a large scale. The answer in these circumstances is to convince management by successfully operating a small-scale pilot scheme. Evangelical zeal is not enough. Sceptical, hard-nosed line managers need proof that it works.

### References

1. *Industrial Democracy – The Way Forward.* Industrial Participation Association, London, 1976.
2. *Practical Policies for Participation.* The Industrial Society, London, 1974.
3. Brown, W. *Exploration in Management.* Heinemann, London, 1960.
4. Jaques, E. *The Changing Culture of a Factory.* Tavistock Productions, London, 1951.

| 24 | Communications |
|---|---|

## The nature of communications

Communications are concerned with the creation, transmission, interpretation and use of information. The communication can be on a person-to-person basis, as when a boss tells someone what to do and when a subordinate reports back to his superior, or it can be on a departmental/corporate basis when general instructions or pieces of information are passed down the line, and reactions, reports and comments float, more or less effectively, up again.

Communications start with the communicator wanting to say something; he then decides how it is to be said and transmitted. The communication arrives with the recipient who forms an impression of what he has heard and interprets it against his own background of attitudes and experiences (figure 24.1).

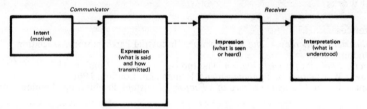

**Figure 24.1 The process of communication**

The basic problem in communications is that the meaning which is actually received by one person may not be what the other intended to send. The communicator and the receiver are two people living in different worlds; any number of things can happen to distort the messages that pass between them. People's needs and experiences tend to colour what they see and hear. Messages they do not want to hear are repressed. Others are magnified, created out of thin air or distorted from their original reality.

## The importance of communications

Organizations function by means of the collective action of people, yet each individual is capable to taking independent action which may not be in line with policy or instructions, or may not be reported properly to other people who ought to know about it. Good communications are required to achieve co-ordinated results.

Organizations are subject to the influence of continuous change which affects the work employees do, their well-being and their security. Change can only be managed by ensuring that the reasons for and implications of change are communicated to those affected in terms they can understand and accept.

Individuals are motivated by the extrinsic reward system and the intrinsic rewards that come from the work itself. But the degree to which they are motivated depends upon the amount of responsibility and scope for achievement provided by their job, and upon their expectations that the rewards they will get will be the ones they want and will follow from the efforts they make. Feelings about work and the associated rewards depend very much on the effectiveness of communications from their boss and within the company.

Above all, good two-way communications are required so that management can keep employees informed of the policies and plans that affect them and employees can react promptly with their views about management's proposals and actions. Change cannot be managed properly without an understanding of the feelings of those affected by it, and an efficient system of communications is needed to understand and influence these feelings.

But the extent to which good communications create satisfactory relationships rather than simply reduce unsatisfactory relationships can be exaggerated. A feature of management practices during this century is the way in which different management theories become fashionable or influential for a while and then decline in favour. Among these has been the 'good communications' theory of management. This approach to dealing with management problems is based upon the following assumptions:

1. The needs and aims of both employees and management are, in the long run, the same in any organization. Managers' and employees' ideas and objectives can all be fitted together to form a single conceptual framework.
2. Any differences in opinion between management and employees are due to misunderstandings that have arisen because communications are not good enough.
3. The solution to industrial strife is to improve communications.

This theory is attractive and has some validity. Its weakness is that the assumptions are too sweeping, particularly that the ultimate objectives of management and workers are necessarily identical. Experiences in countries, such as Yugoslavia, which have had long experience of industrial democracy have suggested that workers' representatives who are appointed to the board of a company concern themselves mainly with pay and conditions and are not greatly interested in other aspects of the company's business. The good communications theory, like paternalism, seems to imply that the company can develop loyalty by keeping people informed and treating them nicely. But people working in organizations have other and, to them, more important loyalties elsewhere; and why not?

The existence of different loyalties and points of view in an organization, however, does not mean that communications are unimportant. If anything, the need for a good communications system becomes even greater when differences and conflict exist. But it can only alleviate those differences and pave the way to better co-operation. It cannot solve them.

## Communication problems

Communication problems fall into four main categories:

1. People are not aware of the need to communicate.
2. People do not know what to communicate.

3. People do not know how to communicate.
4. Proper facilities for communicating are not available.

These problems are equally important, although inadequacy in any one area can lead to communication failures. And they are not easy to solve. To overcome them it is necessary to formulate a strategy for communications which will form the basis for developing communications systems, and to maintain a continuous programme of education and training in communication techniques. The strategy, systems and training programmes should, however, be founded on an understanding of the barriers to communication.

### Barriers to communications
So many barriers exist to good communications that the constant cry in all organizations that communications are bad is hardly to be wondered at — it is amazing that any undisturbed messages get through. Some of the main barriers are summarized below.

HEARING WHAT WE EXPECT TO HEAR. What we hear or understand when someone speaks to us is largely based on our own experience and background. Instead of hearing what people tell us, we hear what our minds tell us they have said. We all tend to have preconceived ideas of what people mean: when we hear something new we tend to identify it with something similar that we have experienced in the past. People like predictability and 'one of the most time-consuming passions of the human mind is to rationalize sentiments and to disguise them as logic' (Roethlisberger and Dickson).[1]

When people receive a communication which is consistent with their own beliefs they will accept it as valid, seek additional information and remember accurately what is heard.

IGNORING INFORMATION THAT CONFLICTS WITH WHAT WE ALREADY KNOW. We tend to ignore or reject communications that conflict with our own beliefs. If they are not rejected, some way is found of twisting and shaping their meaning to fit our preconceptions. Communications often fail when they run counter to other information that the receiver already possesses, whether that information is true or false.

The technical term for what happens when people receive irreconcilable information is *cognitive dissonance*, a theory developed by Festinger, which asserts that an individual experiences discomfort when he holds logically inconsistent 'cognitions' (a person's individual views or images of events which shape his social behaviour) about an object or an event, and that he is thus motivated to reduce the discomfort or dissonance by changes to his views or his attitudes. Cognitions are selectively organized to reflect an individual's own environment, experience, wants and goals, and his physiological structure. This provides the frame of reference against which the properties of a particular object or piece of information are judged. People resist change or the communication asking them to change because the new ideas are outside their frame of reference.

Where communication is inconsistent with existing beliefs, the receiver rejects its validity, avoids further exposure to it, easily forgets it and, in his memory, distorts what he hears.

PERCEPTIONS ABOUT THE COMMUNICATOR. Not only does the receiver evaluate what he hears in terms of his own background, but he also takes the sender into account. Experience or prejudice may ascribe non-existent motives to the communicator. Some people see every collective action as a conspiracy. Others look behind the message to read into it all sorts of different motives to those apparent on the surface. It is extremely difficult for us to separate what we hear from our feelings about the person who says it.

INFLUENCE OF REFERENCE GROUP. The group with which we identify — the reference group — influences our attitudes and feelings. 'Management' and 'the union' as well as our family, our race, our political party and our religious beliefs (if any) constitute a reference group and colour our reactions to information. What each group 'hears' depends on its own interests. Shared experiences and common frames of reference will have much more influence than exhortations from management, where people with whom employees feel they have nothing in common hand on messages containing information which conflicts with what they already believe.

WORDS MEAN DIFFERENT THINGS TO DIFFERENT PEOPLE. This is the problem of semantics. As Strauss and Sayles put it: 'Essentially language is a method of using symbols to represent facts and feelings. Strictly speaking we can't convey *meaning;* all we can do is convey *words.* And yet the same words may suggest quite different meanings for different people. The meanings are in the people not the words.'[2]

Words may have symbolic meanings to some people with the result that they convey a quite different impression to the one intended. 'Profits' to management are an essential prerequisite to survival and growth. To employees, they represent ill-gotten gains as a result of keeping down pay or over-pricing. 'Closed shop' to a trade unionist means an appropriate device for maintaining stability and strength and ensuring that employees contribute to the organization. To managers, 'closed shop' may suggest a fundamentally illiberal device restricting the freedom of both management and workers.

In short, do not assume that something which has a certain meaning to you will convey the same meaning to someone else.

JARGON. All professions and trades develop their own special language or 'jargon'. It is a convenient way of communicating technical terms between those who know the jargon, but it is an effective and irritating barrier between those who know and those who do not.

NON-VERBAL COMMUNICATION. In trying to understand what people are saying to us we use many cues besides language — what has come to be called 'body language'. Looking at the eyes, the shape of the mouth, the muscles of the face, even bodily posture, may tell us more about what the other person really thinks than the words he uses. In a sense, this is an aid to communication if the real meaning of what we are saying is conveyed by the expression on our face than the actual message. But it can become a barrier if people misinterpret our 'body language'.

EMOTIONAL CONTEXT. Our emotions colour our ability to convey or to receive the true message. When we are insecure or worried, what we hear and see seems more threatening than when we are secure and at peace with the world. When we are angry or depressed, we tend to reject out of hand what might otherwise seem like reasonable requests or good ideas. During arguments, many things said are not understood or are badly distorted.

NOISE. 'Noise' in the sense of outside factors interfering with the reception of the message is an obvious barrier. It may be literal noise, which prevents words being heard, or figurative noise in the shape of distracting or confused information which distorts the message. The forms in which messages are communicated — unclear syntax, long unwieldy sentences with numerous 'hanging' clauses, polysyllabic words — all help to produce noise.

SIZE. The sheer size and complexity of modern organizations is one of the main barriers to communication. Messages have to penetrate layer upon layer of management or move between different functions, units or locations. They thus become distorted or never arrive. Reliance is placed more on the written rather than the spoken word to get the message through, which seriously restricts the effectiveness of the communication.

With size goes formality, and with formality go restrictions to the freedom with which communcation can take place. E.F. Schumacher has suggested that 'small is beautiful' and this certainly applies to communications. His theme was applied more to the encouragement of creativity than to the development of good communications, but it is equally relevant to both. On the question of creativity he wrote that:

> In any organization, large or small, there must be a certain clarity and orderliness: if things fall into disorder nothing can be accomplished. Yet, orderliness as such is static and lifeless; so there must be plenty of elbow-room and scope for breaking through the established order, to do the thing never done before, never anticipated by the guardians of orderliness, the new, unpredicted and unpredictable outcome of a man's creative idea.[3]

Organizations, he wrote, have to strive continuously for the 'orderliness of *order* and the disorderliness of creative freedom'. He did not say, but well might have, that a free flow of communication is essential to bridge the gap.

### Overcoming barriers to communication

The overall implication of this formidable collection of barriers is that no one should assume that every message sent will be received in the form that he intended it to be. But communications can be improved, even if perfect understanding between people is impossible.

ADJUSTING TO THE WORLD OF THE RECEIVER. When communicating, the tendency is to adjust to oneself. You have the need to say something and to say it in a particular way. But to get the message across, you have to adjust to the receiver. This means thinking ahead and trying to work out how he will perceive the message — understanding his needs and potential reactions. It also means using feedback and reinforcement techniques as discussed later.

The effective communicator tries to predict the impact of what he is going to write or say on the receiver's feelings and attitudes. He tries to tailor the message to fit the receiver's vocabulary, interests and values and is aware of the possible ways his information can be misinterpreted because of the symbolic meanings attached to phrases, the influence of the reference group and the tendency for people to reject what they do not want to hear.

Overcoming barriers requires *empathy* — the ability to put oneself in someone else's shoes and understand how he is likely to hear and interpret the message.

USING FEEDBACK. Feedback is the process of obtaining information on performance in order to take corrective action where this is necessary. In communications, feedback means ensuring that the communicator gets a message back from the receiver which tells him how far understanding has taken place. This is why face-to-face communications are so much more effective than the written word, as long as the communications are truly 'two-way'; in other words, the receivers are given adequate opportunity to respond and react.

USING REINFORCEMENT. The message may have to be presented in a number of different ways to get it across. Good speakers know that if they can get more than three important ideas across in a thirty-minute talk, they are lucky, and they must repeat each idea at least three times in different ways to ensure that the message has been received and understood. In giving complicated directions, it is wise to repeat them several times, perhaps in different ways, to guarantee successful transmission.

USING DIRECT SIMPLE LANGUAGE. This seems so obvious as hardly to be worth stating. But many people seem unable to express themselves clearly and without the use of jargon or an excessive number of adjectives, adverbs and sub-clauses.

REINFORCING WORDS WITH ACTIONS. Communications are only effective if they are credible. If management says a thing then it must do it. Next time, it is more likely to be believed. The motto should be 'suit the action to the words'.

USING FACE-TO-FACE COMMUNICATION. Face-to-face communication is more effective than the written word for the reasons already mentioned. First, the sender is able to experience direct feedback from the receiver on what the latter is or is not hearing. The way in which the message is presented can then be adjusted by being expressed in different terms or reinforced. If necessary, the message itself can be changed in the light of immediate reactions. Secondly, most people express themselves more clearly and directly when they use the spoken rather than the written word. Thirdly, a spoken message can be delivered in a much more human and understanding way — this helps to get over prejudices against the speaker. It also means that criticisms can be expressed in a more constructive manner. A written reproof seems much more harsh and condemnatory than one delivered orally.

USING DIFFERENT CHANNELS OF COMMUNICATION. Some communications have to be in writing to get the message across promptly and without any danger of variations in the way in which it is delivered. But wherever possible, written communications should be supplemented by the spoken word. Conversely, an oral briefing should be reinforced by a written confirmation.

REDUCING PROBLEMS OF SIZE. Communication problems arising from size can be reduced structurally by cutting down the number of levels of management, reducing spans of control, ensuring that activities are grouped on the basis of ease of intercommunication on matters that concern them, and decentralizing authority into smaller, self-contained although accountable units. An appropriate degree of informality in relationships within the structure can be encouraged, and organization development programmes (see chapter 9) can be used to increase trust and understanding. Techniques such as briefing groups, as described later in this chapter, can be used to get oral communications more effectively disseminated throughout the organization;

## Making communications work

Overcoming barriers to communication can be a slow and, for long periods, an unrewarding task. Communications can only be effective in an atmosphere of trust and co-operation. A sudden conversion to the 'good communications' philosophy resulting in a massive communication campaign will not convert a bad situation into a good one overnight. Trust and understanding have to be built up over a long period during which management demonstrates that it really believes in explaining and listening to people about the things that concern them.

To achieve good results, communication should be seen as a strategic matter to be planned, developed and controlled on the basis of a full understanding of the requirements, the problems, and the needs of everyone in the organization.

# Communications strategy

The starting point for the formulation of a communications strategy should be an analysis of the different types of communication with which the strategy should be concerned. Communication studies embrace all human activities in an organization, and the analysis must narrow the field down to well-defined areas in which action can be taken. The main areas and the objectives to be attained in them are set out in table 24.1.

Employee relations are mainly affected by managerial and internal communications, although external communications are an additional channel of information. The strategy for managerial communications is concerned with planning and control procedures, management information systems and techniques of delegating and giving instructions. These matters are outside the scope of this book, except insofar as the procedures and skills can be developed by training programmes.

The strategy for internal communications, which is the main concern of this chapter, should be based on analyses of:

☐ what management wants to say;
☐ what employees want to hear;
☐ the problems being met in conveying or receiving information.

These analyses can be used to indicate the systems of communication that need to be developed and the education and training programmes required to make them work. They should also provide guidance on how communications should be managed and timed. Bad management and poor timing are frequently the fundamental causes of ineffective communication.

## What management wants to say

What management wants to say will depend upon an assessment of what employees need to know which will, in turn, be affected by what they want to hear.

Management should aim to achieve three things: first to get employees to understand and accept what management proposes to do in areas that affect them; second, to get employees to act in the way management wants; and third,

| | Communication Area | Objectives |
|---|---|---|
| **I. MANAGERIAL** | 1. The communication downwards and sideways of corporate or functional objectives, policies, plans and budgets to those who have to implement them. | To ensure that managers and supervisors receive clear, accurate and prompt information on what they are expected to achieve to further the company's objectives. |
| | 2. The communication downwards of direct instructions from a manager to a subordinate on what the latter has to do. | To ensure that the instructions are clear, precise and provide the necessary motivation to get people into action. |
| | 3. The communication upwards and sideways of proposals, suggestions and comments on corporate or functional objectives, policies and budgets from those who have to implement them. | To ensure that managers and supervisors have adequate scope to influence corporate and functional decisions on matters about which they have specific expertise and knowledge. |
| | 4. The communication upwards and sideways of management information on performance and results. | To enable management to monitor and control performance so that, as necessary, opportunities can be exploited or swift corrective action taken. |
| **II. INTERNAL RELATIONS** | 5. The communication downwards of information on company plans, policies or performance. | To ensure that (i) employees are kept informed of matters that affect them, especially changes to working conditions, and factors influencing their prosperity and security; (ii) employees are encouraged to identify themselves more completely with the company. |
| | 6. The communication upwards of the comments and reactions of employees to what is proposed will happen or what is actually happening in matters that affect them. | To ensure that employees are given an opportunity to voice their suggestions and fears and that the company is in a position to amend its plans in the light of these comments. |
| **III. EXTERNAL RELATIONS** | 7. The receipt and analysis of information from outside which affects the company's interests. | To ensure that the company is fully aware of all the information on legislation and on marketing, commercial, financial and technological matters that affect its interests. |
| | 8. The presentation of information about the company and its products to the government, customers and the public at large. | To exert influence in the interests of the company, to present a good image of the company and to persuade customers to buy its products or services. |

**Table 24.1 Communication areas and objectives**

to get employees to identify themselves more closely with the company and its achievements and to help them appreciate more clearly the contribution they make to those achievements.

Communications from management should therefore be about plans, intentions and proposals (with the opportunity for feedback from employees) as well as about achievements and results. Exhortations should be kept to a minimum if used at all. No one listens to them. It is better to concentrate on specific requirements rather than resorting to general appeals for such abstract things as improved quality or productivity. The requirements should be phrased in a way which emphasizes how all concerned will actually work together and the mutual benefits that should result.

## What employees want to hear

Clearly, employees want to hear and to comment upon the matters that affect their interests. These will include changes in working methods and conditions, changes in the arrangements for overtime and shift working, company plans which may affect pay or security, and changes in terms and conditions of employment. It is management's job to understand what employees want to hear and plan their communications strategy accordingly. Understanding can be obtained by making formal inquiries, by means of attitude surveys, by asking employee representatives, by informally listening to what employees say, and by analysing grievances they express to see if improved communications could modify them.

## Analysing communication problems

Specific examples of employee relations problems where communication failures have been the cause or a contributory factor should be analysed to determine exactly what went wrong and what needs to be done to put it right. The problems may be any of those listed earlier in this chapter, including lack of appropriate channels of communication, lack of appreciation of the need to communicate, and lack of skill in overcoming the many formidable barriers to communication. Problems with channels of communication can be dealt with by introducing new or improved communications systems. Lack of skill is a matter for education and training.

## Communication systems

Communication systems can be divided into those using the written word such as magazines, newsletters, bulletins and notice-boards, and those using oral methods such as meetings, briefing groups and public address systems. The aim should be to make judicious use of a number of channels to make sure that the message gets across.

## Magazines

Glossy magazines or house journals are an obvious way to keep employees informed about the company and they are often used for public relations purposes as well. They can extol and explain the achievements of the company and may thus help to increase identification and even loyalty. If employees are encouraged to contribute (although this is difficult) the magazine can become more human. The biggest danger of this sort of magazine is that it becomes a public relations-type exercise, which is seen by employees as having little relevance to their everyday affairs.

## Newsletters

Newsletters aim to appear more frequently and to angle their contents more to the immediate concerns of employees than the glossier form of house magazine. To be effective, they should include articles specifically aimed at explaining what management is planning to do and how this affects the company. They can also include more chatty 'human interest' material about the doings of employees to capture the attention of readers. Correspondence columns can provide an avenue for the expression of employees' views and replies from management, but no attempt should be made to censor letters (except those that are purely abusive) or to pull punches in reply. Anonymous letters should be published if the writer gives his name to the editor.

The key factor in the success of a newsletter or any form of house magazine is the editor. He should be someone who knows the company and its employees and can be trusted by everyone to be frank and fair. Professional expertise is obviously desirable but it is not the first consideration, as long as the individual can write reasonably well and has access to expert help in putting the paper together. It is often a good idea to have an editorial board consisting of management and employee representatives to advise and assist the editor.

Companies often publish a newsletter in addition to a house magazine, treating the latter mainly as a public relations exercise and relying on the newsletter as the prime means of communicating with employees.

## Bulletins

Bulletins can be used to give immediate information to employees which cannot wait for the next issue of a newsletter; or they can be a substitute for a formal publication if the company does not feel that the expense is justified. Bulletins are only useful if they can be distributed quickly and are seen by all interested employees. They can simply be posted on notice-boards or, more effectively, given to individual employees and used as a starting point for a briefing session if they contain information of sufficient interest to merit a face-to-face discussion.

## Notice-boards

Notice-boards are an obvious but frequently misused medium for communications. The biggest danger is allowing boards to be cluttered up with uninteresting or out-of-date material. It is essential to control what goes on to the boards and to appoint responsible people to service them by removing out-of-date or unauthorized notices.

A more impressive show can be made of notices and other material if an information centre is set up in the canteen or some other suitable place where the information can be displayed in a more attractive and compelling manner than on a typical notice-board.

## Consultative committees

Joint consultative committees as discussed in chapter 23 exist to provide a channel for two-way communication. Sometimes, however, they are not particularly effective, either because their thunder has been stolen by union negotiation committees, or because their proceedings are over-formalized and restricted. It is essential to disseminate the information revealed at committees around the offices and works, but it is impossible to rely on committee members to do this. Minutes can be posted on notice-boards, but they are seldom read, usually because they contain too much redundant material.

## Briefing groups

The concept of 'briefing groups' as developed by the Industrial Society is a device to overcome the restricted nature of joint consultative committees by involving everyone in an organization, level by level, in face-to-face meetings to present, receive and discuss information. Briefing groups aim to overcome the gaps and inadequacies of casual briefings by injecting some order into the system.

John Garnett, the Director of the Industrial Society, has defined the briefing group system as: 'A simple checkable routine or drill where explanations can be given at each level by the boss of each work group on a regular basis. Subjects briefed in the group are those matters which help people to co-operate.'[4]

Briefing groups should operate as follows:

1. *Organization*
   - □ cover all levels in an organization;
   - □ fewest possible steps between the top and bottom;
   - □ between four and 18 in each group;
   - □ run by the immediate leader of each group at each level (who must be properly trained and briefed in his task).
2. *Subjects*
   - □ policies – explanations of new or changed policies;
   - □ plans – as they affect the organization as a whole and the immediate group;
   - □ progress – how the organization and the group is getting on: what the latter needs to do to improve;
   - □ people – new appointments, points about personnel matters (pay, security, procedures).
3. *Timing and duration*
   - □ a minimum of once a month for those in charge of others and once every two months for every individual in the organization – but only meet if there is something to say;
   - □ duration not longer than 20-30 minutes.

The merit of briefing groups is that they enable face-to-face communications to be planned and, to a reasonable degree, formalized. It is easy, however, for them to start in a wave of enthusiasm and then to wither away because of lack of sufficient drive and enthusiasm from the top downward, inadequately trained and motivated managers and supervisors, reluctance of management to allow subjects of real importance to be discussed throughout the system and insufficient feedback upwards through each level.

A briefing group system must be led and controlled effectively from the top, but it does require a senior manager with specific responsibility to advise on the subject matter and the preparation of briefs (it is important to have well-prepared material to ensure that briefing is carried out consistently and thoroughly at each level), to train managers and supervisors, and to monitor the system by checking on the effectiveness and frequency of meetings.

## Education and training in communications

Communication is ultimately one person passing on a message to another and listening to their reply. Formal channels of communication have to be provided for, but their effectiveness depends on the attitudes, skills and enthusiasm of those responsible for using the system.

Education and training programmes are required to develop the attitude that communication is an important part of management and thus to ensure that a prime consideration when making any decision is how, where and to whom it should be communicated. Communicators need to be made aware of the barriers to communication and the skills of perception and analysis they need to overcome them. Finally, training should be given in specific communication skills — speaking, writing, running meetings and, most important, listening. The training in many of these skills can be conducted by means of more or less traditional courses but the maximum use should be made of group exercises and role playing so that people can practise and develop their skills. Sensitivity or 'T-Group' training (see Appendix J) is one method of increasing the individual's understanding of the impact he makes on other people and the way in which they hear what he has to say. Such training, as its name implies, should make people more sensitive to the effect they have on others as well as providing them with new tools to analyse the interactions that take place when people are working together.

### References

1. Roethlisberger, F. and Dickson, W. *Management and the Worker*. Harvard University Press, Cambridge, Mass, 1939.
2. Strauss, G. and Sayles, L.R. *Personnel: The Human Problems of Management*. Prentice-Hall, Englewood Cliffs, New Jersey, 1972.
3. Schumacher, E.F. *Small is Beautiful*. Blond and Briggs, London, 1973.
4. Garnett, J. *The Work Challenge*. The Industrial Society, London, 1973.

*Appendix A*
# Statement of Personnel Objectives

The personnel objectives of the company recognize that the achievement of commercial objectives for profitability and growth depends on the quality, effort and co-operation of its staff. They also recognize that the company has a responsibility towards its staff to provide high standards of employment and working conditions, to treat them fairly and to provide them with opportunities to develop and obtain a sense of satisfaction from their work. In accordance with these principles the personnel objectives are to ensure that:

☐ the company develops and maintains an effective organization;
☐ the company obtains, develops and retains the quantity and quality of staff it requires to meet its present and future needs;
☐ the best use is made of staff and the maximum degree of effective effort is obtained from them;
☐ constructive and harmonious relationships are established and maintained with the staff which will encourage the highest degree of co-operation from them;
☐ staff are provided with the maximum scope to use their capacities to the full and to develop within the company;
☐ equal opportunities are provided to potential or existing employees for employment or promotion;
☐ conditions of employment, employee benefits and working conditions are established which will help to achieve the objectives set out above and will also mean that the company meets its social and legal responsibilities towards its employees.

*Appendix B*
# Training Policy

### The overall purpose
To provide advice, opportunities, facilities and financial support to enable employees of the Company:

(a) To acquire the skills, knowledge and related qualifications needed to perform effectively the duties and tasks for which they are employed.
(b) To develop their potential to meet the future manpower needs of the Company.
(c) In exceptional cases to develop individuals beyond the organization's immediate and foreseeable needs.

### Training intent

COMPANY. The Company gives training in basic skills to sufficient people to meet its long-term labour requirements except where specific circumstances prevent this.

All training will be properly planned, programmed and recorded and the results reviewed to determine how training methods can be improved and how maximum benefit can be obtained from resources devoted to training.

A programme of management development will be planned and implemented.

DEPARTMENTAL. All managers are responsible for training their subordinates to improve current and future performance and provide for management succession. The Personnel and Training Department will provide advice and assistance on training activities.

Departmental training plans based on the assessment of individual and departmental training needs are drawn up annually to take full account of the manpower needs of the various departments and shall include budgetary provisions.

INDIVIDUAL. All new staff receive induction training and anyone transferred or promoted will be given the appropriate training.

Instruction in relevant health and safety precautions will be included in all training.

Employees will be released or sponsored for further education whenever appropriate, according to the Further Studies Scheme.

# Health and Safety Policy

The Company regards the promotion of industrial safety and hygiene within its business as an essential part of its responsibilities. Furthermore, it regards the promotion of safety and health matters as a mutual objective of all management and employees.

It is, therefore, the Company's policy to do all that is reasonably practical to prevent personal injury and damage to property and to protect everyone from foreseeable work hazards, including the public insofar as they come into contact with the Company or its products. The Company will:

1. Provide and maintain safe and healthy working conditions at each of its locations, in accordance with the relevant statutory requirements.
2. Provide integrated safety, job training and instruction for all employees, and additional safety training where appropriate.
3. Provide all safety devices and protective equipment required by statute and supervise their use.
4. Ensure that articles and substances purchased for use at work have been so designed and constructed as to be safe and without risks to health; that full information is made available by the suppliers where additional safety precautions are required.
5. Maintain a constant and continuing attention to all aspects of safety in particular by:
   (a) making regular location safety inspections.
   (b) seeking and stimulating consultation and contributions from employees on safety matters.
   (c) ensuring that each location is given adequate health and safety cover by a person well versed in safety requirements relating to the Company's activities.
   (d) ensuring that all means of access or egress are known to persons either on or using the premises.
   (e) to meet regularly with Safety Committee.
   (f) to provide and maintain a place of work that is, so far as is reasonably practical, safe, without risks to health, and has adequate facilities for the welfare of all employees.
6. In particular, every employee has a responsibility:
   (a) to take reasonable care for the health and safety of himself and of all other persons he comes into contact with at work.
   (b) to co-operate with Management to enable them to carry out their statutory duties with the object of raising and maintaining a high standard of safety and health at work.
   (c) to report all incidents that have led, or may lead to injury.
   (d) to co-operate in the investigation of accidents with the object of introducing measures to prevent a recurrence.

# Grievance Procedure

**Policy**
1. It is the policy of the company that members of the staff should:
   (a) be given a fair hearing by their immediate supervisor or manager concerning any grievances they may wish to raise;
   (b) have the right to appeal to a more senior manager against a decision made by their supervisor or manager;
   (c) have the right to be accompanied by a fellow employee of their own choice, when raising a grievance or appealing against a decision.

The aim of the procedure is to settle the grievance as nearly as possible to its point of origin.

**Procedure**
2. The main stages through which a grievance may be raised are as follows:
   (a) The employee raises the matter with his immediate supervisor or manager and may be accompanied by a fellow employee of his own choice.
   (b) If the employee is not satisfied with the decision, the employee requests a meeting with a member of management who is more senior than the supervisor or manager who initially heard the grievance. This meeting takes place within five working days of the request and is attended by the manager, the manager responsible for personnel, the employee appealing against the decision and, if desired, his representative. The manager responsible for personnel records the result of the meeting in writing and issues copies to all concerned.
   (c) If the employee is still not satisfied with the decision, he may appeal to the appropriate director. The meeting to hear this appeal is held within five working days of the request and is attended by the director, the manager responsible for personnel, the employee making the appeal and, if desired, his representative. The manager responsible for personnel records the result of this meeting in writing and issues copies to all concerned.

## Appendix E
# Disciplinary Procedure

**Policy**
1. It is the policy of the company that if disciplinary action has to be taken against employees it should:
   (a) be undertaken only in cases where good reason and clear evidence exist;
   (b) be appropriate to the nature of the offence that has been committed;
   (c) be demonstrably fair and consistent with previous action in similar circumstances;
   (d) only take place when employees are aware of the standards that are expected of them or the rules with which they are required to conform.
   (e) allow employees the right to be represented by a shop steward or colleague during any formal proceedings;
   (f) allow employees the right of appeal against any disciplinary action.

**Rules**
2. The company is responsible for ensuring that up-to-date rules are published and available to all employees.

**Procedure**
INFORMAL WARNING
3. A verbal or informal warning is given to the employee in the first instance or instances of minor offences. The warning is administered by the employee's immediate supervisor or manager.

FORMAL WARNING
4. A written or formal warning is given to the employee in the first instance of more serious offences or after repeated instances of minor offences. The warning is administered by the employee's immediate supervisor — it states the exact nature of the offence and specifies any future disciplinary action which will be taken against the employee if the offence is repeated within a specified time limit. A copy of the written warning is placed in the employee's personnel record file but it is destroyed 12 months after the date on which it was given, if the intervening service has been satisfactory. The employee is required to read and sign the formal warning and has the right to appeal to higher management if he thinks the warning is unjustified.

FURTHER DISCIPLINARY ACTION
5. If, despite previous warnings, an employee still fails to reach the required standards in a reasonable period of time, it may become necessary to consider further disciplinary action. The action taken may be up to three days' suspension without pay, or dismissal. In either case the departmental manager should

discuss the matter with the personnel manager before taking action. Staff below the rank of departmental manager may only recommend disciplinary action to higher management, except when their manager is not present (for example, on night-shift), when they may suspend the employee for up to one day pending an inquiry on the following day. Disciplinary action should not be confirmed until the appeal procedure (paragraphs 7 and 8) has been carried out.

SUMMARY DISMISSAL

6. An employee may be summarily dismissed (i.e. given instant dismissal without notice) only in the event of gross misconduct, as defined in company rules. Only departmental managers and above can recommend summary dismissal and the action should not be finalized until the case has been discussed with the personnel manager and the appeal procedure has been carried out.

## Appeals

7. In all circumstances, an employee may appeal against suspension, dismissal with notice or summary dismissal. The appeal is conducted by a member of management who is more senior than the manager who initially administered the disciplinary action. The personnel manager should also be present at the hearing. If he wishes, the employee may be represented at the appeal by a fellow employee of his own choice. Appeal against summary dismissal or suspension should be heard immediately. Appeals against dismissal with notice should be held within two days. No disciplinary action which is subject to appeal is confirmed until the outcome of the appeal.

8. If an appeal against dismissal (but not suspension) is rejected at this level, the employee has the right to appeal to the chief executive. The manager responsible for personnel and, if required, the employee's representative should be present at this appeal.

*Appendix F*
# Redundancy Procedure

### Definition
1. Redundancy is defined as the situation in which management decides that an employee or employees are surplus to requirements in a particular occupation and cannot be offered suitable alternative work.
2. Employees may be surplus to requirements because changes in the economic circumstances of the company mean that fewer employees are required, or because changes in methods of working mean that a job no longer exists in its previous form. An employee who is given notice because he or she is unsuitable or inefficient is not regarded as redundant and would be dealt with in accordance with the usual disciplinary procedure.

### Objectives
3. The objectives of the procedure are to ensure that:
   (a) employees who may be affected by the discontinuance of their work are given fair and equitable treatment;
   (b) the minimum disruption is caused to employees and the company;
   (c) so far as possible, changes are effected with the complete understanding and agreement of the unions and employees concerned.

### Principles
4. The principles governing the procedure are as follows:
   (a) The trade unions concerned will be informed as soon as the possibility of redundancy occurs.
   (b) Every attempt will be made to:
      (i) absorb redundancy by the natural wastage of employees;
      (ii) find suitable alternative employment within the company for employees who might be affected, and provide training if this is necessary;
      (iii) give individuals reasonable warning of pending redundancy in addition to the statutory period of notice.
   (c) If alternative employment in the company is not available and more than one individual is affected, the factors to be taken into consideration in deciding who should be made redundant will include:
      (i) length of service with the company;
      (ii) age (especially those who could be retired early);
      (iii) effective value to the company;
      (iv) opportunities for alternative employment elsewhere.

      The first three of these factors should normally be regarded as the most important; other things being equal, however, length of service should be the determining factor.

## Procedure
5. The procedure for dealing with employees who are surplus to requirements is set out below.

### REVIEW OF MANPOWER REQUIREMENTS
6. Management will continuously keep under review possible future developments which might affect the number of employees required, and will prepare overall plans for dealing with possible redundancies.

### MEASURES TO AVOID REDUNDANCIES
7. If the likelihood of redundancy is foreseen, the company will inform the union(s), explaining the reasons, and in consultation with the union(s) will give consideration to taking appropriate measures to prevent redundancy.
8. Departmental managers will be warned by the management of future developments which might affect them so that detailed plans can be made for running down staff, retraining or transfers.
9. Departmental managers will be expected to keep under review the work situation in their departments so that contingency plans can be prepared and the manager responsible for personnel warned of any likely surpluses.

### CONSULTATION ON REDUNDANCIES
10. If all measures to avoid redundancy fail, the company will consult the union(s) at the earliest opportunity in order to reach agreement.

### SELECTION OF REDUNDANT EMPLOYEES
11. In the event of impending redundancy, the individuals who might be surplus to requirements should be selected by the departmental manager with the advice of the manager responsible for personnel on the principles that should be adopted.
12. The manager responsible for personnel should explore the possibilities of transferring affected staff to alternative work.
13. The manager responsible for personnel should inform management of proposed action (either redundancy or transfer) to obtain approval.
14. The union(s) will be informed of the numbers affected but not of individual names.
15. The departmental manager and the manager responsible for personnel will jointly interview the employees affected either to offer a transfer or, if a suitable alternative is not available, to inform them they will be redundant. At this interview, full information should be available to give to the employee on, as appropriate:
    (a) the reasons for being surplus;
    (b) the alternative jobs that are available;
    (c) the date when the employee will become surplus (that is, the period of notice);
    (d) the entitlement to redundancy pay;
    (e) the employee's right to appeal to an appropriate director;
    (f) the help the company will provide.
16. An appropriate director will hear any appeals with the manager responsible for personnel.
17. The manager responsible for personnel will ensure that all the required administrative arrangements are made.

18. If the union(s) have any points to raise about the selection of employees or the actions taken by the company they should be discussed in the first place with the manager responsible for personnel. If the results of these discussions are unsatisfactory a meeting will be arranged with an appropriate director.

## ALTERNATIVE WORK WITHIN THE COMPANY

19. If an employee is offered and accepts suitable alternative work within the company it will take effect without a break from the previous employment and will be confirmed in writing. If the offer is refused the employee may forfeit his or her redundancy payment.

## ALTERNATIVE EMPLOYMENT

20. Employees for whom no suitable work is available in the company will be given reasonable opportunities to look for alternative employment.

## Appendix G
# Promotion Policy
# and Procedure

**Policy**
1. The promotion policy of the company is based on three main principles:
    (a) whenever possible, vacancies shall be filled by the most effective people available from within the company, subject to the right of the company to recruit from outside if there are no suitable internal candidates;
    (b) the excellence of an employee's performance in his or her present job in the company or the absence of a suitable replacement shall not be a valid reason for refusing promotion to a suitable post, provided that the procedure set out below is complied with;
    (c) promotion is not affected by race, creed, sex or marital status.

**Procedure**
1. When a vacancy arises, the head of the department concerned shall obtain the necessary authority, according to company regulations, and notify the personnel department, which will be responsible for submitting suitable candidates. The departmental manager has the final decision in accepting or rejecting a candidate.
2. Except for the circumstances set out in paragraph 5, the personnel department shall advertise supervisory, managerial or specialist posts in grades C and above (works) and 3 and above (staff) on company notice-boards for at least three days.
3. The personnel department, with the agreement of the departmental head, can advertise the vacancy concurrently outside the company.
4. Applications from employees should be sent to the personnel department, which will carry out the following actions:
    (a) notify departmental managers of the departments in which candidates are employed;
    (b) notify the application to the manager of the department in which the vacancy occurs;
    (c) notify candidates whether or not they are required for interview;
    (d) notify candidates of the result of the interview.
5. Internal advertising can be dispensed with where management considers that:
    (a) there is a natural successor (who may have been specially trained to fill the vacancy); or
    (b) because of unusual requirements there is no suitable candidate within the company; or
    (c) the vacancy can be filled by the transfer of an employee of equivalent grade.
6. Where a departmental manager feels that the loss of an employee to another department would vitally affect the efficiency of his department he can appeal to the personnel manager against the transfer, provided that:

385

    (a)  the employee has served less than 12 months in his present occupation and grade; or

    (b)  the rate of transfer from his department of employees of similar grade has exceeded 1% per calendar month over the previous six months.

If the personnel manager is unable to resolve the matter the appeal should be submitted to an appropriate director.

7.  Except in the event of a successful appeal against a transfer on the grounds stated in paragraph 6, no employee shall be refused a transfer within a reasonable time by his departmental manager. The date of the transfer should be determined between his present and future departmental managers. A failure to agree on a suitable date should be referred to the personnel manager for resolution himself or, if that fails, for reference to an appropriate director.

# Job Analysis Checklist:
# Clerical Staff

The following are examples of the questions that might be asked in analysing a clerical job. The questions would not necessarily be put in exactly these words or in this order and it would be necessary to ask a number of supplementary questions to clarify replies.

*Job title*
1. What is the title of the job?

*Responsible to*
2. To whom are you directly responsible?

*Responsible for*
3. Are there any staff directly responsible to you? If so, describe briefly the main purpose of the jobs of each of your immediate subordinates.
4. Have your immediate subordinates any staff responsible to them? If so, what is the total number of staff under your control?

*Main purpose of job*
5. What is the main purpose of your job, i.e. what, in general terms, are you supposed to do?
6. How does your job fit in with the work of your section or department as a whole?
7. How can the results you achieve in the job be measured or assessed?

*Main tasks*
8. What tasks or duties to you carry out? Describe them either in chronological order (that is the order in which you do them during the day or week), in order of importance or in order of frequency.
9. Where does your work come from? e.g.:
   ☐ From outside the organization by post or telephone
   ☐ From another department or section
   ☐ From your superior
   ☐ From colleagues.
10. Where does your completed work go to?

*Volume*
11. How often and in what quantities, is your work received, e.g. does it reach you as a single item, in batches or continuously?
12. For each of your main tasks or group of tasks:
   (a) How often has the work to be done – continuously, daily, weekly, monthly or intermittently?

(b) What is the volume of work you are expected to complete per hour, day or week, as appropriate?

(c) Approximately how long does it take to complete the work?

*Forms and equipment*

13. Do you have to complete or maintain any forms or records? If so, give examples and describe how they are completed.

14. Do you use any machines or equipment? If so, give details of the machines used and how often you use them.

*Contacts*

15. To what extent does your work bring you into contact with:
    □ Members of other departments?
    □ Other organizations
    □ Members of the public?
    In each case indicate the frequency of the contacts and describe what they are about.

*Discretion*

16. Is the way you do your work laid down in a procedure manual or in any other written instructions? If so, give details.

17. To what extent are you able to vary:
    □ The methods of work you use
    □ The order in which you carry out your tasks?

18. Whom would you go to if you were in difficulties over an aspect of your work?

*Checking*

19. Who checks your work and how frequently?

20. How is your work checked?

*Supervision received*

21. On what matters and how frequently do you receive direct instructions from your supervisor or manager?

22. What matters have to be referred by you to your supervisor or manager either for him to deal with or to obtain his approval for an action you propose to take?

23. How often do you have to refer matters to your supervisor or manager?

*Supervision given*

24. What authority have you got in respect of your subordinates to:
    (a) Assign work
    (b) Check work
    (c) Correct and discipline
    (d) Deal with grievances
    (e) Recommend appointments, salary increases, transfers, promotions, discharges
    (f) Assess their performance?

*Working conditions*

25. What are the conditions under which you carry out your work?

26. What qualifications and experience do you think are necessary to carry out your work?
27. What specific training is needed to carry out your work?
28. How long did it take you to learn to do the work?

# Example of Job Description

## Job description

**Job title**: Works manager

**Responsible to**: Production director

**Responsible to him**:
- ☐ Production superintendent
- ☐ Production controller
- ☐ Chief inspector
- ☐ Personnel officer

**Main role**:
To achieve agreed budgets, quality standards and delivery requirements by the efficient control of manufacturing operations, by developing and maintaining good labour relations and by ensuring that his staff work together as a team.

**Main activities**

PLANS
1. Develops manufacturing plans and budgets in line with estimated market demands and ensures that production capacity, equipment and labour are available to achieve agreed output and forseeable additional demands.

DEVELOPMENT
2. Continually seeks to improve production methods and techniques and to this end makes full use of company engineering research and development services.

OPERATIONS
3. Maintains close liaison with company production control to ensure economic loading on the works and to progress availability of supplies.
4. Ensures that production scheduling fulfils its objectives of meeting programmed delivery dates and optimizing wastage, downtime and stock levels.
5. Ensures that all production operations are progressed and the distribution department is informed of expected departures from programmed delivery dates.
6. Maintains the security of the works and all property, stocks and other assets within it and takes suitable precautions against fire.
7. Maintains in good order the works and the equipment in it.

390

PERSONNEL
8. Ensures that the works organization is the most appropriate for achieving company objectives.
9. Recruits, trains and develops effective personnel to meet present and future needs.
10. Implements company personnel policies and national agreements.
11. Maintains sound labour relations and morale.

CONTROL
12. Develops an effective reporting system on works performance and directs a continuous programme of monitoring productivity, quality and costs.
13. Ensures that corrective action is taken where required to meet budgets and standards and reports deviations outside agreed control limits to the production director.

## Job analysis

**Job title**: Works manager

**Resources controlled**:
☐ Assets: £765,000
☐ Turnover: £3,100,000
☐ Personnel: 750

**Decisions**:
☐ The basic production technologies are determined by the company engineering department. The works manager is simply concerned with ensuring that the equipment operates as specified and that it is maintained properly. He can introduce changes to meet special requirements but these are minor modifications which do not affect the basic technology and can be installed within one or two days by maintenance craftsmen.
☐ The overall production programme and quality and cost standards are laid down at company level. The works manager, however, has complete authority to schedule production within the works.
☐ Buying is conducted centrally but the works manager is responsible for ensuring that stocks are maintained at the minimum level required to maintain an economic production flow and an agreed standard of customer service.
☐ The works manager has authority to spend on revenue items within the agreed annual company budget. Capital expenditure has to be authorized by the production director.
☐ The works manager has complete authority to recruit, discipline and, where necessary, dismiss hourly and weekly paid staff in accordance with company personnel policies and procedures. He also has authority to deal with union issues, except those affecting terms and conditions of employment which are dealt with at company level. He must report any major issue to the production director.

**Complexity**
☐ The product is not a highly technical one and most of the production employees, except in the foundry and in the development shop, are semi-skilled

391

assembly line employees. There are nine product lines and three main processes. Some problems are caused when product lines are changed but they are fairly easy to overcome if scheduling is carried out carefully.
☐ The main difficulty to overcome is ensuring that quality standards are maintained and that downtime is minimized. Maintenance is a key factor and fairly complex procedures have had to be developed to overcome serious problems in the past.
☐ Labour relations do not present a problem.

## Knowledge and skills
☐ The technical knowledge required is not very high. Anyone with experience in controlling assembly lines or a flow process operation should quickly be able to understand the techniques involved. The main requirement is skill in planning and controlling a high output, fairly high quality plant to meet critical delivery schedules and in motivating a labour force which is engaged on monotonous although well paid work.

*Appendix J*
# Training Techniques

The training techniques analysed in this Appendix are classified into three groups according to where they are generally used:

1. *On the job techniques* – demonstration, coaching, do-it-yourself training, job rotation/planned experience.
2. *On the job or off the job techniques* – action learning, job (skill) instruction, question and answer, assignments, projects, guided reading.
3. *Off the job techniques* – lecture, talk, discussion, 'discovery' method, programmed learning, case study, role playing, simulation, group exercise, group dynamics (team-building).

## On the job techniques

### Demonstration
Demonstration is the technique of telling or showing a trainee how to do a job and then allowing him to get on with it. It is the most commonly used – and abused – training method. It is direct and the trainee is actively engaged. Reinforcement or feedback can be good, if the supervisor, trainer or colleague (that well-known character, Nellie, by whom the trainee sits) does it properly by clearly defining what results have been achieved and how they can be improved. But demonstration in its typically crude form will not provide a structured learning system where the trainee understands the sequence of training he is following and can proceed by deliberate steps along his learning curve. This is more likely to happen if job (skill) instruction techniques are used, as described later.

### Coaching
Coaching is a personal on the job technique designed to develop individual skills, knowledge and attitudes. The term is usually reserved for management or supervisory training where informal but planned encounters take place between managers and subordinates.

The agenda for such meetings may be based on a performance review system which includes some elements of management by objectives or target setting. This would identify strengths to be developed or weaknesses in performance to be overcome, and the counselling sessions that should be part of the performance review process would indicate career development needs and the additional knowledge or skills that can be acquired on the job.

Coaching is even more effective if it can take place informally as part of the normal process of management. This type of coaching, as suggested by Hawdon Hague, consists of:

☐ making a subordinate aware of how he is managing by, for example, asking questions on how well he has thought through what he is doing;

☐ controlled delegation;
☐ using whatever situations which arise as teaching opportunities;
☐ setting individual projects and assignments;
☐ spending time in looking at higher level problems as well as discussing the immediate job.

Coaching may be informal, but it has to be planned. It is not simply going from time to time to see what a subordinate is doing and advising him how to do it better. Neither is it occasionally telling a subordinate where he has gone wrong and throwing in a lecture for good measure. So far as possible, coaching should take place within the framework of a general plan of the areas and direction in which the subordinate should be developed.

Coaching should provide motivation, structure and effective feedback, if the coacher is skilled, dedicated and able to develop mutual confidence. Its success depends on a clear definition of work and training objectives, and this can be a time-consuming process; ultimately, success depends upon managers and supervisors recognizing that it is one of their key responsibilities and they should be encouraged and trained to do it.

### Do-it-yourself training
Do-it-yourself training aims to apply the principles of the discovery method (see below) to training on the job. The principle behind it is that people will learn and retain more if they find out for themselves, as long as they are given direction on what to look for and help in finding it.

Do-it-yourself training operates by:

☐ starting from a definition of what someone needs to know and do to perform a job;
☐ establishing where the information required is available;
☐ giving the trainee an outline of the information he has to obtain and where and from whom he can get it. He may be given questions to answer or mini-projects to complete.
☐ briefing those concerned (mainly the trainee's boss and his colleagues, but also people in other departments) on the help they should give the trainee;
☐ preparing a timetable for the learning programme;
☐ arranging for someone (the trainee's boss or the executive responsible for training) to monitor his progress. This should include periodic meetings to check on what has been learned and to provide extra encouragement and guidance.

It is not quite as simple as it may appear to implement do-it-yourself training techniques. They must still be based upon job analysis leading to a full understanding of the knowledge and skills required to do the job. The trainee should be given careful guidance on how to set about getting the information required, and he has still to be movitated to understand the reasons for getting this information and how he will benefit.

The managers or supervisors of those under training should be prepared to spend time and trouble helping and coaching their staff. And it is not always easy to persuade busy people to do this, as every training officer knows. The only way is to convince them that this approach will produce better results more quickly and cheaply than other methods. They have to be persuaded that the technique will have a measurably beneficial effect on the performance of the individuals concerned and on the performance of the department as a whole. Training managers have to be salesmen – they have to demonstrate the benefits of the product rather than describe its inherent features.

The only other drawback to do-it-yourself training is that it is more applicable to the development of knowledge than skills. It is therefore more likely to be useful for managers, supervisors and administrative staff than for training machine operators or those in occupations where manual skills are of primary importance. Nonetheless, do-it-yourself training as an embodiment of the voluntary spirit as well as a practical application of learning theory can play an important part in a training programme, especially when shortage of funds precludes any more elaborate approach.

### Job rotation/planned experience

Job rotation aims to broaden experience by moving people from job to job or department to department. It can be an inefficient and frustrating method of acquiring additional knowledge and skills unless it is carefully planned and controlled. What has sometimes been referred to as the 'Cook's tour' method of moving trainees (usually management trainees) from department to department has incurred much justified criticism because of the time wasted by trainees in departments where no one knew what to do with them or cared.

It may be better to use the term 'planned sequence of experience' rather than 'job rotation' to emphasize that the experience should be programmed to satisfy a training specification for acquiring knowledge and skills in different departments and occupations. It can be argued in support of job rotation that if it is by experience that adults learn, then that experience should be planned.

Success in using this method depends on designing a programme which sets down what the trainee is expected to learn in each department or job in which he gains experience. There must also be a suitable person available to see that the trainee is given the right experience or opportunity to learn, and arrangements must be made to check progress. For apprentices this will mean the use of training supervisors within departments to see that the training syllabus is followed, and the use of log-books to record what experience has been gained. The syllabus within a department should include specific assignments or projects. A good way of stimulating trainees to find out for themselves is to provide them with a list of questions to answer. It is essential, however, to follow up each segment of experience to check what has been learnt and, if necessary, modify the programme.

## On or off the job techniques

### Action learning

Action learning, as developed by Professor Revans, is a method of helping managers to develop their talents by being exposed to real problems. They are required to analyse them, formulate recommendations and then, instead of being satisfied with a report, actually take action. It accords with the belief that managers learn best by doing rather than being taught.

This approach conforms to the principle on which all good training should be based – i.e. it is problem-based and action-orientated. It recognizes that the most perplexing task managers face is how to achieve change – how to persuade their colleagues and others to commit themselves to a different way of doing things. An action-learning programme therefore concentrates on developing the skills which managers need to take action effectively, without ignoring the need for knowledge of relevant techniques.

The concept of action learning is based on six assumptions:

1. Experienced managers have a huge curiosity to know how other managers work.
2. We learn not so much when we are motivated to learn, as when we are motivated to learn something.
3. Learning about oneself is threatening and is resisted if it tends to change one's self-image. However, it is possible to reduce the external threat to a level which no longer acts as a total barrier to learning about oneself.
4. People only learn when they do something, and they learn more the more responsible they feel the task to be.
5. Learning is deepest when it involves the whole person – mind, values, body, emotions.
6. The learner knows better than anyone else what he has learned. Nobody else has much chance of knowing.

A typical action learning programme brings together a group or 'set' of four or five managers to solve a problem. They help and learn from each other, but an external consultant or 'set adviser' sits in with them regularly. The project may last several months and the set meets frequently, possibly one day a week. The adviser helps the members of the set to learn from one another and clarifies the process of action learning. This process involves change embedded in the web of relationships called the 'client system'. The web comprises at least three separate networks: the power network, the information network and the motivational network (this is what Revans means by 'who can, who knows and who cares'). The forces for change are already there within the client system and it is the adviser's role to point out the dynamics of this system as the work of diagnosis and implementation proceeds.

The group or set has to manage the project like any other project; deciding on objectives, planning resources, initiating action and monitoring progress. But all the time, with the help of their adviser, they are learning about the management processes involved as they actually happen.

### Job instruction

Job instruction techniques should be based on skills analysis and learning theory as discussed in chapter 20. The sequence of instruction should follow four stages:

☐ Preparation
☐ Presentation – explanation and demonstration
☐ Practice and testing
☐ Follow-up.

*Preparation* for each instruction period means that the instructor must have a plan for presenting the subject matter and using appropriate teaching methods, visual aids and demonstration aids. It also means preparing the trainee for the instruction that is to follow. He should want to learn. He must perceive that the learning will be relevant and useful to him personally. He should be encouraged to take a pride in his job and to appreciate the satisfaction that comes from skilled performance.

*Presentation* should consist of a combination of telling and showing – explanation and demonstration.

*Explanation* should be as simple and direct as possible: the trainer explains briefly the ground to be covered and what to look for. He makes the maximum use of films, charts, diagrams and other visual aids. The aim should be to teach first things first and then proceed from the known to the unknown, the simple to the complex, the concrete to abstract, the general to the particular, the observation to reasoning, and the whole to the parts and back to the whole again.

*Demonstration* is an essential stage in instruction, especially when the skill to be learned is mainly a doing skill. Demonstration takes place in three stages:

1. The complete operation is shown at normal speed to show the trainee how the task should be carried out eventually.
2. The operation is demonstrated slowly and in correct sequence, element by element, to indicate clearly what is done and the order in which each task is carried out.
3. The operation is demonstrated again slowly, at least two or three times, to stress the how, when and why of successive movements.

*Practice* consists of the learner imitating the instructor and then constantly repeating the operation under guidance. The aim is to reach the target level of performance for each element of the total task, but the instructor must constantly strive to develop co-ordinated and integrated performance; that is, the smooth combination of the separate elements of the task into a whole job pattern.

*Follow-up* continues during the training period for all the time required by the learner to reach a level of performance equal to that of the normal experienced worker in terms of quality, speed and attention to safety. During the follow-up stage, the learner will continue to need help with particularly difficult tasks or to overcome temporary set-backs which result in a deterioration of performance. The instructor may have to repeat the presentation for the elements and supervise practice more closely until the trainee regains his confidence or masters the task.

JOB INSTRUCTION GUIDELINES. These are the most important guidelines to follow in giving job instruction:

☐ Keep instruction and practice within reasonable time limits to avoid boredom and fatigue.
☐ Arrange demonstration and practice so that trainees can experience some success early in training, thus maintaining interest and providing incentive.
☐ Ensure that trainees know how they are getting on, but present feedback in an encouraging and constructive way.
☐ Provide useful and productive tasks to do.
☐ Recognize that all learners do not develop at the same rate.
☐ Provide ample opportunity for practice so that trainees can become used to carrying out the job at the experienced worker's standard of quality and speed and in complete safety.

## Question and answer

The question and answer technique consists of an exchange between trainer and trainees to test understanding, stimulate thought or extend learning. It may take place during a job instruction programme or as part of a discussion period on a formal management course. It can be used to increase involvement, to check progress and to explore attitudes to learning. Considerable skill is required to use this method. The questions should be open — they should not lead to 'yes'/'no' answers, but they should also be clear and concise. They should always be asked in an encouraging and supportive manner.

### Assignments

Assignments are a specific task or investigation which an individual does at the request of his trainer or manager. The assignment may be used as a test at the end of a training session and, as long as it is realistic, it should help to transfer learning to the work situation. The trainer may still have to provide some guidance to the trainee to ensure that the latter will not lose confidence if he meets difficulties in completing the task.

Assignments may also be given by managers to their subordinates as a means of extending their experience. They should be linked to a coaching programme so that the lessons from the assignment are fully absorbed.

### Projects

Projects are broader studies or tasks which trainees are asked to complete, often with only very generalized guidelines from their trainer or manager. They encourage initiative in seeking and analysing information, in originating ideas and in preparing and presenting the results of the project. For apprentices, especially students and graduates, the project can be a practical exercise in which the trainees are required to design, manufacture and test a piece of equipment. Projects for managers may consist of an investigation into a company policy issue or operating problem.

Like assignments, projects give trainees or managers an opportunity to test their learning and extend their experience, although the scope of the study is likely to be wider and the project is often carried out by a group of people.

### Guided reading

Knowledge can be increased by giving trainees books, hand-outs or company literature and asking them to read and comment on them. Guided reading may take place before a course when the members are asked to read 'pre-course' literature. They seldom do. Or it may be given during a training course and used as reinforcement. The beautiful hand-outs that lecturers prepare are often allowed to gather dust when the course is over. They can be far more effective if they are distributed at appropriate points during or immediately after the lecture and those attending are required to discuss specific questions arising from them.

Reading as part of a development programme may be a valuable way of broadening knowledge as long as the material is seen by the trainee as relevant and there is follow-up to ensure that learning has taken place. The best way is to ask the trainee to read a handbook or one or two chapters from a longer text and then come back to the trainer or his manager to discuss the relevance of the material and how he can use his knowledge.

## Off the job techniques

### Lecture

A lecture is a talk with little or no participation except a question and answer session at the end. It is used to transfer information to an audience with controlled content and timing. When the audience is large, there may be no alternative to a 'straight lecture' if there is no scope to break it up into discussion groups.

The effectiveness of a lecture depends on the ability of the speaker and the way in which he presents his material with judicious use of visual aids. But there are several limits on the amount an inert audience can absorb. However effective the speaker, it is unlikely that more than 20% of what he said will be remembered at the end of the day. And after a week, all will be forgotten unless the listener has put some of his learning into practice. To maximize its effectiveness, the lecture must never be longer than 30 or 40 minutes; it must not contain too much information (if the speaker can convey three new ideas, which more than one half of his audience understands and remembers, he will have been successful); it must reinforce learning with appropriate visual aids (but not too many); and it must clearly indicate the action that should be taken to make use of the material.

## Talk
A talk is a less formal lecture for a smaller group of not more than 20 people which gives plenty of time for discussion. The encouragement of participation and interest means that more learning is likely to be retained than in a lecture, but the discussion may be dominated by the more articulate and confident members of the group unless carefully controlled.

## Discussion
The objectives of using discussion techniques are to:

☐ get the audience to participate actively in learning;
☐ give people an opportunity of learning from the experience of others;
☐ help people to gain understanding of other points of view;
☐ develop powers of self-expression.

The aim of the trainer should be to guide the group's thinking. He may, therefore, be more concerned with shaping attitudes than in imparting new knowledge. He has to stimulate people to talk unobtrusively, guide the discussion along predetermined lines (he must have a plan and an ultimate objective), summarize the discussion from time to time, and sum up at the end.

The following techniques should be used to get active participation:

☐ Ask for contributions by direct questions.
☐ Use open-ended questions which will stimulate thought.
☐ Check understanding; make sure that everyone is following the argument.
☐ Encourage participation by providing support rather than criticism.
☐ Prevent domination by individual members of the group by bringing in other people and asking cross-reference questions.
☐ Avoid dominating the group yourself. The leader's job is to guide the discussion, maintain control and summarize from time to time. If necessary, 'reflect' opinions expressed by individuals back to the group to make sure they find the answer for themselves. The leader's job is to help them reach a conclusion, not to do it for them.
☐ Maintain control — ensure that the discussion is progressing along the right lines towards a firm conclusion.|

## Discovery method

The discovery method is a style of teaching that allows the pupil to learn by finding out principles and relationships for himself. The essence of the method is that the training designer thinks out the progression of problems which the trainee is required to solve, relates this progression to the capacity of the trainee, and ensures that learning is based on intrinsic rather than extrinsic factors. In other words, the trainee does not need to rely on previous knowledge and experience, nor does he depend on outside assistance (i.e. extrinsic factors). The learning, however, is not a random process. The trainee progresses through a series of planned steps, using the intrinsic information provided at each stage.

The discovery method is a demanding one to develop properly. It goes far deeper than skills analysis which simply lists all that has to be learned. Instead, it first identifies the crucial concepts and removes all the non-essentials so that the training material can be appreciated in its most simple form. The next stage is the most difficult: the training designer has to get inside the learning situation to decide what are the principal obstacles to understanding and to find out why trainees have problems in learning. The next stage is to design a discovery programme specially for the needs of a group of trainees.

The best results from discovery training techniques are achieved with middle-aged and older learners and on tasks that demand the development of concepts and understanding. The method has three main advantages:

1. *Motivation* – the adult is more motivated towards discovery learning because he is involved from the start and involved on his own terms.
2. *Control* – the discovery method reveals the trainee's progress and level of understanding to the instructor and enables easier control to be exercised over performance.
3. *Retention* – learning from experience is easier for adults than learning from words; there is no stress on memorizing, hence this sort of learning is remembered.

The main disadvantage of the discovery method is that it has to be specially designed for limited groups. A further disadvantage is that its benefits are not as evident in the short term as more conventionally based training schemes. But where real understanding and retention of knowledge about the whole job is required for older trainees or people undergoing re-training, the discovery method has a lot to offer.

## Programmed learning

Programmed learning consists of a text which progressively feeds information to trainees. After each piece of information, questions are posed which the trainee should answer correctly before moving on.

The basic principles of programmed learning are as follows:

☐ The subject matter is presented in small units called frames.
☐ Each frame requires a response from the trainee. Thus he is actively involved in the learning process.
☐ The trainee is told if his answer is correct at once. This rapid feedback gives immediate reinforcement to the trainee or immediately corrects a misunderstanding.
☐ The units of information are arranged in correct subject matter sequence and pose increasingly difficult questions. This means that the designer has had to

analyse the learning steps required with great care.
☐ Trainees work independently and at their own pace. Thus they work as quickly or as slowly as they like.

Programmed instruction is primarily a method of systematic presentation which relies a great deal on the self-motivation of the trainee. In its usual form it is quite different from discovery learning which is more concerned with skills than knowledge and allows the trainee greater scope to find out for himself.

Programmed texts may result in an over-mechanical learning process and this could hinder retention. But there are considerable advantages in using this method in conjunction with others as a means of ensuring that the trainee is ready, willing and able to deal with the material confronting him and take an active part in learning.

## Case study
A case study is a history or description of an event or set of circumstances which is analysed by trainees in order to diagnose the causes of a problem and work out how to solve it. Case studies are mainly used in courses for managers and supervisors because they are based on the belief that managerial competence and understanding can best be achieved through the study and discussion of real events.

Case studies should aim to promote inquiry, the exchange of ideas and the analysis of experience so that the trainees can discover underlying principles which the case study is designed to illustrate. They are not light relief. Neither are they a means of lightening the load on the instructor. The trainer has to work hard in defining the learning points that must come out of each case and he must work even harder to ensure that these points do emerge.

The danger of case studies is that they are often perceived by trainees to be irrelevant to their needs, even if based on fact. Consequently, the analysis is superficial and the situation is unrealistic. It is the trainer's job to avoid these dangers by ensuring that the participants are not allowed to get away with half-baked comments. He has to challenge assumptions and pin people down to justify their reasoning. Above all, he has to seize every chance to draw out the principles he wants to illustrate from the discussion and to get the group to see how these are relevant to their own working situation.

## Role playing
In role playing the participants act out a situation by assuming the roles of the characters involved. The situation will be one in which there is interaction between two people or within a group. It should be specially prepared with briefs written for each participant explaining the situation and, broadly, their role in it. Alternatively, role playing could emerge naturally from a case study when the trainees are asked to test their solution by playing the parts of those concerned.

Role playing is used to give managers, supervisors or sales representatives practice in dealing with face-to-face situations such as interviewing, counselling, coaching, dealing with a grievance, selling, leading a group or running a meeting. It develops interactive skills and gives people insight into the way in which people behave and feel.

The technique of 'role reversal', in which a pair playing, say, a manager and a supervisor run through the case and then exchange roles and repeat it, gives extra insight into the feelings involved and the skills required.

Role playing enables trainees to get expert advice and constructive criticism from the trainer and their colleagues in a 'protected' training situation. It can help to increase confidence as well as developing skills in handling people. The main difficulties are either that trainees will be embarrassed or that they will not take the exercise seriously and will overplay their parts.

## Simulation

Simulation is a training technique which combines case studies and role playing to obtain the maximum amount of realism in classroom training. The aim is to facilitate the transfer of what has been learned off the job to on the job behaviour by reproducing in the training room situations which are as close as possible to real life. Trainees are thus given the opportunity to practise behaviour in conditions identical to or at least very similar to those they will meet when they complete the course.

## Group exercises

In a group exercise the trainees examine problems and develop solutions to them as a group. The problem may be a case study or it could be a problem entirely unrelated to everyday work. The aims of an exercise of this kind are to give members practice in working together and to obtain insight into the way in which groups behave and arrive at decisions.

Group exercises can be used as part of a team building programme and to develop interactive skills. They can be combined with other techniques such as the discovery method to enable participants to work out for themselves the techniques and skills they need to use.

For example, a course run for managers in a large firm of chartered accountants dealt with problem solving in the following way:

1. The course was divided into three groups of six, all sitting in the same room.
2. Each group was given three linguistic/mathematical problems to solve and was then asked to discuss how the problem should be tackled.
3. Each group was then asked to develop a better problem-solving method which could be used in future.
4. Further exercises were given to the groups for them to test out their problem-solving method — the exercises were again abstract problems, unrelated to work. Managers were selected in each group to act as observers and to feedback to the other members how they behaved and how effective their problem-solving method was.
5. After each exercise, the observers from each group were asked to summarize their observations to the whole course, and a general discussion took place on the lessons learnt.
6. The groups were then asked to get together and work out between them a problem-solving method incorporating the best elements of the three group methods. Again, observers were appointed to report on how effectively this negotiating exercise was conducted.
7. The jointly agreed problem-solving method was tested on further case studies which became progressively more realistic. Some of these were developed into role playing exercises, each designed to illustrate the use of management skills such as working in groups, leadership, delegation, coaching, appraising performance and handling disciplinary problems.

Group exercises may be introduced as part of a formal off the job management or supervisory training course. They are also an essential element in an organization development programme, as described in chapter 4. Group exercises use many of the principles of group dynamics training, as discussed below, and may constitute a major part of a group dynamics course.

## Group dynamics

Group dynamics training is largely based on the work of Kurt Lewin and the Research Centre for Group Dynamics at MIT in 1946. It has three interconnected and often overlapping aims: first to improve the effectiveness with which groups operate (team building); second, to increase self-understanding and awareness of social processes; and third, to develop interactive skills which will enable people to function more effectively in groups. Group training can also help in modifying individual attitudes and values.

Group dynamics programmes may emphasize one of these aims more than the others, and they come in a number of forms. The basic variety is 'T-group' training, but this approach can be modified for use in courses primarily designed to improve interactive skills. There are also various packaged group dynamics courses, of which the best-known are Blake's Managerial Grid and Coverdale Training.

T-GROUP TRAINING. 'T-group' stands for 'training group', which is not a very helpful description. It is also referred to as sensitivity training, group dynamics and group relations training. T-group has three aims:

1. To increase *sensitivity* – the ability to perceive accurately how others are reacting to one's behaviour.
2. To increase *diagnostic ability* – the ability to perceive accurately the state of relationships between others.
3. To increase *action skill* – the ability to carry out skilfully the behaviour required by the situation.

In a T-group, the trainer will explain the aims of the programme and may encourage discussion and contribute his own reactions. But he does not take a strong lead and the group is largely left to its own devices to develop a structure which takes account of the goals of both the members of the group and the trainer and provides a climate where the group are sufficiently trusting of one another to discuss their own behaviour. They do this by giving 'feedback' or expressing their reactions to one another. Members may not always accept comments about themselves, but as the T-group develops they will increasingly understand how some aspects of their behaviour are hidden to them and will, therefore, be well on the way to an increase in sensitivity, diagnostic ability and action skill.

The design of a T-group 'laboratory' may include short inputs from trainers to clarify problems of group behaviour, inter-group exercises to extend T-group learning to problems of representation, negotiation and conflict management, and application groups where members get together to decide how they can best transfer what they have learned to their actual job behaviour. As much opportunity as possible will be given to members to test out and develop their own behavioural (interactive) skills – seeking or giving information, enlisting support, persuading and commanding.

Follow-up studies have noted three principal areas of change following the attendance of trainees at an external T-group laboratory:

1. Increased openness, receptivity and tolerance of differences.
2. Increased operational skill in inter-personal relations, with overtones of increased capacity for collaboration.
3. Improved understanding and diagnostic awareness of self, others and interactive processes in groups.

T-groups have been attacked because of the possibility of negative or detrimental effects. But none of the follow-up studies has detected any significant problems. A more valid basis for doubt is that it has been difficult to prove that they have been cost-effective for organizations who have used them in company or have strongly supported external programmes.

This criticism could be levelled at any other form of group training or, indeed, most off the job training. The degree to which it can be invalidated will depend on the effectiveness of the training design and of the trainer.

T-group laboratories in their purest form are unlikely ever to become a major part of company training programmes, but the group dynamics approach has valid uses in the modified forms described below.

INTERACTIVE SKILLS TRAINING. Interactive skills training is defined by Rackham as: 'Any form of training which aims to increase the effectiveness of an individual's interaction with others.'[1]

As developed by Rackham and others at the British Overseas Airways Corporation in 1968, interactive skills training has the following features:

☐ It is based on the assumption that the primary limitation on supervisory or managerial effectiveness lies not within each job boundary, but on the interface between jobs.
☐ There are no preconceived rules about how people should interact. It is assumed that the way interaction happens is dependent upon the situation and the people in it – this is what has to be analysed and used as a basis for the programme.
☐ The training takes place through groups which enables people to practise interactive skills – such skills can only be acquired through practice.
☐ Participants have to receive controlled and systematic feedback on their performance – this was achieved by using specially developed techniques of behaviour analysis.
☐ The analysis of behaviour was used to structure groups to avoid the restrictions on behaviour change which might result from relying on arbitrarily composed groups.

A typical design for an interactive skills programme as developed by Rackham consists of three stages:

1. *The diagnostic stage* in which the groups undertake a wide range of activities. These are designed to provide reliable behaviour samples which the trainer records and analyses.
2. *The formal feedback stage* in which the trainer gives groups and individuals feedback on their interactive performance during the diagnostic phase.
3. *The practice, monitoring, feedback stage* in which the group undertakes further activities to develop and practise new behaviour patterns and receives feedback from the trainer to gauge the success of attempts at behaviour change.

COVERDALE TRAINING. Coverdale training is a more structured form of interactive skills training which is described by Training Partnerships as: 'A system of planned experience, by which a man may begin to discover for himself certain lessons – and then go on learning from his subsequent experience.' The four main characteristics or principles of Coverdale Training are that:

☐ managers learn by doing – practising the skills they need to get things done;
☐ the training is centred around practical tasks – tasks which are actually performed rather than just talked about;
☐ managers learn a systematic approach to getting things done;
☐ learning takes place in groups.

THE MANAGERIAL GRID. The managerial grid training as developed by Blake[2] and his colleagues consists of a simple diagnostic framework provided to members to aid them in describing one another's behaviour. The basic philosophy of grid training is that the task of the individual manager is to achieve production through people. In achieving this task, the manager has to show concern both for productivity and people.

Blake suggests that managers can be characterized by their location on a two-dimensional grid – the managerial grid – one axis of which is labelled concern for production and the other concern for people. Each axis is a scale with nine points and so the location of a manager on the grid can be specified by two co-ordinates. Five principal managerial styles are described in Blake's grid:

1,1 *Impoverished management* – exertion of minimum offer to get done the work required to maintain membership of the organization.
9,1 *Task management* – where a person is high in task efficiency but low in human satisfaction.
1,9 *Country club management* – high human satisfaction but low work tempo.
5,5 *Middle of the road management* – adequate task performance while maintaining morale at a satisfactory level.
9,9 *Team management* – high task achievement from committed people. Production is achieved by the integration of task and human requirements into a unified system.

A grid seminar is used to teach each participant to see his managerial style. Trainees are first familiarized with grid language and theory and then work in groups through a series of exercises and case problems which allow each individual to exhibit his management style. This behaviour then becomes the object of feedback. Trainees acquire skills in the perception of their own and other people's style of behaviour, and the aim is to move them towards the 9,9 region of the grid.

Grid training consists of a series of seminars intended to develop the application of the message throughout the organization. In this respect, it is a type of organization development 'intervention' designed to increase organizational effectiveness rather than to concentrate on the improvement of individual interactive skills.

The grid has sound theoretical foundations, being based on a number of research studies. It recognizes the importance of developing an appropriate management style to obtain results by the effort and commitment of work groups. It has plenty of face validity – ex-grid trainees usually speak highly of it – but research studies are only partially conclusive on its overall effectiveness.

## References

1. Rackham, N., Honey, P. and Colbert, M. *Developing Interactive Skills.* Wellens Publishing, Northampton, 1967.
2. Blake, R.R., Mouton, J.S., Barnes, J.S. and Greiner, L.E. 'Breakthrough in Organizational Development', *Harvard Business Review*, Vol. 42, 1964, pp. 133-35.

# Index

# Index of Authors Cited